THE ULTIMATE GUIDE TO
HORSE FEED, SUPPLEMENTS, AND NUTRITION

THE ULTIMATE GUIDE TO
HORSE FEED, SUPPLEMENTS, AND NUTRITION

Lisa Preston

Skyhorse Publishing

Skyhorse Publishing books may be purchased in bulk at special discounts for sales promotion, corporate gifts, fund-raising, or educational purposes. Special editions can also be created to specifications. For details, contact the Special Sales Department, Skyhorse Publishing, 307 West 36th Street, 11th Floor, New York, NY 10018 or info@skyhorsepublishing.com.

Skyhorse® and Skyhorse Publishing® are registered trademarks of Skyhorse Publishing, Inc.®, a Delaware corporation.

Visit our website at www.skyhorsepublishing.com.

10 9 8 7 6 5 4 3 2 1

Library of Congress Cataloging-in-Publication Data is available on file.

Cover design by Tom Lau
Cover photo credit Aly Rattazzi

Print ISBN: 978-1-5107-0535-7
Ebook ISBN: 978-1-5107-0536-4

Printed in China

Table of Contents

Expanded Table of Contents   vi

List of Tables   viii

Foreword by Joseph J. Bertone, DVM   ix

Foreword by Andrea Ellis, DVM   x

1 Introduction: How to Skip the Math and Source with Science   **1**

The Ultimate Chart: Feeding Formulas Solved   2

2 The Horse: Nutritional Physiology   **10**

Teeth to Tail: The Gastrointestinal Tract   10

When and Where Horses Eat: Preempting Stereotypic Behavior   20

Macronutrients for Maintenance Metabolism   24

3 Understanding Feed Labels: Ash? What Ash? And Why Is the Protein Crude?   **37**

4 The Food: Forages and Non-Forage Supplementary Feeds   **47**

Forage: Safe Pastures, Hay, and Other Roughages   48

Non-Forage Supplementary Feed: Grain, By-Products, Oil, and Proprietary Feeds, and Treats   61

5 Alternative Supplements and Nutrition   **84**

6 Dental Care for Optimal Nutrient Absorption   **93**

7 Parasite Control for Gastrointestinal Health   **102**

8 Poisonous Plants and Other Environmental Threats   **115**

9 Special Diets: Athletes, Broodmares, Growing Youngsters, Senior Horses, Draft Horses, Ponies and Miniature Horses, Donkeys and Mules, Recovery from Neglect, Overweight Horses, and Medical Problems with Nutritional Implications   **128**

10 Assessing the Individual Horse: **207**

Weight, Condition, Workload, and Nutritional Needs   207

Resources: Suppliers, Feed Testing, and Further Education   220

References   222

Index   241

Expanded Table of Contents

List of Tables viii

1 Introduction: How to Skip the Math and Source with Science **1**
The Ultimate Chart: Feeding Formulas Solved 2
  Critical Thinking: Avoid Errors, Bust Myths, and Get Metric 2

2 The Horse: Nutritional Physiology **10**
Teeth to Tail: The Gastrointestinal Tract 10
  Feed-Induced Medical Problems: Choke, Colic and Laminitis 14
When and Where the Horse Eats: Preempting Stereotypic Behavior 20
  Slow Feeders and Ground-Level Feeding
Macronutrients for Maintenance Metabolism 24
  Water, Carbohydrates, Fats, Proteins, Vitamins, and Minerals

3 Understanding Feed Labels: Ash? What Ash? And Why Is the Protein Crude? **37**

4 The Food: Forages and Non-Forage Supplementary Feeds **47**
Forage: Safe Pasture, Hay, and Other Roughages 48
  A Bit of Botany: How Essential Carbohydrates Become Dangerous 48
  Pasture Management and Safe Grazing 52
  Hay: Selection, Storage, Serving, and Soaking 57
  Other Roughages: Silage, Haylage, Chop, Cubes, Pellets, and Sprouts 58
Non-Forage Supplementary Feed 61
  Grain: The Common Concentrate 61
  By-Products: Brans, Pulps, Hulls, and Meals 64
  Oils: Fatty Acids from Alpha to Omega 68
  Proprietary Blends 70
    Complete and Sweet Feeds 70
    Probiotics and Prebiotics 72
    Balancers: Vitamins, Minerals, and Electrolytes 74
    Homemade Electrolyte Recipes 79
      Synchronous Diaphragmatic Flutter 81
  Treats: Always, Sometimes, and Never, Plus Recipes 82

5 Alternative Supplements and Nutrition **84**

6 Dental Care for Optimal Nutrient Absorption **93**

7 Parasite Control for Gastrointestinal Health **102**
  Worms, Fecal Egg Counts, and Anthelmintics 102

8 Poisonous Plants and Other Environmental Threats **115**

9 Special Diets Part 1: Life Situations **128**
    Athletes 128
        Ergogenic Supplements 133
        Three Days at a Time 138
    Broodmares 139
        Zikoma is Coming 143
    Growing Youngsters 144
        One Quarter Horse's First Two Years 153
    Seniors 154
        Arthritis and Joint Supplements 155
        The 31-Year-Old Dressage Horse 158
    Draft Horses 159
        Pulling on the Island 160
    Ponies and Miniature Horses 161
        The Guide Horse and the Riding Pony that Believes He's a Horse 163
    Donkeys and Mules 164
        Hugo, the Mule Selected as the Best-Conditioned Horse 169
    Neglect and Starvation 171
        Rescue Success on a Pedestal 174
    Overweight Horses 175
        A Missouri Foxtrotter Slims Down 180
  Special Diets Part 2: Medical Problems with Nutritional Implications 182
    Equine Metabolic Syndrome 182
    Hepatic Impairment or Disease 185
    Hyperkalemic Periodic Paralysis (HYPP) 187
    Insulin Resistance 189
    Neuromuscular Disorders: EMND, Shivers, and Stringhalt 192
    Pituitary Pars Intermedia Dysfunction (PPID) 193
    Renal Impairment or Disease 197
    Respiratory Disorders: IAD, RAO, and SPAOPD 198
    Rhabdomyolysis and Polysaccharide Storage Myopathy (PSSM) 201
    Ulcers: EGUS, EGUD, and RDC 203

10 Assessing the Individual Horse **207**
    The Ultimate Chart to Determine Weight 208
    Condition: Body Scoring, Workload, Fitness, and Vital Signs 212
    Finding Nutritional Needs with the Ultimate Chart 216

Resources: Suppliers, Feed Testing, and Further Education 220
References 222
Index 241

List of Tables

Table 2–1	The Obel Laminitis Grading Scale	19
Table 2–2	The Pros and Cons of Meal Feeding Versus Trickle Feeding	22
Table 2–3	The Effects of Ground-Level Feeding Versus Raised Feeders	23
Table 2–4	Vitamins Required by the Horse	26
Table 2–5	Minerals Required by the Horse	28
Table 2–6	Essential and Non-Essential Amino Acids	33
Table 2–7	Nutrient Requirements of a 1,100 pound (500 kg) Horse at Maintenance	35
Table 3–1	Feed Analysis Abbreviations and Measures	38
Table 4–1	Common Forage Grasses and Legumes	54
Table 4–2	The Impact of a High-Grain Diet Versus Best Practice	62
Table 4–3	The Sweat Scoring System	77
Table 4–4	The Comfort Index	78
Table 4–5	Recipe Matrix for Baked Horse Cookies	83
Table 5–1	Common Supplements Suggested in Alternative Equine Nutrition	86
Table 6–1	The Dental Scoring System	101
Table 7–1	Common Anthelmintics and the Targeted Worms	112
Table 8–1	The Top Forty-Plus Poisonous Plants of Concern to Horse Owners	118
Table 9–1	Equating Pulse to Energy Demand	130
Table 9–2	A Broodmare's Monthly Increase in Energy Requirements	140
Table 9–3	The AAEP Lameness Scale	156
Table 9–4	Weight Estimation for Ponies and Miniature Horses	162
Table 9–5	Key Nutritional Differences Between Donkeys and Horses	165
Table 9–6	Intercontinental Study by the Donkey Sanctuary	165
Table 9–7	The Cresty Neck Score	177
Table 9–8	Equine Ulcers: Risk Factors and Prevention	204
Table 10–1	The Henneke (et al.) Body Condition Scoring System	210
Table 10–2	NRC Definitions of Workload and Equivalent Feed Needs	216

Foreword

It is important to know where one should and should not spend resources in horse ownership. One of my mentors told me that "a veterinarian's most important job is to shepherd a client's time and money." Owners need to be part of that process as well. That capability only comes with factual knowledge and insight. This book helps you get there. Lisa Preston's book is an excellent referenced resource of information relevant for horse owners, and all the shareholders in the horse industry. While reading, I was more than excited by the intense review of topics, as well as the practical and easy to read language of the work. There are always questions, but this book gets you to what we know and what we don't know. Every section is well written and concise. I read it cover to cover and learned a great deal. Ultimately, Preston's work will go in my references for students, and further it should be on the reference shelf of every horse person.

—Joseph J. Bertone, DVM, MS, DACVIM
Professor Equine Medicine, College of Veterinary Medicine
Western University of Health Sciences

Foreword

The Ultimate Guide to Horse Feed, Supplements, and Nutrition is for horse owners, horse managers, and students of equine science who wish to learn and expand their knowledge and to challenge the old myths and traditions they may have grown up with. Lisa Preston gently guides her reader through the equine science and brings up to date understanding into a world where things are often done just because they were always done that way.

The tie between nutrition and the horse's health and welfare is undeniable: linking how horses have evolved into a roaming herbivore, able to survive the harshest winter or desert conditions on minimal quality forage, to the rich environment we keep them in today. Often this environment leads to obesity and related disorders, indeed not unlike those in humans. In addition, we exercise our horses and demand athletic performance while trying to balance their natural, species-specific needs (very low quality herbage, foraging up to fourteen hours per day) with our own lifestyle demands. It is inevitable that sometimes conflict arises between these demands and the health and welfare of the animal, but thanks to a plethora of research over the past twenty years, our understanding of how to prevent and treat nutrition-related problems has advanced considerably.

The Ultimate Guide to Horse Feed, Supplements, and Nutrition has been carefully constructed to give practical advice based on the latest knowledge and is clearly built on systematic, in-depth research. It translates the science into every day, applied situations—from nutrition for work, for breeding-stock, feeding before exercise, dealing with stomach ulcers, to prevention of laminitis and colic. Even feeding of donkeys, mules, draught horses, and miniature horses is discussed.

This book is a perfect learning and reference resource which anyone working with horses should have on their shelves and at hand in the barn, with the pull-out chart hanging up in their tack room or office.

—Andrea Ellis, DVM,
Professor of Equine Nutrition,
Behavior and Welfare UNEQUI LTD.
Research, Education, Innovation

CHAPTER 1
Introduction: How to Skip the Math and Source with Science

A HEALTHY HORSE in its natural state requires only water and grass, yet the feed bill is the largest continuing expense of ownership. The nutrition-related purchasing choices made by owners impact their horses' vitality and performance, as well as the owners' budgets. Smart choices improve the health of both the horse and the wallet, but many horse-feeding practices are the result of habits rather than carefully selected choices based on scientific data.

A large body of tradition exists in horse care, some of which runs counter to well-researched science. Habit, combined with inadequate or poor evaluation of information, often leads people to continue unsound feeding practices, no matter how well-intended those practices may be. Intelligent evaluation of information and reevaluation of habits challenges our critical-thinking skills. Many find it easier to just follow old ways.

Often, an obstacle to learning is accessing the latest information. Recent science has expanded what is known about feeding horses into better and better understanding that, when applied, translates into better care of the horse. As demonstrated by the References section of this book, barn managers and owners who want to stay current on new findings in equine nutrition would have to gather and wade through enormous amounts of research. In this book, stellar, evidence-based studies and guidance are presented and explained.

Owners have faced one big problem in applying the science of evidence-based equine nutrition: the math. Good equine nutrition can be calculation-heavy. Professionally validated mathematical formulas exist for determining these factors: the horse's weight; the minimum forage requirement; the dietary needs, based upon the horse's workload; the percent of increased feed required for special conditions like pregnancy, early growth, or athletic endeavors; the redline maximum of starch a horse can safely intake; the amount of oil the horse can process; and the percent of his crude protein that should be a particular amino acid. Levels of various electrolytes needed daily change under strenuous conditions. It's possible to calculate the amount of certain minerals in the diet to identify a deficit requiring supplementation or an overload that requires diet change.

Further calculations may be required as many readers prefer either the American imperial system or the British imperial thus they must first convert their measurements of pounds and ounces into kilograms and grams, or inches into centimeters, before accessing the formulas, then must convert the formulas' answers back into the imperial system in order to use the results with familiar measurements.

Resources on equine nutrition that provide these formulas usually come with a warning to get a calculator and a software program, or to hire an equine nutritionist. Most people intend to crunch the

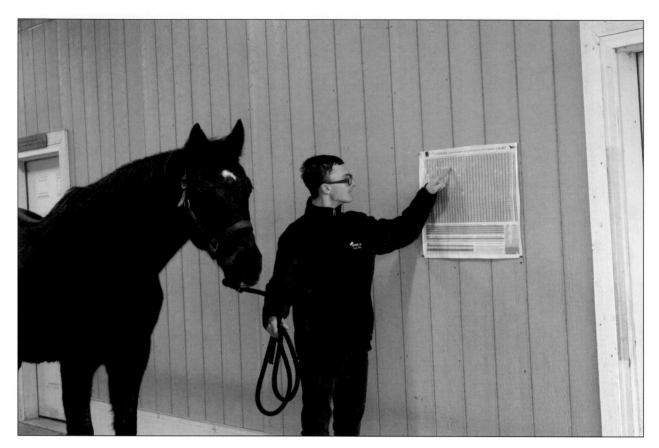

ABOVE: **Feed is a significant cost in horse ownership and the driving force in animal health. The Ultimate Chart solves the equine-nutrition formulas to enable instant access to the answers.**

numbers sometime in the future, but instead continue to guess and feed their horses today the same way they did yesterday. These calculations have been daunting, but now there is a way to skip the math.

The Ultimate Chart: Feeding Formulas Solved

Here, the formulas are provided, but so are the answers. Precalculated for common weights and uses, the formula solutions are available for instant access on the Ultimate Chart.

Equine nutrition formulas are a result of good research and science. Good science does not occur without careful critical thinking. With the math set aside, it's worth reconsidering how to feed a horse by first reviewing critical-thinking skills.

Critical Thinking: Avoid Errors, Bust Myths, and Get Metric

Engaging critical-thinking skills enables owners to reexamine common horse-feeding habits. This can create dramatic improvements in the quality of care horses receive. First, these skills recognize that it is worth asking why a feeding belief or practice exists. It's a good question, and forming a good question is the first step in finding a good answer.

Some sub-optimal horse-feeding habits have confounding factors that seem to support the habit. Sometimes a part of a related truth seems to support a myth. It is an error in thinking to not examine the basis of a habit or myth. Consider the following common assertions related to equine nutrition:

1. Alfalfa makes a horse excitable, and oats make a horse spirited.
2. Sugar beet pulp is bad for horses, because beets are genetically modified and sprayed with Roundup.
3. Canola oil is an industrial lubricant and toxic to horses.
4. Corn is a heatening feed.
5. The right alternative supplements will improve a horse's behavior.
6. Some horses require a low carb diet.
7. Ulcers can be prevented and treated by providing the proper supplements.
8. Donkeys need about 75% of the food a similarly sized pony needs.
9. Horses need high quality hay plus a vitamin and mineral supplement.
10. Bran mashes help a horse's digestion and should be fed regularly.
11. Underweight horses usually have worms and/or bad teeth.
12. Horses must be wormed every eight weeks and dosed according to a weight tape.
13. The horse knows what it needs: when an animal eats dirt, wood, or an entire salt block, it is seeking to replace minerals or another missing nutritional need.

Avoid Errors

The facts that clarify and correct these assertions are not difficult to find or understand, but people often form opinions and habits prematurely and without good information. They unintentionally misinterpret an issue through avoidable errors, including a failure to evaluate information well. They cling to bad information or myths.

At a conference where a panel of veterinarians gave horse enthusiasts a learning opportunity, a questionnaire completed by owners showed that a *majority* harbored a mistaken understanding of some basic horse-feeding principles.

Make an effort to gather quality evidence before forming an opinion. When owners recognize that an assertion is baseless, or is formed on factors other than demonstrable and convincing evidence, they can then seek better evidence for their horse care practices.

Identify and select current, good research. Good studies are well-designed, look for measureable factors, and account for the placebo effect. They are designed to eliminate bias by the researchers; they are double-blind, randomized, and peer reviewed. When repeated, they reliably produce the same result. Good studies produce good science. Competing opinions and interests routinely give conflicting advice, yet so can the results of scientific research. This underscores the need for a disciplined approach in evaluating information.

By contrast, in emotional thinking, riders might choose a product because they like the horse or rider displayed on the package, or they like the person who taught them a particular feeding practice. Sometimes people engage in a horse-feeding practice because it makes *them* feel good. An example is when owners give a particular supplement to their horses, even though there is no definitive benefit to the product or practice, but the product smells good, and the horse seems to find it highly palatable, so it is enjoyable to give it to the horse. This mistake is related to wishful thinking when people want a feed to be helpful and simply choose to believe that it is. Our egos can be threatened by acknowledging that an old habit runs counter to best practices for the horse. No one likes to be wrong, and people often do not welcome information that conflicts with their views.

People also tend to favor whatever method they learned first, no matter whether it is based on good or bad information. Be sure that a belief has a well-founded basis rather than accepting it without good reason. When faced with high quality evidence, be willing to change rather than cling to the old way.

Another persistent error in thinking is confirmation bias. People sometimes make the mistake of accepting different levels of proof based on whether or not they expect or want a conclusion to be true. An example of this is accepting a friend's experience as proof that a particular addition in a supplement improves a horse's temperament, yet rejecting a double-blind, large sample, peer-reviewed, randomized scientific study with a high correlation factor that indicates the additional mineral, vitamin, herb or other additive does not affect a horse's behavior.

Another common fallacy is misattribution. People often imagine correlations or confuse correlation with cause. An example is a study on human joint pain and the weather. Three factors were documented: the joint-pain sufferers' complaints of pain, their actual mobility, and the weather. It was found that patients commonly believe the weather influenced their symptoms, but in fact their complaints did not correlate to temperature, barometric pressure, or precipitation.

Read advertisements with careful critical thinking. When a slick testimonial ad promises, for example, to boost a horse's performance, improve its bloom, or optimize its health, it's reasonable to ask what is meant by those claims. Anecdotes and testimonials are not proof of an assertion. The term "anecdotal evidence" is an oxymoron. When someone says that a nutritional supplement works, ask how the person knows. Be wary of vague appeals or muddy suggestions. A claim that a product improves circulation should first establish that circulation *should* be improved. Also watch out for emotional language, including guilt-inducing pitches along the lines of whether or not owners want what is best for their horses, or ego-stroking slogans that a product is intended only for those who demand the best.

Finally, people can choose to delude themselves in the face of empirical evidence. This is a common failing when horses are at extreme ends of the body condition score. Owners with overly thin horses—or at the other end of the spectrum, those who consistently over-feed their animals into obesity—are often delusional about weight assessment. People regularly make similarly deluded assessments about other facts.

Asking a good question is the first step. The old adage that there are no stupid questions is off the mark. There really are poor, unserviceable questions. Asking "Is it A or B?" is not a good question, if it has not yet been established that one of those two answers must be correct. A good question does not carry a presumption.

Many of the methods in which people care for their horses are rooted in habit, adopted from someone else's habit. Learners recognize that good information is supported by science, but might not realize they sometimes employ bad thinking by accepting bad science.

Bust the Myths

All of that good critical thinking, careful evaluation of evidence, rejection of poor studies, and avoidance of errors in thinking let us go myth-busting.

1. *Alfalfa makes a horse excitable, and oats make a horse spirited.*

Neither alfalfa nor oats have any special, stimulating properties. Both alfalfa and oats provide energy, also known as calories. When a horse, just like a person or any other living animal, has plenty of energy, it can be more engaged and physical. There are ways to add energy to a horse's diet, however, that do not have a reputation for making a horse reactive, and are healthy. Chapter 2 addresses the nutritional needs of the horse, and Chapter 4 addresses the pros and cons of each horse feed, including low-cost, safe ways to add energy to a horse's diet.

2. *Sugar beet pulp is bad for horses, because beets are genetically modified and sprayed with Roundup.*

Sugar beet pulp—more commonly referred to simply as beet pulp in many locales—is a by product from processing sugar beet roots into sugar. Sugar beet plants are sometimes sprayed with various herbicides and pesticides during farming. Related arguments against beet pulp as a horse feed raise concerns about the GMO (genetically modified organism) nature of the crop in some areas, the land on which the root is grown, and the chemicals used in processing the beets. Another complaint is that beet pulp is mere filler.

The truth is that beet pulp is not toxic and is an excellent feed for horses, with highly digestible and beneficial fiber. For a complete discussion of the glyphosate, heavy metal, and disodium cyanodithiomidocarbonate concerns that have been raised about feeding beet pulp to horses, see Chapter 4.

3. *Canola oil is an industrial lubricant and toxic to horses.*

Detractors of using oils to supplement the energy or calories in a horse's diet sometimes mistakenly make this argument against Canola, along with the unfounded assertion that the product has murky origins or is poisonous. Many oils produced from foods that are safe to eat are also used for non-food purposes; thus they can also be termed "industrial lubricants." Canola is a portmanteau derived from the words *Canada* and *oil*. Canola oil is the result of processing the seeds of a plant in the Brassica genus called *rape*. Other healthy food plants in this genus include cabbage, cauliflower, broccoli, and Brussels sprouts. Rapeseed oil (canola oil) has a good profile of omega-3 to omega-6 fatty acids, unlike another common oil more often fed to horses, to be discussed in Chapter 4.

LEFT: **How much is a handful? Feed should be measured by weight, not volume.**

4. *Corn is a heatening feed.*

This is a very old assertion, similar to the claim that alfalfa and oats make a horse high-spirited. Heat-processed corn can be fed safely, but it is high in starch. When starch intake exceeds the small intestine's processing ability, the excess is passed on to the large intestine, where a cascade of negative effects occurs. These disruptive changes can cause colic and laminitis. A horse fed excess corn might not be overheated or acting up so much as experiencing a bellyache (colic). Mild cases of colic can manifest as negative behavioral changes, often with mild aggression. a sour attitude or increased reactivity and spooking.

A horse's limited ability to process starch in the small intestine is detailed in Chapter 2. Unfortunately, owners easily, unknowingly exceed the starch redline when apportioning grain. The starch redline is precalculated for various horse weights on the Ultimate Chart.

Many people fail to measure hay and concentrates, which is a critical step in feeding. Also, people make the mistake of measuring by volume rather than by weight. Corn is physically heavy. Any volume of corn weighs more than the same volume of oats and is thus a larger serving. People sometimes use undefined volumes, too. A scoop is no more meaningful an amount than a handful. Corn and other concentrates are detailed in Chapter 3. Measuring is discussed later in this chapter under *Get Metric.*

5. *The right alternative supplements will improve a horse's behavior.*

As discussed above in reviewing critical-thinking skills, confirmation bias and other avoidable errors can lead people to believe an additive has a particular effect. Proving that a supplement—alternative or mainstream—provides a specific benefit is challenging.

Horses are excellent mirrors of human emotion. A rider who is apprehensive about a horse's behavior transmits that anxiety to the horse, who then realizes he has drawn a poor leader in his human partner. Rider-induced anxiety in horses is a common phenomena, one that is easily misattributed to feeds and supplement. Also, training problems will never be fixed with nutrition. Chapter 4 discusses mainstream supplementation, and Chapter 5 covers alternative supplements.

6. *Horses with certain medical conditions require a low carb diet.*

There is no such thing as a low carbohydrate diet for horses. Horses exist on a diet of plants, which are largely composed of carbohydrates. Within the classification of carbohydrates, there are simple sugars, complex sugars (examples are starch and fructan), and structural carbohydrates. The latter is the mainstay of a healthy horse's diet, yet is a plant constituent that the horse cannot break down to use. The horse depends upon a symbiotic relationship with the microbial population in his gastrointestinal tract to provide fuel, and we must protect these beneficial microbes through sound feeding practices, as is discussed in Chapter 2. Horses with certain medical conditions must be fed a diet that is particularly low in specific carbohydrates, as discussed in Chapter 9.

7. *Ulcers can be prevented and treated by providing the proper supplements.*

There are many causes of ulcers, and no single prevention effort addresses every cause, but proper feeding practices are the first fix. Equine Gastric Ulcer Syndrome (EGUS) and many other medical problems that require special dietary considerations are discussed in Chapter 9.

8. *Donkeys need about 75 percent of the food a similarly sized pony needs.*

The old standby of giving a donkey the same rations as a similarly sized pony typically over-feeds donkeys. The improved suggestion to give donkeys three-quarters of what similarly sized ponies eat is also excessive. Further, donkeys, unlike horses, must browse, which means to eat woody, twiggy material from shrubs, rather than only graze grasses. The pastures and hays horses live on are generally too rich for donkeys. Also, grain is contraindicated for donkeys, as discussed in Chapter 9.

9. *Horses need high quality hay plus a vitamin and mineral supplement.*

Horses evolved eating low quality forage in small amounts throughout a day. Most pleasure horses actually need medium quality hay. Further, horses can often get *all* of their vitamins and minerals from a decent forage diet, as discussed in Chapter 2. Assessing feed quality is detailed in Chapter 3.

10. *Bran mashes help a horse's digestion and should be fed regularly.*

The tradition of bran mashes may have arisen from people noticing that the fiber in bran helps keep the human gastrointestinal tract moving. Horses eating a normal diet of grass or hay already receive enormous amounts of roughage. Bran has an inverted calcium:phosphorus ratio, which can impair bone density, and it easily exceeds the starch redline. This is discussed in Chapter 4.

11. *Underweight horses usually have bad teeth and/or worms.*

The primary reason most underweight horses are too thin is that they are underfed. Chapter 6 reviews dental care, Chapter 7 details parasite control, and Chapter 9 has a special section on how to safely feed and rehabilitate an underweight horse to avoid the dangerous condition called refeeding syndrome.

12. *Horses must be wormed every eight weeks and dosed according to a weight tape.*

The current guideline is that deworming a horse should be guided by an assessment of the horse's living situation, as well as his egg shedding status as verified by fecal egg count testing. Chapter 7 details parasite control.

With regard to approximating a horse's weight with a weight tape, see the photograph in Chapter 10 of two horses whose weights are indicated as the same on a weight tape, yet one weighs about 880 pounds, and the other weighs nearly 1,100 pounds. That chapter returns the reader to the Ultimate Chart for the calculated answers to a proven formula that determines a horse's weight by considering the heart girth, as a weight tape does, while also accounting for the horse's length, as shown in Chapter 10.

13. *The horse knows what it needs: When an animal eats dirt, wood, or an entire salt block, it is seeking to replace minerals or another missing nutritional need.*

If this were true, horses would never poison themselves by eating a toxic plant. Wood chewing is a behavioral problem strongly associated with specific and unnatural horse-keeping practices, as is discussed in Chapter 2. Two types of pica (the eating of non-nutritive substances) are geophagia (eating soil) and coprophagia (eating manure) are discussed in Chapters 2 and 9.

While poisoning scenarios more frequently occur with hungry horses kept on overgrazed land or other conditions with inadequate forage, they also occur with well-fed horses kept on pastures that are in overall good condition, as discussed in Chapter 8.

Get Metric (In Multiple Ways)

Science measures things. A testable hypothesis, for example, that a particular feed supplement will improve a condition, is measureable, not subjective. This is what is meant by the need to find metrics.

Measuring nutritional parameters is the starting point for well-managed nutrition. This requires measuring both the horse and the food. Monitoring and recording the effects of the dietary regimen allow the careful owner to then make adjustments as needed.

LEFT: **A feed room doesn't need to be fancy, but it needs a scale to enable accurate measuring.**

Scientific studies employ numerous measures that readers may have heard of or noticed on feed labels (examples are CP, ADF, and NDF), in addition to many more factors and their acronyms. The Chapter 3 section on reading feed labels and analyses explains what these measurements mean.

The metric system of measurement is the gold standard in research and medicine. Because the units are smaller, centimeters and grams are more accurate than the whole inches or ounces of either the American or British imperial systems. The Ultimate Chart uses half-inch increments in order to determine a horse's size and offers the necessary conversions already calculated for the reader's convenience.

Another way to think about measuring or metrics is the use of standardized grading or scoring scales. Scoring systems included in this book are: the Obel laminitis grading scale, the AAEP lameness scale, the sweat score, the dental scoring system, the cresty neck score, and the Henneke Body Condition Scoring (BCS) System. These grading systems numerically denote the severity of a specific problem and are standardized by verifying a high incidence of intra-observer agreement on the specific signs and symptoms present.

A solid understanding of horse feeds, supplements, and nutrition begins with a foundation in the specific nutritional and behavioral needs of the horse, then a review of the feeds and supplements and the associated factors of dental care, parasite control, and special diets. Putting all of these parameters together enables the owner to monitor and adjust an individual horse's nutrition program as required.

is normally 6–7. The pH of the lower stomach is normally 2-3.5; when fasting it becomes as low as 1.5–2. A cuticle-like ridge (the margo plicatus) divides the upper and lower stomach. Unlike a human stomach, which only secretes digestive acid when a meal is ingested, the horse constantly secretes hydrochloric acid in the lower stomach.

Zymogenic cells in the lower stomach release enzymes that begin to break down food. (Lipase works on lipids (fats); protease and pepsin break protein into amino acids.)

The stomach empties into the duodenum, which is the first part of the small intestine. This gastric emptying is fairly rapid, beginning in about twenty minutes after eating. The digesta (food bolus being digested) will normally have a pH between 2.5 and 3.5 as it enters the duodenum.

The small intestine (SI) is about seventy-five feet long, thus comprising about 75 percent of the entire length of the GIT, but the lumen of the SI is small, so the SI accounts for only about 30 percent of the GIT's volume. A normal rate of passage for digesta through the entire SI, connecting the stomach to the large intestine, is between forty-five minutes and two hours. The SI should always be moving digesta. Intestines can become tangled when empty. The three parts of the SI are the duodenum, the jejunum, and the ileum.

In the duodenum, food is further mixed, and the pH is neutralized. Brunner's glands secrete bicarbonate, and while horses do not have a gall bladder, bile is constantly secreted from the liver into the SI. The bicarbonate and bile increases the pH of the digesta in the SI to the range of 7–7.5. This neutral pH environment is necessary for nutrients to be properly broken down by enzymes and transported across the SI wall.

The lining of the small intestine consists of tiny, finger-like projections into the lumen of the small intestine, called villi (plural of vilus), and projections extending away from the lumen into the body, called crypts. The mucosal lining of the villi and crypts is where starch, simple sugars, fats, proteins, and minerals are absorbed into the body.

In addition to protease and lipase, the SI releases an enzyme called amylase, which breaks down starch into simple sugars. The pancreas secretes insulin, which helps transport glucose into cells throughout the body. Blood levels of insulin rise after eating, rise higher with the ingestion of large meals, and rise even more with the ingestion of large, starch meals. This has management implications for all horses, but especially for those with insulin resistance, as discussed in Chapter 9 under Special Diets.

The small intestine has a limited capacity to digest starch and sugars. A cascade of undesirable effects can occur when a large-starch load overwhelms the SI and must be passed on to the hindgut. Researchers formerly placed the starch redline at two grams of starch per kilogram of the horse's body weight (two g/kg), but recent studies (Vervuert, et al.) have lowered the safe threshold to one gram per kilogram. This figure is calculated in both imperial and metric measurements for a wide range of horse weights on the Ultimate Chart.

Assuming the horse eats a normal, healthy diet of grass or hay, the digesta leaving the foregut is highly fibrous and resistant to enzymatic breakdown in the small intestine, so the bulk of digestion occurs in the hindgut. Digesta leaves the ileum (the last section of the SI) through the ileocecal valve, and enters the cecum, the first part of the hindgut.

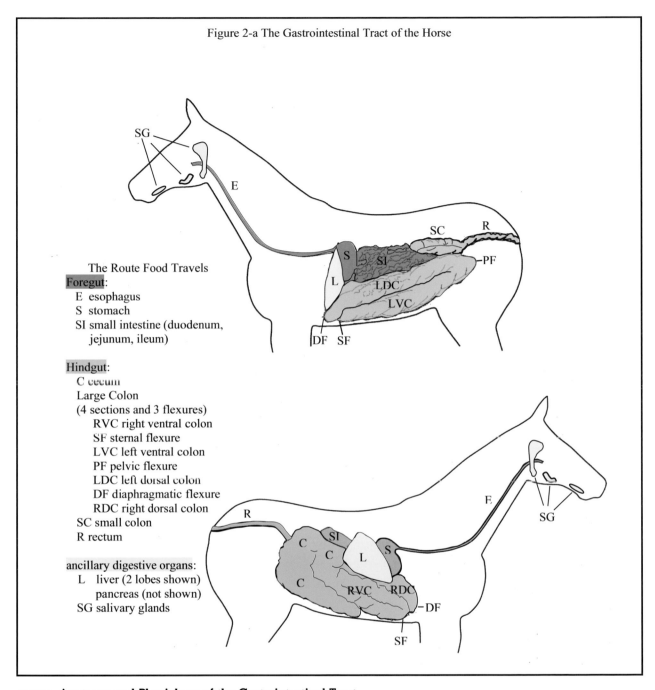

Figure 2-a The Gastrointestinal Tract of the Horse

The Route Food Travels

Foregut:
E esophagus
S stomach
SI small intestine (duodenum, jejunum, ileum)

Hindgut:
C cecum
Large Colon
(4 sections and 3 flexures)
    RVC right ventral colon
    SF sternal flexure
    LVC left ventral colon
    PF pelvic flexure
    LDC left dorsal colon
    DF diaphragmatic flexure
    RDC right dorsal colon
SC small colon
R rectum

ancillary digestive organs:
L   liver (2 lobes shown)
     pancreas (not shown)
SG salivary glands

ABOVE: **Anatomy and Physiology of the Gastrointestinal Tract.**

The Hindgut: Where Fiber is Degraded by Microbial Fermentation

The large intestine is only about fifty feet (15 meters) but at about 125 quarts, it holds about 60 percent of the volume of the entire GIT. The large intestine is comprised of the cecum, large colon, small colon, and rectum.

The cecum is a large, blind sac about four feet long (1.2 meters), with a volume of about thirty-five quarts (thirty-three liters). It's populated by microbes that live in a symbiotic relationship with the horse. Horses do not break down their primary food—the fibrous material of grass and hay—but rather fiber is degraded by the microbial population. (Some fermenting of digesta occurs even in the stomach and small intestine.) The cecum's primary function is to operate as a fermentation vat.

The hundreds of species of microbes naturally populating the hindgut are bacteria, fungi, and protozoa. This microbial population is also referred to as microflora, microbiota, the microbiome, or cellulytic microbes, meaning that they break down plant cells.

The pH in the hindgut should range from 6 to 7; in this environment, the healthy bacteria flourish and do their job of degrading fiber.

Microbial fermentation of forage produces volatile fatty acids (VFAs), primarily acetate (74 percent), butyrate (6 percent), and propionate (17 percent), with the remaining 3–4 percent being isobutyrate, valerate, and isovalerate. (Another by-product of microbial fermentation is gas, in the forms of carbon dioxide and methane.) The VFAs are a horse's primary energy source.

Leaving the cecum, digesta passes into the large colon through the cecocolonic valve, which prevents backflow. The large colon has a total length of about thirty-two feet (10 meters) and a capacity of up to seventy quarts. It also hosts fiber-degrading microbes. (Before learning the names of the four compartments of the large colon, it helps to understand that the term *ventral* refers to near the stomach, and the term *dorsal* refers to near the back.)

From the cecum, the four sections of the large colon and the three flexures joining them are the: right ventral colon (RVC), sternal flexure, left ventral colon (LVC), pelvic flexure, left dorsal colon (LDC), diaphragmatic flexure, and right dorsal colon (RDC). The pelvic and sternal flexures are common sites for impaction colic.

Listen to different quadrants of your horse's abdomen with a stethoscope, and notice that all areas normally have gut sounds at all times. This is good gut motility. A quiet, inactive gut is unhealthy for a horse.

Digesta leaves the right dorsal colon and enters the small colon, which is about twelve feet long and has a capacity of about twenty quarts. The primary function of the small colon is the absorption of water. Fecal balls begin to form near the end of the small colon and are stored in the rectum—which is about one foot (30 centimeters) long—prior to excretion.

Feed-Induced Medical Problems: Choke, Colic, and Laminitis

Choke

Choke, properly called esophageal obstruction, occurs when the esophagus is blocked by something the horse has ingested. This is not a blockage of the trachea (airway), like when a person chokes. Horses with choke usually have a partial blockage of the esophagus. They appear distressed, withdrawn, or restless, and usually exhibit ptyalism (excessive saliva) which may run out of the nose. They may become agitated or depressed and exhibit bruxism (grinding of the teeth). Because of the ptyalism, horses may inhale secretions that could cause a secondary respiratory infection.

Do not delay in summoning veterinary care for a horse that may have an esophageal obstruction. While choke may resolve spontaneously, veterinary intervention may be required to administer smooth muscle relaxants or, more likely, to pass a nasogastric tube to, and through, the obstruction, lavaging (washing) the obstruction away. Have gallons of body-temperature (99–101° F for adults) water ready for your veterinarian to administer through the tube so that the horse does not become unnecessarily chilled.

Obstructions are almost always food particles and seem to be more common when the food is particularly dry or coarse. Horses that bolt their feed may also be more prone to choke. Moistening concentrated feeds makes horses eat faster, so do not moisten pellets unless they are wet enough to dissolve. Ingestion time can be increased with the use of slow feeders for forage and multiple buckets, pocket buckets, or several fist-sized obstacles of stone or wood distributed in the pans when concentrates are fed.

Colic

Colic is a lay term for abdominal pain. It has long been one of the leading causes of death in horses and is so common the word is used as a verb, with people commenting that a horse colic'd. While numerous metabolic processes can induce colic, the condition can arise from mismanaging your horse's feed.

Recall that the pH in the hindgut should range from 6 to 7 and that if the small intestine is overwhelmed by too much sugar and starch, it passes the undigested sugar and starch to the hindgut. The hindgut is meant to process fiber and does not have enzymes to break down sugar and starch. The beneficial bacteria that degrade fibrous feeds are relatively slow growing, doubling their population in eight to ten hours. However, bacteria that degrade non-structural carbohydrates (sugar and starch) are fast growing, doubling their population in fifteen to sixty minutes. Thus, large loads of sugar or starch reaching the hindgut are rapidly digested by lactic acid bacteria (LAB), which then grow in population and give off lactic acid as a by-product of fermenting the sugar and starch. This lowers the pH of the hindgut, creating hindgut acidosis. The acidic environment makes the gut wall overly permeable and kills off desirable microbes. This sudden large load of dead microbes is toxic and can enter the body's systemic circulation, where it may trigger laminitis.

Colic may be referred to as ileus, referring to pain in the ileum, blockage, or an overall lack of motility in the gut. While there are numerous metabolic pathologies that could provoke colic, preventable colics that arise from unsafe feeding practices are the focus here. The classic error horse people fear is a gate or barn door left open, accidentally allowing a horse access to a grain bin. More commonly, lush pasture, loaded with sugars, causes colic that can ultimately lead to laminitis.

Colic can also arise from other pathologies. The mesentery that keeps the various sections of the foregut and hindgut in place can become disrupted, entrapping and strangling a segment of bowel. An example of this is a small opening called the epiploic foramen (hole) on the right side of the abdomen near the liver and pancreas. When a section of the small intestine from the left side of abdomen passes through the epiploic foramen to the right side of the abdomen, the condition is called epiploic foramen entrapment (EFE). Another example is called nephrosplenic entrapment, which occurs when the large colon has left dorsal displacement in the abdominal cavity. Nephrosplenic entrapment appears to be more common in geldings.

Surgery may be required to relieve EFE, intussusception (when a section of bowel telescopes inside itself or an adjoining section), displacement, distention, a section of necrotic bowel, or a bowel twist (most commonly a small intestine volvulus).

The veterinarian can administer analgesics and better assess the location, type, and severity of the colic. The vet can decompress the stomach via insertion of a nasogastric tube or give laxatives (cathartics), such as mineral oil, hydrated magnesium sulfate (Mg SO4, popularly known as Epsom salts), dioctyl sodium sulfosuccinate (DSS), or psyllium hydrophilic mucilloid. A vet might administer enteral or intravenous fluids; the former are given through the nasogastric tube for direct delivery into the stomach, and the latter are given through a catheter inserted into a vein. Finally, a veterinarian can administer drugs that act directly and indirectly to stimulate activity in the foregut and hindgut, for example: neostigmine methylsulfate, cholimimetics and sympatholytics, bethanechol chloride, benzamides, metoclopramide, cisapride, and/or lidocaine.

Yohimbine, derived from a west and central African tree called the *pausinystalis johimbe* or yohimbe, is a supplement that can increase motility in the cecum and RVC, but has not been shown to increase cecal emptying. One study suggested that if administered with the drug bethanecol, yohimbe could be helpful in relieving equine colic.

Colic may also arise from enterolithiasis (the condition of an enterolith or stone being present in the GIT) or parasites. A horse may swallow a lot of air while cribbing or windsucking, and this condition, called aerophagia, can lead a horse to colic as the air moves through the GIT. Colic can also result from intestinal spasms or the impaction of feed or foreign matter, such as dirt or sand.

Assessing Your Horse's Sand Burden

The amount of sand in the feces can be assessed by placing several fresh fecal balls into a clear container with a quart of water, then allowing dirt and sand in the feces to settle to the bottom. If more than two teaspoons of sand are in the bottom of the water container, some owners feed a standard serving of psyllium.

Psyllium Supplementation for Sand in the Gastrointestinal Tract

When colic is caused by the ingestion of dirt or sand (even from consuming pasture grass grown on very sandy soil), it is referred to as sand colic. Horses on sandy ground or dirt lots without a steady supply of forage in a slow feeder have the greatest risk for ingesting enough sand to cause sand colic. Horses that engage in the specific form of pica (eating non-nutritive substances) called geophagia (dirt eating) are also at high risk for sand colic.

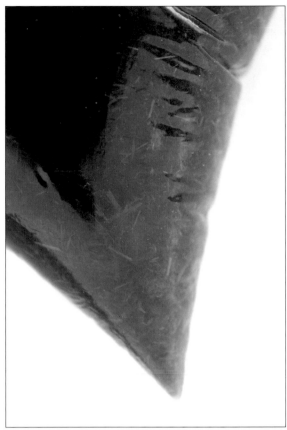

ABOVE: **To check a horse's intestinal sand burden, place fresh fecal balls in water. Agitate the mixture—or simply wait—and let the manure disperse in the water for an hour.**

ABOVE: **Plant fiber floats, but sand that was in the feces settles. This close-up of the bottom of the container shows an insignificant sand burden.**

Sand in the intestine can sometimes be heard on a stethoscope and may be seen with radiographs or an ultrasound. Sand can cause colic either through obstruction of the intestinal lumen or by irritating the mucosa lining the GIT.

Psyllium powder has commonly been administered both to relieve sand colic and prophylactically for horses at risk for sand ingestion. However, two good studies have presented strong evidence that psyllium actually does not have any special ability to move sand through the GIT. In one study, sand was placed into horses' stomachs via a nasogastric tube. Sand excretion was monitored but found not to be affected by whether or not the horses received psyllium. In another study, sand was surgically placed into the cecums of ponies (that were already destined for euthanasia). Half of these were treated with psyllium, and all were examined post-mortem. Psyllium administration had no bearing on how much sand remained in the ponies' hindguts. It appears that some horses tolerate sand better than others, and most clear it from their bowels well on their own if they are not continually subjected to sand ingestion.

Colic Prevention

While ground feeding has many positive effects, discussed below, care should be taken not to make the horse susceptible to ingesting excessive amounts of dirt or sand. Place a stall mat below the hay feeder if needed. If the horse eats concentrates from a pan on the ground and tends to dribble food out of the pan, use a taller pan or place the pan on a tarp or stall mat.

Consistency with the amount and type of feed offered is healthy for the horse. The microbial environment in the horse's GIT takes time to adapt to dietary alterations. A sudden, large change in feed will cause a change in the gut microflora that day. Ideally, feed changes are made incrementally, allowing the microbial population to adapt to the new feeding practice. The GIT could need a month to safely and fully adapt to new feed.

The first week after a feed change carries the highest risk of colic, so be sure to initiate changes in feeding programs gradually.

Medications, strenuous activity, and stress can induce colic, so be vigilant in monitoring a horse that must be medicated, don't overwork your horse, and take steps to mitigate distress he may experience due to the living environment, transportation, or other anxiety-producing situations.

A horse with colic can quickly become obtunded. Signs that his condition is worsening include tachycardia (increased heart rate), tachypnea (increased respiratory rate), pawing, kicking at the abdomen, and the absence of borborygmi (gurgling bowel sounds). Any horse with even mild colic requires careful monitoring. Be prepared to summon a veterinarian.

Horses with recurring colic may be tested with a SmartPill. The horse swallows this monitoring device, which records pH, pressures, and transit times throughout the gastrointestinal tract until it is excreted.

Overall, colic prevention is centered on being mindful of risks and avoiding them. Allow your horse to slowly eat a diet wholly or heavily based on forage, throughout the day, without meal feeding, with little or no concentrates, and with good dental care and a good parasite control program.

The likelihood of a horse experiencing colic increases with grain feeding. A horse fed five pounds of grain is about twice as likely to colic as a horse not fed grain. A horse fed ten pounds of grain is six times more likely to colic.

Horses on pasture have a reduced incidence of colic if they are also provided with hay.

A horse that colics is three times more likely to colic again.

Horses with chronic or recurring colic need a full veterinary workup to rule out or identify underlying medical pathology. Recovery from colic requires careful reintroduction of safe feed.

Subclinical colic, in which the signs of the horse's gastric distress are much less noticeable, can still provoke laminitis.

Laminitis

The laminae (plural of the word lamina) are tiny, finger-like projections binding the soft tissue and bone within a hoof to the interior of the hoof wall. Inflammation of the laminae is called laminitis or founder. Laminitis is extremely painful and dangerous to horses, because as the condition worsens, the laminae can detach, no longer providing the bone with foundational support. This detachment usually occurs at the toe first, causing the internal hoof joint to rotate. With this rotation, the point of the bone can press down on the interior of the hoof's sole, which then must bear the horse's massive weight.

Warning signs of laminitis are bounding digital pulses (Chapter 10 reviews how to check the pulse) and excessively warm hooves, especially in the presence of colic or nutritional conditions known to provoke laminitis (typically lush spring pasture or a grain overload). Due to the pain, the horse may shift its weight constantly, lifting one front hoof then the other, and it will usually show obvious lameness at the trot.

Laminitis typically affects front hooves first; the horse may stand with its forelegs extended ahead of the shoulder rather than under the shoulder, bearing as much weight as possible on the hind legs. This is the classic laminitic stance. A laminitic horse may be reluctant to allow a hoof to be lifted, because doing so increases the weight carried by other hooves.

The scoring system veterinarians use to grade the severity of laminitis symptoms is the Obel scale.

Table 2-1 The Obel Laminitis Grading Scale	
Veterinarians grade the severity of laminitis symptoms according to the Obel Scale. Note that this is not the same scale as the AAEP 0-5 lameness grading scale.	
Grade	**Symptoms**
I	shifting weight, lifting feet, no lameness at walk, shortened trot stride
II	both walk and trot show a shortened stride; horse allows a hoof to be lifted
III	horse is reluctant to move or allow a hoof to be lifted
IV	horse extremely reluctant or refusing to move

Laminitis is a medical emergency, and a veterinarian should be called immediately. Keep the horse on soft ground with as little movement as possible. Apply cold water or ice to reduce the inflammation. Do not add stress to a laminitic horse. If he is happier with a particular pasturemate nearby, keep that other horse close.

A good farrier working with the veterinarian's radiographs can make the horse as comfortable as possible. Veterinary therapy will focus on reducing the inflammation.

Bacterial toxins known as lipopolysaccharides (LPS) appear to play a role in laminitis, and some research has shown promising work with the administration of the antibiotic polymixin B that binds the LPS. Silymarin, an extract from the milk thistle plant, has also been shown to reduce inflammation and may bind to LPS, but polymixin B has shown a much greater capacity to bind LPS.

Horses on pasture make up about half of the laminitis cases every year. Spring growth, when the grass plant is producing and storing high levels of sugar, is the time of greatest incidence for these pasture-associated laminitis (PAL) cases. It is vital for you to know the environmental factors that spike sugars in forage; these are discussed in Chapter 4.

Ponies seem particularly susceptible to laminitis, as do horses that are obese, easy keepers, or those with the medical conditions of insulin resistance or Equine Metabolic Syndrome. In the case of the latter two conditions, there is new research into insulin-sensitizing drugs, but the best approach is prevention rather than treatment. Chapter 9 details caring for—and the prevention of—these conditions.

The extent of rehabilitation of the hooves is determined by the severity of the laminitis. Horses will likely display some continued lameness as they recover. Lameness, whether from laminitis or any other source, is commonly graded on the American Association of Equine Practitioners (AAEP) lameness scale, provided in Table 9–3 on page 156.

Recovery from laminitis requires careful nutritional management. Grain concentrates are not safe for laminitis-prone horses. Pasture grazing must be very carefully monitored so as to not expose the horse to excess sugar in the grass. Many laminitis-prone horses cannot be on pasture at all. Forage low in sugar, presented in a slow feeder, is safest for laminitis-prone horses.

When and Where the Horse Eats: Preempting Stereotypic Behavior

Many people provide a significant portion of their horses' total energy intake through pounds of grain, which is much more convenient than hay to buy, store, and handle, but—as is seen in reviewing the horse's digestive system—is unhealthy for the horse. Not only should forage be the horse's primary diet, the very act of foraging is germane to nutritional physiology, because it is an essential behavioral need of all horses. Ethologically, the horse is driven to find and eat its food while roaming for at least sixteen hours every day.

Confinement is unnatural for horses, and turnout time is essential. Horses in active riding use kept on pasture—especially in a small-herd situation with a few pasturemates—spend between sixteen and eighteen hours per day foraging, even when they have free-choice access to hay in slow feeders.

LEFT: **Excessive confinement often leads to stereotypic behavior, such as cribbing, weaving, and pawing.**

How Much Does Your Horse Roam?

People might dismiss a horse's roaming nature now that the majority of horses live in smaller enclosures. It's easy to assume that a horse in an enclosure doesn't appreciably roam, but it's easy to *know* by placing a GPS unit on a horse for several twelve-to-twenty-four hour periods and downloading the information into any of several free programs (Strava, Garmin, endomondo, and mapmyrun are examples.) Small GPS units and wristwatches with GPS capability are now common and relatively inexpensive. Secure the GPS unit or cellphone in front of the horse's withers at the roots of the mane or behind the withers on a surcingle or bareback pad (rather than on a halter, so as to eliminate the unit tracking the horse raising and lowering its head). A study of horses on a ten-acre pasture showed horses roaming about ten miles per day, but a horse in a half acre can still cover many miles per day.

Many domestic horses are not allowed to roam, nor to eat little and often as a forager should. They are kept in small pens or stalls and fed in meals. Inadequate forage and excessive confinement can lead to a host of problems that often manifest as stereotypic behavior, discussed below. When forage is provided free choice to horses turned out on large lots, they get to satisfy their physical and behavioral needs. Ideally, forage and other feeds are offered in a physical presentation horses would encounter naturally, which is slow consumption from the ground level.

Slow Feeding

Many horses are fed in meals, usually twice per day, with a morning and an evening feeding. They eat all of their presented feed in an hour or less, then must fast for the next eleven hours. People probably feed their horses in meals, because they themselves eat in meals.

Large meals cause the horse's insulin level to spike. A steady level of insulin without large spikes is desirable for optimum health. The solution is to provide hay in slow feeders, allowing the horse constant or near-constant access to forage. People mistakenly anticipate that if they provide free-choice hay in slow feeders that the horse will overeat and then colic or succumb to laminitis due to gorging. In addition to expecting the horse to overfeed, they anticipate hay wastage. On the contrary, most horses adjust very happily to free-choice, slow-feed forage in just a few weeks.

Horses fed in meals often eat all of their hay immediately, in a manner known as compensatory eating. These horses have learned there will be no food available for many hours and that anxiety provokes gorging. A horse will not naturally choose to fast or go without food for more than three hours. Fasting places a horse at risk for ulcers, colic, and the development of stereotypic behaviors.

Another advantage of this system of trickle feeding is the peace of mind that comes from always knowing your horse has forage should you be delayed in getting to the barn that morning or evening.

Table 2-2 The Pros and Cons of Meal Feeding versus Trickle Feeding		
Method	**Pros**	**Cons**
Meal Feeding	traditional	hydrochloric acid still produced in the stomach when the horse has no forage, insulin spikes when eating large meals, significant ulcer risk, colic risk, which brings laminitis risk fasting periods result in insufficient bolus of long fibrous material moving through the tract, horse frustration and misbehavior
Trickle Feeding	steady insulin level, improved gastric health, reduced colic risk, improved horse behavior, convenience for the owner, reduced ulcer occurrence	not traditional

Ground-Level Feeding

A grazing horse is in a natural physical posture that provides numerous healthy pluses not granted to the horse eating hay from a high, wall-mounted feeder. When a horse reaches to eat from the ground, its abdomen is raised, and its back is stretched. The jaw is allowed to slightly subluxate, which may improve the production of saliva. The nasal passages are aided by gravity to discharge inhaled foreign matter, and the eyes are not subjected to a spray of debris pulled from a high feeder.

High feeders promote the opposite effects in every way, spraying the eyes and nose with dust and hay particles as the horse pulls hay from the feeder. These particles are then more likely to be inhaled farther into the airway, rather than discharged with the aid of gravity. The back is inverted and tight instead of long and stretched, the abdomen is pushed down, and the hinge of the lower jaw is held in tightly.

Dusty or silty ground does indeed make a horse more likely to intake more undesirable foreign matter, but this can be avoided by offering hay in

ABOVE: **High wall feeders force horses to eat in an unnatural posture that inverts the back, tightens the jaw, and exposes the eyes and lungs to an irritating spray of dust and food particles.**

Table 2-3 The Effects of Ground-Level Feeding Versus Raised Feeders		
Body Part	**Ground-Level Feeders**	**Raised Feeders**
Eyes	not subjected to hay particles	subjected to hay particles and dust
Jaw	allowed to subluxate	not allowed to subluxate
Sinuses	inhalation of dust and foreign bodies is minimized	foreign body inhalation is increased
Back	lifts and stretches	inverts and tightens
Abdomen	raised	sagging

contained slow feeders and providing loose feeds in low, flat pans. Horses that dribble feed beyond their pans can eat on a tarp or stall mat in order to keep the spilled feed clean.

Together, turnout (always with access to water) and low, slow feeding mimic the horse's natural diet and environment, significantly reducing the likelihood of the horse developing stereotypic behavior.

Stereotypic Behavior

A stall-kept, meal-fed horse is completely removed from the nutritional, physical, and social life of a forging, pasture-kept horse. These stall-bound horses frequently develop one or more of the following habits, which are collectively referred to as stereotypic behavior: cribbing, windsucking, weaving, nodding, pacing (also called stall walking), pawing, shrill calling, aggression, and an overly alert stance. Frustration arising from an inability to engage in hours of chewing forage, the stress of social isolation created by stalls, and a lack of turnout space and time have all been implicated as triggers of stereotypies.

In a study of 100 mares in dry lots, half were given constant forage access, while the other half were fed in meals. The foraging mares were more relaxed than the meal-fed mares. The foragers spent less time moving about or in an alert stance than did the other mares. Foragers also engaged in more positive social interactions, were less aggressive, and were more fertile. Foraging mares had a conception rate over 80 percent while the meal-fed mares' rate was only 55 percent. Fertility and stress are known to have an inverse relationship.

Cribbing, also called crib biting, is when a horse grabs and holds an object—usually a stall door or fence board—in its mouth. When the cribbing horse also sucks in air while its mouth is clamped onto an object, it is called windsucking. The grabbing and neck flexion can lead to undesirable over-developed muscling in the jaw and neck. The horse may damage the object it grabs. Cribbing is one of the most annoying stereotypic behaviors, and it has been treated with muzzles, collars, and even surgery called the Forsell's procedure, severing muscles and nerves that enabled the horse to crib. These interventions are problematic, because the horse is denied a stress-alleviating behavior. Also cribbing can increase salivary flow, which supplies antacid, alleviating the acidic stomach that develops from fasting between meals.

Horses with stereotypic behavior lie down less and can be slower to learn new tasks. These two characteristics could be linked through the explanation of sleep deprivation.

There is a well-established phenomenon in animal training called extinction behavior, which describes an animal's effort when an act that was rewarded is no longer rewarded. Before the animal stops making the effort or action, it initially increases the effort or action, trying to make the reward reappear. The short-term increase in effort is extinction behavior, and it has been observed to be stronger in animals who already engage in stereotypy. In other words, stereotypic behavior, an obsessive habit, leads to other obsessive, negative behavior.

In one study of weanlings that had never been in stalls, half were housed one per stall, and the other half were stalled in pairs, two to a stall. The paired weanlings displayed no stereotypic behavior, while two-thirds of the solo weanlings displayed some stereotypic behavior. Established stereotypies can persist even when the living situation is corrected.

Some people believe horses copy bad behavior from another horse, although no evidence supports this belief. Fearing that a cribber might lead other horses into cribbing, barn managers often isolate a cribber, which worsens the horse's distress. Cribbing horses tend to be subject to frequent re-sells as well, which adds more stress to their lives.

Prevention is the best antidote to stereotypic behavior, and that preventative treatment is turnout with forage, preferably in the company of another horse. A life that includes the opportunity for mutual grooming—standing peaceably and companionably together, swishing flies from each other's faces, nibbling at itches along the pasturemate's shoulders or spine—as free as possible from fasting and excessive confinement, is a life that meets the horse's behavioral and social needs.

Macronutrients for Maintenance Metabolism

The final component to meeting your horse's feeding needs are the nutrients that provide for maintenance metabolism. An astounding number of reactions and interactions occur between vitamins, minerals, fatty acids, amino acids, hormones, or precursors to these and other compounds. An excess or deficiency in one biochemical can have a cascade of effects in others. In the big picture, these compounds all arise from six macronutrients: water, vitamins, minerals, carbohydrates, fat, and protein.

Water

Water is the most critical macronutrient. An average, 1,100 pound (500 kilogram) horse at maintenance (not engaged in any riding or other work) that is living in a mild climate environment requires about 6.5 gallons (25 liters, calculated at 5 liters per 100 kg of body weight) per day when it is eating 1.5 percent of its weight in feed per day. If fed a more-usual 2 percent of its weight in hay alone, the water needs almost double. Sweat losses from work or hot weather, or fluid loss from lactation, can more than triple the water needs.

Generally, plenty of clean water should always be available to horses, except for during brief medical circumstances that contraindicate drinking. Intentional deprivation in order to teach the horse to drink when presented with water has been practiced by some owners in preparation for treks that will involve waterless hours before reaching a stream or puddle, but this is a special circumstance not applicable to the vast majority of horses.

More likely, owners are seeking ways to increase their horses' intake of water, especially in circumstances of weather extremes or travel where a horse may become distracted by surroundings or finicky about its water change and then become dehydrated. Horses can be mildly dehydrated, with a loss of up to 4 percent of their fluids, but not display symptoms. A moderately dehydrated horse may exhibit decreased urination, inappetance (anorexia), a delayed capillary refill time, skin tenting, and dry feces. When these signs present, the horse has already lost 4-9% of its body fluid.

Counting Swallows

I was a little rummy eighty-five miles into the Tevis ride when I reached the veterinary checkpoint called Francisco's, right before fording the American River. After presenting my wonderful horse for examination by veterinarian James Kerr, I hand-jogged her, so he could evaluate her gait.

"Have you been counting swallows?" he asked me.

I imagined a flock of birds and stared at him. It was after midnight by then (we'd started riding around 5:00 AM), not a great time for birding. He repeated his question. Blanking, the best I could come up with was, "What?"

"Count swallows when she drinks. Thirty swallows is a gallon," he said. "Don't ever forget that."

Water intake may be improved by adding flavor (a spoonful of fruit juice or apple cider vinegar but never an artificial sweetener), especially when water sources are unfamiliar to the horse.

Hard-working horses regularly drink from both plain and salt water buckets when provided with the two options. During strenuous work, especially in hot or humid weather, providing a bucket of salt water in addition to a bucket of plain water may help restore fluids and electrolytes. One ounce of table salt in a gallon of water approximates an isotonic saline solution. (Isotonic matches the salinity of body fluids and is described pharmaceutically as 0.9 percent, meaning that there are nine grams of sodium chloride per liter of water). Chapter 4 offers more on information on sweat loss and electrolytes.

Hard water with a high mineral content is associated with enteroliths (the stones that form in some horses' gastrointestinal tracts), but it is difficult to separate this finding from the high-mineral soils and hard water in the same location. Those enteroliths could be caused by the feed as well as the water.

Finally, horses are known to reduce their water intake in inclement weather when only very cold water is available. Heaters in the buckets and troughs can dramatically improve these horses' water consumption. In very hot weather, shaded water will be more appealing than water out in the sun.

Vitamins

Vitamins are quantified in international units (IU) or milligrams. The vitamins a healthy horse requires are listed in Table 2–4, but only vitamins A, D, E, B1, and B2 have specific, estimated daily-requirement levels. Estimated needs simply based on body weight can lead to oversupplying our horses with vitamins, but a better, broad method of recommending needs has not been identified.

Some vitamins are made by the microbes in the horse's gut, some he must consume in feed, and some he synthesizes on his own. Good pasture and decent, free-choice hay generally provides sufficient vitamin material. If your horse is receiving these, he is unlikely to be vitamin deficient. Vitamins are classified as fat soluble if they are stored in body fat and organ tissue, and water soluble if they are not. Choline, sometimes classed as a vitamin, has not been well-studied in horses.

You may see products advertised as having provitamins. This terrific-sounding term just means that the substance is one that the body naturally converts to a vitamin. A provitamin is a precursor, or necessary for the chemical reaction in the body.

Vitamin A occurs naturally as of beta-carotene. Deficiency causes night blindness; the minimum requirement was established by determining the amount needed to prevent night blindness and then adding a safety margin. Toxicity causes birth defects and bone problems.

B-complex vitamins are water soluble. The microbial population of the hindgut synthesizes B-complex vitamins. A horse lacking a healthy microbial population (think of a rescue horse that has been malnourished for a protracted period), could be deficient in B vitamins. Additionally, a horse poisoned by any plant classified as a thiaminase—which destroy thiamin (B1)—will need urgent, massive thiamin supplementation. Veterinarians carry a concentrated, injectable form of

Table 2-4 Vitamins Required by the Horse	
Water Soluble	**Fat Soluble**
C	A
B-complex:	D
B1 thiamin	E
B2 riboflavin	K
B3 niacin	
B5 pantothenic acid	
B6 pyridoxine	
B7 biotin	
B9 folic acid	
B12 cyanocobalamin	

thiamin for these situations. Biotin is frequently supplemented to promote hoof growth, though it generally takes a year to notice improvement. These hoof supplements often come with a host of other vitamins, minerals, or precursors to other compounds, so it is difficult to isolate the singular effectiveness of one component of these supplements.

Vitamin C is an antioxidant that works in concert with vitamin E on many body functions. Neither deficiencies nor toxicities are generally encountered in horses, but their bodies adapt to supplementation by reducing their own manufacture of vitamin C. Because of this, if you have been supplementing vitamin C and wish to stop, taper off rather than abruptly stopping.

Vitamin D is vital to how the horse processes calcium. It is found in plants, and the horse makes it when exposed to sunlight. Two forms are ergocalciferol (D_2)cholecalciferol (D_3). A deficiency can occur in a horse that is always blanketed or indoors. The bone deformities of rickets or osteomalacia in adult horses occur with deficiency; toxicity leads to calcified soft tissues.

Vitamin E is stored in the liver and other tissues in the body. It is an antioxidant, important in the absorption of the trace mineral selenium, and it potentiates vitamin C. A deficiency is associated with equine motor neuron disease (EMND) and equine degenerative mycloencephalopathy (EDM). Vitamin E is abundant in fresh pasture. A horse with no access to fresh gazing likely needs supplementation. Hay loses more vitamin E the longer it is stored.

A study of three groups of unfit horses administered either no vitamin E, a medium dose (in the form of 5,000 international units (IU) of dl-a-tocopheryl), or a high dose (10,000 IU) found that the dosed horses did not experience lower oxidative stress than the control group. Moreover, the horses receiving the high dose vitamin E had lower blood levels of beta-carotene, which implies that the high dose vitamin E inhibits beta-carotene.

In a study of natural versus synthetic vitamin E given to needy foals (all were from mares that had previously produced foals with neurological problems—neuroaxonal dystrophy (NAD) or equine degenerative myeloencephalopathy (EDM)—helped by vitamin E supplementation), the foals given synthetic vitamin E needed twice the dose of foals given natural vitamin E.

Vitamin K is vital to blood clotting and important in many amino acid reactions, and scientists know that they do not know everything vitamin K does in the body. There are three sub-categories identified in vitamin K: phylloquinone (K1), menaquinone (K2), and menadione (K3). Phylloquinone is readily found in forage, and the other two are synthesized by microbes in the GIT. The minimum daily-required level of vitamin K has not been established in horses. There have been no reports of natural (not clinically induced for laboratory study or by a trainer injecting an overdose in the form of menadione sodium bisulfate) deficiency or toxicity of vitamin K.

Minerals

Much of the knowledge about minerals is extrapolated from other species. There is still no agreed-upon, established level of the amount of some minerals that a horse needs. There are seven macrominerals required in grams per day. The microminerals, also called trace minerals, are required in milligrams per day. There is some debate about what qualifies as a trace requirement, because some are acquired along with more prevalent minerals, and therefore it is difficult to know if a microscopic amount that cannot be excluded from the diet is actually vital. Boron and vanadium are examples of trace minerals required at levels so low that neither a deficiency nor a required level have ever been identified. A horse must have a trace amount of chromium too, but he gets it with good nutrition, and there's no convincing evidence to show that he needs extra, thus it may not be listed as a mineral.

Key points of primary minerals pertaining to the horse's nutritional physiology are covered here. Providing these nutrients in feedstuffs is detailed in Chapter 4.

Minerals interact with each other, as well as other chemicals in the body, each filling various roles under different body systems. The interplay between different minerals is complicated and not entirely known.

An example of the complex interplay is that a diet high in calcium and phosphorus seems to impair magnesium absorption or availability. The bioavailability of minerals varies greatly depending on the feed in which it is found. A deficiency of cobalt would theoretically render microbes unable to produce the cobalamin for vitamin B12. (A lack of cobalt has never been identified in a horse.)

Mineral requirements may also be listed as parts per million (PPM) on many proprietary feeds. One PPM is equivalent to one milligram in one kilogram. The Chapter 4 section on proprietary feeds walks you through converting feed constituents listed on a feed label out of PPM.

Some minerals are individually discussed below, but in a nutshell, sodium is usually the first to consider supplementing, in the form of sodium chloride. The ratio between the macrominerals calcium and phosphorus is also a critical consideration. Amongst microminerals, selenium merits special attention, because both deficiency and toxicity can be found in the diet due to regional variations, and the ratio of copper to zinc must be balanced. Minerals are also electrolytes; primarily the electrically charged forms of sodium, chloride, calcium, potassium, and magnesium.

Table 2-5 Minerals Required by the Horse	
Macrominerals	**Microminerals (trace minerals)**
calcium Ca	chromium Cr
chlorine Cl	cobalt Co
magnesium Mg	copper Cu
phosphorus P	fluoride F
potassium K	iodine I
sodium Na	iron Fe
sulfur S	manganese Mn
	molybdenum Mo
	selenium Se
	zinc Zn

Calcium

Calcium is the most prevalent mineral in the body. A rough estimate of its abundance is to consider the skeleton of a 1,000 pound horse to weigh 200 pounds, and assume that twenty pounds of that skeleton is calcium.

The hormone calcitonin influences the movement of calcium in the body. An excess of calcium hampers the processing of magnesium. The calcium:magnesium ratio should be between 2.5:1 and 3:1. Calcium is mostly absorbed in the small intestine with help from parathyroid hormone and physiologically active vitamin D_3. Young horses are much more efficient than mature horses at absorbing calcium. Absorption can be diminished by the presence of other cations (positively charged ions), especially phosphorus. Calcium and phosphorus are readily absorbed as dicalcium phosphate or monosodium phosphate, so these forms are often included in supplements or fortified feeds. Calcium absorption can also be impaired by the plant compounds of phytate and oxalate. Phytic acid deters absorption of calcium and phosphorus, as well as the microminerals of iron, manganese, and zinc. The addition of phytases have improved the digestibility of calcium, but not phosphorus.

The calcium:phosphorus ratio is a primary concern in balancing a horse's diet. A general healthy ratio is to have about twice as much calcium as phosphorus. Much higher ratios are common for horses primarily fed alfalfa; horses do all right with higher calcium but if the potassium level reaches or exceeds the calcium level, they will become unhealthy. A painful condition called nutritional secondary hyperparathyroidism (NSH) results, with the bones demineralizing and being replaced with cartilage.

An excess of both calcium and phosphorus can diminish magnesium absorption.

Most animals excrete excess calcium in their feces, but horses are unique in that they excrete excess in the urine. Because of this, a horse with impaired kidney function is a candidate for urinary stones in the form of calcium oxalate. The risk of these renal and bladder stones are why horses with impaired kidney function should not be given an excess of calcium and phosphorus.

Chloride, Copper, Iodine, Iron, Magnesium, Phosphorus, Potassium, Selenium, Silicon, and Sulfur

Chlorine is the elemental complement needed to form chloride salts with sodium, potassium, and calcium in various body functions at the cellular level. Deficiencies do not occur unless a horse is actually sodium depleted due to very poor nutrition or artificially depleted through the administration of sodium bicarbonate (also called bicarb). This serves as another caution against "milkshakes" of bicarb given by some trainers of athletic horses.

Copper helps detoxify superoxide, works with numerous enzymes in the body, and interacts with other minerals. High molybdenum in ruminants interferes with copper function, but horses can have much higher molybdenum levels and still have good copper distribution. Copper deficiency may play a role in some developmental orthopedic disease.

The copper:zinc ration should be 1:3 or 1:4. Copper and zinc tend to be adequate or oversupplied in diets of hay and most compound feeds.

Iodine is integral to proper thyroid function. Both severe deficiencies and toxicities, although uncommon, can cause hypothyroidism. Raw soy products, kale, and cabbages have a goiter-producing effect that is neutralized by cooking or significant iodine supplementation.

Iron is central to the oxygen-carrying capacity of blood, but deficiencies available in supplements have not been reported. Toxicity does occur in over-supplemented horses, especially young stock.

Magnesium is the fourth-most prevalent electrolyte in the horse's body, after calcium, sodium, and potassium. Sixty percent of the horse's magnesium is in its skeleton, 38 percent is in soft tissues, and about 2 percent is in extracellular space. It is found in alfalfa, beet pulp, molasses, and grain. The uptake of magnesium occurs in the small intestine, primarily in the duodenum and upper jejunum. Most equine diets meet or exceed the recommended level of magnesium. Absorbable forms are magnesium citrate, magnesium aspartate, magnesium sulfate, magnesium oxide, and magnesium carbonate. Some owners become concerned about which form to use and point to details like, for example, magnesium aspartate, an organic compound, is absorbed better than inorganic magnesium oxide, or the fact that magnesium oxide may depress the horse's appetite. Magnesium could form salts with potassium, reducing the absorption of magnesium. Calcium and magnesium may compete for the same absorption sites in the small intestine. It is interesting to note that a person with adequate calcium and phosphorus but inadequate magnesium can get osteoporosis, showing again that the balance of minerals is vital.

A magnesium deficiency has been linked to fractious behavior that is corrected through supplementation. This has led to the regular suggestion of magnesium as a calming supplement, but there is no evidence that magnesium calms a horse that does not already have a magnesium deficiency.

Your horse is unlikely to be deficient in magnesium if he receives a healthy diet. If you want to supplement magnesium, there are a number of safe supplements (discussed in Chapter 4).

Phosphorus is always considered in conjunction with calcium, where various ratios are encountered, but the key point is the amount of phosphorus should always be less than that of calcium. Phosphorus works with proteins and lipids for various functions. It is abundant in a normal equine diet. In grain, the majority of phosphorus present is contained as phylate. A gross excess of phosphorus leads to nutritional secondary hyperparathyroidism (NSH). A horse generally does not have a deficiency of phosphorus without also having other significant mineral deficiencies; starved animals are the most commonly encountered cases.

Potassium is vital to cell function, regulating neuromuscular excitability. Because forage is very high in potassium, deficiencies should not normally occur. Oilseed meals (flax, sunflower, et cetera) are another concentrated source of potassium. Because the horse loses a great deal of potassium in sweat and uses it in muscle contractions, potassium is frequently included in electrolyte compounds, but do not oversupply potassium in these preparations. A healthy horse readily excretes excess potassium, but supplementation during extremely hard exercise is not recommended. Excess potassium must be avoided for horses with the inherited disorder of hyperkalemic periodic paralysis (HYPP).

Selenium works in conjunction with vitamin E. It has a narrow safety range. Horses require about one milligram per day; European law forbids feeding more than 5 milligrams per day to a 500 kilogram (1,100 pound) horse. The most common way horses get toxicity is grazing on high-selenium pasture. Selenium toxicity has been called alkali disease, because alkali soils tend to be high in selenium; thus feeds grown in regions with these soils (the central part of North America is an example) tend to have high selenium. Signs of toxicity are weight loss, jaundice, inappetance, and blind staggers. Selenium deficiency may cause immune problems, tying up, and white muscle disease. The northwest and the northeast regions of the United States tend to have soils that are low in selenium.

Silicon has a role in forming the cartilage matrix. A deficiency may lead to osteochondrosis, but high forage diets should supply adequate silicon.

Sulfur is vital to countless functions, yet deficiencies are not generally encountered. Sulfur-containing amino acids include methionine, cysteine, and the related compound, cystine. The only toxicity reported has been when horses were given a pure-sulfur product called flowers-of-sulfur, which contains far too much sulfur to be healthy for horses.

Carbohydrate

Whether discussing forages or non-forages, remember that carbohydrate is king with horses. Most plants for horses are largely carbohydrate based. Even legume hay, which is known for being higher in protein and calories than grass hay, is mostly carbohydrate.

Within the class of carbohydrate are simple sugars, complex polymers (notably fructan and starch), and the structural carbohydrate that comprises plant fibers. Sugars are also called saccharides. The simplest are monosaccharides, then disaccharides, and finally polysaccharides. Glucose, fructose, and galactose are monosaccharides. Sucrose (made of glucose and fructose), maltose, and lactose are disaccharide. Starch is a polysaccharide composed of amylopectin and amylose. Fructan is a polysaccharide and may also be referred to as an oligosaccharide or a short-chain fructooligosaccharide (scFOS), depending upon the chemical bonds in place. Hemicellulose, cellulose, raffinose, and arabinose are examples of complex, structural carbohydrates.

The Glycemic Index

The concept of a glycemic index (GI) began in the world of human nutrition. The focus is to identify foods that cause rapid rises in the blood sugar (and thus a rise in insulin levels), as well as foods that do not provoke a strong glycemic response. In order to have an index, one food was selected and given a number, then other foods are compared to this standard. In the glycemic index for people, white bread is often assigned the number 100, although the GI began by using fifty grams of glucose as the initial standard of 100. Foods that provoke a lower and slower glycemic response are ranked under 100. Foods that provoke a higher and faster glycemic response than white bread have GI numbers above 100.

A glycemic index for common horse feeds assigned oats the number 100, then tested horses' blood glucose before and after consuming other feeds. They determined sweet feed to have the highest glycemic response at 129, then corn at 117. Feeds with the lowest glycemic response were beet pulp, and alfalfa, both ranked about 20, then rice bran under 20, and finally soybean hulls at 7. Barley and wheat bran had an intermediate response in the 50s or 60s. Jockey oats—a choice classification of oats also called racehorse oats—ranked slightly above regular oats.

Lay publications offer various unattributed permutations of the equine GI, giving very different numbers for different feeds. Some rank beet pulp at 24, corn at 112, and barley at 81. Others rank barley at 101, while placing beet pulp at 1. Some of these numbers may have arisen from a research paper that was later pulled from publication, because the scientists noted flaws in the study.

Research has proven that the glycemic response to a feed by an individual horse is affected by the feed's nutrient composition, the horse's rate of consumption, and the speed of gastric emptying. Also, studies have shown that processing grain (usually by heating or grinding) influences the horse's glycemic response, especially as the quantity of starch per meal is increased.

One study examined the difference in horses' glycemic response to corn processed by three different methods: cracking, grinding, and steam processing. The point of this research was to assess how digestible the grain is in the small intestine, before it can reach the cecum. Good pre-cecal digestibility means that fewer undigested sugars or starches will reach the cecum, where they can overload the microflora and trigger hindgut acidosis, colic, and laminitis. Grain always has a higher glycemic index than forage. Many healthy by-products have a low-glycemic index, but some carry a lot of starch and provoke a strong response.

Horses with the medical conditions of equine metabolic syndrome (EMS), insulin resistance (IR), pituitary pars intermedia dysfunction (PPID), and polysaccharide storage myopathy (PSSM) will all do better with feeds that do not provoke a high or fast glycemic response. Most animals do better under most conditions on low-GI feeds. Because there is no universal GI for horses (or for humans), it is better not to get hung up on the numbers. You only need to incorporate the concept that a low and slow glycemic response is healthiest—just as offering forage low and slow is healthier.

Fat

A normal horse diet of grasses contains as little as less than 1 percent fat, ranging up to 4 percent. The enzyme lipase in the horse's foregut breaks fat down into fatty acids and glycerol. Two fatty acids (alpha-linolenic acid and linoleic acid) are called essential fatty acids, because the horse cannot make them. They are supplied in good forage. Much is made by some owners of the profile or balance of these fatty acids and others that the horse makes from them, but the research is not yet clear.

It is clear that for the majority of horses whose energy needs cannot be met through forage alone (growing youngsters, athletes, and late-gestation mares are prime examples), fat—not grain—is an excellent source. Among horses requiring extra energy to a good forage diet, fat-supplemented horses are less reactive than horses supplemented via carbohydrate concentrates (grain or grain-fortified feeds). This effect was shown in another study in which horses with a 3 percent fat diet were compared to horses with a high fat (10 percent) diet; the high fat horses were less reactive. You'll find more information on supplementing fat via oil in Chapter 4.

Protein

Horses need 8 to 10 percent protein, although active broodmares, growing youngsters, and extreme athletes require more. An excess causes the horse to lose electrolytes through the added urination required to eliminate the excess nitrogen that comes from eating too much protein. Calculating protein requirements is complicated, so the amounts needed for various weights of horses at various work levels are listed for you on the Ultimate Chart.

Enzymes break protein into amino acids (AAs), which are classified as essential or non-essential. Essential means that horses cannot make or synthesize the substance; they must consume it. Amino acids that the horse can produce internally are classified as non-essential.

Some owners get very concerned about different amino acids. They worry about getting enough branched-chain amino acids (BCAAs). (Three of the essential AAs—leucine, isoleucine, and valine—are called BCAAs due to their chemical structure, which also influences the roles they fulfill.) They confuse the amino acid cysteine with cystine. (Cystine is formed by two cysteine molecules and is more stable.) They get concerned that their horses don't make enough of the compounds AAs create. (Acetyl-L carnitine, which horses make out of lysine and methionine, has been suggested as an ergogenic and plays a role in hoof health, among other functions.) They worry about what substances are really amino acids. (Hydroxylysine and hydroxyproline are versions of lysine and proline, although they are sometimes listed as additional AAs.) Similarly, some sources do not markedly differentiate between glutamate and glutamine, or between aspartate and asparagine. They worry about which are really essential. (When sufficient methionine is present, cysteine may be considered a non-essential AA.) They worry about having enough of the chemical precursors the horse requires to make certain AAs. (Methionine and cysteine contain sulfur, and theoretically, a sulfur deficiency would render a horse unable to process them.) They worry about zwitterion amino acids, because they do not know what it means, but someone said their horses need them. (Zwitterion is a name for a compound that can have both a positive and a negative charge; amino acids are zwitterions.)

Table 2-6 Essential and Non-Essential Amino Acids	
Essential	**Non-Essential**
arginine	alanine
histidine	asparagine
isoleucine	aspartate (aspartic acid)
leucine	cysteine
lysine*	glutamate (glutamic acid)
methionine	glutamine
phenylalanine	glycine
threonine	proline
tryptophan	serine
valine	tyrosine
*denotes the first-limiting AA	

Worrying about the entire amino acid profile is unnecessary. Here's why: lysine is known as a first-limiting amino acid, because it's present in only small amounts in most feed; it is hardest to acquire. In evaluating the amino acids in feeds, look at the lysine level. If the horse is getting enough lysine, you can be comfortable that he is getting enough of all of his amino acids. The recommendation for lysine has been revised and increased to 4.3 percent of a horse's total crude-protein intake. This level is precalculated for various horse weights on the Ultimate Chart.

Metabolism: Maintenance and More

The six macronutrients (water, vitamins, minerals, carbohydrate, fat, and protein) combine to provide complete nutritional requirements for the horse. All of the energy or calories needed for metabolism come from carbohydrate, fat, or protein.

Energy requirements are determined by workload. A horse that is not in riding, driving, or any other training, and is not in use as a breeding animal but is simply at rest only needs to intake enough energy for basic metabolism, or maintenance. To maintain its body weight, a horse needs to consume about 2 percent of its weight per day in forage. This amount is precalculated for various horse weights on the Ultimate Chart.

Metabolism is affected by a horse's individuality. A reactive horse that alerts and responds to every stimulus burns more energy than a calm animal. Reactive personalities tend to be more active in turnout as well; a docile horse will be more sedentary, burn fewer calories, and need to consume less energy.

Quantifying Energy (counting calories) in Equine Nutrition

Horses' nutritional needs and feeds are measured in *megacalories* or *megajoules*, but these two terms are not synonymous.

- A calorie (lowercase c) is the amount of energy required to raise the temperature of 1 gram of water 1° centigrade
- 1,000 calories = 1 kilocalorie, abbreviated 1 kcal, or 1 Calorie (uppercase C);
  Calories and kilocalories are both too small to quantify the large-energy requirements of horses, so megacalories are used
- 1,000,000 calories = 1 megacalorie, abbreviated as 1 Mcal
  However, the internationally accepted unit for measuring energy is *joule*.
- 1,000,000 joules = 1 megajoule, abbreviated 1MJ
- 1 Mcal = 4.184 MJ
- Carbohydrates have about 4.2 Mcal/kg
- Fats have about 9.5 Mcal/kg
- Proteins have about 4.1 Mcal/kg

Table 2-7 Nutrient Requirements of a 1,100 pound (500 kg) Horse at Maintenance Per the National Research Council (NRC)

Constituent	Amount
energy	16.7 Mcal
crude protein	630.0 grams
lysine	27.1 grams
vitamin A	15,000 international units
vitamin D	3,300 international units
vitamin E	500 international units
vitamin B1	30.0 milligrams
vitamin B2	20.0 milligrams
calcium	20.0 grams
chloride	40.0 grams
magnesium	7.5 grams
phosphorus	14.0 grams
potassium	25.0 grams
sodium	10.0 grams
sulfur	15.0 grams
cobalt	0.5 milligrams
copper	100.0 milligrams
iodine	3.5 milligrams
iron	400.0 milligrams
manganese	400.0 milligrams
selenium	1.0 milligram
zinc	400.0 milligrams

Quantifying Energy

A calorie is too small a measure for equine food; it is also too small for human nutrition. People discussing calories in human nutrition are usually actually talking about kilocalories but are abbreviating the word kilocalorie as calorie—although it would properly be written as Calorie. A kilocalorie is the amount of heat required to raise the temperature of one kilogram of water one degree centigrade (Celsius). Energy for horses is quantified in megacalories or megajoules.

One academic body that determines horses' nutritional requirements is the National Research Council (NRC), which is based in the United States. Their standard is used throughout North America and the United Kingdom. The NRC offers a free, online program (the website is provided in the Resources section and on the Ultimate Chart) to calculate the estimated requirements for any weight and working level of horse.

There will be adverse effects on the horse's health and performance if its nutritional requirements are undersupplied or oversupplied. Remember that maintenance means an idle horse in a neutral environment. In cold weather, your horse may need half again as much hay in order to keep warm. If a horse is maintaining its body condition with adequate but not excessive fat cover, then its energy intake and workload are balanced. Increase the feed if the horse is losing condition; decrease the feed if the horse is over-nourished.

Beyond the starting point of a primary diet for a horse at maintenance, other dietary situations are either additive or reductive. Bred or lactating mares, growing horses, breeding stallions, and horses from moderate to extreme levels of activity all have special, amplified dietary concerns and are examined separately under Chapter 9, Special Diets, as are safe reducing diets for overweight horses. The calculations for these special diets are also provided on the Ultimate Chart. Coupling knowledge of the horse's nutritional physiology with a solid understanding of feed labels and analyses enables intelligent consideration of your choices among the many forage and non-forage supplementary feeds.

CHAPTER 3
Understanding Feed Labels: Ash? What Ash? And Why is the Protein Crude?

RATHER THAN BEING swayed by the attractive photos, testimonials, and colorful advertising on feed sacks, smart owners read the small, black-and-white label on the bag. The habit of reading feed tags—whether the bag contains one generic component, such as oats, alfalfa pellets, beet pulp, or soy hulls, or whether it is a proprietary feed with over a dozen ingredients—gives buyers familiarity with the numbers.

There are numerous types of feed analyses in use, each providing different degrees of information. Some testing methods are old, but because they are still used by the feed industry, it's important to understand them, as well as more recently developed methods. Also, forage producers often offer measures that are more useful in feeding cattle than horses, so a familiarity with these commonly encountered measurements is helpful.

Finally, we'll review hay sampling procedures. Owners who do not have their hay analyzed still need to learn about sampling and feed analysis in order to understand the average values of hays and other feeds, compare them, and make intelligent purchases.

ABOVE: **Understanding the information offered by the labels on horse feeds helps owners make smart purchases.**

Ingredients

Constituents or ingredients in a feed bag are listed in descending order of prevalence by weight. For example, a complete feed that lists alfalfa meal and then soybean hulls contains more alfalfa meal than it does soybean hulls. Even a package that is expected to contain only one ingredient will have an ingredients list. Near this list of ingredients is the manufacturer's analysis.

Table 3-1 Feed Analysis Abbreviations and Measures

Abbreviation	For	Measures
ACP	adjusted crude protein	CP - (minus) UP
AD	apparent digestibility	(feed intake-nutrients in feces) ÷ feed intake
ADF	acid detergent fiber	primarily report cellulose and lignin content
ADFCP	acid detergent fiber crude protein	insoluble protein in post-ADF residue
ADICP	acid detergent fiber insoluble protein same as ADFCP	
ADIN	acid detergent insoluble nitrogen	nitrogen in post ADF residue (estimates heat damage)
ADL	acid detergent lignin	lignin
AIA	acid-insoluble ash	silica component of the sample's ash
aNDF	amylase-treated NDF	improvement on NDF for total insoluble fiber (treated with solutions of amylase and sulfite)
AP	available protein	protein in the feed the horse can process
CF	crude fiber	structural carbs: cellulose, hemicellulose, & lignin
CP	crude protein	est. protein by evaluating nitrogen content
DDM	digestible dry matter	88.9 - (.779 x %ADF)
DE	digestible energy	megacalories per lb. or kg of feed - fecal loss
DM	dry matter	FW - WM, given as a %
DMD	dry matter digestibility	(DM in feed - DM in feces) ÷ DM in feed
DMI	dry matter intake	120 ÷ %NDF
DW	dry weight	the weight of dry matter
EE	ether extract	lipids or fats, plus indigestible waxes
ESC	ethanol soluble-soluble carbohydrates	simple sugars + pectin
FW	fresh weight	weight prior to drying
GE	gross energy	total energy in a feed, although not all is available
IVDMD	in vitro dry matter digestibility	lab estimate of DMD
ME	metabolizable energy	DE - energy loss from urine & gas
ND	not detectable	constituent not found in the analysis
NDF	neutral detergent fiber	cellulose, hemicellulose, and lignin
NDICP	neutral detergent insoluble CP	6.25 x NDIN

NDIN	neutral detergent insoluble nitrogen	nitrogen in the NDF residue
NE	net energy	ME – heat increment (energy lost in heat)
NFC	non-fiber carbohydrates	100 - (CP + (NDF - NDICP) + fat + ash)
NFE	nitrogen-free extract	rough carb count: 100 - (water+ ash+CP+CF+EE)
NPN	non-protein nitrogen	nitrogen determined not to be part of a protein
NSC	non-structural carbohydrates	WSC + starch content
NSP	non-starch polysaccharides	fructan + pectin + non-simple sugars
OM	organic matter	DM minus ash
RFQ	relative forage quality	(TDN x DMI) ÷ 1.23
RFV	relative feed value	(DDM x DMI) ÷ 1.29
SDF	soluble dietary fiber	cellulose + hemicellulose
TDF	total dietary fiber	insoluble + soluble fiber, little used for animals
TDN	total digestible nutrients	calculated from ash, CP, ADF, and NDF
UP	unavailable protein	protein bound in fiber or carbohydrate
WM	wet matter	FW minus DM, given as a %
WSC	water soluble carbohydrates	simple sugars + fructan

Knowledgeable owners understand the critical difference between non-structural carbohydrates and structural carbohydrates measured in some feed analyses. The section on botany in Chapter 4 clarifies these distinct types of carbohydrates in plants, including the critical environmental influences that impact their levels.

Buyers who know what should be in a feed—whether for a horse at maintenance, with insulin resistance, heavily pregnant, in hard physical training, or just a weanling—can read only the small tags on a bag of feed and be able to predict the life situation and workload of the horse the feed is intended for without looking at the front of the package. The mineral balance, fat and protein levels, and kinds of carbohydrates listed will suit a particular level of activity or other physical need.

In the United States, feed manufacturers may advertise that their ingredient suppliers are approved by the FDA and/or the American Association of Feed Control Officials (AAFCO). This approval process excludes grain suppliers.

Caution

Animal feeds are not necessarily interchangeable between foraging species. Additives for some ruminant feed, for example ionophores in cattle feed, are lethal to horses. No matter how reputable the feed manufacturer is, never give your horse a bag of grain or mixed feed labeled for cattle.

Label Factors

Typical labels on horse feeds, or from laboratory analyses of feed samples, include a variety of abbreviations that refer to various measurements. These factors reveal what is contained in the feed, its value, and enable a useful comparison of one feed to another. The table below defines these factors and their abbreviations. The number of abbreviations and tests in feed analysis can initially seem overwhelming, but after a read-through, the factors do fall into place and make sense.

The most important fractions to note in a feed analysis are overall energy, the types of carbohydrate present, protein and fat content, and the vitamin and mineral content. However, not all of these factors will be listed on every commercial feed tag, so this book provides average values for feedstuffs.

Some factors are more important than others, and some information is simply not available. For example, complete vitamin and mineral assays are not available for most feeds. This fact often surprises customers who thought analysis of every feed constituent factor is available or who thought they knew their feeds better than they actually do.

Feed Analyses

Many feed analysis tests overlap each other, because there are several ways to derive the same or similar information. Some values found in various feed analyses are indirect measures, calculated from other known factors.

Proximate analysis, detergent fiber analysis, and specific chemical analysis through near infrared spectroscopy (NIRS) or high-performance liquid chromatography (HPLC) are used to analyze feedstuffs. Some feed-analysis reports can also identify undesirable components of a sample that provide no nutrition or, worse, are evidence of a bad feed. Examples are mycotoxins, fungicides, herbicides, pesticides, weeds, or other plants that should not be in the sample.

It is disappointing but essential to recognize that feed analyses are not standardized. This stems from the fact that forage analysis began as an aid to raising beef and dairy cattle, which has very different nutritional goals from what horse owners want. Analyses have only recently been used to guide horse nutrition. The result is that four laboratories may offer four different methods for determining the sugar level in hay. When purchasing forage analysis, always specify that you want it for equine nutrition.

Proximate Analysis

Proximate analysis dates from the 1860s and is sometimes called Weende analysis, as the methods were developed at the Weende Experimental Station in Germany. It reports the dry matter, ash, and crude estimates of the levels of protein, fat, and fiber. It indirectly gives the level of carbohydrate.

DRY MATTER

All feeds are composed of both dry matter (DM) and wet matter (WM). Freshly cut hay, for instance, might have a DM content of only 15 percent and a WM of 85 percent. The fresh weight (FW) of this just-cut hay is mostly water. Ten pounds of fresh grass or freshly cut hay is desirable food to the horse, but because it's 85 percent water, it's equivalent to only 1.5 pounds of common, dry hay.

In order to compare feeds, compare the dry matter. Once cut grass or hay has dried or cured, so much water has evaporated that the feed weight is greatly reduced. Although hay seems dry, with no moisture at all, it does contain moisture. A figure of 90 percent DM, implying a 10 percent WM, is not unusual in a hay sample.

Commercial laboratories often list both an analysis of the DM and an analysis of the feed sample before drying, or *as fed*. This *as-fed* analysis reports exactly what is contained in the amount fed, while the DM analysis enables direct comparison to another feed.

Dry matter contains both organic and inorganic material. Organic material includes the three forms of energy (carbohydrates, proteins, and fats), vitamins, organic acids, and nucleic acids. Inorganic material includes factors like dirt, sand, and minerals, which are referred to in the analysis as *ash*.

ABOVE: **Ash is a measurement of a feed's mineral content. Photo courtesy of Dr. Lynn Van Wieringen.**

ASH

After the dry matter (DM) of a feed sample is assessed, part of the sample is burned (ashed) to remove the carbon portions, which are organic, leaving the inorganic matter. Weighing the sample before and after ashing lets the analyst know the weight or amount of the organic matter (OM) the sample contained, thus DM - ash = OM.

Notice that some feed-sample results are determined indirectly, by calculation, as above when OM is determined by burning the dry matter feed sample and measuring the remaining ash. This is an indirect measure, because OM is reported from the DM minus the remaining ash content. A sample that was found to contain 0.7 percent ash is deduced to have contained 99.3 percent organic matter.

A feed tag that lists an ash level is not reporting that the bag contains that percent of ash, but rather that when analyzed, the feed was found to contain that percentage of inorganic material. Buyers who mistakenly equate ash content with the hygienic quality of a feed think that a feed should have 0 percent ash. Remember that the ash content includes all of the minerals present in the feed. Minerals are an essential macronutrient.

CRUDE FAT

A crude estimate of a feed sample's fat content is derived by extracting the lipids (fats) from the sample with ether. This ether extract (EE) is only an estimate of the fat or lipid content, because waxes and other fat-soluble matter are also extracted, which can lead to an overestimation of the feed's fat content.

Grasses and hays tend to range from less than 1 percent to perhaps four precent fat, while grains or seeds can range between 1 percent in some barley to a high of forty-three perecent in flax.

Complete feeds manufactured for horses often have higher fat levels than a horse's natural diet offers. Commercial feeds are formulated with higher fat levels in order to raise the overall energy content so that smaller quantities can be fed. This is more convenient for the owner, but the physically smaller ration can be less satisfying to the horse. On the other hand, some horses benefit from high fat feeds; these include athletes, growing youngsters, underweight horses, horses with poor appetites, lactating mares, and pregnant mares, especially those in late gestation when they can have difficulty eating enough feed to meet their needs.

CRUDE PROTEIN

The crude protein (CP) is commonly estimated either by what is called the Kjeldahl method for its developer, Johann Kjeldahl, or the Dumas method, named for Jean-Baptiste Dumas. Both methods determine how much nitrogen the sample contains. Because protein is composed of about 16 percent nitrogen, multiplying the nitrogen content by 6.25 provides a crude estimate of the protein level but this will be higher than the digestible protein.

The crude protein level is only a rough estimate and not more accurate, because not all protein in a feed is digestible, and there can be nitrogen in a feed that is not part of a protein. For example, some proteins react with fiber or carbohydrates during fermentation and become indigestible. This protein is referred to as acid detergent insoluble crude protein (ADICP) or unavailable protein (UP).

CRUDE FIBER

In proximate analysis, carbohydrate levels are found in two fractions: the crude fiber (CF) and the nitrogen-free extract (NFE). CF is chiefly the cellulose and a portion of the lignin, both of which are parts of the plant known as structural carbohydrate. (More on this later.) Adding together the water, ash, crude fat, crude protein, and crude fiber, then subtracting that total from 100 gives what is known as the nitrogen-free extract (NFE), which estimates the soluble carbohydrates (mainly the sugars, starch, and pectin of the plant).

While CF is still listed on many feed labels and is useful for comparing the CF of one feed to another, CF analysis has largely been supplanted by detergent fiber analysis in order to know more about the types of fiber in a feed, especially in forage. CF remains a useful comparison number for grains, because they do not have large amounts of lignin. (You'll learn more about lignin in Chapter 4.)

Detergent Fiber Analysis

Detergent fiber analysis (DFA), also known as Van Soest analysis, for Peter J. Van Soest of Cornell University, provides a better measure of the types of fiber in a feed sample than the crude fiber and nitrogen-free extract level measured in proximate analysis. Detergent fiber analysis uses detergent to make the fiber soluble. It has two primary types of tests, acid detergent fiber (ADF) and neutral detergent fiber (NDF).

Acid detergent fiber measures the cellulose and lignin (an indigestible fiber) in the plant. Neutral detergent fiber measures the cellulose, lignin, and most of the hemicellulose, but includes some starch as well. Because the ADF test removes starches and hemicellulose, it identifies the less digestible fibers. Overall, it underestimates the fiber and overestimates the feeding value. A feed with a high ADF value is less digestible to a horse than a feed with a lower ADF value. Higher ADF forages may be desirable for a horse with insulin resistance, but are undesirable for an extreme athlete, a growing youngster, or a broodmare. Higher quality, more digestible forage has an NDF of 35 to 55 percent and/or ADF of 25 to 35 percent. Lower quality forage has an NDF above 55 percent and/or an ADF above 35 percent. Most horses will not eat forage with an NDF above 65 percent or an ADF above 45 percent.

Lay articles commenting on ADF and NDF values in horse nutrition sometimes suggest that the two tests were designed to mimic the acid foregut digestion and the microbial hindgut digestion; this is not true. They are tests for ruminant feed that are commonly used in assessing forage.

VITAMINS AND MINERALS: ADDITIONAL ANALYSES

Additional feed analysis can be done by near infrared spectroscopy (NIRS), atomic absorption, calorimetric reactions, high-performance liquid chromatography (HPLC), spectrophotometric techniques, and the ANKOM systems.

NIRS has the advantages of not destroying the sample, being less expensive, and being faster than other analyses. NIRS can determine the DM, TDN, CP, ADF, and NDF, as well as the calcium, phosphorous, magnesium, and potassium levels of a feed sample. However, a NIRS analysis, while useful, is based on equations and prediction models that compare the NIRS to the chemical analysis of a feed and assume that the near infrared spectra absorbed or emitted by the components of different feed-sample types are similar. Therefore, analyses of forages from different areas that are significantly dissimilar to the forages used for calibration could be inaccurate.

Minerals are often reported in parts per million (PPM) in a feed analysis. (Chapter 4 explains PPM.) As noted in Chapter 2, the most important macrominerals are sodium, which is the most likely deficient macromineral in equine diets, and the calcium:phosphorus ratio, which should range between 1.7:1 and 2.5: 1. The most important micromineral to notice is selenium, as it has the smallest safety range. Finally, the copper:zinc ratio should range between 1:3 and 1:4.

Remember that various minerals can interfere with the digestion of other minerals. For example, the absorption of selenium is perturbed by aluminum, arsenic, copper, and molybdenum. Randomly supplementing a few minerals can have unanticipated, negative consequences.

Macromineral assessments are available from many laboratories, but few labs test for microminerals. Most labs can determine the vitamin A level by assessing the amount of carotenid present (although this method can overestimate Vitamin A). Further assay of vitamin content is so specialized that only research labs have the capability of reporting just a few of the B vitamins, usually niacin, riboflavin, and thiamine (also written as thiamin).

ENERGY

Energy is not a specific nutrient, but it is the single most important characteristic in feed. It is the caloric value present in a feed, comprised of the total amounts of carbohydrate, fat, and protein.

Not all energy in feedstuff is available to the horse. Energy is lost through solids in the production of feces, liquids in the production of urine, gas in the production of methane and other gaseous losses, and heat by the fermentation of feed, primarily fiber. The digestible energy is calculated from the gross amount fed to the horse minus the gross amount still available in the feces. The portion of energy that is not lost in urine and gaseous losses is called metabolizable energy (ME). Feeds with a high ME have a high nutritive value, because the horse can efficiently extract the nutrients. Subtracting the heat increment (the amount of energy the horse uses to ferment the feed) from the ME gives the net energy (NE).

There are additional ways to measure energy in feedstuffs. The total digestible nutrients (TDN) is a primary way to compare feeds as a whole before looking at individual constituents. The total digestible nutrients (TDN) are calculated with a formula that uses the ash, CP, ADF, and NDF values to estimate the total energy in the feed. A good equine TDN is 40 to 55 percent.

Additional comparative measures of the total energy of feeds are the indices of relative feed value (RFV) and the relative forage quality (RFQ); these measures are commonly offered by forage producers that also sell hay to cattle ranchers. RFV is a calculated index that accounts for the animal's anticipated intake, along with the available energy in the forage or feed. The baseline for RFV is full bloom alfalfa, assigned a value of 100. Other hays are compared to this standard. RFQ is another index to compare hays that uses full bloom alfalfa as a baseline value of 100. RFQ is calculated from a formula using the TDN and dry matter intake (DMI) to allow a comparison of the value of different hay species, for example, a load of annual rye grass and a load of Bermuda may cost the same, but if the ryegrass is more digestible and more readily consumed, and thus has a higher DMI, the RFQ of the ryegrass is higher than the RFQ of the Bermuda load. An RFQ of 100 might be fine for a horse at maintenance, while a hardworking horse could require forage with an RFQ of 120. These are measures often offered on forage reports that are more pertinent to raising cattle. Horses may retain very low quality hay longer; this retention causes a hay belly.

Another method of quantifying the carbohydrate portion of the energy in a feed is to evaluate the ethanol soluble carbohydrates (ESC), which will include both pectin and the WSC. Important details about these different plant carbohydrates are in Chapter 4 under A Bit of Botany.

A lab providing analysis specific to horses may offer the partial energy calculation of the non-fiber carbohydrates (NFC). With the growing interest in excellent horse nutrition, tests for carbohydrates that ferment at different rates may replace old tests. Carbon, hydrogen, and oxygen are abbreviated on the periodic table as C, H, and O, respectively, which is why you see the term *carbohydrate* abbreviated as CHO. Researchers measuring forage safety for horses distinguish CHO by fermentability; tests may be labeled as CHO-F_R and CHO-F_S for how rapidly or slowly the fiber ferments, and CHO H for hydrolyzable (breaking down in water) forms of sugar.

NITRATE AND MOLD CONTENT

Feed analysis reports may also provide the nitrate and/or mold content of the sample. Nitrate occurs naturally in the environment, but it's also found on land and water due to the application of fertilizers. Nitrate becomes a danger to the animal when their bodies convert the nitrate to nitrite, which poisons the horse. Horses appear to have a higher tolerance than ruminants for nitrate in hay and water, because ruminants are more efficient at converting nitrate to nitrite.

Hay that is baled when it's too wet creates circumstances for microorganisms present to produce nitrate. The percent of nitrate in hay samples commonly ranges from 0.06 to 0.09, which is a safe level for horses.

Mold content is similarly susceptible to spiking if the hay is baled or stored in wet conditions. There are countless varieties of molds. Few molds, if any, will be specifically identified by the lab. Never feed moldy hay to a horse.

Independent Feed Sampling and Testing

The best way to determine your hay's nutrient content is to submit a composite sample of cores for independent analysis. In North America, local agricultural extension offices can direct owners to additional resources. In the United States, analysts may be certified by the Association of Official Analytical Chemists, American Association of Cereal Chemists, American Oil Chemists Society, or the National Forage Testing Association. The Resources section of this book can help you find a suitable laboratory.

ABOVE: **In laboratory analysis, only a small sample of ground feed is tested, but that sample should come from cores of ten percent of the bales considered. Photo courtesy of Dr. Lynn Van Wieringen.**

Hand grabbing some hay will not offer an accurate, representative sample. Sampling is properly done with a tool that drills a core out of a bale. The standard for good sampling is to deeply core 10 percent of the bales. In a lot of 200 bales, twenty cores are submitted for analysis. The lab will grind the entire sample down and perform its analysis on a small amount of the ground hay.

The reality is that most owners do not have their hay tested. They buy hay in small loads of a few dozen bales or less, and they rely on local feed dealers to provide suitable purchasing options. Typically, owners do not submit core samples from numerous hay bales on every large hay purchase, nor do most barn managers routinely send grain or other feed samples for independent laboratory analysis. This is reasonable, because buyers should be able to rely on retailers for a quality product. Buyers should still understand feed labels and lab reports offered by hay producers.

Finally, owners need to know enough about the different plant carbohydrates and the environmental conditions that change these carbohydrate levels. This vital aspect of equine nutrition, covered in Chapter 4, is much too often overlooked, but is key to fully understanding feed analysis and how to care for your horse.

CHAPTER 4
The Food: Forages and Non-Forage Supplementary Feeds

SELECTING FORAGE AND non-forage supplementary feeds in order to provide an individual horse with the right type and amount of carbohydrates, fats, and protein is the essence of equine nutrition. Assessing a horse's needs individually is key, because horses with diverse workloads, genetic differences, and medical problems require different diets. Owners who understand the variable contents of forage and non-forage feeds can supply a healthy diet for any horse.

Mistakes in feeding can result not only in the immediate health complications of choke, colic, and laminitis (discussed in Chapter 2), but also in dangerous long-term problems, such as obesity, insulin resistance, and equine metabolic syndrome (discussed in Chapter 9). Also, many medical conditions—polysaccharide storage myopathy (PSSM), pituitary pars intermedia dysfunction (PPID), hyperkalemic periodic paralysis (HYPP), and more—must be managed with careful attention to the diet.

The array of non-forage supplementary feeds available to adjust the equine diet is staggering, but the foundation of a horse's diet remains forage, supplied by pasture, hay, or a hay product such as cubes or pellets. However, the percent of nutritional factors (primarily different carbohydrates and protein) varies wildly, not just between different forages, but within the average value of specific forages. For example, a grass hay may average a protein level of 8 percent but range from 2 percent to 19 percent. In another example, the non-structural carbohydrate (NSC) level (more on this below)

LEFT: **Grazing provides a natural diet and way of life, but sunlight and stress rapidly alter the carbohydrates in forage. This sunny pasture is producing more sugars than it would on an overcast day. Shaded pasture is less dangerous; temporary cross-fencing can restrict a horse to safe areas.**

of one forage may average 18 percent but can spike to 40 percent under certain environmental conditions. Because the carbohydrates in forage are so inconsistent, owners must learn the factors that cause variation and learn how to adjust the diet through non-forage supplementary feeds.

Forage: Safe Pasture, Hay, and Other Roughages

Horses naturally graze grasses, forbs, herbs, sedges, and legumes. We generally provide hay from grass or legumes. The varying levels of different plant constituents in grazed pasture, hay, and hay products (silage, cubes, and pellets) greatly affect the nutritional value and safety of the forage. This variability cannot be overemphasized. A failure to understand these influences has led many owners to err in their pasturing, hay purchasing, and supplementary-feeding decisions.

It would be wonderful if an owner could rely on average values as hard figures for different hays, then buy brome for one horse, alfalfa for another, and timothy, bluegrass, or Bermuda for yet another horse's needs. An owner may, for instance, desire hay or pasture with 10 percent non-structural carbohydrates (NSC) and 8 percent protein for an easy keeper at maintenance while allowing over 20 percent NSC and 12 to 14 percent protein in hay for an athletic horse in hard work. There are tables that offer the average values of simple sugars, starch, protein, and other constituents in various forages, but the factors that influence contents allow hay to vary so widely that average figures are not sufficiently useful. If you have a tall Arabian or a small Warmblood, it does not affect your horse's height to know that the average Arabian is under fifteen hands and the average Warmblood exceeds sixteen hands. The average does not affect the individual.

Environmental factors affect plant constituents day by day and hour by hour; they apply whether the forage is fresh or conserved. Understanding this demands familiarity with how the forage grows but gives you a much more complete grasp of equine nutrition and impacts your forage selection.

A Bit of Botany: How Essential Carbohydrates Become Dangerous

The energy available in plants is mostly carbohydrate, with lesser amounts of protein and some fat. A plant's ability to photosynthesize—turn water and sunlight into carbohydrate for growth—is why forage becomes more or less beneficial (or dangerous) under certain conditions. Four factors dictate how safe or dangerous grass is: the growth stage, the amount of sunlight received in recent hours, environmental stress (drought, freezing, or poor soil), and the forage species.

GROWTH STAGE: NON-STRUCTURAL AND STRUCTURAL CARBOHYDRATES

An immature forage plant cell is composed mostly of cellular contents with a minimal cell wall. As the plant matures, the cell's contents are used for growth. They diminish while the cell's wall strengthens and thickens. Forage carbohydrates are classified as either structural or non-structural carbohydrates (NSC), which generally identifies whether or not they are part of the plant's cell wall structure or part of its cellular contents.

Structural Carbohydrates

The structural carbohydrates comprising the plant's walls are mostly cellulose, hemicellulose, and lignin. Cellulose and hemicellulose are structural fibers fermented by the beneficial microbes in a healthy horse's hindgut. Cellulose is less digestible than hemicellulose. Lignin is not digestible by horses, although donkeys can digest it. As discussed in Chapter 3, cellulose, hemicellulose, and lignin are measured in a neutral detergent fiber (NDF) test, while cellulose and lignin are measured in an acid detergent fiber (ADF) test. There is an inverse relationship between these test results and the amount of digestible energy in forage—higher numbers equal less value for the horse.

Pectin is a glue-like, highly digestible, water soluble substance that may be classified as a structural carbohydrate, because it is located in the cell wall. It is not measured by either ADF or NDF testing. Pectin is a very safe feed constituent. Beet pulp is high in pectin.

ABOVE: **The dead leaves and stems amidst the new growth in this canary reed grass are the lignin skeletons of last year's grass. Horses can't digest lignin, but donkeys can.**

Non-Structural Carbohydrates (NSC)

Non-structural carbohydrates are those found in the plant's cellular contents. The NSC are mostly simple sugars (glucose, sucrose, and fructose), starch, and a complex sugar called fructan. Simple sugars and fructan are collectively referred to as water soluble carbohydrates (WSC), because they are soluble in water. WSC and starch are collectively called non-structural carbohydrates (NSC). NSCs are all sugars that the horse prefers, but forage with a high level of NSC spikes the horse's glycemic response, presenting a risk of colic and laminitis.

The NSC in grass hay ranges between 2 to 30 percent but averages about 12 to 15 percent. This has significant implications for horses needing a low-sugar hay with a NSC level of less than 10 percent.

Maturity

Plant maturity significantly affects its value. The leaves of grass have a higher nutritive value than the stems; farmers try to produce hay with a high leaf-to-stem ratio. Leaves contain most of the protein and fat.

If the forage plant is allowed to continue growing, it flowers, then forms a seed head. When the seed head begins to show through its sheath, this is called the boot stage. Farmers use either the

Feekes, the BBCH, or the Zadoks scale to classify growth by stages. Hay is usually harvested at boot or pre-boot.

Harvesting after seed heads develop means that the horse will eat the seeds, which are grain that contain a great deal of sugar and starch. Grain hays (oat, rye, and triticale are common examples) can average high combined sugar and starch levels.

After the seed head releases, this very mature hay will have thick stems and drier leaves. This is less desirable to us, because the forage has much more lignin and much less nutritional value; it's less desirable to the horse, because it's less palatable. However, the base of these stemmy plants can still harbor significant NSC. Muzzles—which tend to restrict horses to grazing the upper parts of a plant—can help prevent the ingestion of excess NSC, especially on very mature fields.

SUNLIGHT

Forage plants make more sugar under environmental conditions that promote growth. The sugar level in a grass plant is lowest during the night and begins to climb with increased sunlight, peaking when the sun is strongest, and staying fairly high until dusk. This is why horses sensitive to sugar loads might be turned out only during the night and kept in a dry lot during the sunny hours. In the northern hemisphere, grass growth naturally spikes in May, when the plants make a lot of sugar with good growing conditions. Sugar levels spike again just before winter, as the grass plant stores carbohydrate prior to going dormant for winter.

Forage that has a safe level of non-structural carbohydrates (NSC)—perhaps 11 percent total simple sugars, starch, and fructan—during the night or on an overcast day, might have more than double that NSC level the next day under full sun. The resulting 24 percent NSC level will be unsafe for many horses.

Sunlight intensity is amazingly significant in affecting the sugar load in a forage. Tests comparing unshaded and shaded parts of the same field have shown sugar doubled in the unshaded areas of the field. On a sunny day, if you have a choice between an open field and one shaded by tall trees, choose the shaded field, especially for sugar-sensitive horses.

STRESS

When a plant is not growing because it is stressed by extreme cold, heat, or drought, it stores carbohydrate that would have been used for growth. For this reason, stressed forage is dangerous to horses, particularly those that are overweight, prone to laminitis, or insulin resistant. Fertilized grasses tend to be less stressed overall than those in unfertilized fields.

Cold temperature stress to grass deserves careful consideration. An example is ryegrass, which has a moderate sugar level in the warm climate of New Zealand but tends to be quite high in sugar in the comparatively cooler climate of the UK. Dormant grass that looks dead in the middle of winter can harbor extraordinary amounts of sugar; bluegrass, brome, and fescue sampled in the middle of a cold Colorado drought were causing laminitis, with the fescue reaching nearly 30 percent NSC.

High temperatures during the growing season generally increase the lignin content in all grasses and legumes.

Good hay farmers know that when hay is harvested at times when the plant has stored high levels of simple sugars, starch, or fructan, the hay retains that high non-structural carbohydrate content. They try to harvest at the optimum time for a good, leafy grass that has not been in excessive sunlight or been recently stressed by cold temperatures or drought.

FORAGE SPECIES

There are countless species of forage, broadly classified as legumes or grasses; then grasses are divided into warm season and cool season grasses. Understanding that warm season and cool season grasses have a different storage carbohydrate (explained below) is key to selecting safe grass for your horse, and there are additional differences in legumes.

Legumes

Legumes are part of the fabaceae family, which is distinct from grasses. Legumes have a symbiotic relationship with bacteria, which affix nitrogen from the soil and air to the plant. This high nitrogen content is why legumes average higher protein levels than grasses. Legumes include alfalfa, clover, lespedeza, peas, and beans.

Alfalfa (called lucerne in the UK, Australia, New Zealand, and South Africa) is the most common legume fed to horses. Alfalfa attracts the blister beetle, which is toxic to horses. In areas susceptible to this insect, horses must be kept off of alfalfa pasture when the beetle is on the forage.

Alfalfa is linked to enteroliths, the stones that form in the gastrointestinal tracts of some horses. Enterolithiasis (the condition of having an enterolith) is more common in the Midwest, Florida, and especially California. The stones are made of magnesium ammonium phosphate and often form around a foreign body or nidus, such as an ingested rock or piece of wire the horse acquired from the ground or in a flake of hay. Enteroliths are also more prevalent in horses that drink hard, high mineral water.

Alfalfa can have protein levels as high as 25 percent and NSC as high as 15 percent, which is too rich for sugar-sensitive horses. Alfalfa is a good source of lysine, but excess protein causes horses to drink more, depleting them of electrolytes. Combined grass and alfalfa fields produce hay that is variable, because the two types of plants tend not to mature at the same time.

Bird's-foot trefoil (*lotus corniculatus*) is a legume of the vetch family that can be an appropriate forage, but some vetches—such as hairy (vicia villosa) or crown vetch (coronilla varia)—are toxic to horses. Clover is a legume that horses tend to like very much. It is especially susceptible to molds in warm and humid conditions. White and red clovers are frequently used in pastures and hays, but alsike clover is a variety that can cause liver problems and photosensitivity. Phytoestrogens in clover have been linked to health complications in some horses.

Warm Season Grasses

Warm season grasses are also called C4 plants (because they convert carbon dioxide in the atmosphere to oxaloacetate, a 4-carbon acid). Warm season grasses are also called tropical grasses, because they begin to grow when the soil temperature reaches about 60° F (15.5° C) and grow best at 90–95° F (about 32–35° C). They are chemically more efficient and use less water than cool season grasses. Examples of perennial warm season grasses used as horse forage are Bermuda, big bluestem, and switchgrass. Sudan grass is an annual example.

Starch is the main storage carbohydrate of warm season grasses. Warm season grasses might have moderate sugar content but can have a high starch content. A horse prone to laminitis, insulin resistance, or that is overweight, and on warm season grass needs a field or hay that is as low as possible in starch. Overall, warm season grasses tend to be safer than cool season grasses.

Cool Season Grasses

Cool season or temperate grasses are also called C3 plants (because they form a 3-carbon acid called 3-phosphoglyceric acid). They begin to grow when the soil temperature reaches 40° F (about 4.5° C) and grow best at 65–75 degrees° F (about 18 to 24° C). Examples of perennial cool season grasses used as horse forages are orchardgrass, timothy, brome, fescue, and perennial ryegrass; annual examples include rye and oat hay.

Fructan is the main storage carbohydrate of cool season grasses. A horse prone to laminitis or insulin resistance, or that is overweight and on cool season grass needs a field or hay that is as low as possible in fructan.

PASTURE MANAGEMENT AND SAFE GRAZING

You will have a limited selection of legumes and grasses from your local feed supplier, but you can choose from many more options in managing your pasture. Most horses do well with time on a well-managed, safely-fenced plot of grazing land that is reasonably free of weeds and poisonous or harmful plants. This helps fulfill the horse's behavioral need to forage. Providing safe pasture for horses is predicated first on understanding the factors discussed above that affect the sugar storage in grass. Always consider the amount of sunlight and the other environmental stresses on your pasture before turning your horse out. In the northern hemisphere, May is the riskiest month for pasture-associated laminitis (PAL).

Many horses have health problems, such as equine metabolic syndrome, insulin resistance, laminitis, or obesity that require you to practice extra caution to ensure safe grazing. There are limited times when the risk of exposure to excess non-structural carbohydrates (NSC) in the pasture is

Safe Muzzling

Beware of the risk of your horse snagging its grazing muzzle on fencing or anything else in the turnout area, such as branches or troughs. Muzzled horses should be monitored. Never introduce a new horse into a herd when any of the horses are muzzled. The muzzled horse is at an unfair disadvantage as the horses work out their pecking order. Muzzled horses benefit from having some grazing time without the muzzle. Beware of compensatory grazing, when a horse that is infrequently allowed to graze unmuzzled gorges when the muzzle is off.

very low. It may be safe to turn a sensitive horse out only during the night, for a few hours in the very early morning or very late evening, or in a muzzle. Alternatively, you can hand-graze the horse on a lead line to ensure he eats mature, stemmy, unstressed grasses.

Safe, good grazing also requires maintaining good fencing and practicing good land stewardship. Management begins with grass selection; the practices involved in creating good pasture health never end.

Selecting Pasture Forage

Some grass species make excellent pasture but not good hay because of growth characteristics. An example of this is Kentucky bluegrass, a forage brought to the Americas from Europe, which has a low leaf growth of two to seven inches, while the stems generally grow to a height of one to two feet. A native North American example of this is blue grama. Kochia, also called bassia, has been introduced to some grasslands. Teff is becoming popular for hay, but it has shallow roots so it does not make good pasture. Some forages are less common as hay or pasture yet are excellent grasses for either application. An example of this is crested wheatgrass. Sudan grass and johnson grass are used as forage in some areas, but they can be toxic in the right growth circumstances.

There are numerous varietals of thousands of species of grasses and legumes, and similar plants can be toxic to horses. Also, different regions sometimes call the same forage by different names. *Phalaris angusta* is a toxic grass common in the Americas and introduced to Australia. It is commonly referred to as timothy canary grass, although it is distinct from two appropriate forage grasses called reed canary grass and timothy.

When reseeding, you have the opportunity to choose a mix that maximizes productivity. This means including, if possible, sod-forming and bunchgrasses, both warm season and cool season grasses, and perhaps, both legumes and grasses.

Some landowners seek to restore land to native grasses, which tend to not require irrigation. Native grasses often have lower yields than cultivated forages but require much less care, thus survive without irrigation and fertilization, and they tend to have lower starch and sugar levels. However, they tend to be unable to withstand intense grazing. Warm season native grasses of North America include switchgrass, bluestems, indiangrass, sideoats grama, and eastern gamagrass. Cool season North American native grasses include blue grama, bluejoint, wildrye, and wheatgrass.

Pasture Management

There are separate but overlapping areas of concern in good pasture management. Preserving soil and water quality is important. We want productive growth so that horses can actually acquire nutrition in the pasture and spend as much time as possible in healthy turnout, but we don't want the land overgrazed.

Overgrazing compacts the soil. This compaction reduces air pores in the land and inhibits the ground's ability to cope with water, making it vulnerable to erosion by wind and water. Reduction in soil quality translates into poorer pastures with reduced forage palatability. Overgrazed pastures

Table 4–1 Common Forage Grasses and Legumes

Common Name Varieties	Scientific Name	Type	Comments and Cautions
Alfalfa	*medicago sativa*	L	high in protein and minerals, possible enterolith risk
Bahia	*paspalum notatum*	W	less common warm season
Bermuda Coastal Tifton 44	*cynodon dactylon*	W	most common warm season
Bluegrass, Kentucky	*poa pratensis*	C	common in the East
Bluestem, Big	*andropogon gerardii*	W	common in the Midwest
Bluestem, Little Aldous, Blaze, Camper, Pastura	*schizachyrium scoparium*	W	common pasture
Bluestem, Sand Elida, Garden, Woodward	*andropogon hallii*	W	common pasture
Brome, common	*bromus riparius*	C	found in many pastures
Brome, Meadow Cache, Fleet, Paddock, Regar	*bromus biebersteinii*	W	common hay
Brome, smooth Lincoln, Manchar	*bromus inermis*	C	selected for many pastures
Buffalograss		W	good native pasture
Clover	*trifolium*	L	beware mold
red, Clover	*t. pratense*		fungus causes slobbers
white, Ladino	*t. repens*		
Fescue	*festuca*	C	beware ergot alkaloids
Fescue, tall	*festuca arundiaceae*		
Grama	*bouteloua*	W	needs little care, low producion
Blue grama	*b. gracilis*		
Sideoats grama	*b. curtipendula*		
Indiangrass	*sorghastrum nutans*	W	uncommon pasture
Lespedeza		L	less common
Milk vetch, cicer	*astragalus cicer*		
Needlegrass, green	*nassella viridula*	C	uncommon but good hay
Oat hay	*avena sativa*	C	least cold-tolerant cool season; high NSC;
Orchardgrass/cock's-foot	*dactylis glomerata*	C	high yield, common hay
Red top	*argostis gigantean*	C	regional
Reed canary grass	*phalaris arundinacea*	C	likes wet land
Ryegrass	*lolium perenne*	C	use endophyte-free only
Sainfoin	*onobrychis viciifolia*	L	tends not to cause bloat
Sorghum	*sorghum*	W	caution:
Johnson	*s. halepense*		some varieties are toxic
Sudan	*s. sudanense*		some stages are toxic
Switchgrass	*panicum virgatum*	W	less common pasture

Teff	eragrostis teff	W	increasingly common
Timothy	phleum pratense	C	highly palatable
Trefoil, bird's-foot	lotus corniculatus	L	highly palatable
Wheatgrass, crested	agropyron cristatum	C	common in the Midwest
Wheatgrass, tall	thinopyrum ponticum	C	Midwest
Wheatgrass, thickspike	elymus lanceolatus	W	Midwest
Wheatgrass, western	pascopyrum smithii	C	more common in the west
Wildrye, Russian	psathyrostachys juncea	C	poor hay, good pasture

* Type: L legume, C cool season, W warm season grass

are much more susceptible to weeds, including poisonous plants. Overstocking land and not resting it are the two main causes of overgrazing.

Horses tend to heavily graze some pasture areas and leave others long. These areas are referred to as lawns and roughs. Often, the horse uses the rough for most of its defecation and urination, so these areas are also called latrines. Removing manure from a latrine and using temporary fencing to rest a lawn help keep a pasture evenly used.

ABOVE: **This field is overgrazed. Daisies and buttercups are appearing due to the low grass height.**

Maintaining pasture health can require regular rotation, fertilization, mowing, and weed control. Grazing on parcels of less than ten acres—or even large tracts if the land's forage production is low—requires more intensive land management by the property caretaker. Use cross-fencing to subdivide a large field and rotate between the different smaller pastures created. A ratio of 1 to 4 grazing to resting the land is a good general rule, although climate affects growth; after one week of grazing, allow the land one month of rest. Intensive rotation with smaller strips of land can be done using temporary fencing.

Grasses have an optimum height, depending upon their species, but in general, keep the grass sward no shorter than four inches, but do not let it grow higher than ten inches. Rest and mow as needed to keep a healthy height.

It is beneficial for fields to have another species on them, rather than to always be on a cycle of supporting and resting from horses. Hosting a flock of sheep or herd of cattle is good for the land.

Some owners prefer not fertilizing or not using commercial fertilizers as part of their land stewardship. This is a personal choice. All owners should be aware that fertilization overall reduces stress on land; unfertilized grasses are more likely to have sugar spikes than fertilized fields. Follow all directions carefully when using fertilizers.

Be aware of diseases that can infect your grasses; examples are mold on clover or fungus on rye or fescue. Also be aware of life-threatening insects; the prime example is blister beetles on alfalfa. You must keep horses off of infested fields.

Weed Control

Weed control is the final facet of pasture management. Weeds are just plants out of place, but some of these plants are directly harmful to horses. Invasive weeds displace desirable forages and tend to be less nutritious than forage grasses. Poisonous plants can make horses ill or worse.

Look beyond the border when inspecting your field for poisonous or otherwise problematic plants. Many horses will bend and reach two feet or more through their fence to graze.

Some weeds are palatable to horses and able to store enormous amounts of sugar; dandelions are an example. In some areas, certain weeds are deemed noxious, and landowners are required to control them, whether the land is public or private.

Controlling weeds via herbicides is not without risks and requires careful consideration. Some plants have developed resistance to some herbicides; an example is kochia that is resistant to the broadleaf herbicide dicamba (Banvel, Banvel II, and Vanquish are trade names). Clopyralid, another broadleaf herbicide, is banned in some locations. Herbicides may be more commonly known by their chemical names like 2,4-D (short for 2,4-dichlorophenooxyacetic acid) or by trade names like Ally and Lontrel 360, but they all carry numerous special precautions and warnings. Even if you are not spraying an entire pasture, but just spot treating weeds, perhaps with Roundup, be careful to keep your horse away from the land for the full recommended period. Herbicides often contain salts that actually increase plant palatability for some horses—they may be more apt to graze herbicide-treated plants if given a chance.

Broadleaf herbicides kill legumes and cannot be used on your pastures if you want to keep alfalfa or clover in them.

Five Top Tips for Healthy Pastures

1. Avoid overgrazing. Do not allow the grass to be reduced to less than 4" high.
2. Mow. Do not allow the grass to become overly mature and stemmy.
3. Control weeds early and often.
4. Use a rotational system to rest the land.
5. Periodically graze another species on the pasture.

Hay: Selection, Storage, Serving, and Soaking

Most owners do not have sufficient pasture to meet their horses' forage requirements, so they feed hay or a hay product. Adequately selecting, storing, and serving hay is the backbone of providing nutrition for most horses. Providing hay low and slow, as discussed in Chapter 2, is the natural, healthy way to feed. If your horse is sugar sensitive or prone to respiratory problems, you can soak or steam the hay to make it safer.

Hay Selection

When generally evaluating hay, use all of your senses. It should smell rather sweet, never musty. It should look green but without too many seed heads, with plenty of leaves rather than all stems. It should feel soft rather than overly coarse. If possible, review an analysis of the hay, including the older measures of neutral detergent fiber (NDF) and acid detergent fiber (ADF), as well as newer measures revealing the non-structural carbohydrate levels.

The hay cutting (first, second, third) refers to the number of harvests per season and is often part of an advertisement about hay for sale. Local variances impact hay's quality so strongly that usually generalizations (e.g., first cutting has more weeds, third cutting has less nutrition, first cutting has the most leaves, this cutting is stemmy) about which hay cutting to buy are not useful. Rely on your sound knowledge of the factors that affect carbohydrates in forage and good hay analysis rather than generalizations.

Hay Storage

Barn fires have been caused by improperly stored hay. Even well-cured hay can give off heat, so it is important that the hay storage area have ventilation rather than being a tightly sealed shed.

More vitamins and minerals leach out of hay the longer it is stored. While several tons set aside is a nice, secure supply, owners with only one or two horses shouldn't store so much that they end up feeding hay over a year or so old.

Serving Hay

The bulk and weight of hay is a factor in the common habit of providing a great deal of energy to horses via grain. It is much easier to buy and store a fifty-pound bag of grain than it is to wrestle several bales of hay from the feed store to the feed room. It is physically easier to scoop grain than it is to stuff twenty pounds of hay into a slow feed net and heft that net to your horse's pen. However, free-choice hay, fed low and slow, is the healthy guideline. Slow feeders prolong the horse's intake time, returning him to his natural state of being a forager.

If the horse pulls a lot of hay from the net, a stall mat can reduce waste.

Soaking and Steaming Hay

Hay may be soaked in water to reduce the dust, molds, or other allergens, as well as the water soluble carbohydrates (WSC). Soaking in warm water might work better or faster at removing the WSC than cold water. However, soaking leaches out vitamins and minerals, along with water soluble sugars. There is also an environmental concern about the disposal of water used to soak hay. In some locales, it is illegal to discharge this water into the sewer.

Some owners use hay steamers to reduce mold or bacteria on hay, but steaming does not appreciably reduce the sugar content. Steamers are also expensive, so more owners rely on soaking hay by immersing a filled hay net in a large tub of water.

A study evaluated the effects of four different treatments on removing WSC from hay. Researchers compared: no treatment (dry hay), steaming for fifty minutes, a nine-hour soak in 61° F (16° C) water, steaming and then soaking, and soaking then steaming. The protein and ash (think of this as the mineral content) were unchanged by any of the treatments. The three treatments that use soaking reduced WSC appreciably, but steaming alone did not. Hay that had either of the two treatments using steam as the last step (steaming or soaking then steaming) had less bacteria and mold than other samples. Soaking alone actually increased the bacterial load, although it did not change the mold content. Overall, a nine-hour soak followed by a fifty-minute steaming was the most effective treatment for reducing WSC *and* microbes in the hay.

Other Roughages: Silage, Haylage, Chop, Cubes, Pellets, and Sprouts

While hay is the most common form of conserved forage fed to horses, other conservation methods are in use. These include haylage, silage, chop, cubes, pellets, and sprouts. Sugar beet pulp is sometimes thought of as a roughage, because it is so high in fiber, but it is a by-product and will be discussed under non-forage supplementary feeds. We will discuss one form of forage that you should avoid.

Lawn Clippings

Do not feed lawn clippings. It is tempting to offer this fresh-chopped grass to your horse, but there are several significant health concerns. Remember that good hay farmers choose harvest times when the grass has not been under a great deal of stress or solar radiation. Those conditions make grass store excess sugar, starch, and fructan. That's not something that concerns us when mowing our lawns, so clippings often have extreme sugar levels. Also, hay is properly cured, raked, and tedded to allow air to circulate and dry the forage well. A mower bag is a fermentation vat, where clippings can immediately grow bacteria and mold. Finally, petroleum products from the mower can contaminate lawn clippings.

Silage, Haylage, and Chop

Silage is cut hay that is ensiled or wrapped in plastic. While kept in an airless (anaerobic) environment, it cures, because the captured lactic acid bacteria lower the pH, essentially pickling the forage. There is a risk of lethal microorganisms—notably botulism or molds—growing in improperly ensiled silage. The final moisture content of silage is 35 to 50 percent. In North America, silage is rarely fed to horses, as it is considered cattle feed, but a good quality silage can be appropriate horse forage.

ABOVE: **Ensiled hay in large bales is less commonly fed to horses. In some locales, commercial haylage and silage is sold in small packages for horse feed.**

Chop, or green chop, is a silage method in which cut forage is placed in a bay or container and covered. It is more commonly used in Australia and New Zealand.

Haylage is semi-dried silage with a moisture content of 50 to 70 percent. Packaged haylage intended just for horse feed is increasingly common in Europe.

The higher acid content of silage and haylage concerns some horse owners. Studies have not shown a negative health impact, although the horses did indeed have somewhat lower GIT pH levels. Silage and haylage actually tend to have a higher digestibility than hay. Because the dry matter content is lower in haylage than in hay, you must feed more of it.

In most locales, dried hay products are more common than moist-conservation hay products. These include hay cubes and hay pellets.

Cubes and Pellets

Hay cubes and pellets are made from high-temperature dried hay that is pressed into form. They are usually more expensive than hay, but very consistent in quality and can be fed with almost no waste. In some areas, horses receive only cubes or pellets for their entire forage allotment, and although it is not ideal due to the lack of long-stem fiber, the horses do all right. Circumstances do influence feed choices.

Cubes offer somewhat longer stems than pellets. Both cubes and pellets are usually soaked to prolong eating time and provide more hydration. Adding salt to this water is an excellent way to ensure basic mineral intake.

Alfalfa cubes and pellets are commonly available and a good way to add lysine to the ration of a horse on grass hay. Grass hay pellets are increasingly available, usually in a cool season grass, for example, timothy. Account for hay pellets and cubes by weight; one pound substitutes for one pound of hay.

Hay pellets and cubes make good treats. Soaked cubes or pellets make excellent trailering food. Hay can be too dusty and full of particles to offer during travel, but moist cubes or pellets offer healthy forage during hours on the road.

Sprouts

Sprouts are another method of providing your horse with fresh, green forage. Sprouting a feed seed and providing the horse with the fresh sprouts is not hard. To grow enough sprouts for a beneficial feeding, most people use a commercial system of specially designed trays on a rack.

For just one or two horses, a low budget method can be done with a rotational system, using five to seven buckets. For example, on Monday, place the seeds in a clean bucket and cover them with water. On Tuesday, rinse the wet seeds in the first bucket and start a second bucket. Start a third bucket the next day and so on. By Saturday, feed your horse the sprouts from the first bucket.

Although sprouting systems are often used with oats or other grain seeds, the resulting sprouts are a forage, not grain, because it is the grassy leaves—essentially very early oat hay—not the seeds, that are fed.

Non-Forage Supplementary Feeds

Supplementary feeds for horses are more diverse now than ever. They are found in feed, grocery, discount, and health food stores, as well as online. There is no limit to the amount of attention and money you can spend supplementing your horse's diet.

People often give supplements, because they believe they are doing something good for their horses and that thought makes the owner feel good. A great deal of the supplementation that occurs is unnecessary. Most owners have limited resources, and the vast majority of healthy idle and pleasure horses require only good forage and salt. However, athletes, broodmares, growing youngsters, underweight, and geriatric horses often need the caloric boost of supplemental energy and added high quality protein, vitamins, and minerals.

In addition to the common concentrate of grain, numerous other seeds, by-products, and oils are used as supplemental horse feeds. Feed manufacturers offer proprietary vitamins and mineral mixes, as well as blended supplementary and complete feeds. Finally, you can buy or make treats, but there are certain foods horses should never eat.

Grain: The Common Concentrate

Grain has long been the traditional supplementary feed for horses, and it remains a favored method with many owners, although fats, not grain, should generally be the first way we add energy to a healthy horse's diet. Worse, many horses that do not need supplementary feed at all still receive daily grain. Unfortunately, the habit of delivering a significant portion of the energy in the horse's diet by feeding grain is supported by how much easier it is to scoop a few pounds of grain instead of a wrestle with a quarter of a bale of hay. The horse's nutritional physiology (Chapter 2) teaches us that the average horse needs little or no grain.

When feeding grain, we want the horse's small intestine to absorb the sugars and starch in grain. The two strategies we use to get grain absorbed in the small intestine are processing and portion control. Grain is processed by soaking, heat, or pressure. Cooking, cracking, flaking, rolling, micronizing, and steaming are all processing measures that enhance pre-cecal digestibility of grain to some degree. Remember that grain not digested in the small intestine will be passed on to the hindgut, where it will be digested by lactic acid bacteria that then flourish. This lowers the pH of the hindgut, which kills off the beneficial bacteria and presents an immediate risk of colic and laminitis. The best practice is portion control; feed no more than one milligram of starch per kilogram of your horse's body weight. The Ultimate Chart precalculates this amount for you.

Parts of a grain are healthier than others. The largest portion of an individual grain is the endosperm, composed of stored sugar and starch. The endosperm increases as the grain ripens. Within the endosperm of cereal grains is the embryo, also called the germ; it is highly nutritious, containing vitamins and fat. Coating the endosperm is the seed's bran, which is high in fiber and protein. Fibrous hulls form a chaff-like coat over some seeds. Hulls tend to have a lot of fiber and protein, but not all hulls are good feed. Legumes, such as soybeans, also have hulls. The skin on the common green pea is a hull. These may be added to commercial horse feeds, but listed merely as

Table 4–2 The Impact of a High-Grain Diet Versus Best Practice	
High Grain Diet	**Best Practice: Little or No Grain**
hindgut acidosis	hindgut is not overwhelmed by large starch loads
laminitis	less risk of laminitis
glucose/insulin spikes	steady glucose and insulin levels
higher colic risk	less colic risk
diarrhea	
misbehavior	

"plant protein product." Hulls, germ, and bran can all be milled out of a grain as by-products and become horse feed.

When feeds are analyzed, the amount of endosperm versus bran and germ, the digestibility of the grain, and the processing method are all factors that influence how nutritious or desirable the feed is.

In evaluating grain, it should never have a foul odor. You should never see excess foreign matter in the grain. Purchase grain from reputable sources, never as field oats, which have not been cleaned and sorted to remove weed seeds.

Moldy grain and by-products can harbor toxins that are lethal to horses. Mold is a form of fungus. Aflatoxin is a common mold-produced toxin (mycotoxin) that can make your horse sick. Fungi called fusarium produce fusariotoxins. Fumonisin, trichothecenes, and zearalenone are the fusariotoxins most commonly found in grain. Grain that forms when conditions are cool and wet is particularly susceptible to developing the fusarium-produced toxin called deoxynivalenol (DON, also called vomitoxin). Fungal-caused problems might show within hours, but it could take weeks of feeding a contaminated product for symptoms to develop.

There is a false misconception that grain should be stored in airtight containers. Such containers do not allow for healthy air circulation and can trap moisture occurring from condensation caused by normal temperature changes, thus offering a warm, moist environment that fosters mold.

There are countless cultivars and variations of grain species. Some graminaceous crops (those usually grown for their seeds) may also be forage crops through the curing of the leaves before maturity to make hay. Oats and rye are examples. Remember that if grain hay is not harvested before the plant produces a full seed head then the horse will be eating the grain in addition to the hay.

The most commonly encountered grains in horse feed are barley, corn, and oats. By-products of these grains are discussed separately.

Barley

Barley (*hordeum vulgare*) is the oldest cultivated grain. It averages about 55 percent starch and is also high in sugar. Straight barley is not commonly fed to horses, as most of the crop is directed for human food. However, a non-proprietary, three-grain mix of corn, oats, and barley (called COB) is a pre-mix feed commonly fed to horses as a concentrate. It is palatable and may be sold with or without the addition of molasses; these two products are termed wet COB and dry COB, respectively.

Processed barley it also found in proprietary commercial blends.

Corn

Corn (*zea mays*), also called maize, has a very high starch content of about 70 percent, so it raises the overall starch content of COB or other blends to which it is added.. Corn is a heavy grain; a quarter-pound of corn fills a smaller scoop than a quarter-pound of oats. Always remember that feed should be apportioned by weight, not volume.

Corn is the lowest of these three grains in lysine content, making it the poorest in protein quality. Corn has about twice as much fat as barley. Corn readily grows lethal mold.

Oats

Oats (*avena sativa*) are a favorite of horses, and the grain highest in fiber if the hulls are not removed. Different varieties, such as high fat oats and hull-less oats (the latter also called naked oats) have been developed. Jockey oats or racehorse oats are another term for premium horse oats. Oats average about 45 percent starch.

Compared to regular oats, high fat oats are an excellent way to boost the caloric intake while decreasing the starch fed. Because of the higher overall energy content of high fat oats, remember to decrease the amount fed.

Of these three grains, oats have the highest level of lysine, making them the best-quality protein.

Additional Grains and Seeds:

It has become common to supplement horses with grains and seeds beyond those traditionally used in feeding. (All grains come from the grass family and are seeds, but most seeds are not grain due to botanical distinctions.)

Rice, rye, and wheat are largely directed toward human consumption, which makes them too expensive for horse feed, but they are important in horse nutrition because of the by-products they offer. Wheat (*triticum aestivum*) is the highest in quantity of protein, but it is not highest in the protein quality, because it is relatively low in lysine. The whole grain of wheat is hard; it should be processed by cooking or some form of grinding to make it more digestible. The by-products of wheat bran and wheat middlings offer good nutrition and are common in commercial blends.

Sorghum, also called millet or milo, is a seed commonly found in commercial blends. It is high in energy, relatively low in fiber, and is better absorbed by the horse when processed due to the seed's hardness and small size.

Flax, hemp, and chia seeds are popular supplementary seeds, fed whole or ground. The attributes of the seeds are vociferously debated among proponents. The size and hardness of the seed is one factor considered in promoting one seed over another, due to concern about the horse's gastrointestinal tract sufficiently breaking down and using the seed's nutrition, especially in the small intestine, where most of the nutrients in these seeds should be absorbed.

A desirable balance of omega-3 to omega-6 fatty acids is another reason why flax and chia are promoted as a good supplementary feeds. (Hemp is higher in omega-6 than omega-3.) Learn more about these different fatty acids in the discussion of oils, below.

Phytic acid or phytate naturally found in seeds binds some nutrients, making them unavailable to the animal. There is a myth that soaking seeds in water or salt water counteracts the phytate; it doesn't. (However, soaking can indeed soften a hard seed, making it easier for the horse's body to digest.) Researchers have experimented with adding an enzyme called phytase to counteract phytate. Seeds are a nutritious supplement.

Many seeds are high in a compound called lignan (not to be confused with lignin). There are many types of lignans, and they have numerous interactions for the plant and within the plant eater, but it suffices to note that they are antioxidants. Flax, sunflower seeds. and pumpkin seeds are high in a lignan called seicoisolariciresinol diglucoside (SDG); the presence of this antioxidant is another reason why these seeds are touted as a supplemental food for horses.

Sunflower seeds are a popular seed supplement. The black oil sunflower seeds (BOSS) often sold in bird seed mixes (as opposed to the striped variety commonly sold as snacks for humans) are preferred for horses, because the shell is softer. Sunflower seeds are high in magnesium and extremely high in omega-3. Amaranth, buckwheat, and quinoa are all non-grain seeds promoted as horse supplements. Beans, peas, peanuts, and soybeans are legume seeds commonly blended into horse feeds. Whole soybeans are better for the horse after extrusion or roasting (which inactivates a trypsin inhibitor in the legume; the horse produces trypsin to break up protein into amino acids).

These seeds all have healthy attributes as horse supplements, and there is nothing wrong with the modern practice of adding them to your horse's diet.

By-Products: Brans, Pulps, Hulls, and Meals

The term *by-product* is often mistakenly used as a pejorative when discussing feedstuffs. When a plant is processed, its various parts are used for different purposes. Plant pulps, hulls, brans, and meal are all types of by-products blended into horse feeds or offered straight as a non-proprietary supplement. People who believe by-products are fillers that lack nutritional value are misunderstanding feed analysis. By-products are often more nutritious than the principal end product.

Brans

Bran, the outer coating of a seed, is often ground off when grains like wheat or rice are processed for human consumption. When the by-product of bran is referenced without any other distinction, people are generally talking about wheat bran.

Wheat bran is high in fiber, protein, phosphorus, and non-structural carbohydrates. It is a traditional feed for horses, but those receiving it to excess develop a disorder called nutritional secondary hyperparathyroidism (NSH) from the high phosphorus content. The old practice of giving your horse a large, weekly bran mash is not a healthy choice due to the inverted calcium-to-phosphorus ratio and high non-structural carbohydrate content. Fortified wheat bran with added calcium is available.

Wheat middlings or midds, are produced when wheat is milled beyond the bran on its way to becoming white flour. Midds are high in protein (about 16 percent) but have much less fiber than bran. Midds are a common ingredient in commercial horse feeds, although they may be listed as "plant protein." Wheat germ is a relatively expensive by-product not usually fed to horses, as is wheat germ oil, but there are some owners that offer these to their horses.

While rice (*oryza sativa*), is rarely fed straight to horses, rice bran has become a common supplement and an admixture in commercial blends. Rice bran is 19 to 28 percent crude fiber, high in vitamins and phosphorus, and very high in fat. It also contains lipase, the enzyme that helps break down fat. Upon milling, the lipase begins to degrade the fat in the bran, so rice bran can quickly go rancid and grow bacteria such as E. coli. Rice bran can be stabilized by heat and pressure. This processing reduces the fat content, but makes it safe to store. Rice bran should only be fed in this stabilized form. It is a good way to add fat to a horse's diet, although it is much more expensive than the option of adding vegetable oil.

Rice bran oil contains a component called gamma oryzanol (GO), which in turn contains ferulic acid and sterol. Sterols can have some steroid-like effects, thus gamma oryzanol is suggested as an ergogenic (performance-enhancing supplement). This is discussed in the section on ergogenics under Special Diets for Athletes. Rice bran oil is a specialized supplement that is quite expensive.

Beet Pulp

Beet Pulp, more properly known as sugar beet pulp, is the leftover after sugar has been processed out of sugar beets. Beet pulp is relatively high in calcium, has about 10 percent protein, and contains a high level of pectin. Its fiber content is about 18 percent, making it an excellent adjunct to equine nutrition. The NDF varies from 23 to 55 percent, but it is highly digestible over the horse's entire gastrointestinal tract. It is sold with or without added molasses.

Available as shreds or pellets, beet pulp is usually fed after it has been soaked in water. Many people worry about feeding unsoaked pulp, but in studies, horses have received about half of their daily ration as unsoaked beet pulp without suffering esophageal obstruction, gastric distress, or any other complication. However, soaked beet pulp is an excellent carrier for medications, oils, or powdered vitamin and mineral supplements. Soaked beet pulp is also an excellent way to deliver electrolytes to the horse, as the salt can simply be added to the water hydrating the pulp. Because horses like consistency, it makes sense to routinely soak beet pulp if you feed it regularly and will sometimes use it as a carrier for medications or electrolytes.

It is common to begin soaking beet pulp (or other pellets, such as alfalfa pellets) for the next meal at each feeding. However, consider the temperature before simply leaving feed to soak for twelve hours in your feed room. Very cold, soaked beet pulp may not be consumed by horses, so if you are soaking overnight, and the temperature in your feed room will be cold, consider bringing the soaking pulp to the house until morning. In hot weather, soaked beet pulp can spoil, thus rather than soaking it hours in advance, just soak it an hour before feeding.

Owners may become concerned by regularly circulated warnings against the use of sugar beet pulp as horse feed. The arguments against beet pulp center on: the development and farming of beets that are tolerant to the use of glyphosate (Roundup); the use of disodium cyanodithiomido-carbonate (DCDIC), a product that minimizes slime in the water used to process the beets; and the assertion that root vegetables absorb heavy metals in soil, and thus could contain dangerous loads of these elements.

Genetically modified organisms (GMOs) include crops, like some sugar beets, that have been modified through breeding or laboratory manipulation to favor or disfavor different genetic traits. Genetic modification has occurred over centuries—for example as the grass plant of corn went from having a few seeds to having the large, seed-bearing ears we know today—and rapidly, as when scientists developed hardier strains of core crops that forestalled hunger in poverty-stricken parts of the world. In other applications, GMO crops have been developed to, for instance, withstand the application of an herbicide so that the chemical could be sprayed and reduce competing vegetation. Some people are anti-GMO, others are ambivalent or accepting of this step in agronomy; regardless, GMO sugar beets are consumed by people and other animals.

Other claims against glyphosate and DCDIC are that the chemicals used in farming will remain in the food and then have a deleterious effect on the horse's GIT microflora and impair the horse's ability to adequately process minerals or other nutrients. No good studies support these claims. A study in sheep found no difference in the digestibility of glyphosate-tolerant feed products. The U.S. Environmental Protection Agency has studied and approved the use of DCDIC. Regarding the assertion that a root vegetable can absorb soil elements, this is a true general statement; farming in contaminated soil could always produce contaminated food and would never be advisable.

Copra

Copra is the pulp left over from extracting coconut oil from the meat. It is around 22 percent protein, as well as high in fiber and fat, but low enough in non-structural carbohydrate (about 11 percent) to be a good supplementary feed. It may be an ingredient in a commercial feed. Less often, you may find it available for purchase unblended, depending upon your location. If not dried and stabilized, it is susceptible to aflatoxin, so make your purchases from a reputable source.

Fruit Pulp

Apple pulp and citrus pulp are the most commonly encountered fruit pulps mixed in animal feeds. They are low in protein (about 7 percent) and have very little lysine. They are high in fiber and pectin, but often less desirable to the horse. Remember that while pectin is soluble in water, it is not a dangerous carbohydrate; it is actually part of the plant's cell wall, not cell contents, and horses digest it safely. If your horse will eat fruit pulp, and you can locate a good source, it is a healthy supplement.

Brewer's and Distiller's Grains

Brewer's grains and distiller's grains are the pulp leftover from brewing alcoholic beverages. Brewer's grains (also called mash) are removed from the malt in the process of making beer. They usually come from barley and are high in B vitamins, fat (about 13 percent), and protein (about 25 percent). Many horses find them very palatable. If you are near a brewery, and your horse is a finicky eater that needs the enticement of an interesting ration, by all means tempt him with fresh brewer's grains. Alternatively, you can find dried brewer's grains available retail.

Note that brewer's grains are not the same as brewer's yeast. Brewer's yeast (properly called *Saccharomyces*) is also a by-product of beer making, but it is the inactive yeast left over. It is high in chromium and many B vitamins, so some owners feed it as a supplement.

Distiller's grains are the more common by-product of making alcohol. Rye or another grain used to make whiskey or other alcoholic beverages is further processed into distiller's grains, but usually when you see this addition in a commercial horse feed, the original grain was corn, and the end product was ethanol produced for fuel.

In the distilling process, a sticky, vitamin-rich, high-protein residue remains. When it is stabilized by high-temperature drying, the result is *distiller's dried grains with solubles* (DDGS). This supplement is always very low in starch and sugar, because the starch and sugar were converted to alcohol in the distilling process. Straight corn is over 70 percent sugar and starch, while DDGS is only about 10 percent. Other constituents vary, depending on the processing and the original grain. Distiller's grains made from corn result in about 30 percent crude protein and 12 percent fat. DDGS has an inverted calcium-to-phosphorus ratio, so be sure to provide significant sources of calcium.

Hulls

Soy (also called soya) hulls are a bit harder to find as a straight supplementary feed, but are becoming more popular. They are desirable for their very low glycemic response; they are about 8 percent protein and have very safely digested fiber that is nicely low in lignin, The NDF ranges between 53 and 70 percent, and the starch is less than 3 percent. All of this makes them a good feed for horses with polysaccharide storage myopathy (PSSM, described further under Special Diets). Because soy hulls are also comparatively low in potassium, they also make an excellent addition to the diet of horses with hyperkalemic periodic paralysis (HYPP, described further under Special Diets). Soy hulls are a good carrier for medications, salt, or oil supplementation.

Almond hulls may be listed on the label of commercial horse feeds. Their calcium:phosphorus ratio matches the horse's requirement of 2 to 1, and the fiber is digestible in horses. You may see them as a healthy ingredient on the label of a commercial horse feed, but you are unlikely to find them as an individual constituent sold separately. Almond hulls tend to increase the digestibility of the ration they are mixed in.

Oat hulls, left over from making naked or hull-less oats, may be added to commercial feeds as additional fiber. However, oat hulls alone do not offer significant nutritional benefit. Worse are rice hulls, also called rice husks. They are high in lignin and silica, thus are not a good source of energy for the horse. Peanut hulls are very poorly digestible and have a high risk of aflatoxin. They may also be sold as bedding, but if your horse eats them in this application, do not use them.

Meals

Meals are the result of grinding or pressing a grain, seed, or legume. This processing is usually done to extract oil. They are also called seed meals, but they are not the same thing as ground seeds. If you grind flax (also called linseed) seeds for your horse, you are not making flax seed meal. The seed meal is the residue left over after flax oil is produced. Thus, meals have a lower fat content than the original seed.

Meals tend to have a very high protein content (soybean meal is about 44 percent; cottonseed meal is about 48 percent; peanut meal is about 53 percent), which is the main reason they are used as a supplementary horse feed.

Kelp meal comes from seaweeds (algae): dulse, is a red alga (palmaria pamata); alaria is a brown alga. It is high in amino acids, vitamins and minerals, and included in some commercial mixes. It can be very high in iodine, so should only be fed in moderation.

Fish meal and the milk products of casein and whey protein are found in some mixes; both additions are outside the horse's normal food chain but are high in amino acids.

Owners get concerned about how to ensure that all essential and non-essential amino acids are supplied in their horses' diets. Remember that lysine is a first limiting amino acid, so look first for a good lysine source like soy hulls or alfalfa. If your horse's feed includes enough lysine, then it is likely he is receiving all of the amino acids he needs. The Ultimate Chart precalculates the protein need by weight and workload, as well as the percent of that requirement that is recommended to be lysine (4.3 percent).

Oils: Fatty Acids from Alpha to Omega

Before reviewing oils and other fat supplements, let's address the arguments against supplementing a horse with fat. First, oil is not traditional—the well-established method of adding energy to the horse's diet is through grain. Also, a horse receives little fat from his natural diet of grass, so detractors of oil supplementation argue that a horse does not naturally eat high fat foods. They have missed a deeper understanding of equine nutritional physiology. Forage is the horse's primary source of energy, but that energy is not released through the horse's digestion. Remember that microbes in the hindgut ferment the plant fiber and give off fatty acids, specifically the volatile fatty acids (VFAs) acetate, butyrate, and propionate. VFAs are every horse's natural, primary fuel.

When we understand the physiology that explains how fatty acids are actually our horses' normal source of energy, adding fat as a direct path to boosting calories makes a lot of sense.

Still, detractors argue that added fat can interfere with fiber digestion. While a few studies seemed to support the idea that fat supplementation could have a negative effect on the horse's digestion of fiber, these studies concurrently implemented changes in the glucose and starch in the study diets, which makes it difficult to attribute direct cause.

Another study provided horses with a diet of one-third concentrate; the diets had 4 percent, 7 percent, or 8.8 percent fat provided by linseed and palm oil. The study horses were fistulated, meaning that a cannula (tube) had been surgically inserted into their right ventral colons to enable measurement of the digestibility of the dry matter, fat, total digestible fiber (TDF), acid detergent fiber (ADF), and neutral detergent fiber (NDF). Researchers found no difference in the colon pH, the VFA content, or the bacterial composition of the hindgut. This demonstrated again the safety of fat supplementation.

In particular, horses benefit from fat supplementation in the diet if they are underweight or if they require more calories than they are physically able to consume through forage. Examples of the latter include athletes, certain seniors, starvation cases, and late gestation mares. Also, a horse regularly supplemented with fat is also better able to utilize fat during exercise; this lets us quickly provide more energy to a hardworking horse during a very long ride.

Fatty Acids

Fats can be divided into saturated and unsaturated fats, depending upon the chemical structure. Unsaturated fats are subdivided into monounsaturated and polyunsaturated fats. An individual fat molecule or triglyceride is composed of three fatty acids and a glycerol.

Polyunsaturated fatty acids (PUFAs) include alpha-linolenic acid and linoleic acid. Beyond being a general source of calories, these two specific fatty acids offered by fat supplements are what our horses need. As described in Chapter 2, alpha-linolenic acid and linoleic acid are called essential fatty acids (EFAs), because a horse cannot make them; he has to eat them.

Alpha linolenic acid (also called ALA and written α-linolenic acid) is an omega-3 (also written as ʊ-3) fatty acid. From it, the horse can make other omega-3s it needs called eicosapentaenoic acid (EPA) and docosahexaenoic acid (DHA). The horse can turn the two primary EFAs into long-chain fatty acids. Docosapentaenoic acid (DPA) is another ALA derivative. The molecular structure of omega-3 oils is short chain, which explains why supplement manufacturers advertise their products as having short chain fatty acids (scFAs). Omega-3s are abundant in marine-life oils (cod liver, menhaden, general fish oil), but also in flax, hemp, and walnut oil. Soy and canola oils are fairly good sources, although not as high in omega-3 as flax oil, also called linseed oil.

Linoleic acid is an omega-6 fatty acid and also a short-chain fatty acid. Oils of soy, corn, sunflower, and safflower are high in linoleic acid.

Feed manufacturers may advertise a product with free fatty acids (FFAs) or non-esterified fatty acids (NEFAs). Free fatty acids are non-esterified fatty acids (NEFAs) and something the horse makes when its body breaks down fat. (The body hydrolyzes or breaks down triglycerides, which makes the NEFAs available as an energy source. NEFAs are fatty acids that are not esterified by the addition of a glycerol to the molecule, which would form a glyceride.)

Some owners get very concerned about the ratio of omega-3 to omega-6. Studies in humans have associated omega-6 fatty acids with inflammation and immune suppression, while omega-3 is linked to an anti-inflammatory response. However, the biochemistry behind this correlation is complicated. It is true that the horses natural grass diet is much higher in omega-3 than omega-6 and that grain has the inverse balance. Popular articles advise you to avoid, for example, corn oil, because it is heavy in omega-6, but no studies in horses have compared supplementing an omega-6 source versus an omega-3 and found a negative effect.

You may see omega-3 and omega-6 fatty acids listed separately on a label. Read carefully. If a manufacturer guarantees a minimum of 21 percent omega-3 and 7 percent omega-6, do not assume the product offers a 3 to 1 ratio—7 percent was only the minimum of omega-6 promised, it could contain much more.

While fat supplements include bran (especially stabilized rice bran), copra, hulls, nuts, seeds, and meals, the simplest and least expensive method to add fat to your horse's diet is to supplement with oil. Oil is essentially pure fat. It has 2.25 times as much energy as the same-size serving of grain.

Not all oils are equal. Vegetable oils are the most common choice, usually canola, safflower, sunflower, peanut, or corn oil, but you can offer olive oil, coconut oil, or other more expensive and exotic choices. Canola is the most widely available and inexpensive of the oils with a good supply of omega-3. Corn oil is the most palatable to horses. Never feed mineral oil as an energy booster; horses cannot digest it, so cannot extract any calories from it.

A horse can generally process about one milliliter of oil per kilogram of body weight (one mg/kg). This is about two cups of oil per day for a 1,100 pound horse. Dividing the oil into two or three meals, and pouring it on hydrated beet pulp or hydrated alfalfa pellets is an excellent method of serving this fat supplement. The Ultimate Chart converts the ml/kg into ounces for your horse's weight in pounds.

Proprietary commercial feeds are usually 2 to 6 percent crude fat, but you can find high fat mixes with 10 percent or more, and commercial feed supplements with 30 percent fat.

Proprietary Blends

Proprietary commercial products include: complete feeds, mixes intended as supplementary feeds, probiotics and prebiotics, and ration balancers. A balancer may be just a vitamin and mineral supplement or it may include other feedstuffs. The discussion on minerals below also has details on electrolytes and the disorder called synchronous diaphragmatic flutter (thumps), plus homemade electrolyte recipes.

Complete Feeds

Complete feeds can ensure good nutrition for poor eaters or horses with health problems, but no complete feed in a bag has enough long-stem fiber to match a natural horse diet. Horses that do better with the carefully controlled diet of a complete feed should still be given good hay if possible. Be sure to read labels carefully.

Commercial Mixes: Sweet Feed and Specialty Formulations

Proprietary supplemental feeds are extremely popular and a mainstay of the equine nutrition business. They are also called pre-mixes or sweet feeds. Those formulated for the special needs of growing, pregnant, or senior horses are a part of many horses' diets. You may be able to recognize different plants when sifting through the bag, or the feed may be pelleted. A few cautions follow.

In pelleted feeds, the diameter, length, and hardness of the pellet deserves consideration, especially with regard to choke hazard. Case-hardened pellets are a manufacturing fault in which the exterior of the pellet is harder than usual due to excessive compression force in the extrusion process. Extruded pellets that become case-hardened are slower to absorb liquid and break down. A good pellet is dull in appearance, rather than glossy and shiny like a case-hardened pellet. The dull appearance indicates it will more readily break down. Longer and thicker pellets may be softened by soaking them in water prior to serving.

Pelleted feeds have the advantage of preventing the horse from selecting only the most palatable portions of the feed. This is a particular plus for pelleted creep feed given to foals.

One advantage of using proprietary pre-mixes or pelleted feeds is the consistency of the nutrients. This is quite different from buying a single feed product. The crude protein of oats varies from 8 to 13 percent, depending on the time of year and other farming considerations. In proprietary foods, the manufacturer designs the end result with set levels of protein, starch, fiber, et cetera, then achieves that level with a variety of plant products. Because of this variation, a bag of proprietary horse food purchased in one location might not actually include the same ingredients as a bag of the same brand purchased elsewhere. Examples of this regional variation occur when feed manufactured in California more often contains rice bran, while feed manufactured in the Midwestern United States tends to have more soybean hulls, yet both mixes can have the same packaging and label. The information on the feed tag will contain a guaranteed analysis, and a listing of the ingredients, but the names may be broad descriptions. A label listing *grain products* could mean wheat bran, wheat middlings, or a different grain or by-product. Another example is the general ingredient *plant protein*; this might mean cottonseed meal, soybean hulls or meal, alfalfa meal, peas, or a by-product of another plant.

The biggest caution in using commercial feeds is the risk of contamination. Manufacturers may advertise that their ingredient suppliers are approved. In the United States, this approval process may exclude grain suppliers. Certain feed constituents are associated with fungal toxins (mycotoxins). A reputable manufacturer will test every load of corn it purchases for the deadly mycotoxins aflatoxin and fumonisin. (Fumonisin causes equine leukoencephalomalacia.) A different lethal contaminator—ionophores—should never be in horse feed but is sometimes inadvertently added.

Ionophores

An ionophore is an antibiotic agent that improves the transport of lipids in the gut of ruminants. They are used in cattle feed as a growth promoter. Trade names for ionophores include Rumensin (monensin sodium) and Bovatec (lasalocid). Manufacturers that produce feeds for other species may have leftover traces in their mixing and packaging machinery as they prepare a batch of horse feed.

Ionophore contamination has been linked to a number of horse deaths. Horses encountering cattle feed in any setting can be at risk for ionophore poisoning.

There is no definitive test for the presence of an ionophore in a horse's body. Ionophore poisoning is diagnosed from the horse's presentation and the existing feed circumstances. Horses with ionophore poisoning may colic, become ataxic (uncoordinated), exhibit signs of cardiac stress and inflammation (myocarditis), and die.

When poisonings occur in athletic horses, initial changes in blood chemistry—an elevated level of the hormone troponin or a low blood potassium (hypokalemia)—are expected, so trainers might not initially be alarmed by these signs of cardiac stress that are also early signs of ionophore poisoning. As blood chemistry continues to skew in the next few days, the clinical findings are recognized as consistent with ionophore poisoning. Elevated muscle enzymes and myoglobin, both indicative of muscle damage, may also be revealed in blood work with ionophore toxicity. The large release of myoglobin can then damage the horse's kidneys. If you feed a commercial product from a manufacturing facility that is not ionophore-free, be suspicious of ionophore poisoning with any signs of colic or neurological disturbance like ataxia or distinct demeanor changes.

Treatment of ionophore poisoning is supportive care, and may include giving selenium and vitamin E to mitigate muscle damage, but damage to the cardiac muscle can remain. If an owner becomes aware that a horse has just ingested feed containing ionophores, the immediate administration of activated charcoal may absorb the poison before it moves from the stomach farther down the gastrointestinal tract.

Ionophores may also be in mineral blocks for cattle. Never allow your horse to lick a mineral block that has been manufactured for cattle.

Probiotics and Prebiotics

Probiotics (also called direct fed microbials or DFM) are beneficial bacteria fed to increase the microflora population in the horse's gut. Prebiotics are products intended to nourish and encourage the growth of the beneficial microflora already inside the gastrointestinal tract. Both prebiotics and probiotics are purchased under proprietary brands.

There's no doubt that beneficial bacteria in the horse's gut are important—a horse literally cannot live without them. The volatile fatty acids these microbes give off are the horse's main fuel source. Microbes also make vitamin K and the B-complex vitamins. A horse's gut hosts hundreds of millions of bacteria, protozoa, and fungi. However, there are countless strains of these microbes. The general names (*Bacillus, Bifidobacterium, Enterococcus, Lactobacillus, and Streptococcus*) do not provide enough information to know if the strain of bacteria in a probiotic product is the same strain normally in the healthy horse.

One carefully controlled study found limited effects of feeding probiotics on the digestibility of nutrients or on reducing the acidosis effects of high starch diets. A double-blind study of 200 horses that underwent colic surgery, in which half were given probiotics, found no difference between treated and untreated animals. In a study of horses with diarrhea associated with the administration of antibiotics, half were given probiotics, but there was no difference between treated and control animals. Another study showed that the administered probiotic failed to grow inside the horses. Finally, in a study of neonatal foals with diarrhea, those fed probiotics had more colic, depression, inappetance, and diarrhea than untreated foals.

Live yeasts are another form of probiotic. A study of yeast probiotics in exercising horses found no change in the fitness when compared to a control group.

Common General Probiotic Supplements

Bacteria:
Bacillus (B. coagulans, B. subtilis, B. licheniformis)
Bifidobacterium (B., B. bifidum, B. infantis, B. longum)
Enterococcus (E. faecium, E. thermophilus)
Lactobacillus (L. acidophilus, L. brevis, L. bulgaricus, L. casei, L. curvatis, L. helveticus, L. lactis, L. paracasei, L. planatarum, L. rhamnosus, L. salivarius, L. sporogenes)
Streptococcus (S. thermophilus)

Yeast:
Saccharomyces boulardii
Saccharomyces cerevisiae

Some people feed yogurt or buttermilk to their horses in the hope that these will serve as probiotics, because the products contain active bacterial cultures. However, adult horses are lactose-intolerant and cannot digest dairy products.

A product study found that only four of the fifteen probiotics reviewed actually contained what the package promised, and of those four, only two were accurately labeled. While cultures of lactobacillus, streptococcus, and more are advertised as improving the environment for the beneficial microflora or enhancing pre-cecal digestion of starch and sugar, it is difficult to know if the product can actually accomplish that purpose.

Common Prebiotic Ingredients

Fructooligosaccharides
Galactooligosaccharides
Mannooligosaccharides
Pectin

Polydextrose
Psyllium
Xylooligosaccharides

Prebiotics are similarly difficult to prove as beneficial. One study showed that supplementation with short-chain fructooligosaccharides (scFOS), a common prebiotic ingredient, lowered the hindgut pH, which is not desirable.

Antibiotic treatments do damage the beneficial microbial population in the gastrointestinal tract, so horses that are undergoing or have just undergone antibiotic treatment, or horses that do not seem to be recovering well from a prior antibiotic treatment, might possibly benefit from these supplements. A healthy horse on a good diet does not need regular pre- or probiotics, because his gut already hosts a healthy microbial population.

Balancers

Products called balancers or ration balancers are vitamin and mineral supplements; many contain additional ingredients intended to balance whatever is missing from your horse's hay ration. Be sure that the content enhances your forage selection. If your horse has no access to fresh grass, feed vitamin E in a balancer or as a single supplement. If you feed alfalfa, your horse probably does not need added calcium. If your feed comes from an area known to have selenium-deficient soil, look for a product with selenium (and vice versa).

Vitamins and minerals receive a lot of attention from owners and are the most frequently purchased supplements, but you can overfeed and even overdose through supplementation. Consider the many horses given a vitamin and mineral supplement, plus a fortified grain or complete feed, plenty of good hay, and pasture turnout with a salt block. This is very likely an over-supplemented horse that was receiving all of its vitamins and minerals from the pasture, hay, and plain salt block; it not only didn't need the fortified complete feed or grain, it didn't need the added vitamin and mineral supplement. While many vitamins and minerals have a large margin of safety, some do not. It is not hard to give a horse selenium toxicity from over supplementing. It is also easy to unbalance the horse's calcium:phosphorus ratio (which should be between 1.7:1 and 2.5:1) and its copper:zinc ratio (which should be between 1:3 and 1:4). Over supplementing is also expensive.

Sodium and chloride are the two minerals in which hardworking horses may be deficient. Even with the addition of a balancer, diets can be lacking in both of these minerals. Adding salt to the horse's diet is easily done by a free choice, plain salt block, or more precisely, by adding up to a tablespoon (15 ml) of plain salt to his feed every day.

Silicon—in the form of sodium zeolite A (SZA), orthosilic acid (OSA), or clinoptilolite—has been used as a supplement in the hope of preventing skeletal injury. An argument against SZA is that aluminum, which it contains, is known to reduce the uptake of phosphorus in ruminants fed sodium zeolite. One small study found no difference in the calcium, phosphorus, or aluminum in control horses or horses fed 200 grams of SZA for ten days.

Sulfur is often added in commercial mixes, but it is abundant in forage and also used in some feedstuff processing. An example is sulfured molasses, which provides a source of sulfur to the horse in addition to the calories, flavoring, and dust-reduction to feeds with sulfured molasses. It is also fine to choose unsulfured molasses products.

Balancers may also have amino acids, fatty acids, probiotics, or other nutrients. Of the amino acids, lysine is the best addition to balancers, because it is hardest to acquire. If your horse is on grass hay or pasture with no other supplement, a product with added lysine could be beneficial. Fat sources may be included in a balancer to ensure the horse's diet has the two essential fatty acids (see the earlier section on Oils).

Because of the range of products available, careful label reading is required. A product may be advertised as having all of the necessary vitamins, minerals, essential amino acids, and essential fatty acids. This sounds terrific, and yet the product may be useless, because although it contains those nutrients, it does not offer them in sufficient quantities to be worthwhile. The only way to balance your horse's ration is to know exactly what is in all of the forage and non-forage he gets and compare that to estimated needs, yet there are vitamins and minerals for which a horse's required level has not been estimated. Balancing the ration may involve more calculation, because minerals in proprietary feeds, balancers, and salt blocks may be listed in parts per million.

Understanding Parts Per Million (PPM) on a Proprietary Feed Label

Many people measure their feeds in the imperial system, using ounces and pounds, but must use the metric system when quantifying certain feed constituents. For example, the NRC recommends a 1,100 pound horse in light work receives 13.9 grams of sodium, and 400 mg of zinc daily. Some supplementary feeds might list contents in parts per million.

1 PPM = 1 milligram (mg) per kilogram (kg).

If the product lists 200 PPM of zinc, then there are 200 milligrams of zinc in one kilogram of the product.

To know how many milligrams of a feed constituent listed in PPM are in a pound of the product, multiply the PPM by 0.4536 (or divide the mg/kg by 2.2).

A product listing 200 PPM of zinc has about 91 mg of zinc in one pound of the product.

Salt Blocks

Read salt block labels. Some mineral blocks also contain significant amounts of phosphorus, because it comes with the other minerals that are desired, but horses are very unlikely to need added phosphorus. You may have heard the term *blue block*, which refers to a salt block with added cobalt and iodine commonly provided for cattle. You may have bought reddish or brown salt blocks for the trace mineral content. It is largely the addition of iron oxide that colors most commercial trace mineral blocks, and horses rarely to require added iron. A plain white salt block is all your horse probably needs, and this lets you know you haven't disturbed the copper:zinc ratio or added other unnecessary minerals.

Colored Salt Blocks

Salt block colorization is not standardized, but the following is a general guide. Never allow your horse to lick a salt block that may be intended for ruminants—it may contain deadly ionophores.

White   sodium chloride

Yellow   sodium chloride plus sulfur

Red   sodium chloride plus iodide and iron

Blue   sodium chloride plus cobalt and iodine

Black   selenium plus the minerals in brown block salt

Brown   sodium chloride plus any or all of the following: cobalt, copper, iodine, iron, magnesium, manganese, molybdenum, potassium, and zinc

Electrolytes

Electrolytes are minerals that carry an electrical charge. In this form, they help perform cellular functions; one example is causing muscles to contract and relax for countless repetitions.

Minerals can be classified as either cations, which carry a positive charge, or anions, which carry a negative charge. The primary electrolytes for the horse are sodium, chloride, potassium, calcium, and magnesium. Do not casually tamper with your horse's electrolytes. Do the reading and measuring, and begin with quarter doses. The first time you use electrolytes should not be at a competition; instead, train as you would compete.

You are already providing electrolytes with every routine (vitamin and) mineral supplement or salt block. However, hard exercise and hot weather make a horse sweat more, which uses more electrolytes, so you may want to give your horse additional electrolytes in these circumstances. The urge to drink can be triggered by a high concentration of salts in the blood, so adding electrolytes to keep the horse's salts high can encourage more drinking.

Adding salt to water that is used to hydrate soy hulls, beet pulp, or hay pellets is an excellent way to ensure the horse intakes frequent energy and electrolytes. A teaspoon (5 ml) of table salt provides 2,360 milligrams of sodium.

Whether or not a horse needs additional electrolytes depends on the workload, weather, fitness, and individual. Although horses lose fluids through respiration and excretion, the majority of water loss during exercise is sweat. Sweat is also the horse's primary means of relieving itself from the heat produced by exercise. Sweat always carries electrolytes out of the horse. By estimating sweat loss, you have a better idea of the electrolyte loss.

Electrolyte Losses in Sweat

For every liter of sweat lost, a horse requires:

Sodium	3.45 grams
Chloride	2.0 grams
Potassium	5.5 grams

There is a method to quantify your horse's sweating by its distribution and intensity. Zeyner et al. developed the Sweat Loss Score in 2013. Their research carefully determined actual sweat losses by weighing the horses and measuring water loss in the feces and urine; they also monitored the horses' body temperature and water intake. The study horses were worked multiple times by riders of different weights. Sweat patterns were photographed immediately after untacking. This system was first validated on Warmbloods and since then has been used on Thoroughbreds.

Score	Observations	Sweat Loss in Liters (or by percent of body weight)
	Table 4–3 The Sweat Scoring System (Zeyner et al. 2014)	
1	Under saddle partly dry, partly dark, sticky, and moist; sticky throat area; flanks darker than normal	1–4 liters (0.2–0.7% of BW)
2	Wet area under saddle and on throat; small, white areas at saddle edges and where reins touch body may occur, as well as on inner thighs of muscular or overweight horses	4–7 liters (0.7–1.2% of BW)
3	Snaffle leaves a clear, wet impression (often with foam on the back piece and noseband); flanks clearly wet; throat and areas under saddle and girth consistently wet	7–9 liters (1.2–1.5% of BW)
4	Throat and flanks completely wet; moist, dark wrinkles above eyes; pronounced foaming between thighs, especially on muscular or overweight horses	9–12 liters (1.5–2% of BW)
5	Horse is also dripping sweat above eyes and under belly	12–18 liters (2–3% of BW)

Electrolytes cannot solve bad judgment. Do not override your horse. In hot or humid weather, use the Comfort Index (found by adding the temperature and the humidity) as a guideline for exercising your horse. Above all, be mindful of how your horse responds in a workout.

Table 4–4 The Comfort Index	
The Comfort Index (CI) is the sum of the degrees Fahrenheit plus the percent of relative humidity. For example, if it is 82° F and the humidity is 65%, the Comfort Index is 147.	
CI	**Guideline**
<130	Cooling is not a concern.
130–150	The horse will sweat but should be able to exercise if water is provided.
>150 *	especially if humidity is >75% *Heat dissipation will be problematic for the horse. Monitor workout and responses very carefully.
>180	Do not exercise the horse.

Electrolyte Administration

You can make an electrolyte slurry or buy commercial hypertonic (saltier than normal body fluids) products available as powders to be mixed with feed or water, or as pastes to be syringed directly into the horse's mouth.

Loading a horse with electrolytes increases the amount of electrolytes and water in the large intestine. With a healthy reserve of roughage in the large intestine a continued absorption occurs, making these ions available to the horse.

One study dosed half of a group of horses in a fifty mile (eighty kilometer) ride with high dose electrolytes and the other half with low dose. Four weeks later, the two groups were given the alternate dosage and again underwent the same exertion. The high dosed horses drank more and had higher serum electrolyte levels, but there was no apparent competitive advantage observed. Thus administration of electrolytes increases water consumption, which is desirable, but a correlation between using electrolyte pastes and better performance has not been shown.

Strong electrolyte supplementation may cause a transient acidosis in the blood. Hypertonic pastes have also been linked to an increase in gastric ulceration when compared to horses undergoing the same exercise who were not given electrolytes. Never use hypertonic pastes if your horse has not been drinking and will not drink during a ride. Excess electrolytes can dangerously upset your horse's blood chemistry.

One strategy to avoid the rollercoaster of strong salt products, yet still provide the horse with sufficient salts is to give electrolytes much more often, but in much smaller amounts. Instead of a full syringe of paste every five hours, give a fifth of the syringe every hour.

The timing of electrolyte administration is debated. Some riders immediately dose with electrolytes and then let the horse drink, because rinsing immediately after administration keeps the paste from burning the mouth. However, the administration of electrolyte pastes can offend some horses, who may then be less likely to eat or drink. For this reason, in the situation of a horse needing to eat at a stop or veterinary check during a long ride or competition, some riders water and feed free choice before dosing with electrolytes. Alternatively, you may give electrolytes a mile or so in advance of reaching a water source in hope that your horse will drink well at the water.

There is debate about the safety of potassium in electrolyte preparations. The best consensus is to avoid potassium when exercising at upper elite level speeds, which is defined as above eight meters/second (nearly eighteen miles per hour).

Extra calcium can also backfire, especially with a horse in intense exercise. This is because horses routinely provided with extra calcium make less of the hormones needed to mobilize calcium from their own supply. Then during hard exercise that demands more calcium, the body is sluggish to fulfill the need. (This is one theory of the cause of thumps.) If you reduce daily calcium to the minimum—consider all sources, from forage to beet pulp to vitamin and mineral supplements—the horse's body stays used to supplying calcium naturally from its own stores. When you then supplement calcium during hard exercise, it may prevent thumps or muscle cramps.

Some electrolyte preparations contain sugar, usually in the form of dextrose. This addition does not improve electrolyte uptake in the horse's body, but it may make the solution more palatable to the horse.

Homemade Electrolyte Ingredients and Recipes

To understand desirable combinations of minerals, note the sidebars on the electrolyte contents in sweat and common commercial pastes. The ingredients for your preparation can be as simple as: home table salt (sodium chloride, abbreviated NaCl); other versions of sodium chloride (taxidermy salt, kosher salt, sea salt), salt substitutes, or added electrolytes that you probably already have in the house or barn.

Taxidermy salt is bulk sodium chloride without anti-caking agents. Kosher salt also has no anti-caking agents, and the crystals are less salty than standard table salt (280 milligrams of sodium per quarter-teaspoon). Sea salt is over 98 percent sodium chloride with variable but very small amounts of trace minerals and other macrominerals.

Yellow prussiate, also called sodium ferrocyanide, is an anti-caking agent often added to loose salt by manufacturers. Some owners have expressed concern about the safety of this cyanide-related compound being in their horses' salt. However, horses have proved to tolerate the minimal amount of yellow prussiate. You can also buy pure, plain salt in bulk without anti-caking agents.

Iodized and non-iodized cartons of salt are generically available in the grocery store aisle, and it really does not matter which you choose.

Salt alternatives are readily found in grocery stores. They may be labeled as "light salt" or as "no-salt," but note that these are two very different products. Light salt products are generally a mix of regular table salt and potassium chloride. A typical mix has 290 milligrams of sodium and 350 milligrams of potassium per quarter-teaspoon. A no-salt or "sodium-free" salt substitute (intended for people on sodium-reduced diets) is usually only potassium chloride (KCl), offering 530 milligrams of potassium per sixth-teaspoon (about one gram). Light salt is generally much less expensive than no-salt and offers sufficient potassium.

To make a simple electrolyte powder, place one and a half cups of table salt in a baggie, then add half a cup of light salt. A half teaspoon of this mixture provides 880 mg of sodium and 350 mg of potassium. For a horse that has not previously been given electrolytes, you might begin with an hourly half-teaspoon in a six-hour ride under hot conditions.

A tablet of calcium carbonate (a common antacid) adds calcium to your homemade electrolyte mix. Note that the antacid may be advertised as having 750 mg of calcium carbonate, but reading the fine print on the back of the container will reveal that this actually means 300 mg of calcium. A single dose recipe offered by the Old Dominion endurance riders group is: two ground antacid tablets, two teaspoons of light salt, and two tablespoons of sugar.

You may have Epsom salt (magnesium sulfate heptahydrate) in your barn. If it is dry (Epsom salt readily absorbs water, which increases its weight, thus reducing the amount of magnesium in a given weight compared to dry product), it is 9.8 percent magnesium; one ounce of Epsom salts has 2.8 grams of magnesium. You can also buy magnesium in the health food or supplement section of many grocery stores in the form of magnesium gluconate, magnesium citrate, or magnesium oxide. (Magnesium oxide has a reputation in human supplementation for poor absorbability, but horses absorb it well.) One home electrolyte recipe suggests a pound of table salt, two 10-ounce containers of light salt, and two tablespoons of Epsom salt, then feeding one or two ounces per day.

Dolomitic lime (also called dolomite) is a source of both calcium carbonate and magnesium carbonate; it is different from plain agricultural lime, the crushed limestone composed of calcium carbonate without magnesium. Another home electrolyte recipe calls for two parts each regular salt and light salt, plus one part dolomite.

Commercial Electrolyte Contents

Some products contain salts only; other have sugar or other constituents. A spot check of over a dozen commercial pastes and powders reveals this range of electrolytes in milligrams per ounce:

Sodium	1,800–6,600
Chloride	175–14,900
Potassium	792 –5,509
Magnesium	113–1,345
Calcium	71–1,870

There is no end to the combinations you can create in making your own electrolytes. Applesauce, peanut butter, syrup (never use artificially sweetened syrups), or aloe vera can be carriers for a salt slurry. People sometimes use glycerine (a readily available form of glycerol), in homemade electrolyte preparations for themselves, but a study found that exercising horses actually lost more electrolytes in their urine if their electrolyte preparation contained glycerol.

Salt Water

In addition to a bucket of plain water, you may offer salt water to a horse during or immediately after hard training, especially in hot or humid conditions. A benefit of drinking salt water is retention of the drinking response because of the high salt concentration. This helps protect the hard exercising horse from dehydration.

An isotonic salt solution—meaning that it has the same level of saltiness as the blood, plasma, or other body fluids—is called 0.9 percent saline. This percentage is the pharmaceutical way of referring to a solution in which there are nine grams of sodium chloride (NaCl) in one liter of water, easily prepared for horses as thirty-six grams in four liters. This roughly converts to one fluid ounce of NaCl (about thirty grams of table salt) in one gallon of water.

Regularly offering salt water helps accustom your horse to drinking it. If he won't sample the isotonic solution, cut the salt in half. It is common for a

ABOVE: **Offering a horse two buckets, one clean water and one salt water, after hard exercise can improve both electrolyte intake and rehydration.**

horse with buckets of clean water and salt water to drink from both right after hard exercise.

Synchronous Diaphragmatic Flutter (Thumps)

The diaphragm is the large muscle between the horse's lungs and abdomen. When the diaphragm contracts, air enters the lungs; when the muscle relaxes, the horse exhales. In a stressed horse with an electrolyte disturbance, the diaphragm may contract with each heartbeat. This condition is called synchronous diaphragmatic flutter or thumps. It sounds like human hiccups, but it has a different action and cause. You may see the abdomen jerk with each contraction. Thumps may occur on only one side of the horse.

Thumps is an indication of neuromuscular hyper-excitability. (The phrenic nerve, which is located near the heart and controls contraction of the diaphragm, becomes too sensitive, which allows it to be stimulated by heartbeats.) This usually occurs in tired and dehydrated horses. Horses with thumps should not be ridden and should be monitored by a veterinarian. They may require intravenous fluids.

There are multiple theories of why thumps occurs. It has been called hypokalemic (low potassium) diaphragmatic flutter. Currently, veterinarians often administer calcium and magnesium to restore electrolyte balance in these horses. The acid-base balance may be a significant factor because calcium, which is normally bound to protein, binds more tightly when the blood pH is alkaline. This makes calcium less available to the horse. Imagine an overridden horse that is panting. Panting blows off too much carbon dioxide, which alkalinizes (increases) the blood pH.

To avoid thumps, do not override your horse. Also, help keep him from becoming overheated by managing your time in the sun. If your route has two miles in exposed sun and two miles in shade, ride the hot miles faster and ride slower in the shady miles. This reduces your overall sun exposure time and keeps your horse cooler—yes, he worked harder in the sun, but the general key is to keep him cooler overall, which comes down to heat management, including limiting sun exposure. If you stop to rest or water, place your horse in shade rather than leave him in the hot sun. Again, never override your horse.

Treats: Always, Sometimes, and Never, Plus Recipes

Owners enjoy giving their horses treats. There's nothing wrong with sensible treating, but there are a few caveats. Some foods are harmful to all horses, and there are some ingredients that horses with specific conditions should not receive.

Read the labels on proprietary treats. High-sugar treats should never be fed to horses with insulin resistance. In addition to many commercial horse cookies, this warning includes fruit and jaggery, (the Indian treat made from concentrated sugar cane juice).

Sugar cubes are a classic, but poor treat choice. Another classic horse treat is an apple, but many other common foods also make good treats. Parts of plants that you do not eat—watermelon rind or the end of a carrot—are terrific examples.

ABOVE: **Bite-sized chunks of watermelon rind make an excellent, inexpensive treat.**

The best treats are simply regular, healthy horse food. If you normally feed your horse pelleted hay or beet pulp, carry a few pellets to offer as treats.

Treats can be expensive, but they are easy to make, so recipes for horse cookies and no-bake horse treats follow.

You may discover wild treats. On a snowy trail, rosehips from a wild bush are safe and nutritious. Many horses love them.

Forbidden Foods

As a general rule, do not feed horses outside of their normal food chain—offer plant products, not treats made from other animals.

Avocado, tomatoes, and persimmon are examples of plant foods enjoyed by people that should not be given to horses. Avocadoes contain persin, especially in the peel and seed, which is toxic to horses. Tomatoes are in the nightshade family, and the foliage is especially unhealthy for horses. Persimmon seeds can form dyospirobezoars (also called bezoar), that can cause colic. Do not give horses chocolate, as they are sensitive to the theobromine and caffeine in cocoa.

Some horses have specific dietary restrictions due to underlying medical conditions. An example of this is a horse with hyperkalemic periodic paralysis (HYPP), a condition in which added potassium must be avoided. Do not give high potassium foods such as pumpkin, including pumpkin seeds, to HYPP horses. Be sure to use only regular table salt (NaCl), not KCl, in making treats for HYPP horses.

Recipes for Homemade Horse Treats

Both baked and no-bake treats can be made from common kitchen ingredients. The recipes allows substitutions, so you can select from a variety of household and feed room ingredients. Be willing to experiment.

Mix to a smooth texture the consistency of cookie dough. If the dough feels too wet, add more dry ingredients. Some bakers add sugar. Do not add artificial sweeteners; they have not been determined safe for horses. If the dough feels too dry, add a small amount of water. You may also add seeds; consider sunflowers, chia, flax, or grain. Squeeze dough into bite-sized balls and place on a greased cookie sheet. Bake at 350 degrees for about ten minutes, until firm. Allow to cool before serving.

Table 4–5 Recipe Matrix for Baked Horse Cookies						
1/2 cup wet	+	2 cups dry	+	1/2 cup oil	+	1 teaspoon salt
aloe vera		flour		vegetable oil		Kosher salt
apple sauce		oatmeal		flax oil		salt omitted
honey		flax meal		coconut oil		light salt
peanut butter		corn meal		olive oil		no-salt
pumpkin puree		wheat germ		canola oil		table salt
carrot puree		masa harina		safflower oil		sea salt

No-Bake

Make alfalfa or grass hay meal by minimally hydrating hay pellets or cubes. Mix one-third each hay meal, peanut butter, and dry grain (or other dry feed by-product or seeds). Separate the mix into balls for individual treats. You may mix the vitamin and mineral supplement of your choice into no-bake treats.

CHAPTER 5
Alternative Supplements and Nutrition

MANY HORSE OWNERS are interested in alternative supplements and nutritional therapies. *Alternative* implies a product or service outside the realm of mainstream, evidence-based practices that have been proven by scientific standards to work. This distinction is very important to some consumers but less so to others.

Oversight of alternative nutrition products for horses merits discussion, because they are not regulated or monitored by the agencies that have jurisdiction over pharmaceutical-grade products for animals.

This chapter will review the broad classification of nutraceuticals, as well as alternative products for which there is no proven benefit. Readers interested in homeopathic supplements and remedies are urged to understand the section below on how the strength of homeopathic supplements is determined. Finally, common nutrition-oriented alternative services are discussed.

Oversight

Because products that fall under the alternative label are less regulated than products that have been proven under an evidence-based standard, consumers would do well to make their purchasing decisions accordingly, with good use of critical thinking. Recall the discussion in Chapter 1 on the difficulties of genuinely knowing a fact versus believing or hoping something to be true. Recognize the accidental errors that lead people to misattribute cause. An example is when an owner spends weeks giving a mildly lame horse a supplement that is intended to relieve joint pain or repair soft tissue damage. It's entirely possible—in fact, it is *likely*—that the lameness would resolve with rest. Giving a horse days, weeks, or months off heals many minor complaints. It's not possible to accurately say that the supplement healed your horse in this scenario. To know the supplement worked, you would have to have a large sample of horses and give half of them a placebo while half got your study supplement, but you would have to be blinded to which half were treated so that confirmation bias was eliminated. You would also need a measureable test for whatever the supplement was supposed to improve. If a significant portion of horses in your study have measurable results with the use of the tested product that exceed the healing of horses not receiving the product, then it's reasonable to attribute the success to the product. However, in the scenario where a horse is given time off and the owner administers a nutraceutical or other product touted to promote healing, many people simply presume the product works.

In the United States, the Dietary Supplement and Health Education Act (DSHEA) of 1994 provides regulation, only to products intended for human consumption. The National Animal Supplement Council is a private industry group. Packaging and ads may lead the purchaser to think that a product has been proven to alleviate an illness or injury in horses when, in fact, it has not.

Products are often advertised with testimonials from people who claim they know it works or can see the difference in their horses. These products are suggested for specific medical conditions, such as Equine Metabolic Syndrome (EMS) or Pituitary Pars Intermedia Dysfunction (PPID). They are also touted for non-specific, vague desires, for example: claiming that a supplement will enhance, optimize, promote, or support gut health, joint health, immune function, recovery, healing, etc. These claims are often preceded with mild qualifiers in the endorsement language as well. They are not pharmaceutical preparations and are not a shortcut to good equine management nor a guarantee of good health.

Cautions

Horses' bodies have been shown to adapt to less than ideal circumstances and interference with their dietary systems. However, there are limits. One example is when the horse's body ceases production of vitamin C after it has been heavily supplemented with ascorbate or ascorbic acid. Once the supplement is withdrawn, perhaps because the owner lost interest or belief in the product or had a change in financial circumstances, the horse will suddenly suffer a deficiency, because it adapted to the supplement by diminishing its natural vitamin production. A similar example occurs in athletic horses that are over supplemented with calcium by owners who believe the horse requires high supplementation. With an overabundant calcium supply, the horse's natural hormones that signal the body to mobilize stored calcium become less active. Then, unfortunately, the system is sluggish during hard exercise when the horse really needs its stored calcium.

Caution is also due regarding alternative product ingredients, especially unrevealed, proprietary ingredients. Some substances not only have drug-like effects, they are metabolized along similar pathways. Competition horses have failed drug tests after receiving herbal supplements. Some botanicals may have potentiating effects on natural neurotransmitters. An example is valerian, which is linked to the natural, calming neurotransmitter gamma-aminobutyric acid (GABA) and the related compound beta-phenyl gamma-aminobutyric acid; thus the plant has Valium-like effects. (Valium is the trade name for diazepam, a depressant or calming drug.) Alternative supplements and other botanicals banned by some national equestrian organizations include: arsenic, belladonna, camphor, capsaicin, chamomile, comfrey, devil's claw, hops, kava kava, laurel, lavender, leopard's bane, nightshade, passion flower, raowolfia, red poppy, skullcap, tetrahydrocannabinol, valerian, and vervain.

A third warning is the tendency proponents of natural products have to generalize from other species. For example, garlic and St. John's Wort, which are popular remedies in human alternative medicine, are found in products offered to horses, but both plants are toxic to horses. Garlic, and other members of the allium genus, can cause anemia, and Saint John's Wort causes photosensitivity. Numerous plant derivatives and compounds included in alternative supplements are actually unsafe, not determined to be safe, or not beneficial to horses.

Alternative Supplements

Products considered to be alternative supplements can be classified into several categories. A substance may be intended as: an anti-inflammatory; a treatment for a specific problem (for example, anxiety or worms); a broad benefit such as an antioxidant or an immune stimulant; a hematinic (blood builder); or treatment for a specific disease, like EGUS, EMS, or PPID, (the mainstream approach for these conditions is discussed under Special Diets for Medical Problems in Chapter 9).

Table 5-1 Common Supplements Suggested in Alternative Equine Nutrition

Supplement	For*	Comments
aloe vera	various	used orally and topically
bee pollen	AI	has shown some effect at increasing appetite
bitter melon	PPID	has not been proven effective
black cohosh	anxiety	may have general relaxant properties
black tea	A-I	theobromine and caffeine in it are dangerous to horses
chasteberry	PPID	has not been proven effective
cinnamon	EMS	has not been proven effective
chromium	EMS	has not been proven effective
cranberry	EGUS	has not been proven effective
dandelion	swelling	may have a mild diuretic effect
devil's claw	A-I	may have an anti-spasmodic effect, banned by many orgs.
echinacea	infection	promoted as an immune booster, studies not clear in horses
garlic	infection	warning: Heinz Body Anemia developed in horses
ginger	A-I	also used as an antioxidant and against infections
ginseng	A-I	strong potential for side effects and drug interactions
green tea	AO	effects have not been studied in horses
hawthorn	various	used as a general circulatory tonic or hematinic
jingulan	PPID	has not been proven effective
licorice root	EGUS, RAO	promoted as protective of mucosal lining
magnesium	EMS	high dose has not been proven effective for EMS
marsh mallow	EGUS	root has been suggested to heal damaged gastric mucosa
nettle	hematinic	plant is high in iron, vitamin C, calcium, and potassium
orange peel	AO	may help a distressed or ill horse
raspberry	anxiety	leaves commonly given to mares with estrus difficulty
rhodiola rosea	PPID	has not been proven effective
seabuckthorn	EGUS	has not been proven effective
valerian	anxiety	has drug-like actions, contraindicated in pregnant mares
vinegar	various	apple cider vinegar is commonly used as a general tonic
willow bark	A-I, pain	can irritate the gastric mucosa
yucca	A-I, pain	very little research into yucca for horses

* A-I (anti-inflammatory), AO (antioxidant), EMS (Equine Metabolic Syndrome), PPID (Pituitary Pars Intermedia Dysfunction), RAO (Recurrent Airway Disease)

Alternative nutrition supplements may also be classified either as substances with some known benefit or as without a known benefit, but promoted as having a potential benefit. An example of a substance with no known benefit is vinegar, which is commonly promoted as a general tonic, as well as suggested for the specific problem of enteroliths. No study has demonstrated a general health benefit from giving horses vinegar, nor has vinegar been shown to reduce enteroliths. Similarly, diatomaceous earth, which is regularly suggested as an alternative anthelmintic, is known to be effective against bugs in the outdoors, but does not work in a moist environment such as the gastrointestinal tract and thus cannot be an effective anthelmintic. Vitamins are examples of substances with health benefits that are also called nutraceuticals.

Homeopathic Preparations

Homeopathic preparations can also be classified as substances with no known benefit, although they are promoted as having a potential value. Homeopathic supplements, remedies, and nutritional treatments are popular with many adherents of alternative practices. Homeopathic products intended to treat or prevent colic or laminitis are available. It is critical that consumers understand and evaluate the math regarding homeopathic solutions.

Homeopathic preparations are made by repeatedly diluting a tea made from an original substance, such as the arnica plant or part of a honeybee. The dilution process begins with one drop of the tea and a prescribed number of drops of dilutant, then taking one drop of *that* diluted solution and re-diluting it, repeating this process until the desired level of dilution is reached.

Homeopathic products are labeled with a number, for example, 3oc, 200c, or 12x. The c and the x are Roman numerals, indicating respectively that 100 or 10 drops of a dilutant (usually water, although alcohol and sugar are also used) were used in the dilution cycles. The 3o, 200, and 12

ABOVE: **Homeopathic supplements and remedies are so diluted that none of the original herb remains.**

indicate the number of dilution cycles. The common 3oc preparations have been through 3o cycles of diluting one drop from the last cycle of tea-making with 100 more drops of water.

Homeopathy was founded on the belief that the more dilute a remedy was, the better it worked. This is why homeopaths believe that a 200c product—which has undergone 200 succeeding dilution cycles of one drop of the last dilution with 100 more drops of water—is stronger than a 12x product, which has undergone twelve succeeding dilution cycles of one drop of the last dilution with ten more drops of water.

Bach flower remedies, another popular alternative supplement for horses, are named for their original proponent, Edward Bach, who made remedies by diluting—at homeopathic proportions—

the dew collected off of a chosen flower. A particularly popular product with alternative equine nutritionists is Rescue Remedy, a combination of 5 homeopathic Bach flower remedies.

Mathematicians and chemists have shown that none of the original herb (or other preparation) remains after twelve cycles of diluting with ten drops of water, which is a 12x homeopathic remedy, and much less dilute than the common 30c remedies and the touted-as-stronger 200c remedies. Because homeopathic supplements and products actually contain *only* the dilutant of water, alcohol or sugar, they can be considered placebos.

Nutraceuticals

Many products falling under the label of alternative supplements are termed nutraceuticals, a portmanteau of *nutrition* and *pharmaceutical*. A nutraceutical can be any nutritional component (for example, a fatty acid, amino acid, vitamin, or mineral), or a botanical preparation. There are multiple definitions of the term, with some practitioners holding to the strict view that they are products that are *proven* to have a benefit and others defining the category as substances that are *intended* to confer a benefit. Nutraceuticals are certainly asserted by their vendors to have health benefits, and it's certainly true that substances such as vitamins, minerals, amino acids, and fatty acids not only benefit the horse, but are required. What has not been shown is that an excess of any nutritional component has a health benefit. Hyperalimentation (hypernutrition) does not make a healthy animal healthier.

Many nutraceuticals are made from components of foods that a horse would naturally ingest, but there are numerous nutraceuticals that a horse would not normally eat. Examples are products made from fish oils, sea mussels, or cattle trachea. Some researchers caution against feed or supplements outside an equine's natural food chain, and it's hard to argue with this warning.

When categorized by intended benefit, nutraceuticals can be classified as antioxidants, anti-inflammatories, ergogenics, immune system enhancers, and joint supplements. Note the overlap in the intended area of influence of different products. For example, oxidative stress or damage from intense exercise, being febrile (having a fever), or the stress of malnutrition might all be treated with antioxidants, which means the antioxidant is being used to combat inflammation, support the immune system, and enhance the assimilation of nutrients to restore health. Because of this overlap, many individual supplements are marketed as antioxidants, immune stimulants, anti-inflammatory agents, and for joint repair. Examples are high doses of vitamin E or vitamin C.

Antioxidants

Antioxidants are agents that combat oxidation. Oxidative stress is a natural decaying effect that occurs more rapidly with exercise (especially intense exercise), rapid growth, malnutrition, and infection. Vitamins, minerals, and various plant extracts work as antioxidants in the body, meaning that they chemically stabilize the free radicals that are a by-product of oxidative stress.

Commercial antioxidant products often include any of the following: vitamins C and E, beta-carotene, selenium, amino acids (for example, glutathione or cysteine), lipoic acid (also referred to as alpha-lipoic acid, unfortunately abbreviated as ALA, which is also the abbreviation for the fatty acid alpha-linolenic acid), or fatty acids (commonly either alpha-linolenic acid, linoleic acid, or one of the fatty acids made from either of these). Antioxidants may also be present because a botanical ingredient, such as rosehips, which contain vitamin C, or capsicum from peppers, which contain capsaicin (a banned substance in equestrian sports).

Be cautious of hyper-nourishing a horse. Various chemicals react within the body in complex interactions that can be disrupted with supplementation. For example, high levels of vitamin E as an antioxidant, but high levels of vitamin E might be suggested can impair the horse's absorption of vitamins A, D, and K. Also, understand that the interplay between various constituents is not yet fully understood in many cases.

Botanical preparation can also be antioxidants. An example is curcumin, also offered as *curcima longa* or turmeric. A natural enzyme touted as an antioxidant is superoxide dismutase (SOD). However, oral SOD supplements do not increase the body's level of this enzyme.

Anti-Inflammatories

White willow bark, yucca root, and devil's claw root have all been shown to possess anti-inflammatory properties. However, the difficulty in accurate dosing cannot be solved when simply harvesting wild plants. Without a chemical assay and laboratory purification, it is impossible to know if a sub-therapeutic, a therapeutic, or even a toxic dose has been administered. This is true for all botanicals harvested and administered directly to the horse. There is also a difficulty in purchasing products that actually do contain what the vendor promises on the package. The results of studies spot-checking the contents of products have been disappointing. Many product bottles contain much less of the substance than advertised.

Ergogenics

Numerous alternative substances intended to enhance athletic performance are discussed in Chapter 9 under Special Diets for Athletes.

Immune Support

Botanical products with anti-infection properties include Echinacea and garlic. The sulfur contained in garlic may be the beneficial component, but a horse on a diet of good forage should naturally be receiving sufficient sulfur. Garlic may have antibacterial, antiviral, and antifungal effects, but it also contains a chemical called propyl disulfide that is toxic to horses. Propyl disulfide (also written as N-propyl disulfide) reduces the red blood cells' supply of phosphate dehydrogenase, an enzyme that serves to protect the red blood cell from damage. With a depleted supply of phosphate dehydrogenase, an abnormality known as a Heinz body forms on the red blood cells. Many people give their horses some garlic without *apparent* ill effect, but when enough red blood cells are damaged, a horse will get anemia. A safe level of garlic has not been established for horses, although it is found in numerous alternative products.

Hematinics, or blood builders, are often suggested for anemic horses or those that have been ill or are recovering from extreme stress. Supplementation may be beneficial, but the bulk of the diet should come from healthy forage.

Joint Supplements

Numerous substances intended to relieve arthritis or help joints are reviewed in the arthritis discussion under Chapter 9 Special Diets for Senior Horses.

Essential Oils

Essential oils are another alternative remedy that require mentioning, because they can be confused with essential fatty acids. You know that food oils contain essential fatty acids, meaning that the fatty acid must be consumed in the diet. An example of this is alpha-linolenic acid, found in forage; grain, and flax, soy, or canola oils. However, an essential oil is a non-food oil intended as a massage oil or to promote a mood. An example is lavender oil that believers promote as a calming aid. These products are generally an oil base, such as mineral oil, with added distillate from leaves, roots, or flowers that are called the essence of the plant. This explains the term essential oil. Essential oils are not a source of nutrition for your horse.

Honey

Honey is sometimes used as a flavoring to entice horses to eat pills, but some owners alternatively use it as a topical agent. Applying honey to wounds is a very old folk remedy.

When a honey is believed to be derived primarily from the nectar of only one kind of flower, it is called a monofloral honey. One type of monofloral honey increasingly encountered in the horse world is manuka honey, made by bees collecting from the New Zealand tea tree (also called the manuka myrtle or leptospermum scoparium). You will find manuka honey in tack shops and feed stores. There's nothing wrong with giving honey to your horse, orally or topically, provided he isn't sugar sensitive; take care that topical honey isn't just licked off. An insulin resistant horse could be ingesting enough honey to spike his glucose levels.

Alternative Nutrition Services

Hair Analysis

In addition to general consultation and recommendations, alternative medicine nutritionists and alternative veterinarians may offer hair analysis, also called hair mineral analysis, coupled with an individually tailored dietary supplement.

LEFT: Hair mineral analysis is expensive and controversial. A sample from one animal that was split and described to a hair analysis service as two different animals resulted in two different results and sets of nutritional recommendations.

Hair analysis that is intended to guide alternative supplemental nutrition has been confused with hair analysis in mainstream, evidence-based medicine, because the latter analyzes hair samples with attached follicles for genetic testing. DNA testing to scan potential breeding horses for genetic disorders or color-producing genes is not the same test done in alternative-nutrition hair analysis.

Veterinarians and animal nutritionists who offer hair analysis intended for nutritional parameters will submit a hair sample to a laboratory for chemical analysis. Based on the lab report of macrominerals and microminerals present in the hair, the alternative practitioner then recommends specific supplementation.

To test the service of alternative nutrition hair analysis, I collected a hair sample from an animal, separated the sample into two packages, and submitted them to an alternative nutrition service, as though the samples came from different animals. The calcium, chromium, cobalt, copper, and magnesium levels were reported to be significantly different in the two hair samples. The service recommended two separate, expensive nutritional supplements.

Owners unintentionally contaminate hair with grooming and pest-control products. Mineral content in hair is also impacted by air, soil, and precipitation. This contamination cannot be separated during hair analysis from minerals produced in the body.

While extremes of copper and selenium may indeed be detected via hair analysis, a French review of the published studies on hair analysis for nutritional purposes also concluded that it was not possible to make sound recommendations for nutritional supplementation based on hair analysis.

In any case, remember that significant mineral deficiencies in horses are relatively rare.

Surrogate Selection

Another service some alternative practitioners offer is selecting supplements for the horse via another person's body. A practitioner has a human surrogate touch the horse then offers various supplements or remedies and chooses a product based on how the surrogate's body reacts. This is a service that requires belief and cannot pass muster with science.

The Alternative Choice

Alternative supplements, products, and services that are advertised as optimizing a horse's nutrition and health are appealing. Enhancing bloom and boosting vitality sound positive, and everyone wants the best for their animals. It's rewarding to feel good about giving your horse supplements that might make him healthy or healthier. However, critical thinking has its own rewards.

There are numerous products and services under the realm of the alternative label that are intended to enhance equine nutrition in addition to those commonly encountered and discussed here. Readers interested in alternative treatments and alternative nutritional supplements are referred to *Natural Healing for Cats, Dogs, Horses, and Other Animals: 150 Alternative Therapies Available to Owners and Caregivers* (Skyhorse Publishing: New York, 2011) for a complete review of the topic.

CHAPTER 6
Dental Care
for Optimal Nutrient Absorption

THE CONDITION OF a horse's teeth profoundly impacts its ability to acquire and adequately chew food. Neglected dental care is one reason that horses and donkeys, especially seniors, can have difficuly absorbing nutrients. Poor dentition makes a horse more susceptible to choke and colic, too.

Learning to recognize both normal and problematic dentition is the owner's first step in maintaining a proper dental care schedule. This schedule will vary according to the wear pattern, conformation, and age of the individual equine.

Chewing is also directly related to the production of saliva, which serves as an antacid for the horse's stomach. More chewing produces more saliva. Thus, dental condition is another reason to favor high forage diets. The extensive chewing required of prolonged forage consumption provides more normal wear on the teeth. Concentrates require much less chewing, so diets high in concentrates do not provide sufficient wear on the teeth nor sufficient salivia production.

Normal Dentition and Wear

Horse teeth are hypsodont, meaning that the actual tooth is very high or long, extending well below the gum line. This feature allows the permanent teeth to continue to erupt, seeming to grow for most of the adult horse's life.

Horses are also heterodontous, meaning that they have teeth of different shapes for different purposes. The majority of the horse's teeth can be classified as either incisors or grinders. The twelve incisors are in the front of the mouth to grab and cut grass. There are six upper and six lower incisors. Food is ground up by the premolars and molars. A horse has three large premolars in front of three large molars on each side of both the maxilla (upper jaw) and the mandible (lower jaw), for a total of twenty-four grinding teeth. These premolars and molars are collectively called grinders or cheek teeth. A quadrant of cheek teeth, for example all of the left upper teeth, is collectively called an arcade.

An overly slick or smooth surface on cheek teeth is not a good grinding surface. Cheek teeth normally have transverse ridges across the surface (which is also called a table) that meet the opposing tooth. The transverse ridges help provide a good grinding surface.

The space between the incisors and the cheek teeth is called the bar, interdental space, or a diastema (plural is diastemata). If a tooth is missing or there is an unnaturally wide space between two teeth, this space is also called a diastema.

Some horses have additional teeth on the bar called canine teeth and wolf teeth. Do not confuse the two dog-related references; canines and wolf teeth are not in the same location. Neither the canines nor the wolf teeth play a significant role in eating.

A horse with canines will have one on each side of the lower jaw, located roughly in the middle of the bar, and may also have upper jaw canines in the middle of the upper bars for a total of four canines. Geldings and stallions are more likely to have canines, while less than a third of mares have canines. A canine tooth continues to erupt and must occlude (meet the opposing surface) correctly. A permanent canine tooth in a horse is also called a tusk, while a deciduous canine may be called a tush.

Wolf teeth, if present, will be on the upper jaw immediately in front of the first large premolar. Wolf teeth are technically termed the first premolar, but less than a third of horses have wolf teeth. Unlike the large, rectangular cheek teeth, wolf teeth are small and conically shaped. They usually have shallow roots, especially when they first erupt, and are brachydont (short crowned), thus believed to be vestigial. Wolf teeth may fall out when the horse's permanent premolars come in (between two and three years of age). Some owners never notice that their young horses had wolf teeth.

Wolf teeth are often extracted at the first opportunity to forestall future problems with bitting or impaction. Wolf teeth are easily removed when a horse is young, but the roots grow deeper as the horse ages. When a horse has wolf teeth that stay just below the gumline, they are called blind wolf teeth.

Horses are diphyodontous, meaning that they will have two sets of teeth in their lives. The first set of teeth is deciduous, shedding as the adult teeth erupt. A foal's first teeth, called milk teeth, erupt soon after birth. The youngster normally has a set of twenty-four deciduous teeth by the time it is old enough to wean. These non-permanent teeth shed as the adult teeth come in, with the horse getting its last outer incisors around four-and-a-half years of age. The size difference between deciduous and adult teeth is readily evident during the months when the young horse still has some deciduous teeth but also has some of its permanent teeth.

Eating normally wears a horse's teeth down several millimeters per year. While grinding food, the horse moves its jaw up and down, as well as side to side. Due to the normal grinding motion, horses eventually create uneven wear on their teeth, usually on the outside edge (the cheek side or buccal side) of some molars, while the opposing molars develop edges called points on the side next to the tongue.

Problem Dentition

A horse fed on pasture or with free choice forage from slow feeders uses his teeth enough to provide normal wear, but horses with less natural diets generally require more frequent dental care. Horses given a loose pile of hay will not have to use their incisors as they would if they were gripping a few strands of hay from a slow feeder or grazing. Horses fed concentrates will not have to spend protracted periods of time chewing long stem fiber.

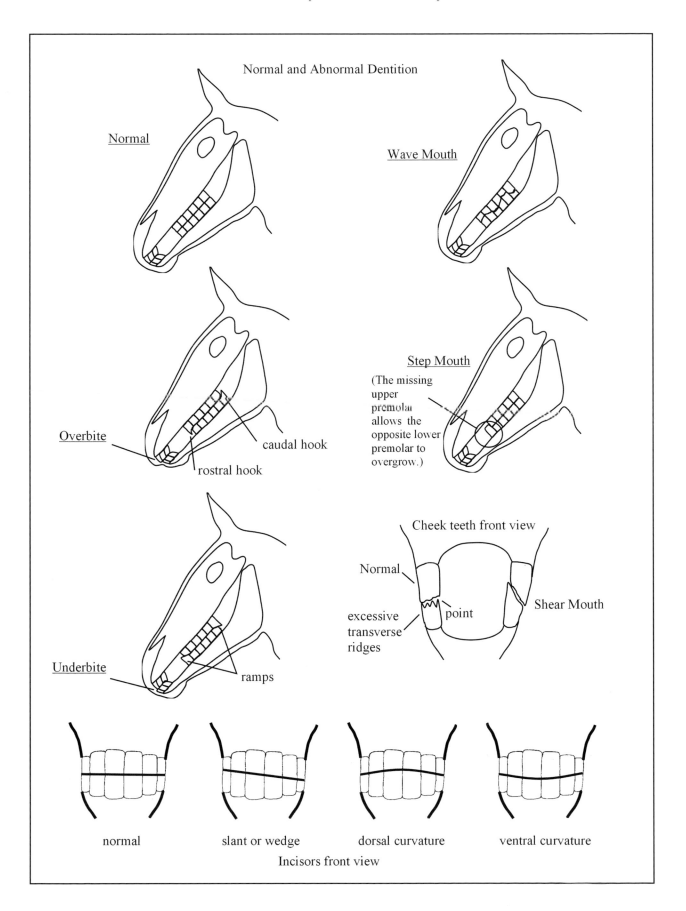

Normal and Abnormal Dentition

Normal

Wave Mouth

Overbite

caudal hook

rostral hook

Step Mouth

(The missing upper premolar allows the opposite lower premolar to overgrow.)

Underbite

ramps

Cheek teeth front view

Normal

excessive transverse ridges

point

Shear Mouth

normal   slant or wedge   dorsal curvature   ventral curvature

Incisors front view

The condition of malocclusion occurs when the upper and lower teeth no longer occlude (meet) as they should. Malocclusion is particularly problematic when it occurs in the cheek teeth, because a good grinding surface requires both the upper surface and the lower surface to meet well. Excessive points, hooks, and transverse ridges, as well as ramps, caps, curvatures, slants, steps, waves, and shear mouth are all malocclusions. Horses with flawed jaw conformation tend to have built-in dental problems that more readily develop malocclusions.

While the development of points is normal, they can injure the horse's mouth as they become more pronounced. Points worn onto the inner cheek teeth edges can damage the tongue. Points on the outer edges can cut the horse's buccal tissue (cheek tissue). In time, the points become longer and sharper, turning into hooks.

Rostral hooks, also called anterior hooks, develop on the front edge of the first upper premolars while caudal hooks develop on the back edge of the last lower molars. Hooks on the outer incisors are also common. When a slope—rather than a hook—wears into the rostral edge of the first cheek tooth (or, alternatively, the caudal edge of the last cheek tooth), the tooth is said to have a ramp or be ramped.

A deciduous tooth that does not shed as the adult tooth erupts, but instead remains on top of the adult tooth is called a cap. This dental cap can interfere with eating if it does not shed quickly, because it makes the permanent tooth underneath it too long and causes uneven wear on the opposite tooth. Caps that remain on the outer upper incisors wear the meeting point of the lower outer incisors, resulting in a downward curve that is termed a dorsal curvature or a frown. When caps remain on the outer lower incisors, they wear an upward curve into the upper outer incisors, which is termed a ventral curvature, upward curvature, or a smile. Another uneven wear pattern on the incisors is a slant, also termed a wedge or a diagonal bite.

If a tooth is lost due to injury or disease, the opposing tooth will overgrow, because it lacks another surface to meet and grind against. This condition of having one overlong tooth extending beyond the other teeth is called a step mouth and is a very difficult situation for the horse.

Poorly aligned front teeth mean that a horse can have difficulty cutting grass while grazing. Horses with flawed oral conformation, for example, an underbite (prognathism of the mandible, also called a sow mouth or a monkey mouth) or an overbite (brachygnathism of the mandible, commonly called a parrot mouth), tend to have additional dental difficulties, because their teeth already do not meet correctly.

Stereotypic behavior such as cribbing (discussed in Chapter 2), can wear the teeth in an abnormal fashion due to the horse repeatedly grabbing and gripping a hard surface with its incisors.

Blind wolf teeth frequently become impacted and painful while staying unerupted. An experienced equine dental practitioner will often be able to detect these unerupted teeth by palpating (feeling) the bars.

Regular dental care keeps points and ridges useable, rather than too long or sharp, and prevents hooks from becoming so pronounced that they cut buccal tissue or the tongue. It will correct cribbing-induced damage to the teeth. Shear mouth, step mouth, and wave mouth are also alleviated through regular odontoplasty (commonly called floating, discussed below).

Oral Assessment and Inspection by the Owner

A cursory oral inspection can be accomplished by carefully pulling the tongue to the side of the mouth in order to examine the surfaces of the premolars, molars, and incisors. Bringing the tongue out to the horse's left side lets the handler view the right cheek teeth. The tongue can then be released, and the horse praised before pulling the tongue out of the right side of the horse's mouth so that the left molars and premolars can be observed.

It is a common misconception that the cheek teeth surfaces should be flat and at about ninety degrees to the tooth edges in order to provide good grinding tables. Unlike the human jaw, horses' jaws and teeth are positioned at angles. The lower jaw is much narrower than the upper jaw. Teeth on the lower jaw angle outward to meet the teeth on the upper jaw. Because the upper jaw is wider than the lower jaw, upper jaw teeth angle inward to meet the lower teeth. A good range for the angle of the occlusal surface of premolars and molars is seventy-two to eighty degrees.

Sinus problems, as well as dental disease and infections, can cause the horse to have difficulty eating. Be aware of unusual drainage or foul smells coming from the horse's mouth. Halitosis (bad breath) or colored drainage could indicate an infection of the tooth or sinus.

ABOVE: **The tongue is held to the horse's left to allow inspection of the upper right and lower right cheek teeth arcades, as well as the surfaces of the incisors.**

While watching the horse eat, be mindful of the chewing manner and rate, as well as the quantity of food processed. When you know a horse's baseline chewing rate and behavior, the difference is noticeable if, for example, a horse with a usual rate of eighty chews per minute begin to have difficulty chewing and slow to a rate of forty chews per minute or anxiously eating at a rate of 120 chews per minute. When bolting, a horse increases its *quantity* per mouthful.

Abnormal eating behavior includes quidding or ptyalism (excessive saliva or drooling). Quidding refers to dribbling food, especially half-chewed hay, and is a strong sign that a horse is overdue for dental care. Swallowing poorly chewed food puts the horse at risk for choke and impaction colic. Inadequate intake and inadequate mastication (chewing) reduces nutrient absorption, leading to poor condition in the horse.

How to Check a Horse's Normal Mastication Rate

When a horse is relaxed and eating normally, count the number of chews in a set time frame and calculate the number of chews per minute. Repeat the check three times, and average the three checks to find the individual horse's normal rate. For example, if you time your horse for thirty seconds on three different checks and note thirty-five, forty, and forty-two chews, this equals chewing rates of seventy, eighty, and eighty-four chews per minute and averages seventy-eight. Most horses chew sixty to eighty times per minute, so your horse falls in the normal range.

If a horse's intake quantity per mouthful is reduced and the length of time it takes to ingest a set quantity of food increases, he is likely *overdue* for dental care. Rather than wait for signs that a horse's dental care has been neglected, it is best to regularly inspect the horse's mouth, observe the horse's daily eating behavior, and schedule routine dental care.

Horses benefit from an annual veterinary examination that includes a dental inspection. Full dental care should be given as soon as possible to any horse that is losing weight while receiving good rations. An exam can include a lab analysis of a blood sample to scan for hints of low grade chronic infection, such as an elevated white blood cell (WBC) count that could indicate periodontal disease.

Equine Dentistry Services

Equine dental care services are offered by non-veterinarians who may or may not have any formal training, by veterinarians who do not specialize in dentistry, and by veterinarians who specialize in providing dental care. Because of this diversity in practitioners' backgrounds, it is important to inquire about the education, training, and experience of anyone offering services.

Floating

Odonoplasty, more commonly called floating, is the procedure of filing the teeth as needed to reduce points and hooks, and restore any other malocclusions. An equine veterinarian can provide sedation to the horse, then float the teeth, including removing caps and wolf teeth.

Competent equine veterinarians who do not specialize in dentistry can generally provide a good inspection and routine float of the horse's teeth.

An oral speculum, or different tool called a gag, holds the horse's mouth open to allow for inspection and to provide access for the teeth to be floated.

Horses' mouths may be sore after odontoplasty, thus horses can go off their feed for a few days, but even the socket left after the removal of a tooth generally heals in about a week.

Dental floats can be either hand-operated dental floats (which look like files on a long handle) or electrically powered. One study showed horses exhibited less heart-rate elevation (which indicates less stress) when power equipment was used. However, these horses may have received more sedation than is required to hand float, thus it is not a fair comparison between the two methods.

Other tooth abnormalities are displaced or rotated teeth and diseased teeth with caries (cavities). Rarely, a horse will have extra teeth (supernumerary teeth) not occurring in a normal mouth. These often become problematic, because they are in an unusual location, and they do not have opposing teeth to keep them worn down.

Frequency of Floating

There is a trend among some owners to increase the frequency of routine dental care to every six months. A healthy horse's teeth generally do not require floating this frequently if it is on a high forage diet. If the owner is obser-vant enough to notice the warning signs of excess wear or

ABOVE: **The speculum holds the horse's mouth open for odontoplasty (also called floating).**

other dental problems, then annual or biennial dental care during a horse's working life should be sufficient to maintain good dental health.

A senior horse, especially one suffering from pituitary pars intermedia dysfunction (discussed in Chapter 9), merits at least annual dental care, as do all donkeys. Any equine with ongoing dental issues (for example, a missing tooth that requires the opposing tooth to be regularly reduced), can be better served by floating every three to four months.

Dental Records

Equine dentistry services include documenting the dentition encountered and floating performed. This record of the horse's dental health is particularly useful if the owner relocates and changes practitioners, or if the horse is sold. Dental records can include documentation using the Triadan system, various indexes to grade the dental health, and the dental scoring system.

Triadan Numbering

In the same way it helps us to learn the names and locations of various body parts—such as the coffin and cannon bones—to better understand and care for our horses, familiarity with the nam-ing system for teeth also lets us communicate clearly. All horse teeth have a three-digit reference number that comes from the Triadan system, or Modified Triadan Tooth Numbering System. Each dental arcade is numbered separately in the hundreds: the right-upper teeth are numbered 101–111;

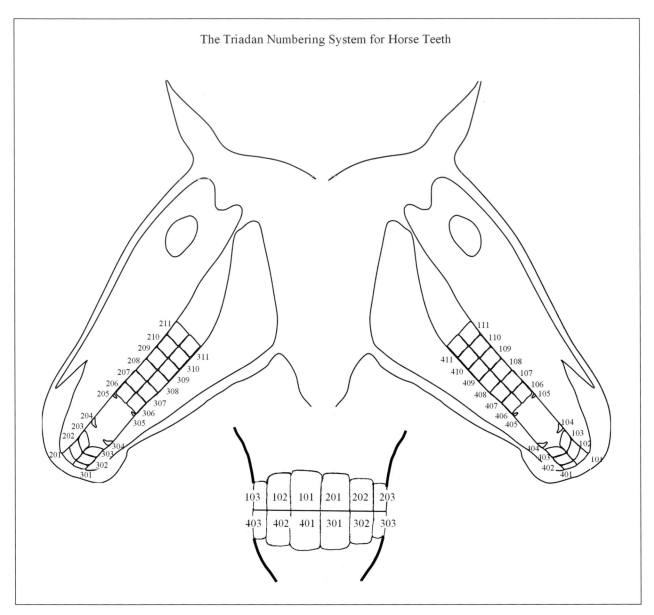

The Triadan Numbering System for Horse Teeth

ABOVE: **The Triadan system assigns a three digit number to every horse tooth.**

the left upper teeth are numbered 201–211; the left lower teeth are numbered 301–311; the right-lower teeth are numbered 401–411. This allows each possible tooth to be accurately referred to in three digits rather than by many words. For example, the back premolar of the upper left jaw is always numbered 208. A lower right canine, when present, is number 404.

Grading Dental Health

Numerous established indexes for grading the status of the horse's teeth and gums exist. The veterinarian may grade the horse's dental health using the equine periodontal disease index, the calculus index (CI), the gingivitis index (GI), the sulcular bleeding index (SBI), and the plaque index (PI). Finally, there is a dental scoring system to grade the wear on the premolars and molars.

Table 6-1 Dental Scoring System (Ellis et al., 2000)	
Score	**Description**
1	flat molar table
2	protrusion but smooth
3	large protrusion, no hook
3.5	large protrusion, no sharp edge
4	large protrusion, hook
4.5	large sharp hook, no damage to soft tissue
5	large sharp hook, damage to soft tissue

The specialized field of veterinary equine dentistry tends to offer a very good result, due to the provider's level of experience and excellent equipment. The sedated horse can rest its 150-pound head on a padded tripod the vet brings or in a sling that places the weight of its head on a ceiling beam instead of the owner's shoulder. This more experienced veterinarian may draw less accidental blood in the process and leave the horse less sore after the procedure, too.

While the dental inspection and float provided by a specialist veterinarian will be safe, thorough, and speedy, it will also tend to be a more expensive veterinary visit. Each owner can decide how often to purchase the services of a specialist in equine dentistry.

By being aware of normal and abnormal dentition, caregivers can ensure that their horses' teeth are in good condition to reap the full benefits of good nutrition.

CHAPTER 7
Parasite Control for Gastrointestinal Health: Worms, Fecal Egg Counts, and Anthelmintics

INTERNAL AND EXTERNAL parasites are natural phenomena in a horse's life. Internal parasites can disrupt the gastrointestinal tract and damage organ tissue as they migrate through the horse's body to complete their life cycles. Having an excessive parasite burden for a protracted period can leave a horse with long term gastrointestinal problems that become increasingly evident as the horse ages. A complete nutrition program includes strategies to control helminth (internal parasitic worms) infestation.

It is important to recognize that the old dogma of a set schedule of regular anthelmintic (dewormer) administration and rotating different commercial products no longer applies. There is no universal deworming program. A one-size-fits-all plan would inherently fail to account for which worms are the greatest threat now (as opposed to a generation ago). It would also fail to account for the individuality of the parasitic burden from horse to horse and from property to property. Additional factors can influence a horse's exposure to parasites, parasitic resistance to anthelmintics, and the practical use of inexpensive fecal egg count (FEC) tests. These can negate the use of any anthelmintic for extended time periods.

Among owners that use FEC tests, some misunderstand and overly rely on the results, then neglect anthelmintic administration to the detriment of their horses. By understanding more about the worms involved, deworming products, the proper use of fecal egg count (FEC) tests, and additional strategies to reduce the worm burden on a horse facility, owners give their horses the best chance for healthy management of parasites, which promotes an effective nutrition program.

The Worms

Although internal parasites are the primary focus, external parasites merit consideration with regard to property management and good grooming.

External Parasites

Ectoparasites include pests such as mosquitoes, chiggers, ticks, lice, fleas, mange, and various flies. Direct management of external parasites requires a two-pronged approach of good general horse care and good property management.

To keep a healthy horse property, compost or remove manure. This dramatically reduces worm survival in the feces. Also, eliminate stagnant water where mosquitoes can breed.

A reputable veterinarian can help the owner determine an appropriate vaccination program to prevent infectious diseases carried by pests, for example, the protozoan-transmitted equine protozoal myeloencephalitis (EPM) or the mosquito-transmitted West Nile Virus.

Bots - gasterophilus

Among the flies that bother horses, the bot fly deserves special attention, because it is both an external and an internal parasite.

There are many species of *gasterophilus*, commonly known as bots. Adult bot flies have a short life cycle of about seven to ten days. When ingested, the bot larvae attach themselves to the horse's mouth or stomach. They can remain in the horse's body for as long as nine months, perhaps having no noticeable effects, but possibly causing a lethal stomach rupture.

Bot flies lay eggs directly on the horse's body, usually on the legs and lower belly, but sometimes on the nose and mane. The eggs are small, off-white or yellow specks that are more visible on dark-colored coats. Bot eggs are easily scraped off with a bot knife, although it is likely that the groomer will miss some eggs and that the horse will have already ingested some.

At the correct dosage, macrocyclic lactone dewormers, discussed below, are effective against internal bots, as well as other internal parasites.

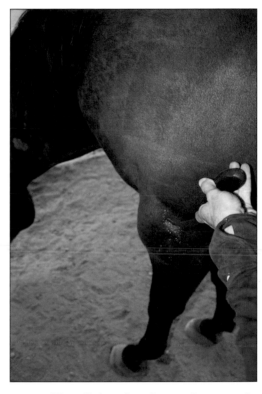

ABOVE: **The light-colored specks on the horse's leg are bot fly eggs. They are removed with a bot knife as shown.**

Internal Parasites

Over one hundred species of helminths (worms) can invade a horse's body. Because these worms provide no apparent benefit and can harm the horse, they are called parasites. The internal parasites affecting horses tend to seek a specific host, rather than infect other species. Parasites infecting other species do not generally bother horses.

While various parasites can infect the horse's eyes, lungs, central nervous system, or musculoskeletal tissues (usually in the neck or legs), worms that affect the gastrointestinal tract most significantly impact the horse's nutritional status, thus are addressed here.

There is tremendous variety in how pathogenic (disease-causing) worms are. Worm species vary in how many weeks or years they live inside and outside of the horse. The prepatent period (the interval between the parasite entering the horse's body to evidence of parasitic infection), varies from one worm species to another. Often a horse with a significant worm burden exhibits no evidence of poor health, and the presence of worms is only detected by checking for parasite eggs in the horse's feces.

Anthelmintics (dewormers) adequately reduce parasite infestations, but owners need to know more about the worms and the dewormers in order to have a good parasite control program. For example, a deworming product advertised to kill worms is claiming to kill *adult* worms, but not necessarily claiming to kill eggs or larvae of that same worm.

The most common category of worms infecting horses are cestodes. There are numerous species of worms within this type, and each can have several different names. After the cestodes, we'll discuss the most common nematode of concern to horse owners.

Threadworms - S. westeri

Threadworms (*strongyloides westeri* or *s. westeri*) are the only worms that a lactating mare can give a nursing foal via milk. Inside the horse's body, the larvae can damage organs as they migrate. A foal with a serious threadworm infestation may be lackluster or have diarrhea and a potbelly, but it might not display any obvious symptoms.

S. westeri larvae can be ingested by a pastured horse or can penetrate the horse's skin. Although the ammonia in urine is toxic to strongyloides, the larvae like warm, moist environments. Skin lesions on a horse that is kept in a warm, moist stall may be evidence of skin penetration by S. westeri larvae.

Threadworms are well controlled with many anthelmintics. Pregnant mares should receive treatment in their last few weeks of gestation to protect the foal from ingesting eggs via mare's milk.

Large strongyles - S. vulgaris

Do not confuse threadworms (*strongyloides westeri*) with another parasite called strongylids or strongyles. Also, strongyles are further divided into large strongyles and small strongyles.

Large strongyles (also called blood worms or red worms, but properly known as Strongylus vulgaris or S. vulgaris) used to be the parasite on which most anthelmintic treatment was centered. Other common species of large strongyles are *S. edentatus* and *S. equinus*.

The adult female large strongyles lay eggs in the horse's intestine. The eggs are excreted in the horse's manure onto the ground, where they mature to larvae. When larvae on grass and other environmental surfaces are ingested, they can migrate through the intestinal wall and into the bloodstream, then damage tissues in organs (such as the pancreas, liver, and heart) before reentering the gastrointestinal tract. The larvae mature into adult worms, and the females lay eggs in the tract. About six months elapse between the horse's initial ingestion to eggs appearing in the feces.

A significant large strongyle infestation is called strongylosis. Signs include poor growth, poor coat, poor performance, weight loss, and colic.

Due to anthelmintic use in the last generation, medical problems due to large strongyles are now fairly uncommon in well cared-for horses.

Small strongyles - cyathostomes

Small strongyles or cyathostomes are now the center of anthelmintic programs for adult horses. This prominence is a matter of default; small strongyles haven't increased in prevalence, but rather the threat of large strongyles has diminished, as noted above.

Cyathostomin larvae go through several stages on pasture grass before the infective stage is ingested. In cold climates, weeks or months can pass before the eggs reach the infective stage. In mild weather, eggs can reach the infective stage in a matter of days. Hot climates can kill the larvae on the ground.

In the interior wall of the cecum and colon, the larvae become encysted and can remain in that state for as little as two weeks or as long as three years before they erupt. The adult worms live near the encysted larvae, feeding on ingesta, and do not generally cause pathology unless their numbers are extremely high.

When large numbers of encysted cyathostome larvae erupt at the same time, a great deal of inflammation occurs. The condition of a horse becoming ill from a massive eruption of encysted cyathostomes is called larval cyathostominosis. It has been theorized that killing large quantities of adult cyathostomes may signal encysted larvae to erupt.

While numerous anthelmintics kill adult cyathostomes, currently only two therapies (moxidectin or a five-day dose of fenbendazole) kill encysted larvae. Cyathostomes have shown a resistance to ivermectin and moxidectin in some locales.

Ascarids - parascaris equorum

Ascarids (properly known as *parascaris equorum* but also called roundworms) are found throughout the equine environment, even in the most meticulously cleaned barns and grounds. While adult horses are not commonly affected by these worms, ascarids are the worm of greatest concern in foal care.

Adult female ascarids, which can reach eighteen inches in length, lay one million eggs per day. The eggs can persist on the ground for years. Ascarid eggs are sticky, clinging to the horse's hair, pasture grass, and other surfaces that horses routinely contact with their muzzles. Once a horse ingests the eggs, larvae emerge in the small intestine, burrow through the gut wall, and are carried to the liver. In a week or more, they arrive in the lungs, where they may soon be coughed farther up the airway only to be swallowed and reenter the gastrointestinal tract. Heavy infestations can manifest as gastrointestinal distress, the horse not thriving, or respiratory colds.

Colic has occurred in heavily infested foals that have been given anthelmintics that paralyze worms. For this reason, benzimidazole compounds, discussed below, are recommended for these foals.

Pinworms - oxyuris equi

Pinworms, technically known as *oxiyuris equi*, live in the horse's colon. After several months, the adult females lay eggs in the rectum and the perianal (around the anus) area. Adult pinworms are sometimes visible at the anus as well. The eggs then drop from the anus onto the ground, ready to be ingested. A horse rubbing its tail in an attempt to relieve the irritation is a classic sign of pinworms, but not every horse rubbing its tail has them. Pinworm eggs die in hot, dry conditions but survive for weeks on moist surfaces.

Since pinworm eggs are not embedded in the feces, fecal egg counts on manure samples usually fail to reveal them, although adult pinworms may be found in the fecal sample. An anal scraping or piece of tape applied to the anus must be examined microscopically to check for pinworm eggs.

Tapeworms - a. perfiolata

Tapeworms are classified as cestodes, as opposed to the nematode class to which the other parasites discussed above belong. There are many kinds of tapeworms, but the tapeworm of most concern in horse care is *anaplocephala perfoliata* or *a. perfiolata*. Tapeworms may cluster at the ileocecal valve, and they have been associated with severe and even lethal colics, yet this parasite is not a great threat overall. Most horses with tapeworms tend not to exhibit pathogenic consequences.

Unlike most worms, tapeworms do not lay eggs in highly predictable cycles.

Horses at pasture have a greater exposure to tapeworms than those that are stabled or dry lotted, because tapeworm eggs must be ingested first by a mite that then must be ingested by the horse. Annual anthelmintic treatment against tapeworms is recommended if tapeworms are known to be a problem in your locale.

Special Considerations for Internal Parasite Problems: Foals and Donkeys

Foals

Remember to protect foals prior to birth by properly deworming the pregnant mare. Ascarids are particularly dangerous for young horses, and foals are predisposed to ascarid infestation. Ascarids have shown resistance to anthelmintics.

Dorsal recumbancy (when a foal lies on its back) is a classic sign of ulcers in a foal. Ulcers may be caused by a worm infestation.

A young horse's first year of life is normally its greatest battle with parasites. In a healthy environment, a normal horse faces less of a threat from worms as it gains maturity around age three. Neglected horses, however, may have high parasitic burdens, so deserve extra monitoring to resolve worm infestations.

Donkeys

Donkeys can present different challenges with regard to parasite control. Horse owners should be aware of the parasitic presentations in donkeys, because contact between the species could create a cross-contamination risk.

Donkeys are subject to a condition called jack sores or summer sores. People once thought these sores were nutrition related and mistakenly ascribed them to excessive protein or non-structural carbohydrates in the donkey's diet. However, these raised areas (usually on the front of the hocks) are actually the result of stomach worms, either *cutaneous habronemiasis* or *draschia megastoma*. Mammoth donkeys seem particularly susceptible. This infestation is effectively treated with ivermectin or moxidectin.

Donkeys are also more susceptible to lung worms (Dictocaulus arnfieldi) than horses and, while harboring these parasites, present a risk of infecting nearby horses.

With regard to external parasites, donkeys seem to attract more than their share of lice and flies, perhaps because of their dense coats. Any new donkey to a property should be examined for lice eggs at the hair follicles before being allowed contact with the resident horse population. A thorough washing and grooming will help alleviate the problem.

Fecal Egg Counts

Three common methods for determining a parasite burden are: (1) examination of the feces for the presence of adult worms; (2) fecal cultures, in which worm eggs are allowed to mature, then the emerging larvae and worms are examined; and (3) fecal egg count (FEC) tests to quantify the worm eggs in the horse's feces. The third is one of the best and easiest tools modern owners have in order to make informed decisions about controlling internal parasites in the horse.

In addition to counting the number of eggs present, FEC testing can be qualitative, revealing to some extent which worm species are present.

A low number of eggs per gram (EPG) of feces is termed a *negative fecal.* Most analysts term an EPG of less than fifty an acceptable, sub-clinical parasite burden, while some would set an acceptable limit at one hundred or even higher. Remember that most horses naturally have some parasites in their gastrointestinal tracts and thus will have some eggs in their feces.

Inexpensive, mail-order fecal egg count tests are now widely available. Simply purchase the service as a package from a feed or supplement supplier (see the Resources section). The package will contain a prepaid mailing envelope, a small plastic fecal-sample container, a rubber glove, and a small plastic spatula for filling the fecal sample container with fresh manure. After collection, mail the fresh manure sample, and soon you will receive the results via electronic mail from the laboratory service which state the number of worm ova (eggs) found.

When you want to do an FEC, keep the sample container handy—perhaps even while riding—to collect a bit of manure the moment the horse defecates.

Collecting a fecal sample early in the week and mailing it early in the day is a good way to ensure the package is not delayed by weekend or holiday mail slowdowns, thus arrives at the lab as fresh as possible.

There are several distinct purposes to FEC tests. The obvious reason is to check the number of eggs in the horse's feces, especially when establishing a baseline, for example, a newly purchased

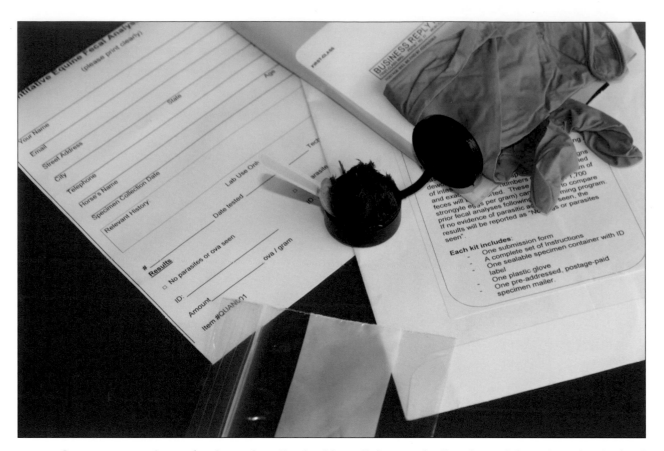

ABOVE: **Owners can purchase a fecal sample collection kit, mail the sample directly to a lab, and receive the fecal egg count (FEC) result via electronic mail.**

horse or one just arriving on a property. Another reason is to determine the egg reappearance period (ERP, discussed below). FECs are also done to determine a horse's normal egg shedding status.

Low, Moderate, and High Egg Shedders

Some horses shed more eggs in their manure than other horses. High egg shedders tend to remain so for life, just as low egg shedders tend to remain low shedders. A low shedder typically has an FEC under 200, while a high shedder commonly has an FEC above 500. Most horses are low shedders, some are moderate, and perhaps 20 percent of horses are high shedders.

High egg shedding horses are also called high contaminators. In a mixed herd, the difference in egg shedding can be that 80 percent of the worm eggs are dropped by 20 percent of the horses. On a property with just a few horses, it may be that one horse is shedding most of the eggs on the land.

Owners make better decisions about parasite control by knowing whether a particular horse is a high shedder, a low shedder, or in between. The high shedders should receive more monitoring and anthelmintic dosing. Less deworming of low shedders helps keep worms from developing resistance to the products.

FEC Reduction Test and the Egg Reappearance Period (ERP)

By doing two FEC tests, you can determine the effectiveness of a recently administered anthelmintic. This is called a fecal egg count reduction test (FECRT). In this case, the anthelmintic is preceded by an FEC, with a second FEC done two weeks after the drug administration.

The time interval after anthelmintic administration up until the significant reappearance of eggs in the feces is called the egg reappearance period (ERP). The ERP varies by worm species and by which anthelmintic was administered.

To determine parasitic resistance to a particular anthelmintic, the administration would be preceded by an FEC test, as well as followed up with a second FEC after the ERP. In this case, the worm species is said to be resistant if the anthelmintic failed to sufficiently suppress the worm presence or if the ERP is shorter than previously noted.

FEC Accuracy and Timing

There are various kinds of FEC tests (generically called flotation tests), which labs perform on a fecal sample. The two most common are the modified McMasters and the modified Wisconsin test, with the latter counting down to one egg and the former having a lower limit of twenty-five eggs.

Different labs and examiners can offer different results. Eggs of some species do not float well and can be harder to count when the sample is separated for the counting process.

Remember that the horse's parasite load cannot be fully determined by fecal egg counts. Only adult female worms and hermaphrodite worms lay eggs. Also, FEC tests do not reveal the number of adult worms and larvae inside the horse. Some worm species lay more eggs than others, and the concentration of eggs in an individual horse's feces can depend on that horse's bowel habits. Also, pinworm eggs tend to be on the anus, not in the feces, and tapeworms only lay eggs intermittently.

The testing purpose, locale, individual horse, and weather influence timing of FEC tests. An unusually warm or cool year can yield atypical worm circumstances for any area. This is another reason why there are no universally applicable anthelmintic protocols. Involve your local veterinarian, and use FEC tests to design a solid parasite control program tailored to the horses, the property, and the current season's weather conditions, selecting effective anthelmintics as needed.

Anthelmintics: The Dewormers

People often refer to dosing a horse with an anthelmintic as worming only to be corrected by others who use the more proper term *deworming*. These people are sometimes corrected in turn by those who recognize that most horses have worms even with excellent management, so horses are never fully dewormed.

Measuring the success of an anthelmintic is complicated by the life stages of the parasites, because a product that kills, for example, five types of adult worms, might not be effective against the eggs or larvae of those worm species.

Understanding all of this, worms are largely reduced with the careful use of anthelmintics dosed according to the horse's weight.

Weight a Minute: Anthelmintic Dosing

Anthelmintics are dosed according to the horse's weight. Underdosing and overdosing can both have negative consequences. Notice the photo in Chapter 10 of two horses that have a 200-pound weight difference but measure within 50 pounds of each other on standard weight tapes. A better approximation of weight also accounts for the horse's length and uses a validated formula. Answers to this formula are provided on the Ultimate Chart.

Commercial Dewormers

Anthelmintics have long been available as: drenches or solutions administered by a veterinarian via insertion of a nasogastric tube passed up the horse's nose, down the esophagus, and into the horse's stomach; or as powders, suspensions, or pastes purchased in a feed store or from a catalog. The owner can easily administer these commonly purchased dewormers.

Veterinary administration of dewormers is now much less common, but there are still owners who believe that administering an anthelmintic via nasogastric tube (a procedure that was called tubing or tube worming) is more effective than over-the-counter pastes and gels. People who believed that tubing placed dewormer directly onto worms misunderstood the anatomy of the gastrointestinal tract and the residences of the worms. Remember that the horse's stomach is many dozens of feet from the lower intestine, where worms primarily reside, and only bot fly larvae attach to the stomach wall.

The most serious potential complication of deworming a worm-infested horse is colic caused by the large number of paralyzed or dead worms inside the intestinal tract. This has particular implications for neglected horses.

Some products are administered daily, some must be administered for five consecutive days to be effective against the targeted worm, and others are only administered every other month or one to two times per year. It is critical to read and comply with the accompanying directions.

It is also important to realize the limitations of the products. Again, an anthelmintic that eradicates worms usually kills adult worms, thus might not be

ABOVE: **Choose anthelmintics carefully and dose correctly.**

effective against eggs or larvae, especially encysted larvae. Match the anthelmintic administration to the individual worm burden of your horse.

The various anthelmintics work in different ways and target different helminth species. They are grouped here by chemical class.

Benzimidazoles

The benzimidazole group includes fenbendazole, oxfendazole, and oxibendazole. These compounds work by interfering with the worms' energy metabolism. They are non-larvicidal in low doses, but a five-day series of fenbendazole is one of the two anthelmintic treatments that can kill encysted cyathostomes.

Heterocyclics

Heterocyclics work by interfering with the worms' muscle function. The only heterocyclic compound used in horses is piperazine, administered by veterinarians via a nasogastric tube. However, it is rarely used now that good, broad spectrum anthelmintics are widely available.

Isoquinolines

The only isoquinoline pyrazine used in horses is praziquantel. It is cestodicidal, thus effective against tapeworms. It is available only as an addition to another product, generally, in a paste with ivermectin or in a gel with moxidectin.

Macrocyclic Lactones

Macrocyclic lactones work by interfering with the worms' nerve signals to the muscles, causing a flaccid paralysis. Ivermectin and moxidectin are the two products in this class used on horses. Moxidectin is also effective against encysted cyathostomes.

Tetrahydropyrimidines

Tetrahydropyrimidines work by interfering with the worms' neuromuscular function, causing the worms to have rigid paralysis. Pyrantel pamoate and pyrantel tartrate are the two products in this class used on horses.

Product Resistance and Rotation

Before the advent of modern broad spectrum anthelmintics, only a few species of worms were targeted. Owners rotated through a series of products in order to kill as many worm species as possible. Some owners mistakenly think they are rotating dewormers when they switch brands. While it is no longer necessary to rotate products, it is necessary to check the chemical names.

Now, well-informed owners know better than to dose horses with dewormers every eight weeks without information on the horse's actual worm burden. Unnecessary anthelmintic use has helped parasites develop resistance to the products.

Table 7–1 Common Anthelmintics and the Targeted Worms		
Anthelmintic	**Efficacy and Limitations**	**Worm Targeted**
Ivermectin	effective on adult worms in the intestine and migrating larvae	s. westeri
		ascarids
		pinworms
		large strongyles
		small strongyles
		tapeworms
Oxibendazole	effective on adult worms in the intestine	s. westeri
		ascarids
		pinworms
		large strongyles
		small strongyles
Moxidectin*	effective on adults worms in the intestine, not approved for migrating larvae	s. westeri
		ascarids
		pinworms
		large strongyles
	can kill encysted larvae	small strongyles
		tapeworms
Fenbendazole	effective on adult wors in the intestine	ascarids
		pinworms
		large strongyles
	5-day treatment can kill encysted larvae	small strongyles
Piperazine	not commonly used	ascarids
		large strongyles
		small strongyles
Pyrantel pamoate	effective on adult worms in the intestine; requires half the dose needed to stop ascarids	ascarids
		pinworms
		large strongyles
		small strongyles
		tapeworms
Pyrantel tartrate	daily use prevents larvae migration	ascarids
		large strongyles
		small strongyles
Praziquantel	sold in combination with ivermectin or moxidectin	tapeworms
*not used on horses under six months		

Parasitic resistance has increased over the last twenty years. The ERP is shortening, and the percentage of worms killed by a dewormer is decreasing. Frequency of treatment is the driving force in promoting parasitic resistance to anthelmintic products.

Parasites with shorter life cycles develop anthelmintic resistance more quickly than longer-lived worms.

Underdosing a horse is ineffective and could promote parasitic resistance to the product. Although modern anthelmintics have wide safety margins, overdosing will not be more effective and might result in toxicity. Toxicosis from ivermectin overdosing has required euthanasia of some horses.

Sometimes when horses are treated empirically for worms and the targeted symptom (tail rubbing or diarrhea) does not abate after the administration of a dewormer, owners erroneously presume they have a treatment failure. Remember that the symptom of tail rubbing or diarrhea may not have been caused by a worm infestation.

The goal of an anthelmintic program is control, not eradication. The well cared for horse won't be completely dewormed, but he will have an acceptably low worm burden. With horses, complete eradication of parasites is not practical.

Alternative and Non-Commercial Dewormers

In the realm of alternative medical treatments, diatomaceous earth is used as a dewormer. Diatomaceous earth (also called diatomite) is an abrasive silica rock powder regularly used as an absorbent in kitty litter, or as an insecticide on the ground in garden applications, where it works by damaging the exterior of bugs' bodies. Diatomaceous earth rapidly loses effectiveness in a moist environment, thus cannot work well inside the horse's gastrointestinal tract.

People have long used any number of other home or alternative deworming remedies (for example, tobacco, pumpkin, or garlic preparations), none of which meet a scientific standard of proven efficacy.

Strategies to Reduce the Parasite Load on a Horse Property

Practices focusing on horse-facility management and the safe introduction of new horses to a property will help lower the parasite burden at your barn.

New Horses

New horses to a property tend to carry a different parasite load relative to the resident horses. The new horse may have been under a very low parasite burden and is now exposed to riskier circumstances, or it may bring new worm adults, larvae, and eggs to the property, exposing the horses already living there. This is one reason why a new horse should not be immediately turned out in a herd, but rather should undergo quarantine.

During quarantining, do an immediate FEC test on the new horse. Find out if the new horse is a high shedder. Rather than accepting the common comment that the horse is "up to date" on deworming, ask for specific information, Find out which anthelmintic was used, at what dose, and on what date. If this information is not available, and an FEC shows a clinical worm burden, administer a broad spectrum anthelmintic, followed up in two weeks with another FEC test.

Manure Management

Prompt removal of manure in common areas is a good policy for any horse facility. Thorough disinfecting of a stall, paddock, or turnout when changing occupants also helps reduce contamination.

Recall the procedures discussed in Chapter 4 on pasture management. Rotating pastures, mowing, grazing another species on the land, removing manure, and spreading composted manure are all measures that help reduce the parasite load, thus reducing the opportunities for your horse to be re-exposed to eggs and larvae.

Note that it is not the general spreading of manure on pastures that can reduce the parasitic load, but rather spreading composted manure. The heat of composting kills many infective agents. Except in very hot climates without grass on the acreage, spreading uncomposted manure actually increases the opportunities for a horse to ingest parasites.

Some facilities amplify standard pasture management practices, removing manure with a vacuum of the sort used on golf courses. This machinery has been shown to better reduce parasite eggs on the land, but is expensive and unsuited to use on rougher ground.

New research with nematophagus fungi (fungi that eat nematodes) that has been shown to destroy parasite eggs in a laboratory setting may someday have practical use for pasture management.

Clean horse facilities with good pasture management and no stagnant water help reduce breeding grounds for both endo- and ectoparasites. Parasite control—an essential part of good equine nutrition—requires a lifelong commitment from the owner in consultation with the local veterinarian, FEC testing, and the careful use of anthelmintics.

CHAPTER 8
Poisonous Plants and Other Environmental Threats

HORSES ARE HERBIVORES, yet many plants are poisonous or otherwise dangerous. Some plants are mechanically harmful, meaning that they physically injure the horse's gastrointestinal tract, beginning in the mouth. Venomous spiders and snakes can pose a threat. Some plants used as forages are potentially toxic. Mycotoxins from fungi can make feed poisonous. Yeasts, mold, and bacteria can spoil feed or bloom on a pasture, making a horse ill. Soilborne organisms can sicken horses. Environmental contamination or changes can cause normally acceptable plants to become toxic.

Early intervention is vital in helping a poisoned horse. Know the classic signs of poisoning. To identify the cause, learn the factors about different plants, feed, the environment, and even the individual horse that complicate pinpointing the toxicity source. Finally, use good poison prevention strategies. These are grounded in owner awareness, coupled with good horse care and land management practices.

ABOVE: **This trail rider has passed through the poisonous plants hemlock, bracken fern, foxglove, field horsetail, and tall buttercup. Riders need to be aware of these toxic hazards.**

Recognizing and Treating a Poisoned Horse

The severity of symptoms can vary not just with the source of the poisoning, but with the individual horse. Poisoned horses may exhibit mild signs, such as a bit of lethargy, minor colic, or going off their feed. More alarming signs include drooling, an uncoordinated gait, staggering, or recumbancy (lying down to an unusual extent). Although there are many causes of colic or sudden behavioral changes (usually manifesting as agitation or depression), consider the possibility of poisoning whenever these symptoms arise. Poisoning should always be considered if your horse has unexplained dark urine or changes in gum color, or color changes in the whites of the eyes.

Common Signs of Poisoning in a Horse

Ataxia: Is the horse uncoordinated or staggering? Does he seem lost? Is he wandering aimlessly or traveling in circles? Is he having difficulty standing?

Color Changes in the Mucous Membranes, Sclera, or Urine: Are the gums bright red or pale? Is there jaundice (yellowing) in the sclera (white of the eyes)? Is the urine dark or red?

Demeanor Change: Is your horse lethargic or depressed? Is he nervous, agitated, or restless?

Gastrointestinal Distress: Does he have diarrhea? Is he pawing, tucked up, or biting at his abdomen? Is there any other behavior indicating colic?

Inappetance or anorexia: Is the horse suddenly off its feed? Does he seem unable to eat? Is he drooling? Does his mouth seem painful? Is the mouth open or is the tongue hanging out?

Photosensitivity: Is the horse blinking or exhibiting extreme shade-seeking behavior? Is he unusually susceptible to sunburn? Are the coronet bands inflamed?

Carefully examine an ill horse's entire body for anything unusual, keeping in mind that he may have been bitten by a venomous snake or spider. Could that spook on the trail ride a few hours ago have been the horse's reaction to a snakebite, even though you never saw the snake? More commonly, horses get bitten in the face by snakes, and the swelling from these bites can progress to the point of needing a tracheotomy to breath. Rattlesnake bites have about a 10 percent mortality in horses, but there is now a vaccine that helps horses build antibodies against the venom. Reactions to spider bites can also be life threatening. In the months after winning a $2,000,000 futurity, a racehorse appeared to have a spider bite on one hind leg that caused the skin nearby to begin sloughing off. This was followed by gross swelling, bilateral laminitis, and then euthanasia.

Poisoning is a strong possibility when a horse exhibits sudden photosensitivity (sensitivity to sunlight). Photosensitivity may present as head shaking, shade seeking, or sunburn, especially on pink skin or the coronet band.

While some poisons have an antidote, most do not. Because of this, the usual treatment in a poisoning is supportive care. In supportive care, the owner and veterinarian seek to stabilize a horse that is deteriorating and ensure its basic needs are met. A dehydrated horse is given fluids. A photosensitive horse is protected from sunlight. Colic is treated appropriately. A severely anemic horse may be given a blood transfusion.

If the poisoning could have been from some part of the feed, immediately remove all feed. Provide fresh, carefully inspected feed. Sniff and examine the removed feed, looking for unusual plants or substances in it. Whether the feed was hay or a commercial concentrate, place it in a cardboard box for transport to an agricultural extension office or laboratory.

In the short term, the effects of recently ingested poisonous plants may be reduced by immediate veterinary care, including the administration of activated charcoal and/or laxatives. If the plant's toxic principle is thiaminase, which destroys the horse's thiamin, a veterinarian can administer large doses of vitamin B1.

Identifying the Source of the Poisoning

When a horse appears to be poisoned, cast a wide net to pinpoint the source. Pastures, paddocks, and stalls are the most likely exposure areas because that is where your horse spends the majority of his time, but also consider brief encounters. A toxic exposure could have occurred while riding past a neighbor's ornamental bushes, at a trailhead, or at a show ground. Examine the feed. Think of every possibility, including far corners of your home pasture where someone may have thrown clippings from unknown plants.

Horses have died when the ingestion of a poisonous plant was suspected but never confirmed, because the source was never identified. Determining which poisonous plant affected an animal is essential to prevent recurrence, but accurate identification can be complicated by numerous factors. The diversity of plant life on the planet is staggering, and globalization permits most plants to be in most locales, even when they are not well suited for the climate. Plants from Florida are now found in Washington State and British Columbia. California poppies are growing in Maine and the Canadian Maritime Provinces. Ornamentals native to India and Southern Africa are in North America, Australia, and Europe. The exchange of flora, both intentional and accidental, occurs in all directions. These scenarios make identifying the poisonous plant a challenge, especially in the long term, when prevention of reexposure is an issue.

A sound knowledge of dangerous plants is made more difficult by the different names plants are called, the number of varietals within a plant family, and the fact that two different plants might have the same common name. For example, in addition to its scientific name *hordeum jubatum*, foxtail is called wild barley or squirrel grass. People

LEFT: **Numerous ornamental nursery plants are toxic to horses. Both oleander and yew are lethal. This garden's poisonous plants include rhododendron, azalea, lupine, cherry, and oak.**

confuse it with another mechanically harmful plant called foxtail grass, which is also known as bristle grass, pigeon grass, or properly, *setaria lutescens*. Locoweed is the familiar name for two distinct poisonous plants, *astragalus* and *oxytropis*. Locoweeds and jimson weed (*datura*) are responsible for large numbers of horse poisonings.

Various plants have different chemical components that affect horses in different ways. In addition, a horse could suffer from a medical condition at the same time as a poisoning, so symptoms—for example, ataxia (a lack of coordination) and laminitis—could have two different causes. A poisoning could cause the ataxia, and equine metabolic syndrome could bring on the laminitis. Also, a horse could have eaten more than one kind of poisonous plant, thus have symptoms that arise from two different toxic principles, with one source in hay and another in the pasture.

The toxic principle in a poisonous plant may be an alkaloid, a glycoside, a phytotoxin, a saponin, cyanide, gallic acid, prussic acid, or another poison. With some plants, the toxicity is understood, examples are the nitrates in *eunymus atropurpreus*—also called burning bush, strawberry bush, summer cypress, or spindle tree—or the cyanide in apple seeds and all parts of cherry trees (including chokecherry) except the fruit. In other plants, the responsible compound has only recently been identified; an example is the gallic acid in maples. There are also plants, such as hoary allysum (*berteroa incana*), in which the toxic principle has yet to be identified.

Table 8–1 The Top Forty-Plus Poisonous Plants of Concern to Horse Owners	
Plant	**Comments**
Black Henbane, *hyoscyamus niger*	usually causes colic
Black Walnut, *juglans nigra*	toxicity can occur from touching
Bracken Fern, *pteridium aquilinum*	extremely common on trails
Butter-and-Eggs/Toadflax, *linaria vulgaris*	affects the grastrointestinal tract
Buttercup, *ranunculus*	spreads rapidly in poor pastures
Canada Thistle, *cirsium arvense*	high in ntrates
Castor Bean, *ricinus comunis*	< 1 lb. seeds fatal to a small horse
Cherry, Wild, Choke, *prunus.*	all but the fruit is toxic
Clover, Alsike, *trifolium spp.*	liver damage, photosensitivity
Fiddleneck, *amsinckia menziesii*	liver damage, photosensitivity
Field Bindweed, *convolvulus arvensis*	multiple poisons and effects
Foxglove, *digitalis purpurea*	cardiotoxic (affects the heart)
Hoary Allysum, *berteroa incana*	can be found in hay
Heliotrope, Common, *heliotropium*	liver damage, photosensitivity
Horsetail, *equisetum arvense*	cumulative effects, all parts are toxic
Hemlock, Water, *cicuta maculatum*	extremely toxic
Hemlock, Poison, *conium maculatum*	extremely toxic
Hound's Tongue, *cynoglossum officinale*	hepatotoxic (affects the liver)

Jimson weed, *datura stramonium*	responsible for many poisonings
Klamath Weed, *hypericum perforatum*	causes photosensitivity
Leafy Spurge, *euphorbia esula*	causes photosensitivity and colic
Locoweed, *astragalus, oxytropus*	responsible for many poisonings
Maple, *acer spp.*	beware of wilted leaves
Monkshood, *aconitum columbianum*	alkaloids and nitrates disrupt the GIT
Nightshade/Horse Nettle, *solanum spp.* Atropa Belladonna, Eastern Black, West Indian	neurotoxic, has many varieties
Oak, *quercus spp.*	tannins in acorns and leaves are toxic
Oleander, Adelfa, Rose Laurel, *nerium oleander*	extremely toxic
Pokeweed, *phytolaca americana*	causes colic
Privet, *ligustrum vulgare*	causes colic
Ragwort/Tansy/Groundsel, *seneccio*	cumulative, irreversible liver damage
Rattlebox, Rattlepod, *crotalaria*	liver damage, photosensitivity
Rhododendrum/azalea/mountain laurel, *ericaceae*	respiratory distress and colic threat
Scotchbroom, *cytisus scoparius*	affects the liver and GIT
Snakeroot/Richweed, *eupatorium*	toxin is excreted into mare's milk
Sorghum/Sudan and Johnson grass, *Sorghum spp.*	causes ataxia and is ardiotoxic
Vipers Bugloss, *echium vulgare*	liver damage, photosensitivity
Water Dropwort, *oenanthe crocata*	extremely toxic
Wild Mustard/Charlock, *synapis*	causes hypersalivation and collapse
Yellow Star Thistle/Russian Knapwood/Barnaby's Thistle, *centaurea*	irreversible damage
Yew, Western, American, Japanese, *taxus*	extremely toxic

Mechanically harmful plants are those that are not poisonous, but that physically injure a horse, sometimes not with large, obvious thorns or burrs, but rather with microscopic barbs. A horse off its feed and showing signs of gastrointestinal distress might well have eaten one of these plants, such as ticklegrass or foxtail. Ticklegrass, *agrostis hyemalis*, is a perennial plant that has microscopic burrs on its seeds and stems that can become embedded in the horse's mouth and entire gastrointestinal tract, causing ulcerations. Foxtail, an annual, has microscopic burrs on its awns that can injure a horse's mouth by burrowing into the soft tissue. Surgery can be required to remove foxtail and ticklegrass burrs, and if the owner will not pay for an extensive procedure, the horse may have to be euthanized.

Whether a horse is at risk from a plant can depend on: the plant part and stage of growth; the plant's health or status; the route, quantity, and duration of the horse's exposure; and the horse's color, health, and individual response level. Consider all relevant factors when trying to locate the source of a poisoning.

The Plant Part and Growth Stage

Different parts of poisonous plants contain more toxin, but the most concentrated site varies from plant to plant. The seeds of poison hemlock are especially toxic, while the roots are the least poisonous part. Water hemlock (also called cowbane) is so deadly that a mouthful of spring growth can make the horse ill in minutes and dead in less than an hour. At other times of the year, the surface parts of water hemlock are less lethal, and the roots are where the cicutoxin alkaloid is concentrated. These roots are accessible to horses, because the plant likes wet, swampy growing conditions, and this type of ground is easily churned up, which exposes the roots. Imagine the horse pulling up the entire plant, roots and all, when snatching a bit of foliage while crossing a boggy section of trail or trampling through a wet corner of the pasture. Wild parsnip (*pastinaca sativa*) is also called cowbane and is also highly toxic.

Toxicity varies with the season or growth stage in some plants. Numerous plants are most toxic as young, green shoots in the spring, but horse nettle (*solanum carolinense*) also called bull nettle, is at its most toxic upon maturity in autumn. Horse owners hate the common cocklebur (*xanthium stumaritum*) when the burrs become matted in a horse's mane, but the young plant was a serious threat to those horses long before those burrs were an annoyance. Green cocklebur shoots are at their most toxic stage, and horses readily eat them at that point.

The Plant's Health or Status

The plant's status can affect whether it is poisonous. Nightshade poisons concentrate when dried, so are more poisonous when accidentally included in hay. Maple leaves are dangerous to horses only when they are green and wilted. The horse trotting down a trail grabbing a fresh, green maple leaf from a tree is not in danger. Piles of dried maple leaves, golden and crisp, are not a threat. However, ingesting one pound of *wilted, green* maple leaves, perhaps blown out of the trees and across a pasture during a storm, lets the concentrated gallic acid affect the horse's red blood cells, causing hemolytic anemia.

The toxicity potential of maples varies. Research has indicated that the ornamental Norway Maple, *acer platinoides*, is less dangerous than the Red Maple, *acer rubrum*. The Silver Maple, *acer saccharinum*, is more dangerous to horses than to other animals. It's safest to consider all trees in the Acer family, including box elders (*acer negundo*), toxic to horses. If there are too many green maple leaves blown into a pasture to remove, the horse will have to be kept off of that pasture until the leaves dry.

The Route of Exposure

Most poisonous plants require a horse to ingest them, but others only require physical contact. Standing on a tack room floor made of black walnut planks or on shavings from that wood can make a horse exhibit the edema (swelling) in the lower legs known as "stocking up."

Wild parsnip can affect a horse merely through external physical contact, because the poison is absorbed through the skin. Wear gloves to pull it out of your pasture, as the painful photosensitivity affects humans as well.

The Extent of Exposure

The duration and quantity of exposure determines how poisonous an exposure is. Some plants are lethal in small doses within minutes or hours; a mouthful of yew or an ounce of oleander is deadly to a horse.

Other plant poisons are cumulative. Consider the scenario of a horse that becomes ill when placed on a new pasture and poisoning is suspected. The new pasture could harbor a toxic plant and must be inspected, but the horse's *former* pasture could be the culprit, too. A new horse might have ingested bracken fern for a protracted period of time at its previous pasture and is now having a seizure.

Like bracken fern, poisonous plants such as tall buttercup and horsetail require prolonged exposure for horses to be affected. Perhaps the last bales of hay came from a corner of the farmer's hayfield that contained horsetail, and after a few weeks of consumption, the horse becomes weak and begins to stagger.

The minimum quantity of an identified poisonous plant varies significantly. A single castor bean can kill your horse. He would need to eat gallons of green acorns to be poisoned by an oak, but pastures with oak trees can provide enough acorns to affect the horse's kidneys. Also, acorns are nuts and the sugar in all nuts and fruits is dangerous to horses with insulin resistance. They can become compromised by fewer acorns than would affect a healthy horse.

Another example of the range of plant toxicity is white snakeroot. Its toxic dose ranges between one and ten pounds. The range may be so large because of growing conditions related to the soil, water, and weather concentrating the tremetol poison.

The Horse

Some horses are what is termed *non-responders* to a particular chemical—they do not react to the drug or poison. About 50 percent of all horses appear unaffected by hoary alyssum, but the other half stock up. The swelling in the legs can progress to laminitis.

Usually, poisonous plants are unpalatable to horses, however there are animals who will try any plant. Most horses don't eat tall buttercups, but some do. Some horses seem to acquire a taste for locoweed.

Hungry horses are more apt to eat poisonous plants. When removing a horse in a rescue situation, examine the land where it was living. Anytime a previous owner didn't provide sufficient forage, a horse may have been desperate enough to eat plants it would not normally consume.

Light-colored horses are more at risk of the effects of plants that cause photosensitivity (sensitivity to light), such as alsike clover (*trifolium hybridum*) or wild parsnip. Grays, palominos, Paints, pintos, Appaloosas, and horses with white face markings are all more quickly sunburned than dark-coated horses. The coronet band is another area of the horse's body that exhibits irritation from poisonous plants that cause photosensitivity. Think of these light-colored horses as the canaries in the herd. The darker horses may also be suffering with painful photosensitivity but not exhibiting the obvious sunburn. A photosensitive horse without shade may blink or try to hide its head under a pasturemate's belly.

Management of these poisonings begins with immediately protecting the horse from ultraviolet light exposure. This horse needs to be indoors immediately, and not just in a stall where it can lean its head and neck out into the sunshine, but completely indoors. Create a shelter of blankets and tarps under a tree if need be, but get the horse full protection from the sun. Photosensitivity may be caused by furanocoumarins or another toxin found in wild parsnip, alsike clover, and other plants. It generally clears in a few days, provided the horse does not continue to ingest the plant. Secondary photosensitivity, however, occurs after ingestion of a plant such as groundsel, heliotrope, or tansy ragwort that damages the liver, which is then unable to clear the phylloerythrin normally produced by the gut in the degradation of chlorophyll. The abundance of phylloerythrin then causes photosensitivity.

Note that the chemical components from poisonous plants may interact with other drugs. Toxicosis from ivermectin, for example, may be exacerbated in a horse that has consumed a poisonous plant, such as silverleaf nightshade (*solanum elaeagniflium*). In any possible poisoning scenario, consider the effect of other medications that horse has received.

The Commercial Feed

If a horse that receives commercial feed exhibits signs of poisoning—ataxia, colic, or lethargy—remember to consider that feed as a possible source of the poisoning. Ionophore poisoning, discussed in Chapter 4, has been responsible for a number of horse deaths. The contamination is traced to a feed manufacturer that prepares a batch of cattle feed containing ionophores and then makes horse feed without adequately cleaning the feed-mixing apparatus. Ionophores (examples are monensin and lasalocid) are common in cattle feed but deadly to horses.

Never give cattle feed to horses. Some owners only buy horse feed from an ionophore-free facility, or a manufacturer that does not produce cattle feed.

The Hay

Countless poisonous plants that grow sporadically in hayfields are inadvertently baled with the good forage. Always check hay when opening a new bale. Identify the leaves, stems, or seed heads of the chosen forage, whether timothy, Bermuda, bluegrass, alfalfa, brome, or another forage, then look for plants amidst the hay that do not belong. Notice any molds, foul odors, or dead animals within the bale. If a horse exhibits signs of poisoning, reconsider the hay.

Some plants, such as kochia (*kochia scoparia*) and the sorghum varieties known as Sudan grass and Johnson grass, are both forage crops as well as potentially poisonous, depending on the growing circumstances or the varieties.

Clover, fescue, and ryegrass are forages prone to fungal infections that make the plant toxic to horses. Clover becomes toxic in pastures when it is infected with molds. One mold converts the clover's natural cumarol to dicumarol, the lethal ingredient in some rat poisons. Clover is also prone to a mold called *rhizoctonia leguminicola*, commonly known as black blotch or black patch, which produces an alkaloid called slaframine that causes hypersalivation or drooling (commonly called slobbers or clover slobbers, but the medical term for excessive salivation is ptyalism). There are usually no other ill effects from clover slobbers, although dehydration is a risk if adequate water is not available.

Another clover mold is visible as rust-colored patches that can cause horses to need vitamin K injections and even blood transfusions. The fungus called sooty blotch forms on alsike clover and causes photosensitivity. Other molds in clover pasture or hay can make horses photosensitive; this reaction has been mistaken for an allergy when actually the horse's irritated skin is sunburnt. These molds, which flourish under warm and humid conditions, clear up in a few weeks with dryer air.

Endophyte is a fungus that lives between the plant cell walls of ryegrass and fescue. It is beneficial to the grass but toxic to horses. Because it improves the grass, turf farms select endophyte ryegrass, while owners should only choose endophyte-free ryegrass. Every year, endophyte causes ryegrass staggers, some broodmares to lose their fetuses through spontaneous abortions, and some lethal poisonings. Generally, the fungus affects extremities first, sometimes to the extent that a horse's ears, hooves, or tail slough off; this condition is a type of gangrene also called dry gangrene.

Broodmares also produce weak or dead foals after dystocia (difficult deliveries) and tend to have agalactia (little or no milk) due to fescue toxicity from endophyte-infested fescue.

A non-endophytic fungus that can infest fescue is called claviceps, which produce sclerotia (the plural of sclerotium, a hardened mass of food reserves for the fungi that can form on forage). More common is ergot, which cause the condition called ergotism. Dallisgrass, also called bahia (paspalum) is a grass naturalized over much of the southern United States that is also susceptible to ergot.

Management is centered on getting the horse, especially a broodmare, off of fescue and ryegrass pastures and fed appropriately.

Other toxins from molds or fungus called mycotoxins may form on hay, especially under humid conditions. A horse exhibiting classic signs of poisoning could have mycotoxicosis, the name for illness due to the ingestion of mycotoxins, most commonly aflatoxin or fusariotoxin.

Blister Beetle

Several varieties of beetles secrete and carry in their bloodstreams a toxin called cantharidin, a powerful blistering agent that damages the horse's gastrointestinal tract if ingested. The hundreds of species of these insects, collectively referred to as blister beetles, feed on or inhabit forages, especially alfalfa, and can be inadvertently included in hay during baling. The problem occurs most frequently in the southern United States. Hay from the northern states and the Canadian provinces tends not to have blister beetles.

Good hay farmers are aware of the danger blister beetles present and watch for the beetles, adjusting their haying schedule accordingly. However, horses are extremely sensitive to cantharidin, and a horse can be poisoned with blister beetles in hay that was thought to be safe.

Hay contaminated with blister beetles can still be dangerous to the horse even if the dead beetles are removed, because the beetles may have secreted cantharidin into the hay. The poison does not safely evaporate with time, so do not be tempted to feed the hay that had blister beetles even after months of storage.

Symptoms of cantharidin poisoning include colic, lethargy or depression, and GIT ulcerations. The ulcers are often visible in the mouth. The toxin can cause renal failure, and the horse may soon exhibit hematuria (blood in the urine). Laboratory analysis of the urine can diagnose cantharidin poisoning. Immediate supportive care is the best treatment, but the prognosis is grave. Numerous horses have died due to blister beetle poisoning.

The Grain

It may seem hard to imagine how a horse could have access to sufficient quantities of some poisonous plants, such as mustard or rape seeds, because the average horse would need two or three pounds for a toxic dose. However, recall from Chapter 4 that owners should never feed bin run or uncleaned grain. Oats, for example, are a weedy crop, and other plants grow among them. If the land also harbors rape or mustard plants, an oat field will yield toxic seeds as well as oats when it is harvested. Grain sold as "field harvest," "bin run," or "pre-cleaned" has not yet undergone the sorting process that removes unwanted seeds.

Grain must be stored properly—with ventilation but protected from moisture—to ensure it does not mold. Mycotoxicosis, described above, can be caused by moldy grain.

ABOVE: **Mold formed on this grain when it was stored in a sealed plastic bag. To prevent mycotoxicosis, never give a horse moldy feed.**

The Environment

Poorly managed pastures are much more apt to contain poisonous plants than well-managed land. Be mindful that the herbicides used to combat poisonous plants in a pasture are toxic. Herbicides often contain salts that some horses seem to find palatable. If using an herbicide in a pasture, be certain to wait the full, specified time on the package directions before allowing a horse back onto a treated field.

Soils and water can harbor toxic elements. One example of this is high selenium, which will be present in the feed grown on the soil and is revealed through feed analysis. Grass along major roadsides could potentially accumulate significant levels of lead from passing motor vehicles. Specific soilborne threats include botulism and equine grass sickness. Finally, an area of concern for some owners is contamination from plastic containers used in feeding and watering.

Botulism

Clostridium botulinum is a common soilborne bacterium. The spores live in about a fifth of tested soils throughout the world and *C. botulinum* also exists—without causing harm—in the gastrointestinal tracts of many mammals. Without the right growing conditions, the bacteria do not produce the toxin that causes botulism infection. However, when the bacteria grow in an anaerobic environment with the right acidity and moisture conditions, they produce the toxins that cause botulism.

The three routes of botulism infection are via a wound, toxicoinfectious botulism (acquired by ingesting the bacteria or spores), or via the consumption of the toxin already produced by the bacteria in poorly conserved feeds, like hay, haylage, or silage (this method of exposure is also called forage poisoning). Botulism in foals is also called shaker foal syndrome and may arise from toxicoinfectious botulism or via a wound, classically the uncleaned umbilical stump coming in contact with the ground.

The early onset of botulism can be difficult to diagnose for several reasons: other conditions give similar symptoms, the bacteria is already harmlessly inside the GIT of many horses, and the toxin is not readily detected in the bloodstream. Signs of botulism can include those related to early muscle paralysis: drooling, quidding, or muscle tremors. As the disease progresses, ataxia will appear, with death coming from the paralysis of respiratory muscles.

There is a vaccine to prevent botulism in horses and an antitoxin to combat the infection. If caught early, some horses survive botulism with the provision of good veterinary care, but the fatality rate in horses is over 80 percent. Careful, regular inspection of all hay and other feeds helps prevent botulism.

Equine Grass Sickness

Equine grass sickness (EGS, also called equine dysautonomia), manifests as dysfunction of the autonomic nervous system. It is rare in North America, with clustered occurrences in Northern Europe and some incidence in South America. Rhinitis sicca (dried secretions in the nostrils) is a sign of chronic EGS, along with colic, ptosis (a drooping eyelid due to paralysis), and ptyalism (drooling).

Its etiology (cause) has not been identified, but it is believed that the pathogenesis might be soilborne. Acute EGS has an extraordinarily high mortality rate, killing over 95 percent of horses that acquire the disease. About half of the horses with chronic EGS may survive.

Plastic Containers Leaching Chemicals into Feed or Water

Some owners have raised concerns that chemicals used in plastic resins could leach out and pose a health risk to horses during feeding or watering, especially when using buckets that were not originally intended to be used that way, but rather are repurposed containers that came with a supplement or another commodity packed inside. Mainstream research has not supported a significant health concern about this, but readers who are interested in taking steps to avoid a specific chemical (for example, bisphenol A, also known as BPA), can see the sidebar to learn how to identify which chemical class was used to make a particular plastic bucket.

Putting Plastics in Perspective.

Plastic containers usually bear on their underside a code number inside of a small triangle that is intended to aid in sorting the plastic for recycling. Owners who are concerned about bisphenol A (BPA) or another plastic classification can check the bottom outside of their buckets for the code.

Number	Abbreviation	Indicates Chemical Class
1	PET	polyethylene terephthalate
2	HDPE	high density polyethylene
3	PVC	polyvinyl chloride
4	LDPE	low density polyethylene
5	PP	polypropylene
6	PS	polystyrene
7	O	other: acrylic, bisphenol A, nylon, polycarbonate, etc.

Preventing Exposure to Poisonous or Dangerous Plants and Other Toxic Threats

The key strategy to prevent toxic exposures is knowledge. Because of the confounding factors of plant dangers, owners are urged to learn about potential problems of every plant on their land and where they ride. Whether or not a plant is expected to be in the area is not the guideline to follow. It doesn't matter what *should be* on the land but rather what *is* on the land. When traveling to different geographical areas with the horse, make the same effort. Do not rely on what someone else says. Remember the rules of good critical thinking discussed in Chapter 1 and get information from the most reputable sources.

The best long term poison prevention plan for the home pasture is good land management. Review the discussion on pasture care in Chapter 4. Remember that well managed pastures out-compete weeds while poorly managed pastures permit weeds to become established. This holds true for land threatened by drought or damaged by wildfire, too. Weeds are opportunistic and likely to germinate on damaged land. Do not overgraze or allow land to have bare patches. Use a multilayered approach of fertilization, mowing, dragging, overseeding, spot control of targeted plants, and fencing off marshy areas if needed.

Be mindful when arriving at a trailhead or show grounds. Is your horse nibbling on a new plant? Is that ornamental wreath on the gatepost a yew? Is the new roadside plant by your neighbor's mailbox an oleander? Aversive conditioning has been used as a training technique with some horses in specific situations to teach them to avoid certain plants, but avoidance remains the most reliable strategy for dangerous plants.

Learn the common signs and symptoms of poisoning in horses to improve the possibility of early detection. Know the individual horse's usual demeanor and vital signs in order to notice early changes that could indicate a poisoning. Review Table 8-1 in this chapter of the most common poisonous plants. Finally, learn the forbidden foods listed under the Treats section of Chapter 4, and review Chapter 5 on Alternative Supplements and Nutrition.

Just like considerable information and effort is required to be a good horse owner in general, considerable knowledge is required to reduce your horse's exposure to poisonous plants and other toxic threats.

CHAPTER 9
SPECIAL DIETS

ALL HORSES ARE special, but some horses require special dietary attention beyond the standard needs of a horse at maintenance. Nine life statuses or situations and ten classes of medical problems with dietary implications are reviewed in this chapter.

The nine life situations detailed in Special Diets Part 1 are athletes, pregnant and lactating mares, growing youngsters, seniors, draft horses, miniature horses and ponies, donkeys and mules, neglect and starvation cases, and overweight horses. One life situation that is sometimes treated as requiring special dietary attention is that of a breeding stallion, but this status is no more physiologically stressful than being a light duty riding horse. For optimum performance, a working stud should be well-nourished, but not overnourished, as both obesity and being underweight can have a negative effect on reproductive performance.

Special Diets

ATHLETES

Whether a horse is ridden or driven for leisure, work, or competition, varying degrees of athleticism are required, and feed must be planned accordingly. Horses with highly athletic lives include those used at elite level competition in the more demanding sports of endurance riding, three-day eventing, polo, foxhunting, racing, and certain rodeo competitions. A true ranching horse may also work as an extreme athlete.

While the majority of horses do not work as hard as these super athletes, many compete at lower levels of these pursuits. Their riders' natural inclination to observe and emulate aspects of top level performance creates additional interest in the nutritional management of ultra-athletes.

Certain considerations set nutritional management of the extreme equine athlete apart from other horses. Their care is grounded in superior daily monitoring, with special attention to pre-competition fueling and then the post-competition refueling called repletion. For work that occurs over extended hours (endurance and all-day ranch riding), the horse should also be refueled *during* the hours of work. Finally, ergogenics, supplements intended to improve athletic performance, are widely available, and a review of the science applicable to these products is provided below.

General Nutritional Needs of Athletic Horses

Several scientific systems have been developed to quantify the nutrient needs of horses under conditions ranging from idle to very hard work. (Chapter 10 provides more information about these systems.) In general, horse diets have long been determined by the additive method, for example an athlete's diet is defined as an addition to the maintenance diet, with the accurately assessed workload being the addition. A horse in light work receives 20 percent more than a horse at maintenance, while moderate, heavy, and very heavy workloads receive, respectively, 40 percent, 60 percent, and 90 percent increases above maintenance. This guideline does not strictly account for the fact that exercise increases metabolism overall and additional extrinsic factors regarding an individual horse that can require more or less feed than would be typically expected.

Intense exercise tends to decrease the horse's voluntary feed intake, a condition known as exercise-induced inappetance. The hormones insulin, ghrelin, leptin, and cortisol all play a part in this response, along with the horse's glucose level. Interval exercise—long touted for its cardiovascular- and strength-enhancing benefits and a reduced overall toll on the body—may exert a less depressing effect on the horse's appetite than more sustained workouts.

Horses in hard exercise may benefit from higher protein diets than idle horses. However, the *quality* of the protein is key. A study comparing horses in hard exercise fed either 16–17.5 percent protein forage-only diets or regular diets of 10.5–11.5 percent protein found no difference in heart or respiratory rates, blood plasma protein and lactate, bicarbonate or blood pH. The high protein diet horses did drink more water and have a higher urine output with higher urea content and lower pH. Note that in these two groups of horses, one group is getting more protein but not more *high-quality* protein. Again, high quality protein is found in alfalfa and soybean meal.

It is well established that diets high in starch and sugar impair energy regulation, a negative effect that is marked in consistent exercise training. A high fiber diet serves horses' physiology. Increased energy, when needed, is best derived from more forage, then added fat.

Intense exercise also influences the retention time of digesta within the gastrointestinal tract. Although fibrous material filling the hindgut creates weight or ballast that the horse must carry, the material also provides a reservoir of fluids and electrolytes. The latter deserve special consideration for all extreme athletes, because improper timing and composition of electrolyte supplementation can contribute to the development of synchronous diaphragmatic flutter, also known as thumps. (Chapter 4 discusses electrolytes, including homemade recipes.)

Glycogen, the stored carbohydrate in muscles and the liver, is a key energy source for athletes. As the glycogen molecule is broken down to provide sugar, released hydrogen and oxygen form water. Glycogen storage capacity can be improved by 33 percent in three months of consistent training.

Assessing Workload

Many people overestimate how hard they work their horses. Consider two groups of riders, both heading out for a two-hour trail ride. The first group's ride might include rest stops, halts to adjust tack, time for photographs or breaks, and stopping to snack or chat. Back at the barn, they might include their tacking and untacking time in their two hours. They may have barely covered three miles. Another group of riders might easily cover twenty or more miles of hard trail in a two-hour ride. While the first group might think their horses require athletic dietary attention, only the latter group merits an athlete's diet.

RIGHT: **Dr. Stephanie Caston Auck of Iowa State University's College of Veterinary Medicine aboard her Akhal Teke x Appaloosa. Speed work and jumping are an increase in workload over riding the same distance slowly or on the flat. Photo Credit: Shane Auck.**

A horse's physical effort is influenced by the duration and intensity of exercise; the footing, including the slope of the terrain; environmental factors (temperature, humidity, and altitude); and finally, by the individual's temperament.

An unfit horse works relatively harder than a fit horse to do the same amount of work. Also different breeds—and individuals within breeds—have variable inherent capacities for different types of work.

The National Research Council defines workload categories with figures for the exercise in hours per week, sustained heart rate, and time at each gait. (Table 10–2 in Chapter 10 offers the NRC definitions of workload, coupled with the feed requirements for the workload categories of light, moderate, heavy, and very heavy.) The NRC defines a very heavy workload as six to twelve hours per week averaging a pulse of 110–150.

Technology for assessing a horse's effort include thermistors and heart monitors. Thermistors provide a measure of the horse's skin temperature. Heart monitors provide the rider with a constant readout of the horse's heart rate.

Anyone can learn how to assess a horse's effort via pulse-checking without using a heart monitor. (Chapter 10 shows three locations to check a horse's pulse.) NRC guidelines also quantify the horse's work by its pulse. The horse's respiratory rate and effort are additional indicators of how hard it is working.

Table 9–1 Equating Pulse to Energy Demand (per the National Research Council)	
Pulse (beats per minute)	Kilocalories per Hour
60	24
90	56
120	99
150	158
180	230

Competition or Workout Feeding

Different equestrian activities impose very different physical demands that require distinct feeding strategies. While racing is extremely demanding physically, an American Quarter Horse or even a Thoroughbred does not work at an intense effort nearly as long as a three-day event horse, and the eventer works less than 10 percent as long as a typical endurance horse. Among endurance horses, mid-pack finishers work much longer but not at the intensity of elite level, top-ten finishers. Thus, specific guidelines for feeding before, during, and after an athletic competition vary depending on the sport involved.

Pre-Exercise Feeding

The overall meal size of all concentrates should not be greater than 0.3 percent of the horse's body weight. Current recommendations are to time the horse's pre-competition meal 3–4 hours prior to the start of exercise. (For endurance horses starting a ride at 5:00 a.m., this means feeding between 1:00 and 2:00 in the morning.)

Grain-based concentrates should not be fed within 3 hours of starting a hard ride, although a small concentrate meal the prior evening may be helpful. The warning in Chapter 4 to not overfeed starch is especially important regarding pre-competition meals. The guideline on starch maximum of one mg/kg of bodyweight has been calculated into ounces and pounds on the Ultimate Chart.

In the days immediately prior to extreme competition, electrolyte loading is no longer recommended, but two ounces (seventy grams) by volume of a 3:1 NaCl/KCl mix about two hours before the ride start may be beneficial. Hay should be available to these horses at all times. Alfalfa will provide high quality protein and a good level of calcium.

Pre-loading a horse with electrolytes in the days prior to competition has often been practiced but is not recommended. Because the body seeks homeostasis, the horse excretes unnecessary salts. It cannot plan ahead for Saturday's need for salts by hanging on to extra salts provided on Wednesday or Thursday. However, for endurance, a small boost of electrolytes in the hours preceding competition might be helpful. Reference the Chapter 4 section on electrolytes.

Feeding During Extended Hours of Hard Work

Remember that a horse in nature does not stop eating for more than two to three hours, which is why its gastrointestinal tract does best with very regular access to forage. During extended exercise (rides lasting more than a few hours, especially at an intense pace or with extensive climbing or jumping), the horse must be refueled during the ride for optimal performance.

Before leaving for a day's ride, determine whether there will be water access and when there might be grazing opportunities. If there will be no forage available, pack a lunch for the horse.

For a lunch during a long conditioning ride of twenty miles or more, place up to a cup each of beet pulp pellets and alfalfa pellets, plus a tablespoon of plain salt, into a gallon-sized plastic bag with several cups of water. If the weather is hot, add ice cubes so that the mix will not become rancid. If the horse is thin, add up to a half cup of canola or other food grade oil to the bag contents.

Horses that regularly receive fat supplementation are better able to use fat during intense exercise. One laboratory method to measure fitness is to determine the volume of oxygen (abbreviated as VO2) the athlete uses during a carefully controlled treadmill test. A higher number generally equates to greater aerobic capacity. Studies have shown that a horse fed a high fat diet tends to have a higher VO2.

If using electrolytes, note that current research suggests using sodium chloride, rather than potassium chloride during extreme exercise, for example, many hours at speeds above three meters per second (about 6.7 miles per hour or 10.8 kilometers per hour). Potassium supplementation during endurance rides ridden at speeds below 6.7 mph can be beneficial. The addition of salts of calcium or magnesium may be beneficial as well. Some horses will eat calcium carbonate tablets (Tum's or an equivalent antacid), as a means of adding calcium as an electrolyte.

Electrolytes are contraindicated if the horse is not drinking well. Hypertonic pastes are not recommended for horses with ulcers at any time. There have been warnings to avoid potassium *during* exercise, but others recommend ensuring adequate sodium, potassium, calcium, magnesium, and chloride salts are provided. The best current advice is to not give potassium *during* exercise at speeds above eighteen miles per hour.

Post-Exercise Feeding

Post-exercise feeding is tailored to provide the horse with the best chance for a full and rapid recovery, called repletion, from an extreme athletic effort.

Glycogenesis is the term for rebuilding the muscles' glycogen supply that was depleted by exercise. A higher glycemic index feed (discussed in Chapter 2) offers material needed for this effect but it is safest to simply feed forage. In people, exercise science has shown that the body is more sensitive to restoring glycogen within the first half-hour after exercise ends. Knowledgeable athletes eat and drink appropriate fuel almost immediately in order to let their bodies have the best chance at rebuilding. With horses, the time frame for repletion is less well established, but one study assessing post-exercise glycogen repletion demonstrated that horses fed within ninety minutes of ceasing exercise had faster glycogen replacement than did horses who were not fed for four hours after exercise.

Recovery electrolytes can improve rehydration. Electrolytes are often given for two to three days after elite level events. Many horses do well when provided with a choice of two buckets, one containing saline and the other clean water. See the section in Chapter 4 on electrolytes for the amount of salt to add to a water bucket to make a drinkable saline.

A study of the antioxidant effect of administering vitamin E (in the form of 250 mg tocopherol), selenium (in the form of 0.5 mg of sodium selenite), and glutathione peroxidase in Arabian race horses in training found the antioxidants remained in the blood. This makes a good argument for the common practice of providing a broad spectrum vitamin and mineral supplement for horses in extreme athletic training. It also brings us to the topic of ergogenic supplements.

Ergogenic Supplements

"Ergogenic" means work-generating. Ergogenic supplements are intended to improve the body's ability to sustain or recover from effort. You may have heard about some of these substances at the gym or in an article on conditioning your horse. Numerous substances are suggested as ergogenics by people interested in sports medicine. However, it is important to recognize the difference between theorizing and proving that a supplement is ergogenic. Also, testing of some ergogenics is done *in vitro* (in a laboratory setting), which is a less applicable test than an *in vivo* (on live horses) study.

Learning whether or not an ergogenic is effective requires delving into physiology (how the body functions). Various ergogenics have been suggested to: increase the availability or transport of key nutrients, improve the body's handling of the oxidative stress (damage) that physical conditioning creates, or delay the onset of fatigue.

Before buying into claims that a supplement is an effective ergogenic, scrutinize the design of the study and then decide how much credence to give the results. Many studies are not conducted over a large sample size. Imagine three horses used as controls in an experiment and three more being given an ergogenic supplement. Then in a resulting physical test, two of the supplemented horses and one of the control horses perform better. This is not convincing data, yet it can be truthfully stated that the supplemented horses showed twice the improvement compared to the control horses.

In other studies, supplemented horses are used as their own controls, and the study is conducted longitudinally. For example, horses are exercise-tested without a supplement and later are supplemented and physically tested again. In this case, it is not possible to know to what extent the horses were benefitting from the conditioning of the first test versus the supplement.

Researchers conduct studies on the various metabolic pathways muscles use to process energy. These studies can involve doing muscle biopsies to ascertain the amount of "slow twitch" versus "fast twitch" muscles the horses have. However, different animals have different muscle composi-

Muscle Fiber Types: I, IIa, and IIb

Type I fibers are called "slow twitch" muscles. They use oxygen efficiently in aerobic metabolism and can fire (cycle through contraction and relaxation) for a relatively long time before becoming fatigued. They are associated with endurance: the low force, but high repetition of a long, relatively easy ride.

Type II fibers are called "fast twitch" muscles. They use oxygen less efficiently and generate more power through anaerobic metabolism pathways. Type IIb, also called type X, are associated with high force, low-repetition efforts: the short, powerful sprints of rodeo events, using a glycolytic energy path. Type IIa are between the extremes of type I and type IIb and use what is called the oxidative energy path.

tion, and it is very difficult to know if the researcher is studying an extraordinary athlete or one who responded to an ergogenic. Similarly, it is hard to discern if an animal is simply a mediocre athlete or if an ergogenic it was given is ineffective. Establishing effectiveness would require a large sample size, which would be very expensive research.

Tremendous numbers of chemical reactions are involved in an idle body, and these processes have additional pathways to support athletic activities. The sheer number of these reactions means there are many possible opportunities to influence the body's ability to produce effort. If an ergogenic increases a chemical that is not a limiting factor in a reaction, it is unlikely to improve the rate of the reaction, thus is unlikely to improve an athletic effort. Making strong links in a chain even stronger will not improve weak links in a chain. For an ergogenic to be effective in improving a chemical reaction, it should target a limiting factor in the reaction.

Protein Manipulation

The building blocks of protein—amino acids, their metabolites, and derivative compounds—are theorized as ergogenics because of their central role in the creation of muscle mass and strength, as well as the numerous other functions these compounds have.

Gelatin provides the amino acids proline and glycine, and some owners feed it to their horses for that reason or in the hope that it will promote hoof growth. It is an incomplete and poorly digested protein extracted from animals, so it is a supplement outside of a horse's normal food chain.

Gamma oryzanol (GO) is a plant sterol compound of ferulic acid esters and triterpene alcohols that occurs naturally in oils extracted from corn, barley, and rice bran, most markedly in the latter. Because it is a sterol, promoters suggest it has anabolic-like, or muscle-building, effects. However, there is no data demonstrating gamma oryzanol is an effective ergogenic in horses.

Branched chain amino acids (abbreviated as BCAAs, which include leucine, isoleucine, and valine) are promoted as ergogenics. In humans, the ingestion of BCAAs post-exercise has been shown to promote anabolic activity. BCAAs are certainly important feed constituents for horses. However, one study in which Standardbreds were supplemented with BCAAs over five weeks and worked three times per week showed no change in the pertinent variables. It is interesting to note that even the reasons why BCAAs might be ergogenic are disputed. BCAAs may serve to increase the concentration of a compound (trichloroacetate intermediates) needed in a chemical reaction (called anaplerosis) that is used in an energy cycle (the acetyl CoA reaction). BCAAs may also take part in the brain's role at regulating effort. BCAAs may be helpful in repletion, but specific, universal recommendations have not been established.

HMB (hydroxy-methyl-butyrate, also called beta-hydroxy-beta-methylbutyrate and written as β-hydroxy-β-methylbutyrate) is suggested as an ergogenic. It is a metabolite of the amino acid leucine. HMB is suggested to affect muscle mass and performance by helping to prevent muscle breakdown, but this suggestion has not been backed by clear clinical studies in horses.

Creatine (also called methylguanidine-acetic acid) is suggested as an ergogenic. It is an amino acid derivative normally synthesized in the liver and stored in skeletal muscles. Some of the stored creatine is phosphorylated (combined with phosphorus). This phosphorylated creatine (also called PCr, creatine phosphate, or CP) serves as a short term source of phosphate for energy production. However, only 5–10 percent of orally administered creatine is absorbed from the equine gastrointestinal tract. [Do not confuse creatine with creatinine. The latter is a by-product of creatine use and is generated when muscles engage in work. A horse with healthy kidneys will effectively clear creatinine from the blood.]

Carbohydrate Manipulation

Carbohydrate loading is suggested as an ergogenic strategy. It is done by depleting the muscles and liver of glycogen through exercise, to trigger fatty acid use then super-supplying carbohydrate in the hope that the muscles and liver will store a larger supply of glycogen; it is a common practice in human athletes but has not been shown to be effective in horses. It is worth remembering that horses are built for a diet very high (over 80 percent) in structural carbohydrate. Even if a horse were given a great deal of a high fat and high protein concentrate, those percentages together would likely range about 30 percent, leaving 70 percent of that concentrate to be carbohydrate calories. The horse should still be on free choice forage, which is of course mostly carbohydrate as well. There is no healthy way to carbohydrate deplete a horse through its diet in the hope of then carbohydrate loading it.

In the *Proceedings of the First European Equine Nutrition and Health Congress* (2002), Ivers reported glycogen loading racehorses with four ounces (128 grams) of maltodextrin with chromium and getting good results, but he did not recommend glycogen loading an event horse, because he thought the high energy level could make the dressage test difficult.

Colostrum is suggested as an ergogenic due to its composition as an extremely high nutrition feed for neonatal foals. It is high in fat and protein, as well as other primary nutrients, but adult horses are naturally lactose intolerant, thus do not digest milk well. Feeding colostrum to adult horses as an ergogenic has not been well studied.

Fatty Acid Manipulation

Free fatty acids and substances involved in their transport or oxidation are frequently suggested as ergogenics. Fatty acids have undeniable health benefits, as discussed in Chapter 4. Examples of naturally occurring fatty acids that you will find in horse supplements include docosahexaenoic acid (DHA), lipoic acid (alpha-lipoic acid), and a reduced form of lipoic acid called dihydrolipoic acid (DHLA); and omega-3 fatty acids.

Omega-3 fatty acids competitively inhibit the enzyme cyclooxygenase (COX, which is also called prostaglandin-endoperoxide synthase or PTGS). Inhibiting COX can help reduce inflammation or the damage caused by oxidative stress.

Medium chain triglycerides (MCTs) have also been specifically suggested as an equine ergogenic (because they do not depend upon acetyltransferase in order to undergo intracellular oxidation.) However, orally supplied MCTs have not been shown to spare glycogen in moderate to intense athletic endeavors.

It suffices to say that the biochemical reactions and interactions of fatty acids are not fully understood, but that a clear ergogenic effect has not been demonstrated in an athlete that is already well nourished and well conditioned.

Carnitine, also called L-carnitine, is suggested as an ergogenic. It is a component of naturally occurring enzymes involved in the transport of fatty acids. (Carnitine also serves in the conversion of acetyl-CoA to acetyl-carnitine. The ratio of acetyl-CoA to CoA is important, because high acetyl-CoA inhibits energy production at the cellular level.) Carnitine is not present in the normal horse diet, but horses synthesize their own supply naturally. Studies in which very large doses of carnitine were given both orally and intravenously showed that while the plasma level of carnitine was raised, the carnitine level in the skeletal muscle was unchanged, thus carnitine appeared not to exert an ergogenic effect in horses. Interestingly, other studies have shown that young Standardbreds given ten grams per day built more type IIa muscle fibers than did control horses. In yet another study, carnitine-supplemented horses had no change in heart rate or blood lactate when compared to control horses.

Co-enzyme Q10 (also called ubiquinone, Co-Q10, or Q10) is suggested as an ergogenic. It is a naturally occurring compound that is important in the intracellular work of oxidative metabolism. However, the horse's Co-Q10 supply does not appear to be a limiting factor in this metabolism.

Fatigue Manipulation

One theory of the general cause of fatigue is that the body has an insufficient capacity to carry oxygen. Another theory is that the primary cause of exercise fatigue is a buildup of biochemical waste products (lactate, hydrogen ions, or free radicals). Products that might improve oxygen-carrying capacity, or those that might mitigate the by-products of exercise have been suggested as ergogenics. Another ergogenic route is to enhance the athlete's repletion after a workout in order to work out again sooner or harder. This strategy and the following substances are covered below: DMG, TMG, hematinics, "milkshakes" of sodium bicarbonate, carnosine, creatine, DCA, SOD, and quercetin.

Dimethylglycine (DMG, also called N,N-dimethylglycine) and its precursor, trimethylglycine (TMG, also called betaine) are purported to mitigate lactate production. (They activate the pyruvate dehydrogenase pathway, a chain of reactions for a body to use energy that turns glucose into pyruvate then into acetyl-A to be used in the primary energy-production process called the citric acid cycle.) However, studies of DMG and TMG supplementation have not borne out good results in clinical testing.

Hematinics (blood builders) are promoted as ergogenics in the hope that an increase in circulating hemoglobin or red blood cells (RBCs) would produce an increased ability to carry oxygen to the muscles. However, an athletic horse should already have normal, healthy blood chemistry. Further, horses, unlike humans, can release large stores of RBCs from their spleens.

Hydrogen ions are another by-product of muscular contractions. Intense exercise produces a great deal of hydrogen ions. This results in acidemia (high blood acid levels). Sodium bicarbonate (abbreviated elementally as $NaHCO_3$, which may be how the supplement is listed on a label) has been administered by racehorse and Standardbred trotting trainers in concoctions called "milkshakes."

Also called jugging, an entire box (500 grams) of baking soda is given to the horse via a nasogastric tube. The milkshake may include DMSO and sugar or other additions as well. While bicarbonate does decrease the hydrogen-ion concentration, studies have shown mixed results, and the greatest effect seems to be in an unfit and overworked horse. A study of horses given just 250 grams of sodium bicarbonate noted the horses had significantly increased water consumption and urinary output compared to undosed horses. Racing authorities ban bicarbonate use, because it is difficult to monitor and may be used to mask the presence of illegal substances.

Hydrogen ions are buffered naturally through phosphates and amino acids. Of the amino acids, histidine dipeptide is especially important, with the horse getting perhaps a third of its buffering effect through a histidine dipeptide called carnosine. Carnosine may be especially buffering for type II muscle fibers. However, studies attempting to increase this effect by supplementing the horse with l-histidine have not shown a statistically significant increase. This led to the suggestion that β-alanine (also written as beta alanine) is a limiting factor in the horse's synthesis of carnosine, however even a low dose administration of β-alanine causes a loss of the amino acid taurine within tissues, which is undesirable.

Phosphorylated creatine is another natural buffer of hydrogen ions, albeit a weak buffer, but attempts to significantly manipulate the horse's supply have resulted in only modest increases.

Dichloroacetate (also called DCA) is an indirect activator of an enzyme (pyruvate dehydrogenase or PDH) that is critical in cellular respiration. (PDH links a chain of reactions called the glycolytic metabolic pathway, which breaks down the body's stored glycogen for use in the routine energy pathway called the citric acid cycle, which is also known as the Krebs cycle.) Both DCA and a related chemical called 2-chloroproprionate (also called 2-CP) initially increase the use of pyruvate during exercise, which is desirable. DCA and 2-CP have not been well studied in horses, but proponents point to a 1982 study in dogs that showed a performance enhancement when DCA was administered along with N,N-dimethylglycine. In a 2013 study, low doses of DCA were shown to lower by about 15 percent the blood lactate in four unfit horses undergoing submaximal exercise.

Superoxide dismutase (SOD) is a naturally occurring enzyme responsible for breaking down a free radical called superoxide. However, SOD does not work when administered orally. In other words, feeding a horse a SOD supplement does not increase its SOD level. Further, although SOD can be synthesized from yeast and certain vegetables, supplement forms are usually synthesized from animal liver, typically cow or chicken, thus are not naturally part of the horse's food chain.

Repletion enhancement is an area of fatigue manipulation that addresses post-workout refueling. By improving recovery from exercise, trainers hope to condition more intensely. Thus, electrolytes, antioxidants, vitamins, and minerals, especially the trace mineral chromium, and BCAAs have been suggested as ergogenics. One example is the combination of calcium, magnesium, phosphorus, and potassium—known elementally as Ca, Mg, P, and K—marketed as CMPK, often with the addition of botanicals and dextrose or another sugar. A study of unfit horses made to exercise, half of which were given the naturally occurring antioxidant quercetin, showed a small reduction in cytokines (a by-product produced within the horse by oxidative stress) in treated horses compared to untreated animals. Quercetin is available as quercetin dehydrate, but it has not been shown to improve performance in an already athletic animal.

It is important to demand the data when considering claims of effectiveness. Imagine a formula consisting largely of vitamins and minerals, some of the substances discussed above that are touted as ergogenics, some form of sugar, and unrevealed, proprietary ingredients. The promotional material may advertise that it contains ingredients proven to increase energy—the claim is truthful because of the sugar included in the formula.

The governing body of any equestrian sport may ban behavior-altering (calming supplements, some of which may be only magnesium, others with herbs or other compounds that have GABA effects, like the drug Valium) or performance-enhancing products, even without naming the substance in question. An example of this is the United States Equestrian Federation, whose rule 410, "Equine Drugs and Medication, The Therapeutic Substance Provisions" forbids substances that "might affect the performance of a horse and/or pony."

Overall, there is little compelling evidence to recommend ergogenic supplements, although this fact does little to dissuade interest in the products by people who do not carefully read the studies. Finally, some ergogenics affect physically unfit animals but have no significant performance-enhancing effect on animals that are in good physical condition. While some ergogenics may help an unfit horse manage an athletic endeavor, no substance can make a fit horse fitter. It is more ethical to compete to the best ability of a horse and rider who prepared by carefully training and conditioning rather than looking for an advantage in a package.

Three Days at a Time

Three-day eventing is an equestrian sport that heralds three classic equestrian sports—dressage, cross country jumping, and show jumping. It is an Olympic sport that originated as a test for cavalry riders.

Elisa Wallace is an elite level, three-day event rider who has trained multiple horses to compete at the Advanced level. Her feeding program for these super athletes is centered on free choice forage. She uses slow feeders that hold a bale of hay, and she estimates that her event horses eat twenty to twenty-five pounds of alfalfa/grass mix per day.

LEFT: **Elisa Wallace aboard Simply Priceless, aka Johnny, during the dressage phase of the 2015 Rolex CCI four star, three-day event. Photo Credit: Aly Rattazzi.**

Advanced level eventing is an expensive sport, and elite competitors sometimes have sponsorships from feed manufacturers or suppliers of other riding-related goods. Elisa relinquished a sponsor after traces of monensin (an additive in cattle feed that is lethal to horses) were found in the manufacturer's horse feed. She now selects feeds from a manufacturer that does not produce cattle feed and can offer guaranteed ionophore-free horse feeds. The concentrate she gives the eventers has 14 percent each crude fat, protein, and fiber. The product has almost 7 percent omega-6 oils and less than 2 percent omega-3. Its first ingredients are wheat middlings, soybean hulls, heat-processed soybeans, ground corn, oat-mill by-product, beet pulp, heat-processed wheat, dehydrated alfalfa meal, and heat-processed flax seed. She weighs her concentrates, and feeds only six to seven pounds per horse although the manufacturer suggests a range of two to sixteen pounds for a 1,200 pound horse in intensive training.

She wets the commercial concentrate feed in order to give the horses a moist feed with the consistency of a mash. Her horses also have free choice access to a salt block. Elisa has never had a horse experience thumps or other electrolyte problems. The only supplements she has used that could possibly be considered ergogenic are the minerals magnesium and calcium.

Elisa notes that these athletes need "the right type of gasoline," and recognizes that there cannot be a universal feeding program for any class of horse.

Her accomplishments as a horse trainer include winning the Extreme Mustang Makeover in which she gentled a wild Mustang in 100 days. These Mustangs make excellent athletes, too. For her exhibition ride in the final competition, Elisa rode bareback and bridleless. For the Mustangs she has trained, she offers orchardgrass instead of alfalfa hay, still offering free choice access in slow feeders, saying, "It makes a lot of sense."

Special Diets: Broodmares

Pregnant and lactating mares have important nutritional differences compared to other horses. Even at the pre-conception stage, a mare's nutritional condition may affect her future foal and certainly affects her ability to conceive and then retain the pregnancy. Beyond affecting the mare, her condition during pregnancy and lactation significantly affects the foal she carries and then nourishes with her milk.

Broodmare Condition

By the time of delivery, a healthy pregnant mare will have increased her body weight 12 to 16 percent, adding placental tissues and fluids plus the fetus. Although pregnant mares in the wild receive no special nutritional attention, they can lose weight to a dangerous extent, using all of their fat stores to support their fetuses. If the mares lack stored fat, they must either use their bodies' protein from their own tissues and bones or have a spontaneous abortion. Never underfeed a pregnant mare.

A negative energy balance can cause an overweight pregnant mare to develop hyperlipemia, a condition in which the body overmobilizes stored fat (discussed under Special Diets for Hepatic

Problems). The greatest risk for this is immediately before and after delivery. Obese mares have a greater risk for this complication.

While a broodmare should not be too thin, she should also not be too heavy. Overweight mares experience insulin levels during pregnancy that can alter their natural biochemistry. Beyond affecting her fertility, obesity in broodmares pre-disposes their young to Developmental Orthopedic Disease (DOD) (discussed under "Growing Youngsters"). In addition to considering the mare's genetic potential and her match with the sire, carefully consider her health prior to breeding. Mares with pars pituitary intermedia dysfunction (PPID, discussed separately), for instance, have a high rate of spontaneous abortion. Choose healthy mares for breeding, and do not rebreed mares that have previously produced unhealthy foals. For example, compared to a mare that has delivered normal foals, mares that have had foals with neuroaxonal dystrophy (NAD), or its more severe variant, equine degenerative myeloencephalopathy (EDM), are twenty-five times more likely to have another NAD/EDM foal.

There are four distinct periods when the broodmare's nutritional needs change. These periods are early gestation, late gestation, early lactation, and late lactation.

Early Gestation

A horse's pregnancy normally lasts eleven months. The first six months of pregnancy are physiologically the least demanding stage. However, it is good to *confirm the pregnancy* and know when the mare conceived because of the coming precipitous rise in feed, seven months into the pregnancy.

During the first months of gestation, the mare's caloric demand is only about 1.03 times that of maintenance. This 3 percent increase is easily met with additional hay but balanced and complete

Table 9-2

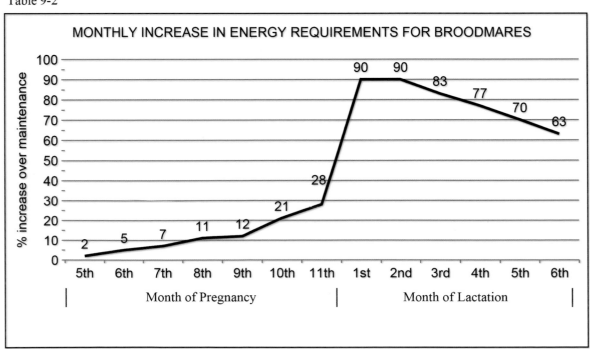

minerals are critical. In horses, fetal growth is not steady. Fetuses average less than 40 percent of their eventual birth weight prior to the ninth month of pregnancy.

Late Gestation

Note in Table 9–2 that at full-term pregnancy, the mare's energy requirements are almost *30 percent above maintenance*. During late gestation, mares can have difficulty consuming sufficient calories through forage alone, because the size of the fetus competes with the mare's gastrointestinal tract for intra-abdominal space. A mare's ability to intake forage typically drops to 1.75 percent of her body weight or less, rather than the usual 2 percent of a horse at maintenance. The energy deficit for this heavily pregnant mare must be made up with high energy supplements, or the mare will lose her own body weight.

In the event of energy deficit in a mare, turn first to fats rather than the traditional grains. Studies have shown that it does not affect the foal or the mare's milk when healthy oils like linseed, soybean, or canola are added to the mare's diet. Also, ensure not just adequate protein but *high quality protein* through sources such as alfalfa and soybean meal. These energy-dense feeds will provide her needed calories and macronutrients without demanding that she intake more bulk than she is able to consume.

Researchers have manipulated broodmares' diets to ascertain the effects on the fetus with dietary imbalances. It is well established that a mare in a dietary deficit supplies the fetus at her own expense, although there is a limit to the losses a mare may endure.

If the mare is receiving a fortified commercial concentrate with a broad spectrum of vitamins and minerals, she should not also need an additional vitamin and mineral supplements or ration balancers.

Late gestation in the Northern hemisphere coincides with the worst winter weather. Ensure that your mare has protection from the elements and is not wasting too much of her energy staying warm.

Monitor the broodmare's condition carefully and aim for keeping her at a body condition score of 6 (Chapter 10 shows the various parameters that equate to this high-normal body score). A lower score will leave the mare less able to withstand the rigors of early lactation. This good body score is especially important if the mare will be immediately rebred.

Rye grass is linked to spontaneous abortion due to endophyte and ergot infection. Pregnant mares should be removed from questionable rye or fescue pastures. Rye straw could similarly pose an infection risk, so choose stall bedding accordingly.

If the mare has not previously delivered a foal by the sire of the current pregnancy, test both the sire and the mare to see whether neonatal isoerythrolysis (NI) should be anticipated. A positive test result will require alternative arrangements for giving the baby milk in its first days. There is more information about NI in the section on feeding growing youngsters.

Parasite Control

Give an anthelmintic to kill threadworms (strongyloides westeri) a few weeks prior to delivery. This will protect the foal from acquiring the parasite in his mother's milk.

ABOVE: **Colostrum, the first milk a mare produces, is vital to the newborn foal's health. Photo Credit: Randy Eiland.**

Contingency Planning

Locate a spare colostrum source for the foal in case the mare is agalactic (producing little or no milk). Colostrum, the first milk a healthy mare produces, is vitally important to ensure a healthy foal.

Early Lactation

The first twelve weeks of the baby's life represent the early lactation phase for the mare, with that first month being the most demanding and the first week of that first month extremely critical. Early lactation is one of the most nutritionally demanding statuses for both the nursing mare and the newborn. The mare's feed intake in the first twelve weeks of lactation will be about *double* that of a horse at maintenance. Light breed mares produce about 3 percent of their body weight in milk per day, which equates to about 4 gallons in an 1,100 pound (or 15 liters in a 500 kilogram) mare.

Mares fed poorer quality protein produce less milk than better-fed mares. The crude protein the mare consumes should be at least 5 percent lysine to be of sufficient quality. Alfalfa approaches this figure. Soybean meal and canola meal surpass it. Of the grains, oats gets the closest, at slightly more than 4 percent.

Water must be readily available to lactating mares, because their intake can more than double. They need about two gallons for every 100 pounds of body weight (12 to 14 liters per 100 kilograms of body weight) in order to produce enough milk.

Manipulations to the dietary intake of lactating mares have shown interesting results. The usual recommended dose of vitamin E is 500–600 milligrams or 1,000 international units for a 1,100 pound (500 kilogram) horse. Mares supplemented with double the recommended doses of vitamins A and E had a higher immunoglobin G (IgG), a factor related to the immunity the foal receives through its mother's milk, in both the colostrum and in the foals. Colostral IgG levels were also increased by supplementing the mare with marine-sourced oils, as opposed to corn oil, but in this study, the foals' IgG levels were unchanged even with the change in colostrum levels.

Broodmares are routinely rebred during this phase. Again, being underweight and being obese have a negative effect on reproductive performance. However, studies have shown that increasing vitamin and mineral supplementation above recommended levels does not equate to higher conception rates.

Late Lactation

In late lactation, the mare's intake will taper down to about 1.75 times her maintenance ration. However, late lactation in the Northern hemisphere tends to coincide with a drop in the quality and productivity of pastures. If the baby is beginning to steal its mother's concentrate ration, the mare may be acquiring less energy from both her pasture and her concentrate than the owner expects.

Zikoma Is Coming

When a beautiful Arabian meets a marvelous American Quarter Horse, an athlete with attitude will be born. And so it was when Zikoma hit the sandy New Mexico soil.

Randy Eiland is known for caring about horses and having long term riding companions. He has some outstanding mares and has produced some excellent horses that can carry a rider all day.

This is a region where excellent alfalfa is readily available. Randy provides his horses with free choice access to the forage, as well as plenty of water, a salt block, and shade. He's straight-

RIGHT: **Late gestation is demanding on the broodmare, and early lactation requires almost double the energy she would need at maintenance. Photo Credit: Randy Eiland.**

ABOVE: **Good nutrition produces good horses. Photo Credit: Fred Eiland.**

forward and does not use an elaborate feeding plan for his broodmares. His mantra is "simple is better than complex."

By a mare's eighth month of pregnancy, he meets the additional energy and nutrient demands of late gestation by supplementing with rolled oats and a mixed commercial grain with a high fat content. To meet the extraordinary nutritional demands of early lactation, Randy increases the amount of this supplemented concentrate again after the baby is born. As the baby increases the amount of forage it consumes, Randy can reduce the supplemented non-forage feed and watch the baby continue to grow at the mare's side.

Special Diets: Growing Youngsters

A horse's first year presents the most marked physiological and nutritional changes it should ever endure. The general key to nutrition in a growing youngster is providing a quality, forage-based diet that promotes slow, steady growth and avoids spurts or lags in development. Specific nutritional guidelines for horses in their first two years of life have been revised by the National Research Council in recent years and thus deserve a new look.

The nutritional stages of a growing horse can be divided into the neonatal phase, the remainder of the suckling phase, and then the weanling and long weanling stage. In most cases, changing from a suckling to a forager is called the weanling phase; this morphs with time into the yearling and then the long yearling phase. The process of weaning is discussed as a separate issue.

Neonatal Nutrition

Certain neonatal nutrition concerns should be addressed weeks prior to birth. Colostrum, the first milk the mare provides, differs from later milk in the key nutritional factors and antibodies it contains. It is vital to the neonatal foal's health. An extra source of colostrum should be located prior to birth in case it is needed.

Two to three weeks before delivery, the mare should receive an anthelmintic as discussed in Chapter 7, so that she cannot pass *S. westeri* to her baby via her milk.

Antibody screening can be done on the sire at any point but should be done on the mare in the last few weeks of gestation to identify neonatal isoerythrolysis (NI), a condition in which the mare has antibodies against the foal's red blood cells. If NI is present, the baby cannot safely ingest its mother's colostrum. Mules and donkeys are at higher risk for NI, with about a 10 percent incidence among neonatal mules. Blood screening must be repeated for each pregnancy if it is by a different sire.

NI is usually lethal if untreated, but if identified and treated promptly, it has a good prognosis. In a scenario where advance screening was not done and NI occurs, the foal will become ill in the first hours or days of life, showing lethargy, tachycardia (high heart rate), tachypnea (high respiratory rate), and icterus (jaundice or yellowing of white membranes, such as the sclera or white of the eye, generally a sign of liver compromise). Veterinary care is urgent for a foal showing post-colostrum-ingestion signs of NI. The foal may recover on its own in mild cases, but the situation can quickly progress to multi-system organ failure and death. Intravenous fluids and perhaps a transfusion are the best chance to save the baby.

The key is advance identification. An NI baby must not nurse from its mother for the first seventy-two hours so that it does not receive her colostrum, because it will destroy the baby's red blood cells. The mare and foal will have to either be physically separated or preferably, the baby must be muzzled and allowed to be with its mother. In either case, the mare should be milked and her colostrum saved and carefully labeled for possible future donation. The baby must be given another source of colostrum by bottle nursing or with access to a surrogate mare for several days. The neonatal foal must be given this different colostrum source as soon as possible after it's born. After the birth mare's colostrum is passed (about seventy-two hours postpartum), the baby should be able to suckle its own mother safely. The NI baby should not be treated as an orphan or rejected foal.

Colostrum

Colostrum is the most important nutrition for a new foal not just because it provides a necessary immune and energy boost. It also contains hormones, helps establish a healthy gastrointestinal tract, and is higher in protein and vitamins A and E than later milk. In cases where the mother's colostrum is not available, donated colostrum or veterinary administration of plasma is necessary.

A foal needs one to three liters of colostrum, most of which should be consumed in its first twenty-four hours, chiefly in the first four hours of life. The foal's immunoglobin G (IgG) level can be checked by a veterinarian to confirm good transfer of immunity from colostrum.

About 200 ml of colostrum is often collected from high-producing mares with good quality colostrum (which is indicated by it having a specific gravity of at least 1.06). Spare colostrum should be saved for donation to another foal. Numerous donations are required to provide initial nutrition for a foal whose mother is not providing colostrum due to the mare being agalactic or ill, rejecting the foal, or bearing antibodies that will attack the foal's red blood cells (NI).

If you are using donated, frozen colostrum, defrost it in warm water. Do not cook it on a stove or microwave. Frozen colostrum can be saved for two years.

Normal Nursing

Foals have an extremely high metabolic rate. They also have very low reserves of energy and nutrients. Their livers and muscles have not yet stored glycogen to any significant degree. Because the neonatal foal's metabolism demands sustenance, and the baby lacks reserves, only a few hours of fasting can cause the foal's body to break down its own tissue for fuel. A newborn with a healthy appetite will in-take about 15 percent of its weight on its first day and about 22 percent on its second, increasing to 25 percent or more by day seven. In these first days of life, the baby should nurse six to eight times per hour.

Later in the first week, the baby should still nurse around five to eight times per hour, consuming about 2.75 ounces (80 ml) at each feeding. Frequent feeding may help to prevent ulcers by keeping the stomach pH from being too acidic.

If the mare's udder appears flat and the foal is constantly trying to nurse, the mare may not be producing enough milk. If the udder is distended or streaming milk, the foal may not be nursing sufficiently. Either case means the foal is undernourished and needs veterinary attention. Another milk source must be located if the dam is incapacitated, not providing sufficient milk, or rejects the foal.

Orphan and Rejected Foals

Being orphaned or rejected is very stressful, and the foal will need exceptional care. Some veterinarians prophylactically medicate orphans with ulcer medication. However, many owners with an orphaned or rejected foal, especially owners who choose bottle feeding, make the critical mistake of failing to provide the foal with equine companionship. These owners may also allow the foal to engage in poor behavior, such as not respecting safe boundaries or engaging in excessive oral behavior, such as nibbling on people. Pasturing the foal with its own kind is socially healthier than raising it wholly in human company. Even if no other youngsters are available, other adult horses make good companions and chaperones from whom the foal can learn both how to forage and how to obey appropriate boundaries. It is possible to milk a mare that rejects her foal and provide the milk to the foal by bottle or bucket.

Bottle and Bucket Feeding

If the mare is incapacitated or agalactic (not producing milk), milk must be provided either by a foster mother, or by milk or a milk replacer product in a bottle or bucket.

When feeding milk or a milk replacement product by bottle or bucket, be sure to thoroughly clean all apparatus between *every* feeding. Bucket feeding is less labor intensive care than bottle-feeding and has the advantage of not flooding the foal with excessive amounts of human companionship. The baby may be shy about the confinement of its muzzle in a deep bucket, so a shallow bucket or wide pan may be needed. Babies really can drink instead of suckle, but do not place the pan on the ground. Make sure to place the pan at an accessible height: chest-high to the baby. The foal's short neck and long legs do not allow prolonged feeding at ground level.

Foals that initially nursed successfully have a harder time drinking from a bucket than those who never nursed. Some foals in the former situation may need a bottle. Keeping a chaperone horse within reach at every feeding will help with the bottle-fed foal's social development. It is essential that orphan foals learn equine behavior from horse role models.

If mare's milk is not available, milk replacements include modified cow milk, goat milk, or a commercial milk replacement product. Mare's milk is about 22 percent crude protein and nearly 15 percent fat. By comparison, cow milk is lower in sugar and higher in fat. When using a cow milk, add 0.75 ounces (twenty grams) of pectin or glucose (not sucrose) to each quart (or liter) of cow's milk. Goat's milk is higher in fat, solids, and calories than mare's milk. Foals digest the fats in goat milk better than they do those in cow milk, but goat milk sometimes causes them constipation or acidosis.

Read commercial milk replacer product labels carefully. Foals do not have high levels of maltase, the enzyme needed to break down maltose, a type of sugar. Because they lack this enzyme, products with maltodextrin are not the best choices. Corn syrup, glucose, and oligosaccharides are undesirable sugars. One study of commercial milk replacers revealed that all products exceeded the mineral content of mare's milk. The excess potassium in these products would be problematic for foals with kidney problems.

Most milk replacement products come in a powder that must be reconstituted with water. A good mixture ratio will be about 1:10 of powder to water, to mimic the solids in mare's milk. Do not make the mix stronger than indicated on the directions in an attempt to boost the foal's nutrition.

When putting an orphan or rejected foal on a milk replacer product after initial feeding of donated colostrum, make the change over the course of several days, mixing the donated colostrum with the replacement. Milk replacer pellets can be a good addition to the diet of orphan foals too, but be sure not to overfeed.

Surrogates

Healthy mares with calm dispositions that have successfully raised foals are the best choices for nursing an orphan foal. There are farms that have nurse mares available to lease. Barren mares can be stimulated to lactate through drug therapy administered by a veterinarian.

When asking a mare that has lost her foal to accept another mare's orphaned or rejected baby, it can be helpful to place the prospective foster mother's scent on the baby by wiping it with her sweat, milk, or manure. Because horses use scent at close range but sight at distance to recognize one another, another technique that has been used to make a mare adopt is to blanket the original foal and then place that blanket on the adoptee.

A foster mare may need to be hobbled, put in stocks, tranquilized, twitched, or corrected for aggression to encourage her to accept another mare's baby. One study showed the technique of cervical palpation on the surrogate mare significantly improved the adoption; fourteen of sixteen mares adopted the presented foal when the presentation occurred with cervical palpation, but only two of sixteen mares that did not receive the technique adopted immediately and the other fourteen were aggressive toward the baby for up to twenty-four hours.

Be cautious of using a much larger foster mother that would have a much higher milk production than the baby would have received from its birth mother. Excess milk is over-nourishing and will make the baby grow too fast, which will make it prone to health problems.

The foster nursing mother can be another species, usually a goat. Be aware, however, that a foal fostered by a goat may learn from the doe to butt its head into others. People must immediately correct a foal that head-butts a person.

Let the orphan foal develop into as normal a suckling as possible for its best chance of becoming a good horse.

Weight Assessment in Foals

A healthy foal's birth weight equals about 10 percent of its future adult weight. A foal's intake should be 25–35 percent of its weight *every day*, and its weight should increase every single day, thus its nutrient needs are higher each day. The nutrition goal is to strive for a lean build, not a fat baby.

A foal that had been steadily growing then suddenly does not gain weight could be exhibiting illness. The more closely the owner monitors the foal's weight, the sooner changes in growth rate can be detected. The following formula uses the heart girth circumference on average or light riding breed youngsters.

Imperial Measurement:

$$\frac{\text{Heart girth in inches} - 25.1}{0.07} = \text{Weight in pounds}$$

Metric Measurement:

$$\frac{\text{Heart girth in centimeters} - 63.7}{0.38} = \text{Weight in kilograms}$$

Suckling or Pre-Weanling

While in the first week, the baby should nurse about seven times per hour, this will decrease over the next month to a rate of about four times per hour by the end of week four.

Some foals begin to consume small amounts of forage or sample their mothers' supplemented feed as early as three days of age but not until three or four months of age will the foal's hindgut have established the necessary microbial population for good fermentation of forage.

Coprophagia, the eating of feces—usually their mothers' feces—is fairly common in foals. Some researchers have suggested that this may be how foals acquire beneficial microbes in their gastro-intestinal tracts. However, foals with access to adequate nutrition should not engage in sustained coprophagia.

For about twelve weeks, a foal can get all of its nutrition through nursing, provided its mother is lactating well. By this stage, the average foal will nurse once or twice an hour and gain about two pounds per day. However, the nutritional content of mare's milk drops at the same time the baby needs more nutrition for optimal growth. High quality, palatable forage—preferably grass—should be available even if the baby does not yet show much interest in consuming forage.

Optimal growth should not be confused with maximum growth. A lean foal is a healthy, normal baby. Also, a lack of exercise has a negative effect on the baby's development. The foal should have ample room to run and play, but forced over-exercising is detrimental to its development.

A youngster may briefly go off its feed after routine vaccinations. Try to entice it to keep eating with small, frequent presentations of palatable forage.

Nutrition may sometimes be attributed a greater role than it deserves in certain problems of growing youngsters, specifically Developmental Orthopedic Disease (DOD) and hoof problems. The latter will be dealt with here and the former is discussed under weanlings. It is important to recognize that horse-care practices such as deworming and hoof trimming depend on a manageable foal that has been trained to accept human control. These care measures are unfortunately often not done when the foal is unmanageable, and the delay can negatively impact the baby's future.

Hoof problems in foals are best attended by a qualified farrier with specific expertise in the area of correcting foals' hooves. These problems are ripe for early correction but can be persistent if not remediated early. They may be later blamed on poor nutrition when really the baby just did not receive adequate farrier service.

Creep Feeding

Creep feeds are pre-mixed commercial feeds formulated for growing youngsters. By two months of age, many breeders offer creep feed to move the suckling to solid food, and keep it on a steady diet through weaning, but creep feed is often unnecessary.

METHOD

Creep feeders are containers that permit a foal's slender muzzle to access the special foal ration while not allowing access by the mother or other adult horses. A barred bucket is a common creep feeder.

A creep feed *enclosure* is a small feeding area created with the erection of a single pole barrier a few feet high. This allows a foal to go under and eat while barring adult horses.

CONTENTS

The creep feed formula differs from commercial feed the broodmare may receive while pregnant or lactating, because it is lower in overall energy but higher in the quality of the protein and the mineral content. Creep feed should not contain much, if any, grain. Excess starch intake promotes rapid growth in youngsters, which is has been linked to Developmental Orthopedic Disease (DOD).

Pelleted creep feed has the advantage of not allowing the foal to selectively take only the parts of the creep feed it most wants.

Lysine is the only amino acid with a well-defined requirement in growing horses. This is not to imply that other amino acids do not have baseline requirements, only to recognize that the numbers have not been established through scientific research. Extra lysine is well supplied in soybean meal, alfalfa meal, and even synthesized lysine has been added to commercial creep feeds.

In 2007, the NRC increased the recommended levels of calcium and phosphorus for growing horses: 35 percent and 25 percent, respectively, over the prior recommendations. The micronutrients of copper and zinc are also extremely important in a young horse. A desire to ensure the healthy, balanced profile of macronutrients and all minerals is part of the reason so many breeders elect to provide creep feed, although there are still breeders who maintain their herds well on pasture or hay.

In *Equine Applied and Clinical Nutrition* (Elsevier, 2013), Feeding the Growing Horse, Staniar offers a homemade creep feed recipe of 35 percent mid-maturity grass hay, 20 percent alfalfa hay, 10 percent beet pulp, 5 percent soybean hulls, 10 percent crimped oats, and 5 percent vitamin and mineral mix.

Deworming

Ascarids in the gastrointestinal tract lining are of primary concern in foals, manifesting with the classic pot-bellied, shaggy, lackluster appearance. While foals are predisposed to ascarid (roundworm) infestation, they should also be protected against threadworms, strongyles, and bots. The first deworming is usually at six to eight weeks.

Work with your local veterinarian and do fecal egg counts on the other horses in the property to be aware of the site's parasite burden. Deworming is discussed thoroughly in Chapter 7.

Equine Gastric Ulcer Syndrome (EGUS) in Foals

A worm-ridden foal is at risk for Equine Gastric Ulcer Syndrome (EGUS). The classic sign of ulcers in foals is dorsal recumbancy, in which the baby lies on its back with its legs in the air. EGUS is discussed separately under Special Diets for Medical Conditions, but good turnout and good forage is the best safeguard against ulcers. Although EGUS is markedly prevalent in foals, there is a strong, avoidable correlation between EGUS and stress. The greatest stress in a foal's life generally comes from weaning.

Weaning

Feral mares often let a baby suckle until the next foal is born. Some breeders no longer wean at all, but leave the babies with their mothers in herd situations. Whether or not a farm weans will depend on its business schedule, wants, and tradition. On farms that do wean, the use of low stress weaning measures rather than the old forced-weaning practices have produced better results in nutrition and sociability.

Low stress weaning occurs best between six and twelve months of age. The foal will already be eating forage and drinking water, may be creep feeding, will have the companionship of other foals and horses, and be accustomed to its pastures. The mares and foals will briefly be separated only by a fence that does not allow the foals to suckle but allows mothers and babies to touch muzzles and nuzzle each other's top lines. Time in those adjacent pastures will gradually be increased.

Weaning should not be added to other stressors, for example, deworming, vaccination, transportation, or new companions.

By contrast, the old forced style of weaning is often done earlier, perhaps at four months, and involves complete physical separation of mother and baby, whether or not they are still in sight of each other. Foals experiencing high stress weaning may react by either gorging or refusing feed, neither of which contributes to the desired steady plane of growth.

Recall the discussion of stereotypic behavior in Chapter 2. Pasture-weaned horses display far less stereotypic behavior than stalled weanlings. Although some research has indicated that stereotypic behavior may have roots in changes in the central nervous system, it is not clear whether or not the stress causes the changes.

Weanlings

Free choice access to good quality forage—possibly with a vitamin and mineral supplement designed to meet the more recently established baseline needs for early growth—can supply all of the weanling's nutritional needs. The youngster does need quality protein, so additional protein can be sourced from alfalfa or soybean meal if the grass pasture or hay is low in protein.

If you are a new owner acquiring a weanling that has been poorly fed, be cautious while increasing its feed. Changes must be made slowly.

DEVELOPMENTAL ORTHOPEDIC DISEASE (DOD)

Weanlings are at a crucial growth stage, and feeding errors in this phase have been implicated in Developmental Orthopedic Disease (DOD), a term for a number of growth-related conditions affecting young horses. This cluster of medical conditions includes physitis (inflammation of the growth plates in long bones, also called epiphysitis or physiolysis), osteochondrosis (a disorder of the growth cartilage, also called dyschondroplasia or (if bone or cartilage detaches) osteochondritis dissecans (OCD), acquired angular limb deformities and flexural deformities, collapse of the tarsal bone (also called cuboidal bone malformation), cervical vertebral malformation (also called wobbler syndrome), and acquired vertebral deformities.

Of these conditions, interesting science has been conducted in the area of silicon supplementation to prevent osteochondrosis. Because silicon deficiency can depress the glycosaminoglycan concentration and cartilage in joints, some breeders supplement their young stock with silicon, usually in the form of sodium zeolite, in the hope of reducing the size or severity of lesions. However, another study found no change in the lesions of horses with osteochondrosis compared to horses fed a placebo.

While genetics, environment, exercise and nutrition have been implicated in DOD, it has a higher occurrence in foals that undergo poor mineral nutrition, excess energy intake, and high exercise stress. There is much more DOD amongst overfed and stalled foals. Compensatory growth, resulting from improved nutrition after a period of reduced intake, has also been implicated in DOD. Excessive starch in the diet is strongly correlated to DOD.

Foals become overfed from creep feed and by eating from their mother's rations. Ensure the lactating mare, not her foal, consumes her feed. When the baby is young, simply use a high bucket placement. As the baby grows, they may need to be briefly separated to ensure the mother eats her supplemented feed. This caution goes for other adults pastured with the foal. Make sure the growing youngster is not cleaning out their buckets and receiving excess calories, especially starch.

To avoid DOD, provide turnout and constant access to quality forage with a balanced vitamin and mineral intake. DOD may be caused by genetics or nutrition, but the pregnant mare must have adequate copper and not be obese; then keep your youngster lean yet eating well for steady growth for its first year.

Yearlings

At one year of age, a healthy, young horse has acquired about 60 to 70 percent of its future adult weight, and its growth begins to slow. Do not expect any measuring tapes or formulas intended for adult horses to apply to growing youngsters. Their developing bodies are not yet carrying sufficient structure to use the Henneke body condition scoring system or commercial weight tapes. A section in Chapter 10 on determining body weight includes a different denominator for calculating the weight of a growing youngster.

Although it is not an adult, the yearling is fully able to eat an adult diet.

Long Yearlings

Youngsters beyond a year but still shy of their second birthday are often called long yearlings. Much is made of some breeds of horse being late maturing, while other breeds are commonly ridden at age two. The truth is that the equine skeleton grows at a predictable rate across the breeds, with no horse fully maturing before six to eight years.

Although it is not generally recommended to place younger horses in hard training, some horses—notably, racehorses—are in that situation. If a youngster is put under saddle, its energy needs will be higher, and these needs are best met through forage rather than grain. Supplemental energy can be given in the form of fat, such as oil, or hydrated beet pulp or alfalfa pellets, served in small, frequent meals as needed. In any case, the growth that slowed at one year of age will further slow by the end of the horse's second year.

ONE QUARTER HORSE'S FIRST TWO YEARS

River has the advantages that come with being wanted before he was born. Katy, the young woman who owns him, hopes to make a cow horse out of this Quarter Horse that she obtained by breeding her mom's mare to a good stallion of the same breed.

River lives on a coastal Bermuda pasture, with free choice access to coastal hay when the pasture is poor in the winter. When he showed interest in the mare's supplemental commercial feed, Katy began giving River a commercial feed with 16 percent protein, 0.9 percent lysine, and 6 percent fat.

River's mother is an easy keeper whose condition was never pulled down or weakened by the growing youngster at her side. She was still producing milk when he was ten months old, and Katy weaned him to prevent a chance in-breeding of him and his dam.

After weaning, Katy kept River at pasture and modified his supplemental feed to a product with 14 percent protein, 0.7 percent lysine, and 6 percent fat. He is still on this feed today and gets one pound daily. He's growing up in a ten-acre pasture in the company of other horses and even shares a fence line with his sire.

"He's a sweet boy with a huge personality," Katy reports.

She's done a lot of ground work with him, plenty of leading, and has saddled him but not been on him at this age.

River was gelded when he reached age two. Katy won't rush his training, but she looks forward to enjoying him all of his days. Look for them in Working Cow Horse classes.

ABOVE: **River at two weeks of age. Photo Credit: Katy Preston.**

ABOVE: **River at four months of age. Photo Credit: Katy Preston.**

ABOVE: **River at two years of age. Photo Credit: Katy Preston.**

COMPLICATIONS IN DRAFT BREEDS

Drafts are prone to obesity and have a higher incidence of neuromuscular disorders and polysaccharide storage myopathy (PSSM) than other horses. Each of these medical conditions with dietary implications discussed here are reviewed in more detail in Part 2 of this chapter.

Allowing a draft horse to be overweight sets it on a path for insulin resistance, metabolic syndrome, and laminitis. If the horse is starting to become overweight, immediately reduce superfluous calories found in supplementary feeds and treats. If the horse is not receiving any supplementary feed and is on forage only, but still gaining weight, select a lower quality forage.

Scientists do not know why draft horses have an increased incidence of neuromuscular disorders (covered later in this chapter), but they recommend providing vitamin E and selenium supplementation if the horse is not receiving good grazing opportunities that would normally fulfill that vitamin requirement.

The muscle disorder of polysaccharide storage myopathy (PSSM) is also over-represented in draft breeds. Use a higher fat diet that excludes high starch and high non-structural carbohydrate supplements, and be aware of the risk of rhabdomyolysis associated with PSSM. Rhabdomyolysis and PSSM are discussed separately under Special Diets for Medical Problems.

PULLING ON THE ISLAND

Sonny and Toots are a father-daughter team working on San Juan Island in Washington State. Sonny is an old-school American Belgian who was bred to a Clydesdale mare to produce Toots, after which he was gelded. Their owner, Greg Lange, is pleased with the working ability, controlled speed, and lack of wasted action this magnificent team possesses. The horses aren't prancers; they are steady and deliberate on their feet.

"They can pull for hours and hours before they start to tire."

Sonny weighs about a ton, and Toots is about one hundred pounds less. They both stand over eighteen hands high and eat prodigious amounts of free choice grass hay.

Greg notes that there are a lot of fads in the world of nutrition, including with horses. With a strong background in physiology, he's not given to following fads. He listened to old-time teamsters

LEFT: **The draft team offers pulling power in areas that machinery cannot access. Photo Credit: Eva Cooley.**

to learn how people cared for their draft teams when their livelihoods depended on the animals' working ability. He found that there's nothing remarkable about a working horse doing a day's work. This is what they are born and bred to accomplish.

When Greg presents a workload that demands a boost in the team's energy and protein intake, he adds alfalfa hay to their diets. If they are working long days for more than two consecutive days, he also supplements them with grain.

The logging on timbered acreage Greg does with this draft team isn't the only pulling they do. He's hauled pickups out of the mud when tractors only spun their tires trying to free the stuck trucks. The team also harrows fields where cattle are grazed, spreading cow manure as a means of improved pasture management. It's good work with a great team.

Special Diets: Ponies and Miniature Horses

Ponies and miniature horses have certain nutritional needs that deserve special consideration. Ponies are defined as horses measuring less than 14.2 hands high. Minis are generally about 8.2 to 9.2 hands high (34 to 38 inches or 86 to 97 centimeters). The Ultimate Chart includes a conversion table comparing hands, inches, and centimeters.

Overfeeding is the single biggest nutritional mistake owners make with regard to ponies and minis. This can set the animal up for laminitis and metabolic problems (insulin resistance is a top concern), in addition to the added burden on the joints from excess weight.

Pony breeds developed in harsher conditions, which contributed to their genetic predisposition to a hardy constitution. Just as with full-sized horses, forage should comprise the bulk of a pony's diet, but because ponies tend to be good doers, they need comparatively less than the 2 percent of body weight per day guideline that maintains horses. A pony, especially a miniature horse, might do well on as little as 1 percent of its weight in forage or forage-based products per day. Use caution if feeding grain to ponies, and keep the quantity of supplemented feeds low while choosing forms that are as low as possible in non-structural carbohydrates so as not to provoke colic with an overload.

Grazing can be risky for ponies, because they are susceptible to carbohydrate overload from grass. While strategies like limiting grazing and using muzzles may help, be aware that ponies have been observed to engage in extraordinary compensatory grazing, consuming a day's ration in just a few hours when they are given access to grazing.

Never try to make a pony lose weight by fasting it (withholding feed entirely). Fasting places him at risk for a serious metabolic condition called hyperlipemia in which fat stores are over-mobilized, because the pony or mini is in a *negative balance* of energy relative to its energy expenditure. This condition, discussed under Special Diets for Hepatic Problems, is more common in females. Hyperlipemia may present with symptoms ranging from inappetance to tremors to colic; it is dangerous and must be treated by a veterinarian.

If a pony or mini is overweight, a severe diet is risky. Instead, reduce the animals weight by offering a lesser quality hay, increase exercise, and limit treats, concentrates, and rich grazing.

When providing pellets or concentrates in a pan, avoid feeding circumstances that encourage the pony, and especially the mini, to ingest dirt or sand. A pony's smaller body is more susceptible to sand colic than a larger horse's body. If your pony tends to drop food as it eats and then pick it up again from the ground, use a larger pan or place the pan on a tarp or stall mat, so dirt is not ingested with every mouthful.

There are vitamin and mineral supplements made specifically for ponies, which enable the owner to offer a more precise allocation than merely scaling back a supplement formulated for a full-sized horse.

Dental care is markedly important for miniature horses, as their teeth are quite large compared to their jaw size. Also, ponies and minis tend to be long lived, making a commitment to their life-long care not uncommonly a promise of thirty-five years or more.

Weight Assessment

The standard formulas for estimating a horse's weight do not apply to ponies and minis. Veterinary scales that accommodate large dogs work well for accurate weight assessment of miniature horses. A pony's weight is often estimated from the formula of assuming seventy pounds for a thirty inch

Table 9–4 Weight Estimation for Ponies and Miniature Horses			
*heart girth in inches ≈ weight in pounds		heart girth in inches ≈ weight in pounds	
30	70	46	278
31	83	47	291
32	96	48	304
33	109	49	317
34	122	50	330
35	135	51	343
36	148	52	356
37	161	53	369
38	174	54	382
39	187	55	395
40	200	56	408
41	213	57	421
42	226	58	434
43	239	59	447
44	252	60	460
45	265	61	471

*Chapter 10 discusses how to measure the heart girth

heart girth and adding thirteen pounds for each additional inch of the heart girth. The table in this section offers those calculations, but as is evident, the formula becomes less reliable as the size approximates small horses. For example, a slim, young Arabian pony could have a heart girth in the low 60s, but will likely weigh closer to 700 pounds or more. The weight of larger ponies may be found on the Ultimate Chart.

The Guide Horse and the Riding Pony that Believes He's a Horse

Panda, a fourteen-year-old miniature horse at a good weight of about 125 pounds, is a guide animal for Ann Edie. Panda regularly guides Ann through foot and vehicle traffic and also travels well inside a car. In addition to the usual commands that the visually impaired use with guide dogs—forward, left, right, find the curb, or find the stairs—Panda retrieves anything Ann drops. This mini has already worked about twice as long as an average guide dog, and she has a long working life ahead of her.

Ann is mindful of not letting her miniature horse become overweight. She provides Panda with a forage-based commercial complete feed that is composed of chopped timothy and oat hays that are low sugar and low starch, wheat middlings, soy hulls, alfalfa pellets, stabilized rice bran, ground flax seed, soybean oil, yeast culture, and vitamin and mineral pellets. Panda also gets timothy hay in a slow feeder and earns treats of light commercial-brand pellets that are based on wheat middling, soybean hulls, and alfalfa. Ann also hand grazes Panda.

Ann also enjoys riding Fengur, her thirteen-hand Icelandic gelding, and she says he would not care to be referred to as a pony. Icelandics have a thrifty constitution, and Fengur does well with 14 percent protein complete feed along with a hay-stretcher pellet made from oat hulls, soy hulls, alfalfa meal, and wheat middlings. The complete feed's primary ingredients are alfalfa meal, soybean hulls, and wheat middlings.

Fengur weighs 650–700 pounds and at age twenty-one, still has a lot of riding life left. He loves to be groomed, and Ann likes to groom. When they ride, usually in an arena, he takes good care of Ann, and she repays him in kind.

LEFT: **Caution must be exercised to not overfeed miniature horses. Panda is at a good weight. Photo Credit: Alexandra Kurland.**

Special Diets: Donkeys And Mules

"Long ears," the equids separate from the familiar horse (*equus ferus caballus*), have some different nutritional and care requirements from horses. The common donkey (*equus africanus asinus*) is a separate species and even bears a different number of chromosomes—62 compared to the horse's 64. The mule, a hybrid between the two species, falls between the horse and donkey in nutritional needs and behavioral manner. Worldwide, there are about as many long-ears as horses, around 55 million each, but the majority of mules and donkeys are working beasts of burden in the less developed parts of the world.

There has been little scientific study in the area of donkey nutrition and even less research specific to feeding mules. The most recent edition of the National Research Council's Nutritional Requirements of Horses was the first time the NRC addressed donkey and wild equid nutrition, and it still offers no guidelines for mules.

The Donkey

Donkeys are genetically adapted to a different environment than horses. The donkey (or burro) is descended from the Somali Wild Ass of Northeastern Africa. Originating in that arid climate and its poor grazing, donkeys browse (eat twigs and similar plant materials projecting from trees and shrubs) in addition to graze. A donkey normally spends fourteen to eighteen hours of every day foraging, selectively eating the more nutritious forages, and roam twelve to twenty miles per day. Thus, meal feeding, especially large meals, is unhealthy for donkeys. They do best with free choice access to lower quality forages.

A donkey's jaw is appreciably thicker and heavier, and thus much stronger, than that of a similarly sized horse or pony. This different bone structure and attendant muscling gives their jaw the necessary power to browse woody forage that a horse would not eat. Unlike the horse, the donkey has some ability to digest lignin. Although there is little research in this area, the donkey may have different gut flora from a horse.

Feed Quantity

A donkey's gastrointestinal tract passes food more slowly than a horse's does, thus extracts more nutrition from plant material. Because donkeys also possess the ability to digest feedstuffs that a horse simply cannot process, donkeys need less food than a horse or pony of the same size requires. People used to assert that a donkey could have three-quarters of what a similarly sized pony would intake, but even that figure has been found to be excessive. Overall dietary energy requirements have recently been found to be much lower in donkeys as compared to similarly sized ponies.

Table 9–5 Key Nutritional Differences Between Donkeys and Horses		
Factor	**Donkey**	**Horse**
browse	needs twiggy foods in diet	does not browse
food type	browse, straw, hay, grass	grass, hay
food quantity	1.5% of body weight/day	2% of body weight/day
pasture	tends to get obese	safe pasture is a good environment
grain	*inappropriate* food	small grain meals are acceptable
fat deposits	crest, rump, *pannier* region	overall
laminitic stance	*rarely* exhibits	exhibits
water	can abstain and guzzle	does not safely abstain or guzzle
dehydration	appetite usually present	appetite usually diminishes

Table 9–6 Intercontinental Study by the Donkey Sanctuary			
Factor	**Pony**	**75% of a Pony Diet**	**Donkey**
Appetite	2–2.5%	1.5–1.7%	1.3–1.8%
Dry Matter Intake	3.6–4.5 kg	2.7–3.5 kg	2.4–3.2 kg
Digestible Energy (summer)	157 kJ DE/kg	117 kJ DE/kg	88 kJ DE/kg
Digestible Energy (winter)	158 kJ DE/Kg	119 kJ DE/kg	117 kJ DE/kg

In the developed world, overfeeding is the greatest nutritional threat facing most donkeys. This mistake is usually made in large meals with overly rich forages and supplements. Meal feeding, instead of slow feeding that approximates a foraging lifestyle, also places donkeys at risk for ulcers.

Feed Quality

Donkeys easily overfeed when placed on pasture. They have relatively low protein needs, doing well on straw and even corn stover (the stalks left over after harvesting) to meet their forage-chewing needs while ingesting less carbohydrate and protein than would be provided by higher-quality forages. Horse people can be reluctant to use straw as feed, equating it to poor forage, but a donkey does not need higher quality grass and legume forages. Grain straws are widely available, and a healthy donkey diet can be composed largely of good, clean straw that does not have seed heads, supplemented with hay as needed to maintain body condition.

Remember that seed heads are grain, and grain contains varying amounts of starch. Grain diets place donkeys at risk for ulcers, and starch is particularly unsuited for these animals. Even an underweight donkey should not receive its extra needed energy via grain, but rather via fat, which is most easily provided with an oil.

Vitamin and mineral requirements for donkeys are extrapolated from what is known about horses because so little research exists on donkey nutrition.

Historically, donkeys were often fed barley, which with its poor calcium:phosphorus ratio, eventually resulted in the side effect of soft, overlarge skulls. This effect led to the terms Big Head Disease, Bran Disease, Barley Disease, or Miller's Disease (because grain millers had excess bran and used it as stock feed) to describe donkeys fed too much barley. Either a deficiency of calcium or an excess of phosphorus can create this imbalance, ultimately causing bones to demineralize and manifesting in lameness. The stoic donkey classically tolerates more pain and lameness than a horse, so did not show signs of the imbalance until its skull was demineralizing and the bone replaced by cartilage. This condition is properly known as nutritional secondary hyperparathyroidism (NSH), often shortened as nutritional parathyroidism.

Pregnant, ill, or hardworking donkeys will have higher protein needs that can be easily met with feeds like alfalfa or soy meal.

Provide browse for all donkeys. In addition to partial fulfillment of its forage requirement, browse satisfies the need to chew, which helps keep donkeys from eating fences, blankets, pasturemates' manes, and the barn.

Hydration

Water-drinking capacity and tolerance of drought is another difference between donkeys and horses. Donkeys can gorge on water and also be remarkably drought tolerant, although they tend to be choosy about the water source and temperature. Donkeys have been documented to endure up to 30 percent dehydration. However, unlike horses, they often still have an appetite when dehydrated, which places them at risk for impaction colic.

Complications

Another impaction colic risk for donkeys stems from their propensity to eat bedding and bark, especially when not provided with browse sources. It is essential that donkey owners allow the animals to fulfill their need to browse by providing straw, or twiggy brush.

Do not try to make a donkey lose weight by fasting it (withholding feed). Fasting places it at risk for a serious metabolic condition called hyperlipemia in which fat stores are over-mobilized. This condition, discussed under Special Diets for Hepatic Problems, is more common in females and can also be precipitated with stress and a gross reduction in water intake. Hyperlipemia may present with a variety of symptoms, ranging from inappetance to tremors to colic. It should be assessed and treated by a qualified veterinarian. Dieting an overweight donkey can be a challenge, because their rations cannot be drastically reduced due to the risk of triggering hyperlipemia. Give an obese donkey exercise by hiking, packing, riding, or driving, and provide it with plenty of straw and perhaps supplementary hay. Provide drylot turnout, not pasture.

Obesity and the associated conditions of laminitis and equine metabolic syndrome are common in overnourished donkeys. (These conditions are covered in detail in this chapter.) They are even more susceptible than horses to getting laminitis due to sudden changes in feed or indulging in non-structural carbohydrates. A key difference in a donkey's presentation of laminitis is that they typically do not assume a horse's classic laminitic stance of trying to keep weight off their front feet by standing with the front hooves extended as far forward as possible. Also, donkeys might have hind-hoof laminitis first, while horses more commonly have laminitis first in the front feet. Donkeys can be remarkably stoic and have been documented to be experiencing severe laminitis without displaying particularly obvious distress.

Dental care is very important. Underweight donkeys that are already provided with adequate nutrition usually suffer from dental pain and poor dental condition. Thin donkeys needs supplementary feeding, but the additional feeds should be given at a trickle rate, not in large meals. Tablespoons of oil, as discussed in Chapter 4, added to alfalfa meal provide a solid protein and energy boost for a donkey in serious need of gaining weight, but the owner must be willing to allow weight to regain over months for a donkey that is not at risk of starvation.

Hepatic (liver) disease is not uncommon in donkeys, with the chief symptom being loss of appetite. Always be suspicious of a donkey going off its feed, and watch it carefully for signs of deterioration. Donkeys have been observed to engage in sham eating when they are ill. It is important to see that the donkey is actually eating and assess the quantity of food it truly consumes in order to know that the donkey really is eating adequate food.

Both internal and external parasites can present and persist differently in donkeys. This has implications for horses in contact with donkeys. The issues are covered in Chapter 7, but it's interesting to note that the donkey's affinity for high tannin plants like Sudan and Johnson grass and even tobacco leaves may have served the purpose of deworming. Tobacco used to be a common anthelmintic administered in the 1800s.

Senior donkeys—their normal lifespan is longer than a horse's, not uncommonly reaching forty years—may have outlived their pasturemates but still need companionship. Seniors may also require raised feeders to continue to eat well. Continue to feed free choice browse forage, small supplementary meals if needed, and no grain or grain products.

Weight Assessment

Evaluate an individual donkey's nutritional status by first assessing its body condition, then adding or subtracting appropriate feed as needed. If a donkey appears to already be at an ideal weight and getting appropriate feed, continue the good work.

As donkeys cannot be fed like small ponies, they also cannot be measured in the same way. Because their build differs from horses', they are not conditioned scored on the usual Henneke Body Condition Score but rather on a simpler scale of 1–5, with 3 being ideal, 5 obese, and 1 severely thin.

To assess condition, it is very important to *feel* as well as observe the animal. Donkeys can grow thick, shaggy coats that hide fat deposition. Rather than overall fat accumulation, overweight donkeys tend to get fat deposits on their crests, rumps, and along their sides in what might be termed fat panniers. It is important to recognize that a large belly on a donkey could be due to a highly fibrous diet. A pendulous abdomen may also be seen in donkeys that have delivered numerous offspring.

The formulas for calculating the weight of a horse do not apply to donkeys. A good donkey-specific formula is: weight in kilograms =

$$\frac{(\text{heart girth in cm})^{2.12} \times (\text{length from point of elbow to point of buttock in cm})^{0.688}}{3{,}801}$$

The Donkey Sanctuary, a foundation based in the United Kingdom dedicated to the welfare of donkeys worldwide, has developed a nomogram for finding a donkey's weight.

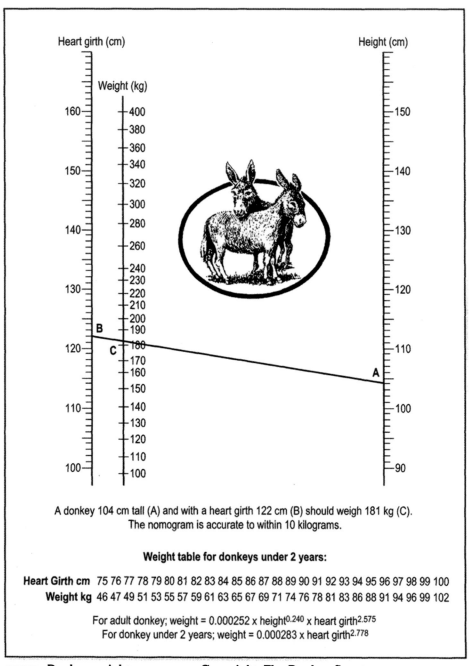

A donkey 104 cm tall (A) and with a heart girth 122 cm (B) should weigh 181 kg (C).
The nomogram is accurate to within 10 kilograms.

Weight table for donkeys under 2 years:

Heart Girth cm	75	76	77	78	79	80	81	82	83	84	85	86	87	88	89	90	91	92	93	94	95	96	97	98	99	100
Weight kg	46	47	49	51	53	55	57	59	61	63	65	67	69	71	74	76	78	81	83	86	88	91	94	96	99	102

For adult donkey; weight = $0.000252 \times \text{height}^{0.240} \times \text{heart girth}^{2.575}$
For donkey under 2 years; weight = $0.000283 \times \text{heart girth}^{2.778}$

ABOVE: **Donkey weight nomogram. Copyright: The Donkey Sanctuary.**

The Mule

A mule is a hybrid achieved by breeding a donkey to a horse or pony. Mules receive 31 chromosomes from the donkey parent and 32 chromosomes from the horse parent for a total of 63 chromosomes. Because of this, mules are usually sterile, but there have been cases of molly mules (mares) reproducing by both donkey jacks and horse stallions.

Most mules are the product of a donkey jack bred to a horse mare, but there are mules foaled from a donkey jenny (also called a jennet) sired by a horse. By convention, such a mule is called a hinny. A donkey jenny's smaller size, lower fertility, and longer gestation contribute to the fact that most mules are a result of a jack bred to a mare, rather than a stallion to a jennet. Hinnies can seem a bit more like a horse than a common mule, which has feeding requirements a bit more like a donkey's than a horse's. However, the physical appearance of a hinny versus a mule is really more a matter of the parents' individual genetics rather than whether the male or female parent was the donkey.

Mule feeding is an area of equine nutrition even less well studied than that of donkey nutrition. Because there are significant blood test differences between donkeys and horses, and because a mule can have traits of either parent, it is good to have routine blood work done on a healthy mule to know its baseline values. Numerous medical conditions have nutritional implications, but knowing that a donkey has, for example, higher plasma triglycerides, higher liver enzymes, fewer but larger erythrocytes, means that the donkey's mule offspring can have blood chemistry that differs from a horse's normal values. A mule's blood panel results could be misunderstood as pointing to a medical problem, when the mule is actually normal for its own chemistry.

Also, mule foals are at a higher risk for neonatal isoerythrolysis (NI, discussed under Broodmares and Growing Youngsters) than any other equid, because all donkeys possess the responsible antigen. It is so common that the blood test to diagnose the problem is sometimes called checking for anti-donkey factor. NI is generally fatal when untreated but has a very good prognosis with early identification and treatment.

Mules seem to have a lower propensity to overeat than horses or donkeys. Good nutrition begins with assessing the mule's current condition and adding or subtracting energy from the diet if the mule is under- or overweight. Very hardworking mules will need improved hays, but be careful when giving grain products. Extra calories can come from fibrous and fat sources, although mules doing extremely athletic activities (all-day ranching, racing, or full-endurance riding) are often supplemented successfully with grain.

Hugo, the Mule Selected as the Best-Conditioned Horse

When Eva Taylor's good friend Mari asked for help in bringing a new horse home, Eva was game. Mari had purchased a beautiful buckskin American Quarter Horse mare in foal to a purebred buckskin Quarter Horse. Arriving to get the mare, Eva noticed a donkey jack in the next pasture and teased her friend that he might have sired the baby the mare was carrying.

The day came when the mare foaled, and Mari called Eva in tears. "It's a mule. It's a mule."

ABOVE: **Eva Taylor and her beloved mule Hugo covered more backcountry miles than most horse and rider teams ever do. Photo Credit: Dan Taylor.**

Again, Eva was game, agreeing to take the unwanted mule baby. She and her husband kept burros. Eva loved to ride the backcountry, but she preferred the resilience of mules to horses. She called the young mule Hugo and brought him home after he was weaned. In due time, Eva sought help from an excellent local trainer to teach Hugo to be a good riding mule.

Hugo became Eva's partner, and they crisscrossed countless miles of the wild Olympic Peninsula's backcountry. They rode tremendous distances, and she cared for him with plenty of local hay, supplemented with rolled oats when he was working hard. Eva made sure Hugo drank well, and she read up on electrolytes, dosing him as needed. She did everything she could to give him excellent care, and he returned the effort. It was early days in the endurance world, but Eva knew about Tevis.

The Western States Ride for the Tevis Cup is legendary. This ride was a founding force in the sport of modern endurance riding and set the standard for a one-hundred-mile ride completed in less than twenty-four hours with a special award to be given to the horse judged to be in the best condition. The point-to-point route for the Tevis crosses the spine of California's Sierra Nevada mountain range, literally over the same territory that stranded the ill-fated Donner Party. Only about half of the annual entrants actually manage to complete the ride. Of those finishers, the first ten stand for an extra inspection by a team of veterinarians to determine which horse is awarded the coveted Haggin Cup for being the best conditioned.

In 1973, Hugo became the first mule ever awarded the Haggin Cup. He finished Tevis five times, a feat only a handful of animals have accomplished.

"Hugo was head over heels in love with Eva," commented one riding buddy. "She couldn't move in the house without him noticing and calling out to her."

In 1976, Eva entered Hugo and her molly mule, Sugar, in the Great American Horse Race, crossing the North American continent from New York to California. They top-tenned again, finishing in seventh place.

Hugo lived nearly thirty years, and his accomplishments with Eva Taylor have never been equaled.

Special Diets: Neglect And Starvation

Insufficient food intake, relative to the amount burned, results in stored body fat being burned to make up the caloric or energy deficit. If there is insufficient stored body fat, the body will break down other tissues in muscle, organs, and bone for energy. Underfeeding can be a touchy subject, with some owners routinely having horses that are thin or too thin. Genetics, health, conformation, and age affect a horse's ability to add and maintain weight, but they are not excuses. Empirical standards for assessing weight and scoring body condition exist, and these are what should be used for evaluation.

The physiological effects of significant malnutrition impact how neglected and starved horses are best rehabilitated. In rescue situations, new owners faced with the task of feeding and caring for the horses must be mindful of precipitous changes in blood chemistry that can occur both while the horse was undernourished and in the critical period when the horse is first reintroduced to food that is healthy in both quality and quantity. Refeeding syndrome is a dangerous potential complication. The severity of underfeeding is directly proportional to the horse's risk for serious medical complications—including death from organ failure—during refeeding.

Financial hardship, an owner lacking education, cruelty, or other factors can result in underweight horses. Whatever the reason for a horse becoming malnourished, success in rehabilitating these animals requires attention to the science of nutrition. Overall, rescue of underweight horses is risky and rewarding.

Assessing Malnutrition

Chapter 10 details the standard body condition score for horse, describing healthy horses that would be scored from 4 through 6, with an ideal horse at a 5. Underweight horses are rated at a body condition score of 1, 2, or 3. Note that even horses rated at 2 and 3 have some palpable body fat.

Of the six areas—neck, withers, loin, tailhead, ribs, and behind the shoulder—assessed individually in body condition scoring, the first four are along the spine. A prominent tailhead (where the dock of the tail joins the rump) rates a horse at 3 for the tailhead area. Prominent ribs rate a horse at 2 for the rib area. Before rating the withers and loin, consider the shape of a vertebrae. Each vertebrae has one bony projection sticking out away from the body called a spinous process and two bony projections sticking out sideways from the vertebrae called transverse processes. A slight fat covering over the transverse processes of the vertebrae in the loins rates a horse at 2 for the loins, and when the transverse processes of the vertebrae are visible in the loin, the loin area is rated at 1. Spinous processes are evaluated in the withers. Hook bones, properly known as the ilia (singular is an ilium) and pin bones (the bone that forms the point of the buttock, properly called the ishial tuberosity) protrude in underweight horses; they are rounded and covered with muscle and fat in healthy horses.

Using objective criteria helps remove subjective opinion and argument from the body condition assessment.

Physiological Effects of Malnutrition

When a horse receives less energy than it requires, its body will first use all of its stored glycogen (which will be depleted in twenty-four to thirty-six hours in a fasting situation), then stored fat, and finally protein. While horses normally have a reserve of carbohydrate in the form of glycogen stored primarily in the muscles and liver, as well as stores of visceral and regional fat, they have no stored protein. Horses reduced to breaking down their own protein for energy to maintain life lose tissues throughout their bodies. Skeletal muscles break down, gastrointestinal tract tissues dissolve, and organs such as the heart, liver, and kidneys give up cells to keep the horse alive.

These animals also deplete their normal stores of various macrominerals and microminerals. When the horse is finally given a significant amount of food, insulin is released to bring glucose into cells, but insulin also brings phosphorus and magnesium from the bloodstream into cells. Horses without adequate circulating phosphorus and magnesium cannot cope with the necessary electrolyte shift. Low blood phosphate, called hypophosphatemia, can result in heart failure.

Additional abnormal blood chemistry is not uncommon in undernourished horses. The prolonged deficit in vitamins negatively impacts many blood values, and the mineral deficit disrupts the electrolytes. The lack of general nutrients means the horses cannot replace their erythrocytes (red blood cells) normally, so they usually have anemia.

Recovery from Malnutrition

As a result of inadequate amounts of energy for a prolonged period of time, the horse's gastric volume and gastric emptying time become greatly reduced. Therefore, a recovering horse must initially be given small, very frequent meals. Soaked beet pulp works well.

In early recovery, these horses are unable to cope with large amounts of food being available. In severe cases, feed three-quarters to one pound of hay per hour (double this if giving chopped fresh grass), every hour, to a horse whose healthy weight should be 1,000 pounds. Be aware that these horses have learned that a food supply is not reliable, so they can become aggressive when refeeding.

In the longer view, malnourished horses are at a greater risk for complications from parasitic burdens than are healthy horses. It all begins with the recovery diet.

One study evaluated the effects of three different, but isocaloric (equal calorie) diets—a complete feed, alfalfa hay, and oat hay—fed to three groups of severely underweight horses. The complete feed offered 19 percent starch. The alfalfa diet offered about 3 percent starch and 20 percent protein. The oat hay diet offered the greatest bulk and was lowest in protein at about 7 percent. Three horses died in this study, underscoring the critical medical danger to severely underweight horses. In general, the horses fed the alfalfa diet showed the best results.

Another study comparing isocaloric recovery diets of alfalfa hay versus alfalfa hay supplemented with corn oil to help moderate the insulin response, determined that the straight alfalfa-hay diet was superior because of the additional minerals in the hay that were not afforded with the oil.

Horses will generally require three to six months to significantly recover from malnutrition, but the first ten days is the most critical period in re-nourishing severely underweight horses. This is the time frame when a horse is at greatest risk for the lethal complication of refeeding syndrome.

REFEEDING SYNDROME

Refeeding syndrome is a potential complication that can occur when nourishing a starved or emaciated animal. It is characterized by peripheral edema (swelling), neurological disturbances, liver failure, kidney failure, and cardiac failure. It is chiefly precipitated by hypophosphatemia, along with hypokalemia (low blood potassium) and hypothiaminosis (low thiamine) that combine to disturb the normal function of critical organ systems. This disruption occurs most easily with hypernutrition—a rapid, rich, and large supply of food. Thus, be exceedingly cautious of offering starved horses concentrates. These animals are not prepared to cope with the imbalanced mineral ratios or the high sugar and starch of grain. Feed hay, preferably good-quality alfalfa.

Similarly, be cautious about overloading these animals with vitamins and minerals, allowing instead a slow adjustment to a healthy mineral balance through prolonged consumption of good hay.

Veterinary care is imperative for these horses. An inappetant horse in particular requires urgent veterinary intervention.

DEWORMING COMPLICATIONS

Colic from a gross parasitic burden is a standing risk in neglected horses. However, a large population of recently killed worms in the gastrointestinal tract of this already physically compromised horse also places it at a significant risk for colic. For this reason, do not immediately deworm a starved horse. Allow the horse to get past its first two weeks of a healthy diet then assess the worm burden both qualitatively and quantitatively through fecal egg counts. Ensure the horse is eating well and exhibiting good mental alertness—a cardinal sign of its physiological status—before deworming.

ABOVE: **This horse is too thin. Photo Credit: Valerie Jones Jackson.**

Rescue Success on a Pedestal

[Author's Note: Photographs and stories of severely malnourished horses are strongly emotive and are often evidence of an unprosecuted crime. Rather than photographing an emaciated horse, I chose a somewhat less traumatic example. As with overfed but not grossly obese horses, it takes more skill and experience to identify horses that are underfed but not extreme examples. Learn this skill by studying how to assess a horse's body condition score with Table 10–1.]

An underfed horse is unfortunately not an uncommon story. An owner with diminished health, finances, or interest often results in the horse not being given enough food. Being an unwanted horse is often the stage an animal goes through before heading for the slaughterhouse—it's happened to backyard horses, champion cutting horses, and even a Kentucky Derby winner.

When Sasha was underfed for a protracted period, volunteers from a horse rescue organization noticed and intervened. They managed to buy her from the neglectful owner.

Sasha did not trust that food and kind handling would be given to her again. However, her rescuers were accustomed to providing good hay, pasture, beet pulp, and senior feed to the rescue horses that came their way, along with a salt block and clean water. They also gave her time.

ABOVE: **Rescue success on a pedestal: Sasha six months later. Photo Credit: Diane Royall**

Although Sasha looked significantly better in a matter of weeks, rebuilding her body and regaining trust took many months. Half a year elapsed before she was in a good working relationship, benefitting from groundwork and then going under saddle.

It is the habit of healthy nutrition and good handling that shows a horse a reason to trust. Sasha returned the kindness and became a healthy, reliable riding horse.

Special Diets: Overweight Horses

Being overweight—or in more severe cases, being obese—makes a horse susceptible to numerous medical problems. Laminitis, insulin resistance, and equine metabolic syndrome are the most common and dangerous risks. Also, obese horses tend to form lipomas (fatty tumors) that, when located near the gastrointestinal tract, increase the risk of colic. Large deposits of fat are more than just stored calories; they become chemically active, releasing messenger proteins called adipokines, essentially functioning as an organ and affecting metabolic functions.

Weight can be a touchy subject, with some owners routinely having horses that are too heavy but denying or excusing the overfeeding. An easy keeper with a thrifty constitution is the most likely candidate for becoming overweight, but any horse can end up overweight. While genetics, conformation, health, and age can affect a horse's ability to gain and lose weight, these factors do not excuse allowing a horse to carry unhealthy weight. Empirical standards for weight assessment are reviewed here.

In general, the cause of being overweight or obese is mismanagement. Instead of the horse's intake and output of energy being in balance, a surplus of energy has been consumed. Excess calories are stored as body fat. The only lasting solution is to rebalance the intake and output of energy. Usually both a reduction in calories and an increase in exercise are required for maximum benefit. Begin with accurately assessing the horse's weight, then reevaluate his intake and output for a results-oriented approach that gives measureable success.

Assessing Weight

Objective criteria help diminish the usual subjectivity involved in assessing a heavy horse's body condition. Weight tapes measure the horse's heart girth circumference and attempt to correlate that measurement into weight, but different tapes give different weights for the same measurement, and the heart girth measurement fails to account for the horse's length and general build. Chapter 10 provides the formula that combines both the heart girth and body length measurements to provide a more accurate weight assessment than heart girth alone can offer. The Ultimate Chart precalculates the answers, turning inches into pounds. The heart girth measurement is, however, good for noticing *change* in an individual horse's body composition.

The Henneke body condition scoring system (BCS), Table 10–2, is a reliable resource for evaluating a horse's fat stores over time. An acceptable BCS for healthy horses is anywhere from 4 to 6, with the ideal being 5. Overweight horses will be scored at 7, 8, or 9. A score of 9 is grossly obese.

In body scoring, it is important to individually assess and score six areas of the body and then average the scores. For example, obese horses can exhibit bulging fat along the neck, withers, and behind the shoulder, but the ribs may be faintly palpable, thus the latter area earns a lower score, but the overall average of all six areas scored will show that the horse is overweight.

In the short term, two circumference measurements specific to weight loss are the neck crest and the umbilicus girth. Document changes in these measurements.

Neck Crest Measurement

To measure the neck crest circumference, measure snugly around the entire circumference of the neck, exactly halfway between the front of the withers and the end poll (of the spine right behind the ears). Part the mane so as not to include large hanks of hair. Let the tape measure contact the body. Consider making a small mark on, or cut in, the coat or mane at the measuring point so that future measurements are taken at the same spot.

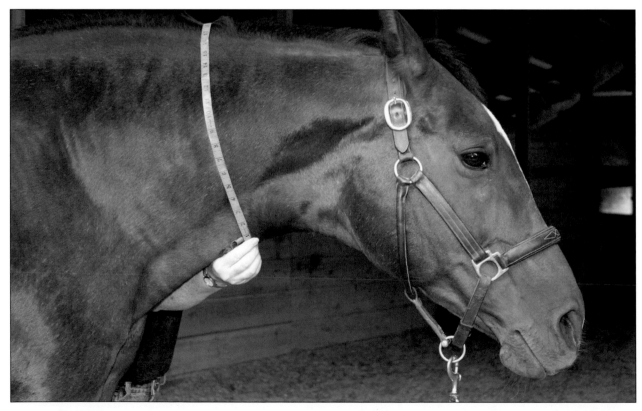

ABOVE: **Checking the neck crest circumference, measured halfway between the withers and the poll, is one way to monitor weight loss. You may mark or cut the coat to enable next week's measurement to be taken precisely in the same location.**

Researchers at Virginia Tech developed a cresty neck scoring system, detailed in Table 9–7, to grade the severity of these fat deposits.

Score	Comments
Table 9–7 The Cresty Neck Score (Carter et al.)	
0	no visible crest
1	no visible crest but slight filling felt by palpation
2	noticeable crest, fat deposited evenly from poll to withers; crest easily bent from side to side
3	enlarged, thickened crest with less side-to-side flexibility; fat deposited more heavily at the middle of the neck
4	grossly enlarged crest cannot be easily moved side to side; may have wrinkles or creases perpendicular to topline
5	crest is so large it permanently droops to one side

Umbilicus Girth Measurement

The umbilicus refers to the area in the horse's abdomen where its umbilical cord was at birth. Notice the umbilical stump on new foals where the cord releases or is cut. The umbilicus girth circumference is a good measure of visceral fat. Changes in this measurement reflect changes in the amount of belly fat.

To measure the umbilicus circumference, locate the hairless centerline of the horse's lower abdomen. It is important to always use the same point. If desired, use a felt pen to mark the measuring point, refreshing the mark as needed.

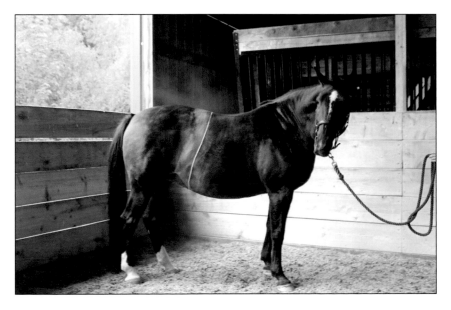

LEFT: **The length of the yellow baling twine around this overweight horse's umbilicus girth will be checked on a tape measure to monitor weight loss.**

Intake: The Food

The best management practice for overweight horses is early intervention. With many horses, however, excess weight is a long standing condition, creeping up year by year. Generally, this results from a combination of owners overfeeding, and overestimating the horse's workload. Consider overweight horses to need only a maintenance ration, unless they are obviously in at least hard work.

Obesity-associated laminitis (OAL) is the most immediately threatening issue for obese horses, especially those on pasture and is likely undiagnosed EMS. The horse may need to be on a dry dirt lot with no grazing, or it may need to wear a grazing muzzle for most of its turnout time. Remember that compensatory grazing can provoke a horse to consume extraordinary amounts of grass in a very short time. Although grazing is behaviorally important to a horse's mental and physical well-being, an obese horse would benefit from being restricted to hand-grazing, where the owner can direct the horse to very mature and sparse grasses. While in dry lot, low quality hay in two slow feed hay nets, one inserted inside the other, can provide the horse with a safe means to fulfill its need to chew forage.

Overnourishment is more challenging to monitor in herd and pasture situation, because a horse can consume more food than it needs. In a herd setting, the turnout may need to be sectioned off to permit a lower quality of hay for the overweight horse, while pasturemates become fence-line mates, and receive their higher quality hay on their side of the shared fence line.

It can come as a surprise to many that reducing a horse's body mass to a healthy size need not involve an actual restrictive diet and that it's best not to force overweight horses to engage in intense exercise.

Counting Calories

Reconsidering the horse's food consumption requires looking not just at the quantity of food the horse is eating but also the quality. Hay with more chaff, lower quality protein and above all, fewer water soluble carbohydrates (WSCs) will be less caloric than richer hay.

As discussed in Chapter 4, there is no such thing as a low carbohydrate diet for horses. A diet low in the specific carbohydrates of simple sugars, starch, and fructan—all of which are non-structural carbohydrates (NSC)—but high in the structural carbohydrates of cellulose and hemicellulose plus the pectin found among those two plant cellular wall components is still a diet composed mostly of carbohydrates. Hay with less than 10 percent NSC is desirable, although difficult to find in good supply. Slow soaking the hay helps lower the water soluble carbohydrate content. Feeding the hay in two or three slow feed hay nets (one inside the other) prolongs the eating time into a more moderate, foraging pace.

TRY MAINTENANCE BEFORE DIETING

Diets and severe diets can be enacted, but the healthiest route is to determine the horse's optimum weight and *feed the horse as though it is already at its optimum weight*. For example, a horse that would ideally weigh 1,000 pounds but has been overfed to the point of weighing 1,200 pounds should be fed the maintenance diet for the 1,000 pounds it should weigh. Take several weeks to decrease feed.

Too often, people want fast results and immediately enforce diet rations, or severe diet rations, on the horse without first giving the necessary 4–6 months at its proper, healthy maintenance hay ration. This is another reason to first determine the horse's target healthy weight and then simply feed the horse at the appropriate level for its target weight and actual workload.

Diets generally fail due to the dieter not maintaining a weight loss, in other words, regaining lost weight. By skipping the diet and simply going to a proper maintenance ration, the weight will, in the time span of several months or half a year, adjust.

Diet

A dieting ration is below the standard maintenance guideline of 2 percent of the horse's body-weight per day, generally between 1.5 percent and 1.75 percent, feeding only forage. Note that this figure is not calculated on the animal's actual weight, but rather the optimum weight. For example, rations for a pony that should weigh 800 pounds but weighs an obese 1,000 pounds, should be calculated on its target weight, not its actual weight.

A diet that is strictly adhered to will give faster results than skipping the diet and going straight to maintenance rations, but it may bring hyperlipemia or negative behavioral changes, for example, stereotypic behavior, aggression, or disobedience.

The Ultimate Chart has precalculated the diet and severe diet hay rations for all weights.

Severe Diet

A severe diet should be veterinarian-monitored; it is 1 percent to 1.5 percent of the horse's calculated ration at its desired weight. It is important to work from the desired weight, not the current weight, and it is healthiest to first afford the horse a number of months to drop weight at a healthy maintenance ration, then try a diet ration, if necessary, before trying a severe diet.

Human compliance is the biggest obstacle to a horse losing weight. If other people are slipping the horse treats or allowing it pasture access, the weight loss effort will be defeated and frustrating for all.

Output: The Exercise

Reevaluate the overweight horse's workload. Believing a horse is in moderate work, when it is really at the very low end of light work, receiving a few hours of very light riding per week, only encourages overfeeding.

Overweight and obese horses tend to be exercise intolerant, which in turn exacerbates the problem of not expending enough energy, and continuing to store the surplus of energy as fat.

The American Association of Equine Practitioners (AAEP) recommends moderate intensity exercise for weight loss. This means working the horse hard enough to attain a heart rate of 90 beats per minute (bpm). It does not mean running the horse or otherwise overstressing the unfit horse. Chapter 10 discusses how to check a horse's vital signs, including the pulse.

The fitness program may start with no riding at all, but rather hand walking, perhaps as easily as two ten-minute sessions per day for the first few days, increasing to two fifteen-minute sessions by the end of week one or two.

Make moderate intensity exercise of a sustained duration the goal of a fitness program once you start riding, but initial efforts should still involve all or mostly walking rather than faster gaits. Be mindful that an overweight horse builds up heat faster, and holds it longer, than a horse at an ideal weight, due to the insulation and physical burden.

As fitness increases, so can the duration of time spent under saddle. An increased duration at a gait faster than a walk will come thanks to the pure pleasure of riding.

A Missouri Foxtrotter Slims Down

Dodger is a kind, trail-loving, nineteen-year-old easy keeping Missouri Foxtrotter whose weight crept up after his owner, Marilyn, broke her back in a bad fall from a less kind horse.

Missouri Foxtrotters tend to have a thrifty constitution. Dodger is believed to have some pony in his breeding as well. Ponies also tend to be hardy, doing well on what would be merely adequate for other equines and doing too well on better food.

Marilyn has always had to be especially careful with Dodger in the spring. With the fresh, new growth of the season's rich grass, she monitored his tendency to grow a cresty neck and have throbbing digital pulses that warn of laminitis. But by the time Marilyn was recovered from the spinal fracture, she found that Dodger no longer had a saddle that fit him. Also, she had relocated and was unfamiliar with local trails. Her work soared beyond fifty hours per week. A new horse on the farm took most of Marilyn's limited riding time, and Dodger—well, Dodger got fat.

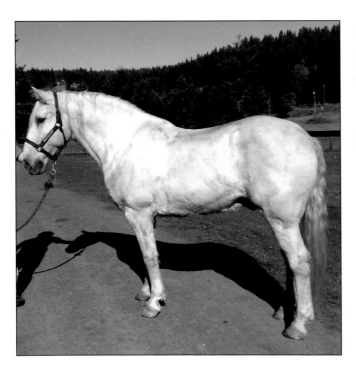

His cresty neck grew thicker and harder. Spongy deposits on his withers, tailhead, ribs, loins, and behind his shoulders all bulged. His blood work showed signs trending toward insulin resistance. A horse that should weigh in three digits was over 1,100 pounds. Most body scorers would have ranked him at 8 or 9.

Marilyn, a lifelong treat-giver to all good horses, made hard changes. It took time but gave results.

LEFT: **Too much of a good thing—Dodger has made good diet success but is still overweight. Photo Credit: Lori Crow.**

She ceased giving treats for her special boy. She had already had her hay tested and selected the lowest sugar hay she could purchase. She soaked Dodger's entire hay ration for at least an hour to remove soluble sugars. He received no grain or other concentrates. She put Dodger on a dry lot when the farm's large turnout paddocks grew fresh grass. She learned the local trails, re opened old ones, built new paths, and found a good saddle that fit him. They began exploring trails at a walk until Dodger was sufficiently legged up. After a few months, Dodger's crest was much diminished, and the fat deposits behind his shoulders were markedly reduced. He was still fleshy, the easy keeper consistent with his pony and Foxtrotter breeding, but his body condition score had dropped to a high 6.

They kept up the good work. Dodger still eats from a slow feed hay net to satisfy his foraging need and prolong his meals.

Dodger's blood work became entirely normal, and his BCS dropped over time to a low 5. He has remained at that healthier weight thanks to attentive management.

ABOVE: **Dodger has made it to svelte. Photo Credit: Lori Crow.**

Special Diets Part 2:
Medical Problems with Nutritional Implications

Many medical conditions with nutritional implications have already been reviewed when the etiology was discussed. These include choke, colic, and laminitis (Chapter 2); synchronous diaphragmatic flutter (also known as hypokalemic diaphragmatic flutter, or thumps, reviewed under Electrolytes in Chapter 4); enterolithiasis, discussed in Chapters 2 and 4; the environmental threats of poisonings, botulism, and equine grass sickness (Chapter 8); osteochondrosis dissecans (OCD) and developmental orthopedic disease (DOD) (see Growing Youngsters, earlier in this chapter); and arthritis (see Senior Horses, earlier in this chapter). The behavioral problems of cribbing and other stereotypic activity, often related to nutrition and management, were also discussed in Chapter 2.

A number of horses have other significant medical conditions that require special diets and additional care measures. The ten classes of conditions reviewed here are: equine metabolic syndrome; hepatic impairment or disease; hyperkalemic periodic paralysis; insulin resistance; the neuromuscular disorders of equine motor neuron disease, shivers, and stringhalt; pituitary pars intermedia dysfunction; renal impairment or disease; the respiratory disorders of inflammatory airway disease, recurrent airway obstruction, and summer pasture-associated obstructive pulmonary disease; rhabdomyolysis and polysaccharide storage myopathy; and ulcers (equine gastric ulcer syndrome, equine gastroduodenal ulcer disease, and right dorsal colitis).

Some of these medical conditions overlap with respect to their symptoms, prevention, and treatment. For example, the distinct problem of insulin resistance is also one of the three primary factors of equine metabolic syndrome.

Special Diets—Medical Problems with Nutritional Implications: Equine Metabolic Syndrome

Equine metabolic syndrome (EMS), or simply metabolic syndrome (MS), is the term for horses generally exhibiting three clinical signs: obesity (with either general or regional excess fat deposits), insulin resistance (IR), and an increased susceptibility to laminitis in the absence of another distinct cause for laminitis. EMS horses tend to have an increased appetite and fertility problems. EMS horses have special feeding and management requirements.

As the name suggests, EMS is a metabolic disorder, with the dysfunction involving the horse's endocrine system and energy metabolism. EMS has been confused with hypothyroidism and was initially referred to by the term peripheral Cushing's syndrome. EMS has also been called Syndrome X, pre-laminitic metabolic Syndrome, or, after an episode of laminitis, obesity-associated

The Three Sides of the
Equine Metabolic Syndrome Triangle

- obesity—general or regional fat deposits
- insulin resistance
- increased susceptibility to laminitis

laminitis (OAL). The hypothyroidism that has been noticed with horses experiencing endocrine problems is more likely a result rather than a cause of the problem.

There may be a genetic component that makes some horses more likely to exhibit EMS. When the genes that give horses a thrifty constitution (being an easy keeper), collide with an environment and management practices that offer excess calories—especially excess non-structural carbohydrates—and a lack of sufficient exercise, there is a high risk for EMS.

What Breeds Are Most Subject
to Equine Metabolic Syndrome?

Pony breeds are overrepresented with respect to the number of EMS cases, notably the Shetland, Welsh, and Dartmoor breeds. In horse breeds, Morgans are overrepresented, as to a lesser extent are Arabians, American Quarter Horses, Spanish Mustangs, Saddlebreds, Tennessee Walkers, Paso Finos, and Warmblood breeds. Thoroughbreds and Standardbreds seem to be underrepresented in EMS cases. There does not seem to be a gender distinction in EMS prevalence. Equine Metabolic Syndrome usually strikes horses between five and fifteen years of age.

Not all overweight horses have EMS, and not all EMS horses are classically fat, but a body condition score of 7 or more indicates a higher risk for EMS. This is usually long standing obesity that developed over a protracted period of time. The horse's obesity can be insidious for the owner of an easy keeper. Because of the horse's tendency to gain weight over the years, the owner can mistake the horse becoming overweight for mere filling out from young adulthood into adulthood.

The obesity may manifest in areas of lumpy fat rather than overall body weight gain. Similar to the research findings that extra adipose accumulation in the abdomen in humans is linked to an increase in medical complications, the horse's dangerous fat area is the neck. The classic regional fat deposit associated with EMS is a cresty neck, with fat deposits over the nuchal ligament. In addition to the cresty neck, EMS horses with regional adiposity often have fatty deposits above the tailhead, along the sheath in males, and at the prepuce and mammary glands in females. Gross fat deposits are more than stored excess calories; the fat is metabolically active, releasing hormones that trigger undesirable body chemistry reactions. Being obese is akin to constantly being in a state of low grade inflammation.

People can err in evaluating a horse's weight, which is why measurement is so helpful. The section on overweight horses reviews the cresty neck score developed by researchers at Virginia Tech to grade the severity of fat deposits on the neck crest. Check the neck circumference between the poll and the withers and record the measurement every week. Monitoring changes in a horse's fat deposits is an important part of regulating its feed.

The second parameter of EMS is the diagnosis of insulin resistance (IR). EMS horses will have hyper-insulinemia (high serum insulin levels). The section on insulin resistance (IR) clarifies this condition.

The third cardinal EMS factor is an increased susceptibility to laminitis, which is often insidious rather than acute, and recurs in cycles. The laminitis may be subclinical, so the owner does not notice the condition. As obese animals are always in a state of inflammation, an inflammatory stimulus like a large grain meal or a pasture rich in sugar and starch, spikes the insulin levels. The resulting increased inflammation can easily tip the horse into danger. Laminitis also limits the ability to exercise, and limited exercise tends to worsen the progression of EMS.

Nutritional Management of EMS

Management of the EMS horse is centered on achieving a healthy weight through diet and exercise. Careful monitoring of the diet will combat the insulin resistance by improving the horse's insulin sensitivity and will also safeguard against high sugar and starch feeds that could provoke laminitis.

It is essential that EMS horses receive feed that is low in non-structural carbohydrates (NSC). Hay that has only 10 percent NSC is desirable, though it is difficult to find. Hay above 16 percent NSC is unacceptable for an EMS horse. Again, the sugar content of hay may be reduced by soaking, and consumption time may be extended by doubling slow feed hay nets. Pasture is often too rich for EMS horses, and grazing opportunities will have to be limited to scrubby, dried, unstressed grasses that are not in an active growing phase.

Supplementary feeds are not usually needed for EMS horses when they are already overweight. If supplementary feeds are used in addition to forage, only low starch feeds like beet pulp or proprietary low starch blends should be given.

Veterinary Intervention

Ensure the EMS horse does not also have pituitary pars intermedia dysfunction (PPID) so that the correct therapeutic regimen is followed. EMS and PPID can occur in the same horse, but they are different conditions. PPID is covered separately.

The veterinarian may find additional medical signs of EMS, such as arterial hypertension, hypertriglyceridemia (an increased concentration of triglycerides in the blood), and hyperleptinemia (increased serum concentrations of the hormone leptin). Monitoring blood levels of insulin and glucose can help differentiate between the two conditions and also verify progress in normalizing the horse's resistance to insulin. Returning this blood chemistry to normal is the goal of nutritional management.

Special Diets—Medical Problems with Nutritional Implications: Hepatic Impairment or Disease

Horses do not regularly or easily acquire liver disease or impairment. A horse with mild liver problems that is compensating well may not require dietary changes, but there is considerable misinformation about how to feed and supplement a horse with a deteriorating liver.

A horse's liver is a spectacular 1 percent of its total body weight. Some people believe that horses with hepatic impairment or disease are poorly tolerant of fat and/or that protein could exacerbate liver problems. For these reasons, horses with liver problems have often been fed diets low in fat and protein. However, this may be a case of failed extrapolation between species. Human patients with liver failure have been noted to decompensate after consuming protein; when the protein in these peoples' diets was restricted to vegetable protein instead of animal protein, the patients improved. Horses should already be receiving no animal protein, only vegetable protein.

Protein restriction in liver-compromised horses could cause the horse to catabolize (burn) protein from its tissues and hasten the progression to hepatic encephalopathy (HE). HE occurs when the liver fails so badly that brain function is impaired due to the overload of toxins in the blood that a healthy liver would have removed.

While horses with liver problems need not be on a protein-restricted diet, they should only be fed high quality protein, and they should not be fed excess protein.

Fat-restricted diets, often suggested for human patients with failing livers, are not a solid assumption for horse. People generally intake a much greater percentage of their diets as fat (15 percent, 20 percent, 30 percent, and even higher) compared to the average horse's intake of less than 5 percent. Also, the human digestive anatomy differs in that people have a gall bladder that secretes bile for fat digestion. Horses have no gallbladder, and they constantly secrete bile. So, do not accept the easy suggestion that a horse with liver problems should be on a fat-restricted diet. The addition of some fat to the diet of a thin horse with hepatic (liver) compromise can provide needed calories.

Steatorrhea (the visible excretion of fat in the feces) or diarrhea is usually present in horses that are poorly absorbing added fat in the diet. Horses with steatorrhea or diarrhea should have fat-reduced diets, whether or not they also have liver insufficiency.

Signs of Liver Problems

Jaundice (also called icterus), is a classic sign of liver problems; it readily shows as yellow in the sclera (white of the eye). Weight loss, inappetance, and lethargy are also common signs. Behavioral changes can include circling or aimless wandering. Because the liver has important functions in the creation of clotting factors, horses with liver problems can have prolonged or excessive bleeding from minor injuries. These horses may also have photosensitivity when the liver fails to remove normally encountered toxins.

A competent veterinary examination, including blood tests, will determine a diagnosis. The blood work will reveal how well the horse is excreting ammonia and other factors regarding liver function. As damaged liver cells become scarred, the condition of cirrhosis exists; as more of the liver becomes cirrhotic, function will decline.

Hyperlipemia

The liver plays a significant role in the normal process of mobilizing (breaking down) stored body fats for use as energy. Hyperlipemia is a serious condition in which the body *over*-mobilizes stored fat. A similar condition called hyperlipidemia (abnormally high lipids in the blood) may occur. The animal becomes dull, weak, and may have muscle tremors or ataxia (a lack of coordination) or any signs of liver problems. Veterinary care is urgent. The serum portion of the blood becomes opaque. Autopsies show greasy organs.

Donkeys, ponies, and miniature horses are more susceptible to hyperlipemia, and females are more susceptible than males. Late pregnancy and early lactation are particularly high risk times for this disorder.

Hyperlipemia can be provoked by a significant negative energy balance, in which the animal requires more energy than is present in its feed, which is another reason why horses should not fast for extended periods. Diets should be done through regular feeding of lower quality feeds rather than withholding feed, and with no sudden changes.

Nutrition for the Horse with Liver Problems

The usual recommended horse feeding regimen of low sugar and low starch feeds must be revisited for the horse with hepatic insufficiency. The animal can do better on added concentrates as these feeds ease the liver's burden of gluconeogenesis (the body's process of creating glucose from non-carbohydrate substrates). Increasing sugar and starch intake through supplementing with grain also improves the appetite.

The horse with a compromised liver still requires mostly fiber, preferably pasture. If only poor pasture is available, or the horse is too photosensitive due to its failing liver to stay outside on pasture for most of the day, then provide plenty of good hay. In addition to grain concentrates, beet pulp with oil can be a way to increase the energy intake of a horse that is losing weight.

Vitamins and Minerals

Fat soluble vitamins (A, D, E, and K) are less well absorbed and stored in these horses. While the daily requirement for vitamin K has not been established, researchers believe the toxicity ranges of fat soluble vitamins allow a comfortable doubling up of the general dose. Regarding the water soluble vitamins, the liver is involved in production of B-complex vitamins, most notably niacin, and vitamin C synthesis occurs in the liver—so supplementation of B-complex and vitamin C may be helpful as well.

However, be cautious with general vitamin and mineral supplements. Copper and iron are hard on an unhealthy liver, so do not give a broad spectrum vitamin and mineral supplement or any concentrate that is fortified with added copper or iron. In a herd living situation, ensure that the salt block is a plain, white sodium chloride block, not a trace mineral block that could burden the horse with added minerals that it cannot excrete well with its unhealthy liver. Better still, remove the salt block and supply the other horses with salt individually, so the liver-compromised horse is not consuming added salt at all.

Finally, horses with liver problems can be low in zinc. Offer treats with zinc; this includes seeds, especially pumpkin seeds, and wheat bran.

Final Considerations

Poisoning scenarios are one of the more likely causes of liver failure in horses. As you were cautioned in Chapter 8, identify the plants where the horse lives and is ridden, and feed the horse well enough, and often enough, that it is much less tempted by unusual plants.

The end stage of liver disease produces a remarkably unpleasant death. Humanitarian considerations might make euthanasia a kinder option.

Special Diets—Medical Problems with Nutritional Implications: Hyperkalemic Periodic Paralysis (HYPP)

Hyperkalemic periodic paralysis (HYPP) is an intermittently occurring partial paralysis of varying severity that is associated with abnormal blood chemistry. Specifically, potassium levels in the blood are too high (hyperkalemia); within muscle cells, there is dysfunction in the sodium channels that are responsible for causing contraction and relaxation, and amino acids responsible for controlling these reactions are not working properly.

Tens of thousands of purebred and half-bred American Quarter Horses have the genetic defect that causes the disorder known as HYPP. Breeds with significant amounts of Quarter Horse blood (Appaloosas, Paints, and Appendix) also have a high incidence of HYPP.

Recognition of HYPP

A horse with HYPP may have general twitching or trembling that can initially be confused with rhabdomyolysis or shivers. Unlike rhabdomyolysis, however, HYPP does not seem related to exertion. Rather, attacks are random, though they do sometimes seem related to weather shifts. Also unlike a horse with rhabdomyolysis, HYPP horses will not have muscle damage in the hours and days following an attack and will not seem painful. Unlike a horse with shivers, an HYPP horse does not seem distressed but may be unable to move, or may abruptly drop into a sitting position due to a sudden inability to control his hind muscles, or he may completely collapse.

While general muscle twitching and hind paralysis are most common, muscles throughout the body may be affected. The third eyelid may droop, but this is distinct from drooping of the main eyelid seen in equine grass sickness. Ptosis, the paralysis of the horse's primary eyelid, is noticeable in onset, as the eyelashes will point downward rather than outward. Neighs and nickers may sound peculiar as the larynx may be weak.

Severe HYPP attacks may be lethal; paralysis of the diaphragm makes the horse unable to breathe. HYPP horses can be distinguished from a horse experiencing seizures in that horses remain lucid and aware of their surroundings during an attack.

Nutritional Management of HYPP Horses

Managing the hyperkalemia (excessively high potassium in the blood) is the central focus of nutritional support. Since forage is the largest source of potassium in a horse's diet, testing hay for potassium can help you select the most appropriate hay supply. Hay fields that are fertilized with potash will be higher in potassium than unfertilized fields. Short term hay soaking of up to thirty minutes may help leach out some potassium.

Be aware that the labels of broad spectrum vitamin and minerals supplements, sweet feeds, and complete feeds may not reveal how much potassium they contain. If the HYPP horse does not truly need these supplements and concentrates, do not use them. Instead stick to feeds that are labeled as having reduced potassium.

Never feed HYPP horses treats that are high in potassium; these include bananas and pumpkins or any products that contain them.

A salt block for an HYPP horse must be a plain, white sodium chloride block, not a mineral block that could contain potassium. Also, do not give mixed electrolytes that could contain potassium.

All horses do best with a healthy insulin response, but because insulin is involved in the uptake of potassium into cells, this is an added concern for HYPP horses. Letting this horse trend towards insulin resistance—through poor diet and exercise habits—can exacerbate HYPP attacks.

Meal fed HYPP horses strongly benefit from numerous meals, rather than a mere twice-daily feeding, so total potassium intake per meal is kept low.

Long term management should involve a qualified veterinarian, who can use diuretics as needed to help the horse eliminate excess potassium. It is up to every owner to help eliminate the disorder from the gene pool by never breeding an HYPP horse.

Special Diets—Medical Problems with Nutritional Implications: Insulin Resistance

Insulin is the hormone responsible for regulating the amount of glucose circulating in the bloodstream. Insulin stimulates the uptake and storage of glucose from blood, into body tissues, specifically muscle, fat and brain tissue. Blood insulin levels naturally rise in response to a meal, rise more with a large meal, and even more so with a meal heavy in non-structural carbohydrates, especially simple sugars and starches.

An insulin resistant (IR) horse has a diminished response to its insulin. The body then struggles to overcome the problem by releasing more insulin. This abnormally high level of insulin in the bloodstream is called hyperinsulinemia.

IR horses are prone to laminitis as well. (In a research setting, laminitis is induced in horses by administering inulin, a polysaccharide.) Because insulin naturally rises after the ingestion of large starch meals, it is important to recognize this risk of laminitis. This is yet another warning against the feeding of large grain meals, as well as any sizable meal with a high glycemic index or large meals of high non-structural carbohydrate feeds. Overweight horses frequently develop IR.

Insulin, like most hormones and other messenger chemicals, has other functions. It may play a role in peripheral vasodilation (expansion or dilation of the blood vessels in the extremities), which may be related to the laminitis risk experienced by IR horses.

Long standing IR is often coupled with Equine Metabolic Syndrome, Equine Cushing's Disease (PPID), or sometimes both. Very early detection and dietary correction of a horse trending toward IR, however, might forestall significant future health problems.

It is often possible to reverse IR and normalize the horse's blood chemistry with a long term effort at a healthy diet and a moderate exercise regimen.

Testing for Insulin Resistance

There are numerous ways to test for IR. Confounding factors of those tests has led to owner confusion and misinformation. First, a horse that is in pain or anxious—perhaps because it initially evaded capture for the testing procedure, or it has been trailered or otherwise separated from pasturemates—may have elevated hormones due to stress. The elevated hormones will skew the results of blood tests. Therefore, maintain a calm, consistent, routine atmosphere for any blood testing, especially hormone testing.

In addition, the blood samples must be handled carefully. The blood sample tubes must be the correct type, must be gently rolled a few times to circulate the blood sample contents, then stored upright to avoid contact with the rubber tube stopper, and immediately refrigerated to slow the metabolization of glucose and insulin.

IR is diagnosed by either static or by dynamic testing, with the former being less reliable than the latter. A static test requires a blood sample drawn and checked by a laboratory to determine the insulin and blood glucose levels. The presence of hyperinsulinemia and normal glucose levels is generally indicative of an IR horse. The presence of hyperinsulinemia and hyperglycemia can be indicative of a horse with Pituitary Pars Intermedia Dysfunction (PPID), which is described separately.

A dynamic test for IR involves placement of an intravenous catheter to permit multiple blood draws. This more time-consuming and expensive test is sometimes called a combined glucose-insulin test (CGIT). It may be combined with an oral sugar challenge, in which the horse is fed a known quantity of sugar. An IR horse will release much more insulin than a normal horse after ingesting sugar.

A less expensive solution is simply to use only the oral sugar challenge test. Here the owner administers a small dose of sugar in the form of light (not lite) corn syrup. A typical dose is 0.15 ml of corn syrup per kilogram of the horse's weight, which translates to 70 ml of light corn syrup for a 1,000 pound horse. (The Ultimate Chart converts your horse's weight from pounds to kilograms.) For a reliable oral sugar test, the horse must fast overnight, be kept calm, given the sugar challenge, and then given a blood draw one hour after the syrup is administered.

Feeding an IR Horse

Management of IR is aimed at improving insulin sensitivity through diet and exercise. Insulin promotes weight gain. Most IR horses are overweight, but there are some at healthy weights, and even animals that are too thin.

All IR horses need forage that is low in non-structural carbohydrates (NSC). A hay at 10 percent NSC is best, but hard to find. Hays above 16 percent are unacceptable for IR horses. Soaking, discussed in Chapter 4, reduces the NSC content of hay.

ABOVE: **Muzzles reduce the horse's ability to gorge on pasture, but sugar-sensitive horses can still acquire too much grass while wearing a muzzle.**

IR horses with pasture access must be monitored very carefully. Be aware of the stress conditions—drought, freezing, and poor soil—that cause forage to store NSC. Cool season grasses can store extraordinary amounts of fructan. Warm season grasses store starch. Hours of sunlight stimulate forage plants to create sugar and starch. Some owners allow IR horses on pasture only at night. If daytime turnout is allowed, consider muzzling the horse, or allow only limited time on shaded pastures because shaded grasses create less sugar and starch than grasses exposed to full sun.

Because horses with insulin resistance are more sensitive to sugar loads, they can be adversely affected by fruits, berries, and nuts, including acorns. Make sure the animal does not have access to them.

Do not give an IR horse sweet feeds, fruit treats, starchy foods, or grain. Many commercial horse feeds and treats are too sweet for these horses. The section on the glycemic index in Chapter 2 further explains feeds that produce low and slow glycemic responses. For the underweight horse, calories can be added via oil on soy hulls, beet pulp, or hay pellets.

If your IR horse is overweight, which is typical, turn this unhealthy trend around. Document weekly progress by measuring the umbilicus girth and neck crest measurements as discussed in the section on Overweight Horses. Try simple maintenance rations before resorting to a diet, and give the horse time to find its leaner weight without cheating the regimen by sneaking in treats and added grazing time.

Hay that is known to be low in non-structural carbohydrates remains the cornerstone of feeding an IR horse at any weight. Frequent, small meals help to lower the body's natural glycemic response.

Improving Insulin Resistance through Exercise

Many IR horses are idle and have been that way for some time. Turnout alone is insufficient exercise. Horses must receive at least light exercise and preferably moderate exercise in order to provoke the biochemical changes needed to improve the horse's sensitivity to insulin.

Initially, the exercise maybe as little as sustained walking in hand rather than under saddle, but exercise tolerance will improve with regular work. Horses with athletic lives are rarely IR. Healthy diet and exercise prevent and combat IR.

Medical Intervention for an IR Horse

A minority of cases do not respond to diet and exercise management. Your veterinarians may administer medications such as levothyroxine sodium (Thyro-L®) or metformin (Glucophage®).

Supplementing with cinnamon, chromium, and magnesium have all been suggested for managing IR horses, but there are no scientifically established levels for the minerals above the standard recommendations, or for cinnamon at all.

Home glucometers for monitoring a person's blood glucose level have been used to check horses. One study showed that these devices do not correlate as well in horses as they do in people. Blood glucose levels obtained by checking a horse on the home glucometer are a guideline, not definitive.

Caretaker compliance is an enormous factor in the success or failure of managing an IR horse. Sometimes owners think a horse is unresponsive to careful diet and exercise efforts and may indeed tell the veterinarian that diet and exercise are not effecting the needed changes, but in reality the owner is not truly following the management plan. A few commericial treats are slipped in here, a couple of carrots and apples there. Hand walking was skipped because of rain, or the person was busy. The one-mile walk was actually a quarter-mile. Make a concerted effort at the diet and exercise plan in order to safeguard your horse's health and give him the best chance to normalize his insulin regulation and sensitivity.

Special Diets—Medical Problems with Nutritional Implications: Neuromuscular Problems: Equine Motor Neuron Disease, Shivers, and Stringhalt

Neuromuscular disorders of various types have been identified in horses, with some common elements and some factors being as yet less well understood. Equine motor neuron disease, shivers, and stringhalt are the most commonly encountered neuromuscular disorders.

Equine Motor Neuron Disease (EMND)

Equine motor neuron disease (EMND), also known as equine degenerative myeloencephalopathy (EDM), is a progressive, degenerative disease that affects the communication of the nerves and muscles. A less severe form of EMND is called neuroaxonal dystrophy (NAD).

EMND horses appear weak and have a short stride. They may elevate their tails and sometimes seem better when moving than they do while standing still. The horses are poorly coordinated (ataxic) when moving and may stand oddly, with very wide or narrow stances. Prior to the onset of symptoms, the horse may lose weight, yet have an increased appetite and be eating very well.

The age of onset is usually between birth and three years. There does not seem to be a gender prevalence in EMND. Although it has been reported in many breeds, American Quarter Horses have a higher incidence of EMND. In the United States, more cases are reported in the Northeastern states.

In a research setting, broodmares in late gestation deprived of vitamin E produced foals with EMND. However, while EMND is most prevalent among horses with that deficiency (for example, those without access to fresh pasture), EMND has occurred in horses that do have good grazing access. Although deterioration may be slowed with vitamin E supplementation, nerve damage that has already occurred is irreversible.

Your veterinarian will want to rule out West Nile virus, equine protozoal myelitis (EPM) or other infections, as well as other neurological problems, such as wobbler syndrome, prior to diagnosing EMND.

Shivers

Shivers is a complex neuromuscular disorder that causes the horse to quiver. The hind limbs are particularly affected. Horses also over-flex their joints and hesitate while walking, sometimes slamming their hooves onto the ground when they move forward. Turning and especially backing, is hard for a horse with shivers.

The problem can affect any breed, although it is predominately found in draft breeds. Up to a third of Belgians exhibit shivers.

Stringhalt

Stringhalt is unmistakable: the horse snaps one hind leg up to its belly while walking and is sometimes unable to continue forward while it stands on three legs with one hind leg contracted abnormally. For unknown reasons, the digital extensor muscles of the hind limb are over-contracting. Stringhalt is not fully understood, but fungal and plant toxins may be a cause, notably false dandelion (hypochaeris radicata).

Some horses with stringhalt continue to deteriorate and others go into lasting remission. Turnout on safe pasture with minimal negative stress can be helpful.

Nutritional Support for Neuromuscular Disorders

It has been theorized that these horses were damaged in utero when their dams were undersupplied with vitamin E or that the horses were deficient in vitamin E as growing youngsters. While magnesium and other supplements have been suggested, vitamin E supplementation is always recommended for these disorders, and it is found naturally on pasture. Confinement and stress exacerbate symptoms of neuromuscular disorders. These horses may still have relatively useful working lives when managed carefully.

Special Diets—Medical Problems with Nutritional Implications: Pituitary Pars Intermedia Dysfunction (PPID)

Pituitary pars intermedia dysfunction (PPID), formerly called equine Cushing's disease (ECD), is the most common endocrine disorder in senior horses. It is classically characterized by a long, hairy coat with delayed shedding (together called hirsutism or hypertrichosis). This distinctive coat is a pathognomonic sign, meaning that no other condition commonly causes it, and 90 percent of the horses with a coat in this condition have PPID. The most dangerous result of this disease is laminitis. Nutritional management is a primary factor in caring for a PPID horse.

Understanding PPID

The disease was named for its discoverer, Harvey Cushing, who identified it in humans in the early 1900s. The problem lies with the pituitary gland, which is located in the base of the brain under an area called the hypothalamus. In horses, the problem resides in the center section of the pituitary gland, which is called the pars intermedia. (This differs from Cushing's Disease in humans, where the problem arises from degeneration of neurons from the hypothalamus that enervate the anterior part of the pituitary gland.)

The dysfunction in horses is with inhibitory neurons from the hypothalamus that enervate the pars intermedia. Those neurons fail to do their job of regulating the pituitary gland, which then grows too large, a condition called hyperplasia. The disorder has been called many other names, including pituitary adenoma, indicating enlargement of the pituitary gland. This is not a cancerous growth or tumor.

The PPID horse has hormones out of balance. (The hyperplasic pituitary pars intermedia becomes overactive and releases excess amounts of chemicals, chiefly proopiomelanocortin (POMC), which then create an excess presence of hormones, notably adrenocorticotropic hormone (ACTH). Excess ACTH causes the adrenal glands, which are located above the kidneys, to release excess hormones, including cortisol. Cortisol is the hormone sometimes referred to as the stress hormone.)

The cause of muscle wasting and poor condition in PPID horses is not fully understood. One study found that older mares with a subclinical presentation of PPID had lower vitamin C concentrations in their blood. Another study found degraded small intestinal mucosa in PPID horses when compared to horses of similar age without PPID (but a related study indicated that the nutrient assimilation problem was not due to transporter proteins).

Evaluating a Horse for PPID: Signs and Concurring Conditions

In addition to the classic PPID sign of a horse bearing a long, hairy coat with delayed shedding, early signs of the disease include: docility; diminished performance; regional fat deposits—often in a cresty neck or in supraorbital (above the eye) fat pads—and the dreaded laminitis. More advanced signs include: general muscle atrophy; poor wound healing or recurrent infections; diaphoresis or hyperhidrosis (excess sweating), or anhidrosis (absence of sweating); polydipsia (frequent or excessive drinking) and polyuria (frequent urination); hyperglycemia (high blood sugar); infertility or, in mares, difficulty maintaining a pregnancy resulting in spontaneous abortion; and again, laminitis. PPID horses might exhibit neurological symptoms, such as ataxia (uncoordinated movement) or seizures, and they tend to have high fecal egg count (FEC) test results.

The disease is usually seen in horses aged fifteen years or more, although it has been documented in younger animals. One study suggested PPID testing middle-aged horses with growth rings in their hooves, because hormonal disturbances may affect hoof growth.

PPID horses often develop insulin resistance (IR). IR horses frequently progress to equine metabolic syndrome (EMS), and EMS horses can become PPID horses.

PPID horses cannot be cured. There is no method to reduce the size of the enlarged part of the gland via surgery, medicine, or other procedures. Even the definitive diagnosis of the disorder has no direct test.

Who Gets Pituitary Pars Intermedia Dysfunction?

Morgans and many pony breeds are overrepresented in the PPID population. A senior Morgan horse or senior pony may be at an especially increased risk for PPID. If you have a middle-aged Morgan or pony, be alert to early detection of initial signs of PPID.

Testing

Testing, using indirect methods, has implications for early detection. Prior to the appearance of the classic shaggy coat, older horses with laminitis for no obvious reason, or displaying the demeanor change of a PPID horse should be tested.

There are numerous indirect tests for PPID, but veterinarians have commonly used either the adrenocorticotropin (ACTH) test and or the overnight dexamethasone suppression test (ODST). More recently, recommendations for *early detection* suggest a thyrotropin-releasing hormone (TRH) stimulation test. However, these tests can give false positives between late July and November in the Northern Hemisphere, because during the autumnal reduced daylight, the horse's body normally elevates chemicals and hormones to prepare for winter; these elevations can skew results of tests intended to determine if a horse has PPID. In the Southern Hemisphere, false positives are likely from late January through May.

Many PPID horses are also insulin resistant (IR), which is determined by tests described earlier in this chapter.

Testing centers on various hormone levels. Stress can significantly elevate a horse's hormones. Horses experiencing pain or stress can have unreliable blood tests, especially tests for hormone levels. A horse should be caught and haltered in a calm manner, without being upset by a disruption of its usual routine, including the location of its usual stablemates.

TRH Stimulation Test

Thyrotropin-releasing hormone (TRH) causes the pituitary gland to release adrenocorticotropic hormone. In the TRH test, a baseline blood sample is drawn, then the horse is given a dose of TRH intravenously, and a second blood sample is drawn ten minutes after the TRH injection. A PPID horse will have a higher resting ACTH and will release more ACTH in response to the TRH injection.

ACTH Test

In the ACTH test, a blood sample is drawn and submitted to a laboratory for analysis of the horse's resting level of adrenocorticotropic hormone. Difficulties with this test include making the mistake of drawing the blood sample in the usual glass tube rather than the required plastic tube, and the need to ice the blood sample continuously enroute delivery to the lab. However, the ACTH test only requires one veterinary visit, one blood sample, and no injections of other drugs or administration of sugar, as would be needed to assess the horse's insulin status.

The Overnight Dexamethasone Suppression Test (ODST)

A dexamethasone suppression test involves giving a horse dexamethasone, and then testing the horse's blood level of cortisol seventeen hours. The dose of dexamethasone mimics effects of cortisol release. A healthy horse given this dexamethasone dose will automatically compensate by decreasing its release of cortisol, essentially suppressing the dexamethasone. The endocrine system in a PPID horse will fail to properly respond to the challenge of the dexamethasone dose and continue to release cortisol. The blood sample is drawn so many hours after the dexamethasone administration in order to give the horse's body time to react to the dexamethasone.

Nutritional Guidelines and Management for PPID

General management is centered on maintaining a healthy weight. If needed, energy can be added to the diet through palatable, high quality forage, with additional calories supplied as required via oils, seed meals, or commercial senior feeds. Increase calories through added fat, not extra carbohydrates. If your PPID horse is also IR, follow the IR feeding guidelines as well.

PPID horses merit early attention to even minor injuries, because they have poor wound healing. For the same reason, dental checks are particularly important. An oral infection or problem could become a much more serious.

Maintain muscle tone through exercise. Clip the coat when it is over-insulating the horse. This will help alleviate the sweating (hyperhidrosis) and prevent hyperthermai (overheating).

Close parasite control monitoring—more frequent FEC tests—and anthelmintic administration will help these infection susceptible horses cope with worms.

Veterinarians can get a special use permit in order to obtain pergolide mesylate (more simply called pergolide) for PPID treatment and may use additional drugs, such as cyproheptadine, bromocriptine, and trilostane. Pergolide treatment can cost one thousand dollars per year and will likely continue for the rest of the horse's life.

Alternative medicine supplements in use for PPID are herbal preparations usually made from chasteberry (the berry of the plant *vitus agnus castus*). Unfortunately the alternative remedies have not been shown to help. A study by a manufacturer of a popular PPID remedy observed more than one hundred PPID horses for a year. Over eighty of the horses died, and several had to be placed on pergolide during the study.

A well-respected group of veterinarians came together as the Endocrine Study Group to examine the evidence and offer the best treatment protocol. Their recommendation is for owners to allocate their financial resources to treatments that are known to help. A PPID horse can do well with good nutrition and careful management that includes evidence based veterinary treatment.

Special Diets—Medical Problems with Nutritional Implications: Renal Impairment or Disease

Acute renal failure can be triggered by poison or rhabdomyolysis but chronic kidney disease (CKD) is fairly uncommon in horses. Extreme overconsumption of salt blocks can cause it. When kidney function declines, it tends to be a progressive disease, so an awareness of the problem helps ensure early intervention, which can slow the disease's progress.

SIGNS OF RENAL PROBLEMS

Horses with kidney impairment may seem to have difficulty in urinating, may urinate more frequently than healthy horses, may dribble while urinating, and may have discolored, thick, or cloudy urine. They may become inappetant and lose condition.

Being aware of the horse's usual pattern of behavior as it urinates is required before change can reasonably be noticed. It is normal for horses to initially urinate with significant force then spurt and dribble to some extent.

Laboratory analysis is critical in detecting kidney impairment. This includes not only chemical analysis of the blood and urine, but microscopic inspection of any crystals or sediment found in the urine to determine the exact content, which can be indicative of the nature of the problem. It is possible to free-catch urine for inspection in a clean, plastic gallon jug in which the upper quarter—on the side away from the handle—has been cut away. Be sure to catch urine all the way to the end of the horse's effort. Sediment and calculi (stones) are more often expressed toward the end of urination, so catching only the initial urine could miss important findings.

Nutrition for the Horse with Kidney Problems

Whether the problem stems from acute or chronic renal failure, horses with impaired kidney function should receive diets low in protein (less than 8 to 10 percent), calcium, and phosphorus. Pasture is the first and best option. Fresh grass is so much better a diet for a horse with renal compromise that some owners without good pasture cut swaths of long, fresh grass and bring it to the horse.

After pasture, grass hay is the next best option. Alfalfa hay is a poor choice due to the higher general mineral content of legumes, specifically the calcium level. The protein in alfalfa also places too large a burden on unhealthy kidneys. However, for the inappetant horse with kidney problems, very small amounts of alfalfa can be added to the grass hay to encourage intake. Keeping the weight up on these horses is the first goal.

Remember that beet pulp, and to a lesser extent wheat bran, are high in calcium, so do not feed significant quantities to horses with renal impairment.

SUPPLEMENTATION

Because it is important to avoid excess minerals, be cautious about feeding general vitamin and mineral supplements. Remember that many complete feeds and other fortified grain products have added calcium and salt, which is an unnecessary burden to the horse with kidney problems.

Urolithiasis (stones in the urine, formed in the bladder from sediment or crystals) can be a recurring problem in horses with compromised kidneys. Your vet may recommend anionic salts, which were developed to combat milk fever in cattle. Anionic salts are available in pelleted form. They acidify the urine, which helps prevent crystals from accumulating within the bladder or ureters. However, the body tends to adjust, so acidifying the urine may only help for a few months.

WATER

This horse merits extraordinary attention to its water to ensure the greatest intake possible. If it likes clean water, scrub the bucket or trough daily. If the weather is cold and the horse likes warmer water, use a bucket heater at the first sign of cold weather, and leave the warmer on all day, not just overnight. If your horse likes cold water in hot weather, shade and insulate the trough. If it dislikes hard ground near the trough, place stall mats around the trough. Some horses drink more with the addition of flavorings, so try adding apple juice and similar to enticements. Take whatever measure is required to ensure the horse drinks well.

Special Diets—Medical Problems with Nutritional Implications: Respiratory Disorders

Recurrent Airway Obstruction (RAO), Inflammatory Airway Disease (IAD), and Summer Pasture-Associated Obstructive Pulmonary Disease (SPAOPD)

Respiratory problems can often be improved or worsened by particular feeding practices. Horses with respiratory distress may have a respiratory rate higher than a relaxed, healthy horse's rate of six to twelve breaths per minute, may have flared nostrils and an elevated pulse, and are usually exercise-intolerant or have reduced performance due to their labored breathing. They may also exhibit a heave line in their lower lateral abdomen, which is evidence of abdominal muscles being engaged to assist in breathing, especially in exhaling.

Note that this discussion is not investigating airway problems stemming from infections of a bacteriological, viral, or other nature. Infectious agents should first be ruled out in any horse with respiratory problems. A fever, cough, or nasal discharge can indicate infection and the need for veterinary attention.

RAO, IAD, and SPAOPD are the primary classes of respiratory problems with nutritional implications. Failure to relieve the horse's symptoms can result in permanent lung damage, so be attentive to the appropriate nutrition and other management practices that help alleviate respiratory problems. These horses often benefit from a veterinarian's bronchodilators and anti-inflammatory drugs. However, medical treatment will fall short when the owner does not attend to feeding and housing concerns that help alleviate respiratory problems.

Recurrent Airway Obstruction (RAO)

Recurrent Airway Obstruction (RAO) is also called Chronic Obstructive Pulmonary Dsease (COPD), or heaves. An older lay term for the disorder was to say the horse had broken wind. (The term COPD is less often used now, because COPD in horses is so distinct from the human COPD conditions of emphysema and chronic bronchitis, which generally come from prolonged tobacco smoking.) In equine emphysema, alveoli (terminal air sacs in the lungs where gas exchange with the capillaries occurs) become overinflated and collapse, trapping air in the lower lungs as the horse exhales.

RAO is also associated with bronchitis (inflammation of the mainstem bronchii, that branch from the trachea to bronchioles, which then branch down into smaller and smaller airways in the lungs) and bronchiolitis (inflammation of the bronchioles).

About 12 percent of RAO horses develop emphysema from chronic hyperinflation of their alveoli and changes in the levels of two enzymes (protease and antiprotease) that affect the lining in the lungs.

An RAO horse can have labored breathing even when at rest. Environmental irritants are a primary factor in RAO, and it is fairly common in older horses, with a usual onset at age nine. The primary feeding guideline for horses with these respiratory challenges is to reduce their exposure to dry, dusty feeds and environments to every extent possible. Horses feeding on pasture have less RAO than do horses eating hay, which is likely due to both the feed and the housing.

With the goal of reducing dust to relieve irritation in the horse's airways, hay should be thoroughly soaked. Note that this is not the long-soak method used to reduce the quantity of water soluble carbohydrates in the forage, but just a thorough submerging for about ten minutes to rinse, and weight surface dust and very fine vegetative matter so that these particles are not inhaled.

Round bales should not be offered in a pasture as supplementary roughage, because they can gather excessive dust and mold. Instead, offer soaked hay in slow feeders. Ensure that the wet hay is changed often enough that it does not begin to mold.

ABOVE: **A brief but thorough soak reduces the hay's dust and particles that can irritate the respiratory tract. Longer soaks reduce the water soluble carbohydrates, which gives safer hay to sugar-sensitive horses.**

Horses with severe RAO may not be helped enough by soaked hay, thus may have to be maintained on soaked cubes or pellets, or commercial complete feeds to reduce dust and particle inhalation.

Being in a stall is associated with increased inflammation of both the lower and upper respiratory airways. Because RAO is worsened by dusty living conditions, these horses do best living outdoors as much as possible. If an RAO horse must be stalled, keep its diet on the low side of protein requirements, because excreted excess protein means the caustic scent of ammonia will be in the stall. Also, keep the stall as clean as possible, wiping down the walls to reduce dust and cobwebs. Similarly, these horses do better ridden in the open air, provided dusty settings are avoided. Even well-ventilated indoor arenas are often too dry and dusty for RAO horses. Feed forage at ground level.

If RAO horses must be in stalls, use minimal, dust-free, particle-free bedding (cardboard, paper, or peat moss); do not use straw. Low dust shavings that do not have small particles are acceptable. These horses should not be in stalls that are under hay lofts, and they should be out of the barn when stalls are cleaned, aisles are swept, or hay is delivered.

Inflammatory Airway Disease (IAD)

Inflammatory airway disease (IAD) is distinct from RAO in several respects. IAD horses are usually asymptomatic (without symptoms) at rest or have only subtle signs when not working. While RAO tends to affect mature horses, horses of any age can exhibit IAD.

Decreased performance, a chronic or intermittent cough, and increased mucous secretions are the three cardinal signs of IAD. Veterinarians confirm the diagnosis by analysis of the bronchoalveolar lavage fluid (BALF). A horse with lungworms (Dictyocaulus arnfieldi) can be mistaken for an IAD horse. Worm larvae can be detected in microscopic examination of tracheal fluid.

IAD horses exhibit exercise intolerance through an increased respiratory rate and exaggerated respiratory effort while working. Veterinarians may administer steroids to reduce inflammation, expectorants to help clear mucous, and bronchodilators to widen the airways, but these medical methods will likely fail if the horse is continually exposed to irritating aerosolized particles. The same precautions for dust free housing and feeding as RAO apply to IAD. In one study, the dust burden in the diet for IAD horses was reduced 97 percent by eliminating hay and using a soaked complete pellet diet.

Summer Pasture-Associated Obstructive Pulmonary Disease (SPAOPD)

Summer pasture-associated obstructive pulmonary disease (SPAOPD) is also called heaves. It is akin to asthma in people and seems to be triggered by outdoor allergens such as molds or pollen. SPAOPD is seasonal and most strongly associated with increases in temperature and humidity, occurring throughout the Southeast United States during summer.

While RAO and IAD horses tend to do best with outdoor turnout—thus avoiding the respiratory irritants that can be inhaled indoors—SPAOPD is unique in that the horse should be protected from pasture irritants. Reduce their turnout time during pollen or mold conditions that trigger their respiratory distress. It is critical that the housing for these horses be clean and as dust-free as possible, following all the recommendations for indoor housing of an RAO horse.

For a moist, dust-free forage, thoroughly soak a net of hay. Other options are to feed haylage, or hydrated hay cubes, hay pellets, and beet pulp. At each feeding, you can soak the next meal's cubes or pellets. The feeding and housing practices that improve respiratory distress in RAO, IAD, and SPAOPD horses are not curative. They must be done for the entire life of the horse, but they do make a difference in how worthwhile that life is.

Special Diets—Medical Problems with Nutritional Implications: Rhabdomyolysis and Polysaccharide Storage Myopathy (PSSM)

Rhabdomyolysis is a pathological breakdown of muscle tissue; this results in the release of myoglobin (muscle protein) into the bloodstream. The kidneys must filter out the myoglobin. The condition, also called rhabdo, is painful due to the cramping and destruction in the muscles. It can be fatal due to the toxic load of myoglobin in the circulatory system. Proper management of the horse's nutrition and exercise is the key to avoiding rhabdomyolysis.

The condition has previously been called azoturia for the excess nitrogen compounds in the urine, due to protein breakdown. Other older terms for the disorder are tying-up or "Monday morning sickness," so-called because many pleasure horses were typically idle all week and then ridden hard on the weekend.

Rhabdomyolysis can also be triggered by the underlying condition of polysaccharide storage myopathy (PSSM), a genetic disorder in which the horse uses certain sugars abnormally. It is quite likely that before the condition of PSSM was identified, many of the horses exhibiting Monday morning sickness were PSSM horses that could have been helped with the specific PSSM diet.

Equine rhabdomyolysis syndrome (ERS) is the term for a horse without PSSM that has repeated bouts of rhabdomyolysis. When the onset is always precipitated by exercise, the disorder has also been termed exertional myopathy, recurrent exertional rhabdomyolysis (RER), or equine exertional rhabdomyolysis (EER).

About 5 percent of Thoroughbreds are predisposed to rhabdomyolysis, although the disorder occurs in most breeds. Within the racing industries, Thoroughbreds and Standardbreds with RER have been shown to utilize calcium in the muscle cells abnormally.

Signs of Rhabdomyolysis

Pain, sweating, reluctance to move, and muscle fasciculation (twitching), especially of the large hip muscles, are classic signs of rhabdomyolysis. The muscles may be swollen or hardened as well.

Dark-colored urine is a warning sign that the kidneys are processing myoglobin out of the blood.

Prevention and Treatment of Rhabdomyolysis

Overworking a horse, especially an unfit horse or one that has not been exercised in some time, presents a risk for rhabdomyolysis. Exceptionally hot and humid weather further increases the risk.

Stress may play a role in precipitating a bout of rhabdomyolysis. Be mindful of extended anxiety in horses that have shown themselves to be prone to rhabdomyolysis. If the horse is particularly reactive, take care to limit or incrementally build up to circumstances that challenge the animal's security.

Feed a high forage diet of grass hay instead of alfalfa Use low starch, low non-structural carbohydrate options, such as soy hulls or beet pulp, when supplementing. Avoid grain, especially prior to exercise. Provide a full supply of vitamins and minerals. These horses do best with turnout.

Protect the horse from the elements during an episode of rhabdomyolysis. Provide shade on hot and sunny days. In inclement weather, blanket the horse. When riding in cold or wet conditions, use a quarter blanket to keep the hip muscles warm. Offer plenty of water and hay. Do not wait to summon a veterinarian. Intravenous fluids may well be required to correct dehydration and relieve the kidneys of the burden of clearing myoglobin from the bloodstream.

If your horse has had a true episode of rhabdomyolysis, be forever cautious in feeding and exercising. Take care not to overexcite, overfeed, or overwork this horse.

Microscopic examination of the muscle cells of RER horses reveals changes in the location of the cells' nuclei when compared to normal muscle cells. In the racing industries, RER is exhibited strongly along genetic lines, more prevalent among younger horses, and somewhat more prevalent among females. RER appears more commonly in exercise situations that increase the horse's mental stimulation or anxiety. An example is a horse that anticipates its exercise while a string of horses is worked ahead of him. Exercise the RER horse first, so that it does not become agitated while waiting for his turn.

Polysaccharide Storage Myopathy (PSSM)

Polysaccharide storage myopathy (PSSM, also called equine polysaccharide storage myopathy or EPSM) is an inherited disorder that triggers rhabdomyolysis. The muscles are glycogen-overloaded because the horse cannot break it down. PSSM occurs most frequently in Belgian draft horses, American Quarter Horses, and breeds with strong Quarter Horse influence, such as Paints and Appaloosas, but is seen in many other breeds.

There are two sub-types of PSSM in adult horses, type I and type II. Type I can be diagnosed with a genetic test done on hair follicles. Testing for type II PSSM is done via muscle biopsy.

The biochemical process by which the Belgian and American Quarter Horse breeds have the disorder may differ. American Quarter Horses with PSSM have excessive uptake of glycogen into their muscle cells or a decreased use of glycogen. Belgians with PSSM synthesize excess glycogen. Unlike Belgians with PSSM, American Quarter Horses with PSSM seem to have a marked sensitivity to insulin, which in turn affects glucose use in the muscle cells.

Not only is PSSM a genetic disorder, it is a dominant trait. Horses with PSSM should not be bred. However, horses with PSSM can have useful working lives if their owners are attentive to managing diet and exercise but should not be bred.

SIGNS OF PSSM

Muscle atrophy and an irregular gait are possible indications. While the etiology (cause) is different from non-PSSM horses with rhabdomyolysis, the same signs appear: sweating, muscle fasciculation (twitching), cramping (especially of the large muscle groups of hindquarters and shoulders), and a reluctance to move.

Exercise intolerance in a PSSM horse is remarkable. As little as ten minutes of walking may induce rhabdomyolysis in a PSSM horse. Reintroducing exercise to these horses after an episode of rhabdomyolysis should be kept to five minutes or less. This is not a casual estimate, as exceeding the amount by only a few minutes will increase the risk for another episode. Remember that rhabdomyolysis can permanently damage the kidneys, leading to renal failure (a condition discussed separately).

Once a PSSM horse tolerates five minutes of exercise on a daily basis, you can slowly increase the amount of time under saddle. Regular, daily exercise is one of the keys to preventing rhabdomyolysis in a PSSM horse. Make exercise a daily routine. If your horse has been given weeks off, start again with five-minute sessions.

Dietary management helps control PSSM. Any amount of sugar, starch or other non-structural carbohydrate dramatically increases the risk of rhabdomyolysis. Feed hay that has less than 10 percent NSC, and use fat, not grain, if the diet requires energy supplementation. Limit the starch and simple sugars, including lush pasture. Make sure the horse is receiving a healthy supply of vitamins and minerals.

When their owners follow these diet and exercise precautions, PSSM horses can have useful working lives.

Special Diets—Medical Problems with Nutritional Implications: Ulcers: Equine Gastric Ulcer Syndrome (EGUS), Equine Gastroduodenal Ulcer Disease (EGUD), and Right Dorsal Colitis (RDC)

A stomach ulcer is a lesion, sore, or erosion in the gastric mucosa (lining). Ulcers of the foregut, primarily in the stomach but also in the duodenum, can only be definitively diagnosed by a veterinary procedure called endoscopy: a small camera is passed through the esophagus and into the stomach to permit the veterinarian to visually inspect the stomach lining and evaluate the severity of the ulcers.

The ulcer scoring system begins with grade 0 signifying no ulcers at all, grades 1, 2, and 3 showing increasing number and severity of lesions, and grade 4, the worst, with extensive, deep ulceration of the gastric mucosa. Prior to endoscopy, the horse must be fasted for about six hours. Many horses are treated presumptively for ulcers, meaning that the diagnosis of ulcers was presumed but not verified by endoscopy. Remeber, fasting is stress-inducing and irritates the stomach.

Ulcers also occur in the hindgut, usually in the colon and called colonic ulcers and may be caused by worms. The right dorsal colon (RDC) is a likely site. However, when the disorder of equine gastric ulcer syndrome (EGUS) is discussed, these are foregut ulcers, in the stomach. Equine gastroduodenal ulcer disease (EGUD), sometimes called gastroduodenal ulcer disease (GDUD), refers to ulcers at the lower stomach where it empties into the duodenum.

Signs of Ulcers

Grinding the teeth, known as bruxism, is the classic sign of EGUS. Additional signs include: being girthy or cinchy (when a horse objects to the girth or cinch being tightened); recurrent colic; pawing or kicking, especially kicking at its own abdomen; poor body condition; a poor or variable appetite; diarrhea; and excessive salivary flow (ptyalism). In foals, dorsal recumbancy, when a foal lies on its back, is a cardinal sign.

Colic signs may indicate right dorsal colitis (also referred to as RDC).

Causes of Ulcers

Ulcers have numerous, often overlapping, causes. Bacterial contamination and duodenal reflux carrying bile salts are endogenous causes. A virus called rotovirus is thought to play a part in EGUD in foals. Reactive, high stress horses may have a higher incidence of ulcers. Diet, exercise, and other stressors are management causes. Not surprisingly, the risk factors tend to run counter to the safest and most natural horse management practices, while the prevention measures are concurrent with basic good equine management standards.

Strenuous exercise is linked to ulcers. Race training is the exercise most frequently linked to ulcers, although it is difficult to separate the exercise as a cause of ulcers from the confinement and high starch diets racehorses receive. The gastric compression in strenuous exercise (from the horse's abdominal muscles, as well as from the girth) could be a factor in the prevalence of ulcers in horses undergoing very hard work.

A horse secretes gastric acids constantly, rather than just as needed. The acid-buffering function of saliva, and the fact that concentrates require half the chewing of forage—thus the horse

Table 9–8 Equine Ulcers: Risk Factors and Prevention	
Risk Factor	**Prevention**
confinement	turnout
fasting	free choice forage
large starch meals	little or no starch
NSAID use	limit NSAID use
high stress	limit stress
strenuous exercise	careful management of athletes

produces half the saliva when fed a high concentrate diet—mean that concentrates, especially a diet high in concentrates, bring a risk of gastric ulceration.

Finally, frequent use of non-steroidal, anti-inflammatory drugs (NSAIDs), such as aspirin, phenylbutazone (commonly called bute), flunixin meglamine (Banamine), and firocoxib (brand names are Equioxx and Previcox) has been shown to increase a horse's risk of ulcers.

Prevention and Management of Ulcers

Prevention and management of EGUS and the associated conditions of EGUD and RDC is a long term effort. A feeding program combined with management centered on reducing stress to the horse is essential. Free choice forage with turnout and limited starch remain the hallmarks of a healthy equine diet.

Guidelines suggest limiting meal size in the immediate hours prior to hard exercise and not giving any concentrates for two hours immediately after hard exercise.

Two studies with different hay diets, one using alfalfa versus brome and the other using alfalfa versus Bermuda, both found less ulceration in horses on the alfalfa diet. This result was attributed to alfalfa's high calcium working as an acid bufferer, and to the higher protein content of the alfalfa. Given the choice between a higher or lower protein grass hay, a horse being managed for ulcers would likely do better on the higher protein grass hay.

The addition of omega-3 oils—prevalent in soy, safflower, canola, and especially flax oil—may be beneficial by inhibiting enzyme activity, thereby decreasing inflammation in the gut. Additionally, constant access to water is a must.

Straw bedding has also been linked to the prevalence of ulcers in horses that consume the straw. This may be attributed to its dry, coarse fiber causing mechanical injury to the gastric mucosa, as well as the low protein and low calcium content of straw.

A retrospective study correlated EGUS with the presence of enteroliths and enterolithiasis. However, it did not determine whether ulcers or enteroliths came first and could not say that one provoked the other.

The therapeutic modality of electrolyte pastes also comes with cautions. Hypertonic electrolyte pastes commonly administered to horses in very hard work have been implicated in an increased incidence of ulcers. Consider decreasing the dose while increasing the frequency. Alternatively, give electrolytes by adding salt to water that hydrates pelleted feed, then feeding the salt-hydrated pellets to the horse instead of using the hypertonic pastes.

Gastrointestinal-protectant drugs, such as ranitidine, cimetidine, misoprostol, omeprazole, and sucralfate are sometimes administered along with NSAIDs.

Psyllium, in the form of psyllium hydrophilic mucilloid (Metamucil) or psyllium mucilloid (Equisyl Advantage), may help reduce the time ingested food remains in the gut; an improved transit time helps maintain a healthy pH, especially in RDC. Transit time, pH, and pressures within the gastrointestinal tract can be measured with a SmartPill, described in Chapter 2.

Antacids such as calcium carbonate, sodium bicarbonate, aluminum hydroxide, or magnesium hydroxide (Neigh-Lox is one proprietary equine antacid) have been used, but these short lived remedies may last just a few hours.

Colitis may be helped with the administration of di-tri-octahedral smectite (DTO smectite), a natural hydrated aluminomagnesium silicate that absorbs toxins produced by bacteria such as Clostridium perfringens (C. perfringens) and Clostridium difficile (C. Difficile).

Veterinarians may prescribe any of an array of drugs to protect the horse's stomach and let the ulcers heal. These drug classes and examples are: a proton-pump inhibitor (such as esomeprazole, lansoprazole, omeprazole, pantoprazole, or rabeprazole); a histamine antagonist (such as cimetidine, famotidine, nizatidine, or ranitidine); a coating agent (such as bismuth subsalicylate or sucralfate); a muscarine-receptor agonist (bethanechol) to increase gastric emptying; a prostaglandin analog (such as misoprostol, commonly called by the trade name Cytotec); or Pronutrin, a proprietary, pectin-lecithin complex; and finally, antibiotics (such as trimethoprim, sulfadimidine, or metronidazole) for ulcers suspected to have arisen from bacterial excesses of E. coli, helicobacter, or streptococcus.

Seabuckthorn berry and cranberry have been suggested as alternative supplements for EGUS, although no well-designed, published studies indicate these alternatives are effective therapeutic remedies.

Good, evidence-based ulcer medication is expensive. It may be that some ulcer cases are not resolved merely because the horse does not receive a large enough dose for a long enough time period.

Rather than having to turn to medical intervention, it is best to feed and manage the horse in a manner likely to prevent ulcers. A horse that is unduly stressed by travel or showing might simply be unsuited for a competition life.

CHAPTER 10
Assessing the Individual Horse: Weight, Body Condition, Workload, and Nutritional Needs

WHEN WE BRING horses into our lives, we alter their lives. Through selective breeding and exercise, horses' bodies are altered. The welfare of horses and their nutritional needs are a human responsibility. To feed a horse appropriately, we need to know how much of what type of feed to provide. Accepted scientific systems for identifying the horse's nutritional needs are discussed below.

Because feed is apportioned according to the weight and needs, you must accurately assess your horse's weight, body condition, and workload before selecting the ration. Ongoing monitoring involves regularly reassessing the horse's weight, body condition, and workload, then reevaluating the type and amount of feed provided. It's helpful to document these factors, including the associated nutritional parameters of dental care and parasite control measures.

Systems for Determining the Nutrient Needs of Horses

Established systems to determine the nutrient needs for horses are: the United States's National Research Council (NRC) system, the German system (GEH, which translates as Society for Nutrition Physiology for Pets), the French system (INRA, which translates as the National Institute for Agricultural Research), the Dutch system (CVB, which translates as the Central Bureau of Livestock Feeding), and the developing Scandinavian system (SCAN).

The German and Dutch systems account for the weight of the rider and tack, and also factor in exercise speed and duration. Both the NRC system and the German system classify workload as light, moderate, heavy, or very heavy. The NRC system, which is used in the UK as well, applies a percentage increase over maintenance metabolism, ranging between 1 and 1.9 times maintenance. The NRC and Dutch systems have undergone more recent revision, 2007 and 2005, respectively. The German and French systems were revised in 2014 and 2015, respectively. All systems require the user to factor in the workload. The NRC offers a free, online program for the calculation of nutrients (see the Resources section or the Ultimate Chart for the website). This program will let you check the estimated requirement of several vitamins, all macrominerals, and many trace minerals for a horse of any weight and workload.

All systems and advice are necessarily subject to interpretation and are based on averages: an average rider, an average trainer, and an average effort from an average horse. Consider your horse as an individual and make a clear-headed, ongoing assessment of effort and needs. Evaluate the effects of your nutrition and conditioning program by regularly assessing changes in weight, body condition score, fitness, demeanor, and feed intake.

The Ultimate Chart to Determine Weight

The starting point for quantifying the horse's feed is an accurate weight assessment. Knowing his weight is also important for drug dosaging, including anthelmintics. Changes in weight are often an early warning sign of diminishing health. Regularly monitoring the horse's weight takes the guesswork out of weight maintenance.

When a horse has just been fed and watered, or has just urinated or defecated, its weight can be momentarily impacted by twenty pounds or more, so try to assess weight at the same time of day and under the same feeding and relief conditions.

A scale, also called a weighbridge, is the most accurate method of determining weight, but with limited access to a scale that can accommodate a horse, people have long used weight tapes.

ABOVE: **These mares have close heart girth measurements (marked in blue twine), but the buckskin weighs almost 200 pounds more than the palomino. Green dots mark the points of shoulder. The line on the palomino shows the length from point of shoulder to point of buttock.**

Weight tapes are not standardized. Two different tapes often give different weights for the same heart girth measurement. They are also inherently inaccurate, because they *only* measure the heart girth circumference. See the photo of two horses with similar heart girth measurements but significantly different weights. The taller horse is much longer and more heavily built than her smaller pasturemate. The accuracy of weight tapes is improved by using height-specific tapes, but their precision drops markedly during pregnancy and for animals at extremes of condition. The heart girth measurement is, however, useful for noticing change in a horse.

Here is a formula that factors in the horse's heart girth and body length, which is much more accurate than a weight tape.

$$\frac{HG \text{ in cm}^2 \text{ x L in cm}}{11,877} = \text{weight in kilograms then convert to pounds}$$

You don't have to do the calculations; just look up your horse's heart girth and length (in inches) on the Ultimate Chart to find his weight in pounds.

This formula was developed by C. L. Carroll and P. J. Huntington, who studied and measured numerous horses in order to validate the calculations. They also devised a body condition score with a range of 1–5, with 3 being a horse at a healthy weight, 1 being emaciated, and 5 being obese. (For adult riding horses, the formula uses the denominator 11,877. The denominator 12,265 is used for horses scored below 2.5 in body condition. The denominator for overweight horses is 11,706, and 10,080 is used for growing youngsters.)

The formula has been converted for direct use in imperial measurement [(heart girth in inches^2 x length in inches) ÷ 330.] Additional denominators for the imperial formula are: 303 for weanlings and 320 for yearlings. However, it is more accurate to use the original formula, because smaller units of measure are more accurate. There are about two and one-half centimeters in one inch. The Ultimate Chart precalculates the formula by every half inch in length and girth.

How to Measure Heart Girth and Length

Owners encounter two difficulties in measuring heart girth and length. The first is that people do not generally have a soft measuring tape of sufficient length. The second obstacle is a lack of familiarity with the anatomical landmarks. Both concerns are addressed here.

TWINE

Many people own a standard, retractable, metal tape measure, but wisely won't use it on a horse, because the startling noises made as the metal tape bends or retracts spook horses. Measure the horse with old lengths of baling twine (tie two pieces together if needed). Mark a small dot on the twine at the measuring end point. Check the marked point against the metal tape measure.

LANDMARKS FOR LENGTH

Note in photo 10–1 the colored dots on the point of shoulder and point of buttock. These landmarks stem from anatomical points on the skeleton. The point of shoulder is formed by the humeral

Table 10-1 The Henneke (et al.) Body Condition Scoring System (BCS)

Rate each of the six body areas individually, then average the six scores.

Score	Neck	Withers	Loin	Tailhead	Ribs	Shoulder
1 Poor- extremely emaciated	Bone structure easily noticeable	Bone structure easily noticeable	Spinous processes project prominently	Tailhead and hook bones project prominently	Ribs project prominently	Bone structure easily noticeable
2 Very Thin	Faintly discernible	Faintly discernible	Slight fat covering over base of spinous processes; Transverse processes of lumbar vertebrae feel rounded; spinous processes are prominent	Tailhead prominent	Ribs prominent	Faintly prominent
3 Thin	Neck accentuated	Withers accentuated	Fat buildup halfway on spinous processes, but easily discernible Transverse processes cannot be felt	Tailhead prominent, but individual vertebrae cannot be visually identified; hook bones appear rounded, but are still discernible; pin bones not distinguishable	Slight fat cover over ribs	Shoulder accentuated
4 Moderately Thin	Neck not obviously thin	Withers not obviously thin	Negative crease along back	Prominence depends on conformation; fat can be felt; hook bones not discernible	Faint outline discernible	Shoulder not obviously thin
5 Moderate	Neck blends smoothly into body	Withers rounded over spinous processes.	Back level	Fat around tailhead beginning to feel spongy	Ribs cannot be visually distinguished but easily felt	Shoulder blends smoothly into body
6 Moderately Fleshy	Fat beginning to be deposited	Fat beginning to be deposited	May have slight positive crease down back	Fat around tailhead is soft	Fat over ribs feels spongy	Fat beginning to be deposited

Score	Neck	Withers	Loin	Tailhead	Ribs	Shoulder
Table 10–1 Henneke (et al.) Body Condition Scoring System (BCS)						
Rate each of the six body areas individually, then average the six scores.						
7 Fleshy	Fat deposited along the neck	Fat deposited along the withers	May have positive crease down back	Fat around tailhead is soft	Individual ribs can be felt, but noticeable filling between ribs with fat	Fat deposited behind shoulder
8 Fat	Noticeable thickening of neck	Area along withers filled with fat	Positive crease down back	Tailhead fat very soft	Difficult to feel ribs	Area behind shoulder is filled in flush with body
	Fat deposited along inner buttocks.					
9 Extremely Fat	Bulging fat	Bulging fat	Obvious crease down back	Building fat around tailhead	Patchy fat appearing over ribs	Bulging fat
	Fat along inner buttocks may rub together. Flank filled in flush.					

head, which is the top end of the arm bone called the humerus. In humans, the humerus is the upper arm bone. In horses, the majority of the humerus is part of the shoulder.

The point of buttock is formed by the part of the pelvic bone called the ishial tuberosity (also called the tuber ischii). It is not on the side of the hip; rather it faces rearward. On the Henneke BCS, it is called a pin bone. It is easier to identify in slender horses with rangy muscles, especially when the horse's hind leg on that side is stepping well under the belly.

Notice the point of shoulder and point of buttock on a variety of horses. This practice improves your ability to quickly locate the points on fleshier horses.

LANDMARKS FOR HEART GIRTH

The heart girth is the smallest measurable circumference around the horse's ribs, back, and belly. Place the twine into the girth groove (if the horse has this indentation in its chest) and behind the withers to obtain a snug measurement. Blue baling twine is tied on the heart girths of both horses in photo 10–1.

Ultimate Chart

Using the Ultimate Chart, look up your horse's weight in pounds according to the horse's measured heart girth and length in inches, then record this weight on the form at the end of this chapter.

Because most drugs are given in the metric system, it's also good to know your horse's weight in kilograms. Find the weight in kilograms on the chart and record it on the form as well.

The Carroll and Huntington formula converted on the chart is the most widely used for ponies and light riding breeds, although other formulas exist, often utilizing different measurements and landmarks, for example, the length to point of elbow. [The Jones, et al. (1989) formula for larger horses is: (umbilical girth in cm x 1.78) x (L in cm x 1.05) divided by 3011 = body weight in kilograms.]

Most owners will be well served by the weight calculation answers supplied on the Ultimate Chart without having to use another formula. The chart also eliminates math errors and saves you from having to calculate the nutritional requirements after assessing the horse's condition and workload.

Condition: Body Scoring, Workload, Fitness, and Vital Signs

While the Carroll and Huntington weight formula is widely used, their 1–5 body condition scoring system is now less commonly used than the one developed by Henneke et al.

The Henneke Body Condition Scoring (BCS) System rates the horse's condition on a scale of 1–9. A score of 5 is ideal, with normal fat cover. Fat deposits are assessed in six areas: the tailhead, loin, ribs, neck, withers, and shoulder, then averaged to determine the final score. This is not a visual assessment, you must *feel* the six areas and distinguish between fat and muscle.

In the Henneke system, a horse scored at 4 is termed moderately thin, and a horse scored at 6 is moderately fleshy. Any score from 4 to 6 is acceptable, as it is understood that some individuals naturally run heavier or lighter. A score of 1 is severely emaciated, while 2 and 3 are both too thin. A score of 9 is grossly obese, while 7 and 8 are both overweight.

The Henneke BCS reference to "hook bones" and "pin bones" means the bony pelvic prominences called the point of hip and point of buttock, respectively. As with weight assessment, body-condition score is best assessed at the same time of day and under the same feeding, watering, and urination/defecation conditions.

An accurate assessment of body condition score can be hampered by the horse's coat length, gut fill, and muscle development, but the single biggest factor resulting in an inaccurate body condition score is unintentional bias on the part of the evaluator. The Henneke Body Condition Score has been validated and has a high level of intra-observer agreement. With practice and honesty, anyone can reliably score body condition.

After determining the BCS of your horse, record the number on the form at the end of this chapter. If the horse has a BCS lower than 4, he needs more food. If the horse has a body score above 6, he needs less. Weigh how much food he receives so that the amount can be lowered or raised as needed. If your horse is not at an ideal BCS of 5, but in the acceptable range of 4–6, be aware of his trend away from the ideal so that you can make small changes before his BCS strays farther from a 5.

As discussed in the Chapter 9 section on Overweight Horses, the body condition score is not a short term metric, but more useful over a matter of months for comparison. If you are monitoring intentional weight loss on an overweight horse, check the umbilicus girth and the center of the neck crest weekly. Owners monitoring these two weight loss parameters can record the numbers on the form at the end of this chapter.

Assessing Workload

Many riders err in assessing their horses' workloads. They tend to overestimate how far they ride and over-report the amount of time spent at a gait other than a walk. Sometimes people make this mistake because they are really reporting how much they intended to do rather than what they actually did. Sometimes they just haven't checked the numbers. Perhaps a rider goes on an hour-long trail ride and doesn't know how far she rode, but she has heard that her friend rides five, seven, or ten miles in an hour, so she guesses her mileage based on that comment, although perhaps she actually covered two to three miles. Maybe an owner doesn't check the clock and guesses the ride took two hours, but it was really an hour. The owner could be accidentally including time spent tacking up and chatting with friends at the barn.

Remember the advice in Chapter 1 that suggested to get metric, meaning to measure things. By measuring the amount of work a horse does, you enable an accurate assessment of his workload and fitness. Table 10–2 shows NRC definitions of different workloads—from light to very heavy work, by activity, duration, and the horse's pulse.

FITNESS

The term *condition* refers not just to the horse's body condition score, but also to his health and fitness. Ascertaining a horse's weight is separate from assessing his condition. A flabby 1,000-pound horse and a lean, fit 1,000-pound horse are physiologically different. Their bodies process nutrition and drugs differently, they require different feeding regimens, and they are capable of different workloads.

Fitness is a measurable dimension of condition. When noting the effort your horse makes on a ride of a set mileage or time frame, notice changes in his exertion from one week and from one month to the next. If he has to try harder for the same speed or distance, he has lost fitness. If the same ride is easier, he's gained fitness. How long did the last five miles take compared to riding the same route two weeks ago?

Note changes in your horse's body composition. After several months of careful nutritional management—and conditioning with long, steady rides, dressage, and hills—the previously flabby, unfit horse might weigh the same, but now carry more muscle and less fat. Muscle growth may be visible, as well as palpable. The improved tone of well-conditioned muscles feels harder than flaccid, little-used muscle tissue.

VITAL SIGNS

A functional nutrition program keeps a horse as healthy as possible. Part of assessing your horse's health and condition is checking his vital signs. Changes, especially negative changes, may be detected early in his general demeanor and vital signs.

Make a practice of looking at your horse's gums and noticing their normal color. Recall from Chapter 8 that numerous plant poisonings are indicated by bright-red or pale mucous membranes, best observed in the gums. Press a thumb against the gum, blanching the skin, then observe the capillary refill rate when you release the pressure. Normal capillary refill is almost instantaneous.

Observe the normal color in the white of the horse's eye as well. Liver problems and certain poisonings may be exhibited as icterus or jaundicing in the whites of the eye.

Gently grasp and release a fold of skin along the horse's neck, shoulder, and ribs; notice how quickly the skin snaps back into position in a well hydrated horse. When the horse is dehydrated, the skin will tent, and tenting will briefly remain as a pinched fold after the skin is released.

In addition to noticing these parameters on rest days, check your horse's vital signs—including his pulse—before, during, and after rides.

PULSE

Checking the pulse is a terrific way to assess how hard your horse is working. The pulse correlates to workload during an exertion effort (see Table 9–1). Does your horse have a lower heart rate after cantering this hill than he did two weeks ago? Did he recover to a calm rate under 70 beats per minute within minutes of finishing that sprint? Did his pulse come down faster than it did two months ago? After months of incremental fitness workouts, is his resting rate in the morning 36 when it used to be 40?

Any site on the horse's body where an artery's pulse can be felt is acceptable to use. Use the index, middle, or ring fingers when feeling for a pulse, not the thumb, because you may accidentally detect your pulse in your thumb.

The facial artery is a site you can easily reach with your fingertips to feel a pulse. The pulse is commonly auscultated (listened for with a stethoscope) at the apex of the heart. When the pulse is checked at the digital artery, this is to assess blood flow to the hoof, particularly when laminitis is a concern.

ABOVE: **The pulse can be checked by feeling the artery on the inner edge of the jaw.**

To check the pulse at the facial artery, feel along the large curve of the jawbone, until you find the throb of the artery that crosses just inside near the middle of the curve. With practice, your fingertips will develop a muscle memory to locate this small section of artery.

The apical (near the apex of the heart) pulse is usually checked with a stethoscope, but the concussion of the heart within the chest cavity may also be felt by placing your hand along the ribs behind the elbow on the horse's left side.

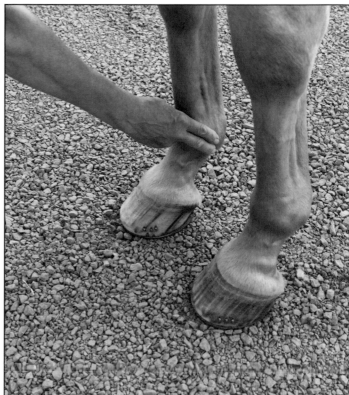

ABOVE: **The apical pulse is usually checked with a stethoscope.**

ABOVE: **A pulse check at the digital artery is usually done to assess blood flow to the hoof, rather than to find the heart rate.**

Count the number of heartbeats in a set time frame, then multiply as needed to get the number of beats per minute. For example, count the beats in fifteen seconds and multiply by four, or count the beats for thirty seconds and multiply by two. The fastest but least accurate pulse check is done by counting the pulse for six seconds, then mentally placing a zero to the right of the number counted: if twelve beats are felt, the pulse is 120; if four beats are felt, the pulse is 40. This is a handy pulse-counting method, for example, in the middle of a competition where a horse must have a pulse below 68 before a veterinary exam. Palpating the pulse for a full minute lets the pulse checker notice rhythmic variances and get the most accurate count.

As mentioned in the Chapter 2 discussion of laminitis, the digital pulse is usually checked to assess the quality of blood flow to the horse's foot. A bounding pulse is a warning sign of inflammation. A diminished digital pulse could indicate that inflammation has progressed to the point that the swelling is now reducing blood flow. Either digital pulse abnormality could come with laminitis.

Your horse's resting pulse is a key piece of health information. Always assess the resting pulse under the same quiet conditions. A pasturemate being led away, feed being distributed, or being tacked up all raise the pulse. Eating raises the pulse. Wait for your horse to be truly quiet and at rest, then calmly note his resting pulse and record it on the form at the end of this chapter.

Table 10–2 NRC Definitions of Workload and Equivalent Feed Needs			
Workload	Hours per Week	Average Pulse	Feed Needs
Idle/Maintenance	0	35–50	2% of body weight per day
Light	1–3	80	maintenance x 1.2
Pace: walk 40%, trot 50%, canter 10% Example: training, recreational riding, light showing			
Moderate	3–5	90	maintenance x 1.4
Pace: walk 30%, trot 55%, canter 10% + 5% jumping or similar effort Example: ranching, polo, school horse, frequent showing			
Heavy	4–5	110	maintenance x 1.6
Pace: walk 20%, trot 50%, canter 15% + 15% jumping or similar effort Example: ranching, polo, low-level eventing, limited-distance endurance, racing			
Very Heavy	6–12*	110–150	maintenance x 1.9
Pace: *many hours at a moderate pace or 1 hour very hard and fast Example: elite level racing, endurance, three-day eventing			

Finding Nutritional Needs with the Ultimate Chart

After assessing your horse's weight, body condition score, and workload, establish the feeding regimen Table 10–2 shows the percent increase over maintenance a horse requires for each assessed workload.

The Ultimate Chart has precalculated these percentages. Find your horse's daily forage requirement on the chart.

Carbohydrate

Remember that equine diets should be forage-based, and forage is mostly carbohydrate. The other two macronutrients that offer energy are fat and protein. All three are calculated independently.

As noted in Chapter 4, there is a starch redline (1 milligram per kilogram of bodyweight), which is the maximum amount of starch a horse may be given per meal. This formula is precalculated for different weights of horse and converted from the metric on the Ultimate Chart. Find your horse's starch redline on the chart.

Fat

Fat is an excellent way to supplement energy for a needy horse. The maximum volume of oil that a horse may be fed per day as a fat supplement is one milliliter per kilogram of bodyweight. This quantity is precalculated for different weights of horse and converted from the metric on the Ultimate Chart. It is the same number as his starch redline.

Protein

The new NRC guidelines now recommend a horse's protein requirement as a percent of the horse's weight rather than the older method of calculating a percent of the horse's diet. Recall that the essential amino acid lysine is minimal in feeds. The NRC also now recommends lysine comprise 4.3 percent of your horse's crude protein intake. Note the crude protein and lysine recommendation for your horse's weight and activity on the Ultimate Chart.

More and more, owners are feeding—in addition to free choice grass hay in slow feeders—a small amount of alfalfa in the form of pellets and providing this twice a day instead of any grain or other concentrate. The owner gets the pleasure of feeding and checking on the horse twice a day. The horse's gastrointestinal tract is not burdened with grain, and he gets adequate lysine. You can salt the water when hydrating the alfalfa pellets to ensure he receives essential minerals.

Monitoring the Individual

After finding your horse's forage requirement, starch redline, oil maximum, and the crude protein and lysine requirements on the Ultimate Chart, record these figures on the form at the end of this chapter.

Identify fitness, weight, and training goals. If your horse is maintaining good weight and condition, evaluate the feeding regimen to ensure a high forage content and adequate supply of fats, protein, vitamins, and minerals. If your horse is too thin, provide more energy in his diet through additional high quality forage and, if needed, supplementation, most likely by adding fat. If he's too heavy, match the feed and workload. Be willing to take time with small changes in feed. Make incremental, safe changes to the workload as needed. Goals for increased fitness will require increased energy in the diet.

Intrinsic factors beyond weight, condition, and workload must be considered to evaluate a horse's nutritional status. Individual animals vary in how efficiently they digest food and in how much they choose to move on their own. Busy, reactive horses do well with consistency in their feeding and exercising schedules. Handle them quietly, and be as low key as possible with regard to stressors like transportation or changes in living situations. Markedly unreactive horses that engage in little voluntary movement often make small weight gains that add up over time. In a herd situation, an individual's rank in the pecking order impacts its motion and its food intake. It is up to you to recognize individuality and work with these traits.

ABOVE: **After assessing the horse's condition and determining a complete nutritional regimen from the formulas calculated on the Ultimate Chart, record your horse's information.**

Dental health and parasite control complete the nutritional program. Monitoring all of these nutritional factors ensures that you will notice changes, not overlook other factors, and meet your goals. Recording the pertinent information is a tool. The first record establishes the individual's baseline and lets you begin to set goals. Quarterly records identify changes and highlight success.

The horse's lifelong health is best protected by science-guided decisions. Despite the wealth of recent research findings available, it can be difficult to break habits and question long standing practices. Remember that myths, misinformation, and misunderstanding cloud good thinking. Protect yourself and your horse from the trap of faulty thinking by looking for good evidence. Accurately assessing information and the individual horse enables smart choices in horse feeds, supplements, and nutrition.

Record of Horse's Condition and Nutritional Regimen

Horse's Name: _____ Date: _____

Heart Girth: _____ Length*: _____ Weight (in lbs.): _____ kg: _____ BCS: _____

Forage Requirement: _____ CP Requirement: _____ Lysine: _____

Starch Redline: _____ Oil Maximum: _____

Feeding Regimen: _____

_____

Resting pulse: _____ Current Workload: _____

Goal(s): _____

Dental

Date of Most Recent Float: _____ chewing rate: _____ comments: _____

Parasite Control

Date of Most Recent Anthelmintic: _____ product: _____ dose: _____

Date of Most Recent Fecal Egg Count: _____ result: _____

Overweight Management Measures to Check Weekly:

Neck Circumference at Midpoint: _____ Girth Circumference at the Umbilicus: _____

Other: _____

_____

* To apply the formula answers provided on the Ultimate Chart, length is measured from *point of shoulder* to *point of buttock*

Resources

Feed and Related Supplies

Tractor Supply Co. www.tractorsupply.com

Doctors Foster and Smith (800) 381–7179 www.drsfostersmith.com

Dover Saddlery (800) 406–8204 www.doversaddlery.com (sells fecal egg count test kits)

Valley Vet Supply (800) 419–9542 www.valleyvet.com (sells fecal egg count test kits)

Feed Testing Services

North America:

National Forage Testing Association:

PO Box 371115

Omaha, NB 68137

(402) 333–7485

www.foragetesting.org

www.dairylandlabs.com

www.equi-analytical.com

www.stearnsdhialab.com

Europe:

www.lab-to-field.com

www.dairyco.org.uk/technical-information/feeding/feed-analysis/

Further Education

Equine Science Society

1800 S. Oak Street

Champaign, IL 61820

www.equinescience.org

European Equine Health and Nutrition Congress

www.equine-congress.com

European Workshop on Equine Nutrition

EWEN is under the EAAP (European Federation of Animal Science, www.eeap.org) and holds a bi-annual conference in various locations with leading scientific research.

International Veterinary Information Service

www.ivis.org

www.myhorseuniversty.com
(webcasts on a host of topics)

www.safergrass.org

PubMed, part of the US National Library of Medicine, contains abstracts of research papers
www.ncbi.nlm.nih.gov/pubmed

National Research Council's Free Online Program to calculate nutrients for horses
www.nrc88.nas.edu/nrh/

References

Åkerstedt, J. Parasite egg counts in faecal samples from horses in South-Western Norway. Proceedings of the 13th International Congress of the World Equine Veterinary Association. Budapest, 2013

Alizadeh, A., Moshiri, M., Alizadeh, J., and Balali-Mood, M. Black henbane and its toxicity-a descriptive review. Avicenna J Phytomed. Sept-Oct; 4(5): 297–311.

Almeida, F.A., Martins, J.A., Sila, V.P., Trigo, P., Pereira, M. B., Galvão, P.M., Silva, A.T., and Miranda, A.C.T. 2012. *In vitro* gas production from colon contents in electrolyte supplemented horses. EEAP Pub. 321: 363–6.

Andrews, F.M. 2009. Overview of Gastric and Colonic Ulcers. In Advances in Equine Nutrition IV. Nottingham University Press: UK.

Andrews, F.M. and Nadeau, J.A. 1999. Clinical syndromes of gastric ulceration in foals and mature horses. Eq Vet J April; (31)S29.

Annandale, V.J., Valberg, S.J., and Essén-Gustavsson, B. 2005. Effects of submaxial exercise on adenine nucleotide concentrations in skeletal muscle fibers in horses with polysaccharide storage myopathy. Am J Vet Res Mar; (66)5: 839–45.

Argo, C.M. 2013. Chapter 29, Feeding thin and starved horses, in Equine Applied and Clinical Nutrition. Saunders Elsevier: NY, Geor, R.J., Harris., P.A., and Coenen, M., eds.

Arias, M., Cazapal-Moneiro, C., Suárez, J., Miguélez, S., Lopéz-Arellano, M.P., Suárez, J.L., Mendoza de Givas, P., Sánchez-Andrade, R., and Paz-Silva, A. 2012. A combined therapy of chemotherapy and biologial control mesures against parasites in grazing horses. EEAP Pub. 132: 413–18.

Bain, F.T. 2011. Medical Management of the Acute Abdomen in the Field: Analgesia and Cardiovascular Support. Proceedings of the American Association of Equine Practitioners Focus on Colic Meeting. Indianapolis.

Bakos, Z. 2013. Pituitary Pars Intermedia in Horse-Practical Hints. Proceedings of the 13th International Congress of the World Equine Veterinary Association. Oct; Budapest.

Baldessari, J., McKeever, K., Malinowski, K., and Horohov, D. 2011. Effects of quercetin on exercise potantial and exercise-induced cytokines in the horse. Rucore http: //dx.doi.org: 10.7282/ T39C6X3G

Benhajali, H., Richard-Yris, M. A., Ezzaouia, M., Charfi, F., and Hausberger, M. 2010. Increasing foraging opportunities improves welfare and reproductive efficiency in Arab breeding mares. Proceedings from the Fifth European Workshop on Equine Nutrition. Wageningen Academic Publishers: Netherlands, 78–80.

Bergin, B.J., Pierce, S.W., Bramlage, L.R., and Stromberg, A. 2006. Oral hyaluronan gel reduces post-operative tarsocrucial effusion in the yearling Thoroughbred. Equine Vet J. Jul; 38(4): 375–8.

Bezdekova, B. 2013. Equine Gastric Ulcer Syndrome (EGUS). Proceedings of the 13th International Congress of the World Equine Veterinary Association. Oct; Budapest.

Bishop, R. 2013. Chapter 21, The manufacturer's role in feed quality and safety: A discussion on methods used in feed manufacturing processes to assure feed hygiene and safety, in Equine Applied and Clinical Nutrition. Saunders Elsevier: NY, Geor, R.J., Harris., P.A., and Coenen, M., eds.

Blundell, E.L., Adjei, L.J., and Brigden, C.V. 2012. The effect of steaming and soaking treatments on respirable dust content of hay and the potential environmental polluting impact of the waste water produced. EEAP Pub. 132: 125–128.

Bohar Topolovec, M., Kruljc, P., Prosěk, M., Jazbec Križman, P., Smidovnik, A., and Nemec Svete, A. 2013. Endogenous plasma coenzyme Q10 concentration does not correlate with plasma total antioxidant capacity level in healthy untrained horses. Res Vet Sci Oct; 95(2): 675–7.

Boyle, A.G., Magdesian, K.G., Durando, M.N., Gallop, R., and Sigdel, S. 2013. Saccharomyces boulardi viability and efficacy in horses with anti-microbial-induced diarrhoea Vet Rec Feb2; 172(5): 128.

Boyle, A.G., Magdesian, K.G., and Ruby, R.D. 2005. Neonatal isoerythrolysis in horse foals and a mule foal: 18 cases (1988–2003). J Am Vet Med Assoc; Oct 15; 227(8): 1276–83.

Brewster-Barnes, T., Lawrence, L.M., Warren, L.K., Siciliano, P.D., Crum, A., and Thompson, K. 2009. The effect of feeding after exercise on glucose and glycogen responses in the horse. In Advances in Equine Nutrition IV. Nottingham University Press: UK.

Bush, J.A., Freeman, D.E., Kline, K.H., Merchen, N.R., and Fahey Jr., G.C. 2001. Dietary Fat Supplementation effects on in vivo nutrient disappearance and in vivo nutrient intake and total tract digestibility in horses. J Anim Sci 79: 232–39.

Burger, S. M. et al. 1996. Horse Owner's Field Guide to Toxic Plants. Breakthrough Publications: Ossining, NY.

Caloni, F. and Cortinovis, C. 2010. Effects of fusariotoxins in the equine species. Vet J Nov; 186(2): 157–61.

Carmalt, J.L. 2013. Evidence-based equine dentistry: Five Years of Peer-Reviewed Literature (2008–2013). Proceedings of the American Association of Equine Practitioners Focus Meeting on Dentistry. Aug: Charlotte, NC.

Carroll C.L., and Huntington, P.J. 1988. Body Condition Scoring and Weight Estimation of Horses. Equine Veterinary Journal; 20 (1): 41–45.

Carter, R., Treiber, K., Cubitt, T., Staniar, B., Harris, P., and Geor, R. 2007. Regional fat distribution in equines associated with metabolic variables and laminitis predisposition. The Faser Journal; 21: 831.11.

Coenen, M. 2013. Chapter 10, Macro and trace elements in equine nutrition, in Equine Applied and Clinical Nutrition. Saunders Elsevier: NY, Geor, R.J., Harris., P.A., and Coenen, M., eds.

Coenen, M., Appelt, K., Niemeyer, A., and Vervuert, I. 2006. Homeotasis of amino acids during a training session and after feed intake in response to supplemental gelatin. Seventh International Conference on Equine Exercise. Aug: Fontainbleu, 196.

Connyson, M., Muhonen, S., Lindberg, J.E., Essén-Gustavsson, B., Nyman, G., Nostell, K., and Jansson, A., 2006. Effects of crude protein intake for forage-only diets on exercise response and acid. Seventh International Conference on Equine Exercise. Aug: Fontainbleu, 207.

Corke, M.J. 1981. An outbreak of sulfur poisoning in horses. Vet Rec 109: 212–13.

Coverdale, J.A., Moore, J.A., Tyler, H.D., and Miller-Auwerda, P.A. 2004. Soybean hulls as an alternative feed for horses. J Anim Sci Jun; 82(6): 166–8.

Crandell, K. and Duren, S. 2001. Nutraceuticals: What are they and do they work? KER, Inc: Versailles, KY, 29–36.

Daels, P.F. 2006. Induction of Lactation and Adoption of the Orphan Foal. Proceedings of the 8th Annual Resort Symposium of the American Association of Equine Practitioners. Jan: Rome.

Dart, A., Kelly, A., Dart, C., Perkins, N., Jeffcott, L., and Bischofberger, A.S. 2011. Effect of manuka honey gel on second-intention healing of distal limb wounds in horses. Proceedings of the 57th Annual Convention of the American Association of Equine Practitioners. Nov: San Antonio.

Dekker, H., Marlin, D., Alexander, L., Bishop, R., and Harris, P. 2006. How closely are apparent energy intake and workload correlated? Seventh International Conference on Equine Exercise. Aug: Fontainbleu, 200.

De Rancourt, B., Petit, S., and Graubner, C. 2011. Is Nutritional Diagnosis and Formulation of Supplementation Possible Through Analysis of Horsehair? Proceedings of the 57th Annual Convention of the American Association of Equine Practitioners. Nov: San Antonio.

DeVries, J.L., Schott II, H.C., Ernst, C.W., Steibel, J.P., Raney, N.E., and Trottier, N.L. 2014. Glucose and amino acid transporter expression across equine small intestinal brush border membrane and gluteal muscle in horses suffering from pituitary pars intermedia dysfunction (PPID) with confirmed insulin resistance. Proceeding from the Seventh European Workshop on Equine Nutrition, The Impact of Nutrition on Metabolism: 16–18.

DeVries, J.L., Schott II, H.C., Lubitz, J., Chamberlin, D.P., and Trottier, N.L. 2014. Small intestine morphology in horses suffering from pituitary pars intermedia dysfunction. Proceeding from the Seventh European Workshop on Equine Nutrition, The Impact of Nutrition on Metabolism: 14–15.

Disodium Cyanodithiomidocarbonate (DCDIC). United States Environmental Protection Agency R.E.D. Facts on Pesticide Reregistration. EPA-738-F-94–017. Accessed 4/19/15. www.epa.gov/oppooool/reregistration/REDs/factsheets/3065fact.pdf.

Dizaji, B. R., Hassanpour, A., Ranjbari, O., Gogdaragi, M.M., Golzar, F.S., and Farsad, A.G. 2012. The effect of selenium and vit E supplement on the sera concentrations of antoxidane in Arabian horses. Proceedings of the 18ᵗʰ Annual Meeting of the Italian Association of equine Veterinarians. Feb: Bologna, 241.

Drasch, G. and Roider, G. 2002. Assessment of hair mineral analysis commercially offered in Germany. Journal of Trace Elements in Medicine and Biology. 16; (1): 27–31.

Durham, A. 2013. Feeding the horse with colic. Proceedings of the British Equine Veterinary Association Congress. Sept: Manchester, UK.

Durham, A. 2013. Chapter 30, Hyperlipemia, in Equine Applied and Clinical Nutrition. Saunders Elsevier: NY, Geor, R.J., Harris., P.A., and Coenen, M., eds.

Durham, A. 2013. Chapter 37, Hepatic insufficiency, in Equine Applied and Clinical Nutrition. Saunders Elsevier: NY, Geor, R.J., Harris., P.A., and Coenen, M., eds.

Düsterdieck, K.F., Schott II, H.C., Eberhart, S.W., Woody, K.A., and Coenen, M. 1999. Electrolyte and glycerol supplementation improve water intake by horses performing a simulated 60 km endurance ride. Equine Vet J Suppl Jul; (30): 418–24.

Ellis, A.D. 2010. Biological basis of behavior in relation to nutrition and feed intake in horses. Proceedings from the Fifth European Workshop on Equine Nutrition. Wageningen Academic Publishers: Netherlands: 53–73.

Ellis, A.D. 2008. Practical assessment of work-level in equines. Proceedings from the Fifth European Workshop on Equine Nutrition. Wageningen Academic Publishers: Netherlands: 147.

Ellis, A.D., Visser, C.D., and Reenen, C.J. 2006. Effect of a high concentrate versus a high fibre diet on behavior and welfare in horses, Proceedings of the 40ᵗʰ International Congress of the ISAE. Cranfield University Press: University of Bristol: 42.

Ellis, A.D. and Hill, J. 2005. Nutritional Physiology of the Horse. Nottingham University Press: UK.

Ferraz, G.C., Brito, H.C.D., Berkman, C., Albernaz, R.M., Araújo, R.A., Silva, M.H.M., de F. D'Angelis, F. H., and Queiroz-Neto, A. 2013. Low dose of dichloroacetate infusion reduces blood lactate after submaximal exercise in horses. Pesq. Vet. Bras. Jan; (1)33: 1–7.

Ferreira, J.R., Moreira, C.G., Rodrigues, F., Taran F.P., Francisco, R., Centini, T.N., Gonzaga, I.V.F., Freitas, Júnior, J.E., and Gobesso, A.O.O. 2012. Effect of omega-3 and omega-6 fatty acids supplementation on development of equine and mule nursing foals. EEAP Pub. 132: 351–6.

Filho, W.H., Fonseco, L., Braga, F., Araujo, J., Milani, J., and Brassiane, D. 2013. Destruction of infective larvae of cyathostomes by nematophagus fungi. Proceedings of the 13th International Congress of the World Equine Veterinary Association. Oct; Budapest.

Finno, C., Pardon Lamas, L., Costa e Cutro, T., and Spier, S. 2012. Lusitano horses in Portugal without access to pasture are at risk of having low serum levels of vitamin E: pilot study. EEAP Pub. 132: 341–2.

Forsyth, R., Brigden, C., and Northrop, A. 2006. Double blind investigation of the effects of oral supplementation of combined glucosamine hydrochloride (CGHC) and chondroitin sulphate (CS) on the stride characteristics of veteran horses. Seventh International Conference on Equine Exercise. Aug: Fontainbleu, 199.

Frank, N., Andrews, F., Durham, A., McFarlane, D., and Schott, H. 2013. Recommendations for the Diagnosis and Treatment of Pituitary Pars Intermedia Dysfunction (PPID). Equine Endocrinology Group.

Frank, N., Geor, R.J., Bailey, S.R., Durham, A.E., and Johnson, P.J. 2010. Equine Metabolic Syndrome. ACVIM Consensus Statement. J Vet Intern Med; 24: 467–75.

Galán, R., Calvo, L.A.G., Mena, M., De Llera, N., Tovar, M.A.A., Calvo, L.J.E., and Martín-Cuervo, M. 2013. Castor Bean Intoxication. Proceedings of the 13th International Congress of the World Equine Veterinary Association. Oct; Budapest.

Galloway, S.S. 2011. How to Document a Dental Examination and Procedure Using a Dental Chart. Proceeding of the American Association of Equine Practitioners Focus on Dentistry Meeting. Sep: Albuquerque.

Gaskill, C. 2009. Nitrate Poisoning in Horses. Eq Disease Quarterly. 10: 18; 4.

Geor, R.J. 2010. Digestive strategy and flexibility in horses with reference to dietary carbohydrates. Proceedings from the Fifth European Workshop on Equine Nutrition. Wageningen Academic Publishers: Netherlands: 17–28

Geor, R.J. 2006. The role of nutritional supplements and feeding strategies in equine athletic performance. Equine and Comparative Exercise Physiology 3(3); 109–19.

Geor, R.J. and Harris, P.A. 2013. Chapter 27, Laminitis, in Equine Applied and Clinical Nutrition. Saunders Elsevier: NY, Geor, R.J., Harris., P.A., and Coenen, M., eds.

Geor, R.J. and Harris, P.A. 2013, Chapter 28, Obesity, in Equine Applied and Clinical Nutrition. Saunders Elsevier: NY, Geor, R.J., Harris., P.A., and Coenen, M., eds.

Geor, R.J. and Harris, P.A. 2007. How to Minimize Gastrointestinal Disease Associated with Carbohydrate Nutrition in Horses. 53rd Annual Convention of the American Association of Equine Practitioners . Dec: Orlando.

Geor, R.J., Harris., P.A., and Coenen, M., editors. Equine Applied and Clinical Nutrition. Saunders Elsevier: NY, 2013

Gieche, J.M. 2013. Oral Examination of Equidae. Proceedings of the American Association of Equine Practitioners Focus Meeting on Dentistry. Aug: Charlotte, NC.

Goachet, A.G., Poncet, C., Boisot, P., Couroucé, A., and Julliand, V. 2006. Feed digestibility, passage rate and fecal microflora in horses conditioned to perform 60 and 90 km endurance races. Seventh International Conference on Equine Exercise. Aug: Fontainbleu,

Gobesso, A.A.O., Françoso, R., Toldeo, R.A.D., Centini, T.N., Gonzaga, I.V.F., Gil, P.C.N., and Baldi, F. 2012. Evaluation on body condition score in horses by ultrasonography. EEAP Pub. 321: 387–90.

Gobesso, A.A.O., Gonzaga, A.V.F., Taran, F.M.P., Françoso, R., Centini, T.N., Moreira, C.G., Ferreira, J.R., Rodrigues, F.P., and Baldi. F. 2012. Influence of fat supplementation on mare's milk composition. EEAP Pub. 132: 347–50.F

Goodrich, L.R. and Nixon, A.J. 2006. Medical treatment of osteoarthritis in the horse: a review. Vet J 171: 51–69.

Gordon, M.B., Betros, C.L., and McKeever, K.H. 2006. Interval exercise alters feed intake as well as leptin and ghrelin concetrations in standardbred mares. Seventh International Conference on Equine Exercice. Aug: Fontainbleu, 195.

Hale, C., Warren, H., and Hemmings, A. 2012. The fermentation of hay and starch when incubated *in vitro* in faecal innocula from either normal healthy horses or horses with a history of laminitis. EEAP Pub. 132: 357–62.

Hallum, S., Campbell, A.P., Qazamel, M., Owen, H., and Ellis, A.D. 2012. Effects of traditional versus novel feeding management on 24 hour time budget of stabled horses. EEAP Pub. 132: 319–22.

Hammock, P.D., Freeman, D.E., and Baker, D.J. 1998. Failure of Psyllium Mucciloid to Hasten Evacuation of Sand from the Equine Large Intestine. Vet Surg 27: 547–54.

Harris, P. 2012. Update on nutrition and pasture associated laminitis. Proceedings of the 51st British Equine Veterinary Association Congress. Birmingham.

Harris, P.A. 2008. Ergogenic aids in the performance horse. In Nutrition of the Exercising Horse EAAP Publication No.125 Proceedings on the Fourth European Workshop on Equine Nutrition. Wageningen Academic Publishers: Netherlands. pp 373.

Harris, P.A., Coenen, M., and Geor, R.J. 2013. Chapter 26, Controversial areas in equine nutrition and feeding management: The Editors' Views, in Equine Applied and Clinical Nutrition. Saunders Elsevier: NY, Geor, R.J., Harris., P.A., and Coenen, M., eds.

Harris, P.A. and Harris, R.C. 1998 Nutritional Ergogenic Aids in the horse-uses and abuses. Physiology Research Group, Chichester, UK: 491–507. In Lindner, A. (ed) Proceedings of the Conference of Equine Sports Medicine and Science. Wageningen Press, The Netherlands. 203-218.

Harris, P., Longland, A., Murray, J-A., Ellis, A., Dunnett, C., Menzies-Gow, N., Bailey, S., and Elliot, J. 2010. Pasture and laminitis: truth or fiction? Vet Times No. 43 Jan 11, in vetsonline.com, accessed March 2, 2015.

Harris, P.A., Pagan, J.D., Crandell, K.G., and Davidson, N. 1999. Effect of feeding thoroughbred horses a high unsaturated or saturated vegetable oil supplemented diet for 6 months following a 10 month fat acclimation. Equine Vet J Suppl Jul; (30): 468–74

Harris, P.A. and Rivero, J.L.L. 2013. Chapter 31, Exercise-associated muscle disorders, in Equine Applied and Clinical Nutrition. Saunders Elsevier: NY, Geor, R.J., Harris., P.A., and Coenen, M., eds.

Harris, P.A. and Schott II, H. C. 2013. Chapter 14, Nutritional Management of elite endurance horses, in Equine Applied and Clinical Nutrition. Saunders Elsevier: NY, Geor, R.J., Harris., P.A., and Coenen, M., eds.

Hartnell, G.F., Hvelplund, T., and Weisbjerg, M.R. 2005. Nutrient digestibility in sheep fed diets containing Roundup ready or conventional fodder, beet, sugar beet and beet pulp. J Anim Sci Feb; 83(2): 400–7.

Hassel, D.M., Smith, P.A., Nieto, J.E., Beldmenico, P. and Spier, S.J. 2009. Di-tri-octahedral smectite for the prevention of post-operative diarrhea in equids with surgical disease of the large intestine: results of a randomized clinical trial. Vet J Nov;182(2):210-4.

Hemmings, A., McBride, S.D., and Hale, C.E. 2007. Preservative responding and the aetiology of equine stereotypy. *Appl Behav Anim Sci* 104(1–2): 143–150.

Henneke, D.R., Potter, G.D., Kreider, J.L., and Yeates, B.F. 1983. Relationship between body score, physical measurements, and body fat percentage in mares. Equine Veterinary Journal Oct 15(4): 371–372

Hess, T.M., Kronfeld, D.S., Carter, R.A., Treiber, K.H., Byrd, B.M., Staniar, W.B., Smith, L.T., Gay, L.A., and Harris, P.A. 2006. Does usefulness of potassium supplementation depend on speed? Equine Vet J Suppl Aug; (36): 74–9.

Hoffman, R. 2013. Chapter 8, Carbohydrates, in Equine Applied and Clinical Nutrition. Saunders Elsevier: NY, Geor, R.J., Harris., P.A., and Coenen, M., eds.

Holcombe, S.J., Jackson, C., Gerber, V., Jefcoat, A., Berney, C., Eberhardt, S., and Robinson, N.E. 2001. Stabling is associated with airway inflammation in young Arabian horses. Eq Vet J 33(3); 244–9.

Hothersall, B. and Nicol, C.J. 2013. Chapter 25, Effects of diet on behavior – normal and abnormal, in Equine Applied and Clinical Nutrition. Saunders Elsevier: NY, Geor, R.J., Harris., P.A., and Coenen, M., eds.

Hussein, H.S., Vogedes, L.A., Fernandez, G.C., and Frankeny, R.L. 2004. Effects of cereal grain supplementation on apparent digestibility of nutrients and concentrations of fermentation end-products in the feces and serum of horses consuming alfalfa cubes. J Anim Sci Jul; 82(7): 1986–96.

Ivers, T. 2002. Carbohydrates and glycogen loading. Proceedings of the First European Equine Nutrition and Health Congress. Feb; Antwerp: 1–14

Jansson, A. 2013. Nutritional Strategies for gastrointestinal health-the basics. Proceedings of the Sixth European Equine Health and Nutrition Congress: Feeding for Gastrointestinal Health. March; Ghent.

Jansson, A. and Löf, F. 2010. Digestibility of calcium and phosphorus in yearlings. Proceedings from the Fifth European Workshop on Equine Nutrition. Wageningen Academic Publishers: Netherlands p. 50

Jarvis, N. 2012. Nutraceuticals and the Geriatric Horse: A Review. Proceedings of the 51st British Equine Veterinary Association Congress. Sep: Birmingham.

Jensen, R.B., Austbo, D., and Tausen, A. H. 2012. Feeding forage before or after oats affects caecum pH profiles of the horse. EEAP Pub. 132: 327–30.

Jouany, J.P., Medina, B., Bertin, G., and Julliand, V. 2008. Effect of live yeast culture supplementation on apparent digestibility and rate of passage in horse fed a high-fiber or high-starch diet. J Anim Sci Feb; 86(2): 339–47.

Jouany, J.P., Medina, B., Bertin, G., and Julliand, V. 2009. Effect of live yeast culture supplementation on hindgut microbial communities and their polysaccharidase and glycoside hydrolase activities in horses fed a high-fiber diet or high-starch diet. J Anim Sci Sep; 87(9): 2844–52.

Julliand, V. and Martin-Rosset, W. (eds.) 2004 Nutrition for the performance horse. EAAP Pub. No 111. Wageningen Academic Publishers: Netherlands, p 158.

Kamphues, J. 2013. Chapter 20 Feed hygiene and related disorders in horses, in Equine Applied and Clinical Nutrition. Saunders Elsevier: NY, Geor, R.J., Harris., P.A., and Coenen, M., eds.

Kaplan, R.M. and Nielsen, M.K. 2010. An evidence-based approach to equine parasite control: It ain't the 60s anymore. E Vet Ed Jun; (22)306–16.

Katy, S. and Ana, M. 2012.Serum triglyceride concentrations during pregnancy in Spanish mares with different body condition scoring. Proceedings of the 18th Annual Meeting of the Italian Association of equine Veterinarians. Feb: Bologna, 235–8.

Kawcak, C.E., Frisbie, D.D. and McIlwraith, C.W. 2011. Effects of extracorporeal shock wave therapy and polysulfated glycosaminoglycan treatment on subchondral bone, serum biomarkers, and synovial fluid biomarkers in horses with induced osteoarthritis. Am J Vet Res Jun; 72(6): 772–9.

Kawcak, C.E., Frisbie, D.D., Trotter, G.W., McIlwraith, C.W., Gillette, S.M., Powers, B.E. and Walton, R.M. 1997. Effects of intravenous administration of sodium hyaluronate on carpal joints in exercising horses after arthroscopic surgery and osteochondral fragmentation. Am J Vet Res Oct; 58(10): 1132–40.

Klohnen, A. 2012. Association between enterolithiasis and equine gastric ulceration. Proceedings of the 51st British Equine Veterinary Association Congress. Sept: Birmingham, UK.

Klohnen, A. 2012. Large colon sand impaction in horses: 1996–2008. Proceedings of the 51st British Equine Veterinary Association Congress. Sept: Birmingham, UK.

Kohl-Parisini, A., van den Hoven, R., Leinker, S., Hulan, H.W., and Zentek, J. 2007. Effect of feeding sunflower oil or seal blubber oil to horses with recurrent airway obstruction. Can J Vet Res Jan; 71(1): 59–65.

Lacombe, V.A., Hinchcliff, K.W., Cohn, C.W., Reed, S.M., and Taylor, L.E. 2006. Effects of dietary glycemic index after exercise on plasma concentrations of substrates used for muscle glycogenesis. Seventh International Conference on Equine Exercise. Aug: Fontainbleu, 193.

Lawrence, L. 2008. Nutrient needs of performance horses. R. Bras. Zootec July (37)

Lawrence, L.M. 2013. Chapter 11, Feeding stallions and broodmares, in Equine Applied and Clinical Nutrition. Saunders Elsevier: NY, Geor, R.J., Harris., P.A., and Coenen, M., eds.

Levine M.A. The Domestic Horse: The Evolution, Development and Management of its Behaviour. Cambridge University Press; Cambridge, 2005

Lewis, C.L. and Underwood, D.D. The Great American Horse Race of 1976. Mennonite Press: Newton, KS, 1993.

Lindberg, J.E. 2013. Chapter 17, Feedstuffs for horses, in Equine Applied and Clinical Nutrition. Saunders Elsevier: NY, Geor, R.J., Harris., P.A., and Coenen, M., eds.

Lindberg, J.E., Essén-Gustavsson, B., Gottlieb-Veti, M., and Jansson, A. 2006. Exercise response, metabolism at rest and digestibility in athletic horses fed high fat oats. Seventh International Conference on Equine Exercise. Aug: Fontainbleu, 201.

Longland, A.C. 2013. Chapter 18, Pastures and pasture management, in Equine Applied and Clinical Nutrition. Saunders Elsevier: NY, Geor, R.J., Harris., P.A., and Coenen, M., eds.

Longland, A.C., Barfoot, C., and Harris, P.A. 2012. The effect of wearing a grazing muzzle vs. not wearing a grazing muzzle on intakes of spring, summer and autumn pastures by ponies. EEAP Pub. 132: 185–186.

Lopes, M.A. and C.J. Pfeiffer Functional morphology of the pelvic flexure and its role in disease: a review. Histol Histopathol 2000 Jul; 15(3): 983–91

Lutherson, N. and Nadeau, J.A. 2013. Chapter 34, Gastric ulceration, in Equine Applied and Clinical Nutrition. Saunders Elsevier: NY, Geor, R.J., Harris., P.A., and Coenen, M., eds.

MacAllister, C.G., Andrews, F.M., Deegan, E., Ruoff, W., and Olovson, S.G. 1997. A scoring system for gastric ulcers in the horse. Equine Vet J. Nov; 29(6) 430–3.

Madigan, J.E. 2015. Gastrodudenal Ulcers, in The Manual of Equine Neonatal Medicine. IVIS: Ithaca. Updated 31 March.

Martin-Rosset, W. 2008. Energy requirements and allowances in exercising horses. In Nutrition of the Exercising Horse EAAP Publication No.125, Wageningen Academic Publishers: Netherlands pp103

Martin-Rosset, W. 2008. Protein requirements and allowances in exercising horses. In Nutrition of the Exercising Horse EAAP Publication No.125, Wageningen Academic Publishers: Netherlands, 183.

Martin-Rosset, W. and Coenen, M. 2006. Energy requirements of exercising horses: scientific bases and recommendations. Seventh International Conference on Equine Exercise. Aug: Fontainbleu, 191.

Matsui, A., Ohmura, H., Asai, Y., Takahashi, T., Hiraga, A., Okamura, K., Tokikura, H., Sugino, T., Obitsu, T., and Taniguchi, K. 2006. Effect of amino acids and glucose administration after exercise on the turnover of muscle protein in the hindlimb femoral region of Thoroughbreds. Seventh International Conference on Equine Exercise. Aug: Fontainbleu, 197.

Maxie, G. and van Druemel, T. 1992. Menadione (vitamin K3) toxicity in six horses. an Vet J Vol. 33 756–7.

McBride, S.D. and Long, L. 2001. Management of horses showing stereotypic behavior, owner perception and the implications for welfare. Vet Rec Jun 30; 148(26): 799–802

McBride, S.D. and Mills, D.S. 2012. Psychological factors affecting equine performance. BMC Veterinary Research 8: 180

McBride, SD and Parker, M.O. 2015. The disrupted basal ganglia and behavioral control: an integrative cross-domain perspective of spontaneous stereotypy. Behav Brain Res Jan 1; 276: 45–58

McGorum, B., Pirie, R.S., and Keen, J.A. 2013. Chapter 38, Nutritional considerations in grass sickness, botulism, equine motor neuron disease and equine degenerative myeloencephalopathy, in Equine Applied and Clinical Nutrition. Saunders Elsevier: NY, Geor, R.J., Harris, P.A., and Coenen, M., eds.

McGreevy, P.D. and Nicol, C.J. 2010. Prevention of crib-biting: a review. Eq Vet J 30(27); 35–8.

McIlwraith, C.W. 2013. Chapter 33, Oral joint supplements in the management of osteoarthritis, in Equine Applied and Clinical Nutrition. Saunders Elsevier: NY, Geor, R.J., Harris, P.A., and Coenen, M., eds.

Medina, B., Girard, I.D., Jacotot, E., and Julliand, V. 2002. Effect of a preparation of *Saccharommycescerevisae* on microbial profiles and fermentation patterns in the large intestine of horses fed a high fiber diet or a high starch diet. J Anim Sci October; 80 (10): 2600–9

Menzies-Gow, N.J., Stevens, K.B., Sepulveda, M.F., Jarvis, N., and Marr, C.M. 2010. Repeatability and reproducibility of the Obel grading system for equine laminitis. Vet Rec Jul 10; 167(2): 52–5.

Merrit, A.M. and Julliand, V. 2011. Equine GI Physiology-Some Species Specific Features. Proceedings of the Sixth European Equine Health and Nutrition Congress: Feeding for Gastrointestinal Health. March Ghent. 93–107.

Moore-Colyer, J.S., Lumbis, M.K., Longland, A., and Harris, P. 2014. The effect of five different wetting treatments on the nutrient content and microbial concentration in hay for horses. PLOS One Nov 26; 9(11)e114079

Morresy, P.R. 2011. How I evaluate the chronic colic. Proceedings of the American Association of Equine Practitioners Focus on Colic Meeting. Indianapolis.

Morresy, P.R. 2011. Medical Management of the Acute Abdomen in the Field: Laxatives, Motility Agents and Nutritional Management. Proceedings of the American Association of Equine Practitioners Focus on Colic Meeting. Indianapolis.

Müeller, C.E. 2012. Impact of harvest, preservation and storage conditions on forage quality. EEAP Pub 13: 237–54.

Murray, M.J. and Grady, T.C. 2002. The effect of pectin-lecithin complex on prevention of gastric mucosal lesions induced by feed deprivation in ponies. Equine Vet J Mar; 34(2): 195–8.

Niedžwidž, A., Krszystof, K., and Nicpon, J. 2013. Plasma total antioxidant status in horses after 8-hours of road transportation. Acta Vet Scand; 55(1): 55–8.

Nielsen, M.K., Fritzen, B., Duncan, J.L., Guillot, J., Eysker, M., Dorchies, P., Laugier, C., Beugnet, F., Mcana, A., Lussot Kcrvcn, I., and von Samson-Himmelstjerna, G. 2010. Practical Aspects of equine parasite control: a review based upon a workshop discussion consensus. Jul; 42(5): 460–8.

Nielsen, M.K., Mittel, L., Grice., A., Erskine, M., Graves, E., Vaala, W., Tully, R.C., French, D.D., Bowman, R., and Kaplan, R.K. AAEP Parasite Control Guidelines. AAEP Parasite Control Subcommittee of the AAEP Infectious Disease Committee. Rev. 2013.

Nielsen, M.K., Pfister, K., and von Samson-Himmelstjerna, G. 2014. Selective therapy in equine parasite control-application and limitations. Vet Parasitol May 28; 202(3–4)95–103.

Nolf, M., Rannou, B, Gestin, C., and Leblond, A. 2013. Prevalence and early clinical signs of equine pituitary pars intermedia dysfunction in horses older than 10 years in France. Proceedings of the 13th International Congress of the World Equine Veterinary Association. Oct; Budapest.

Nutrient Requirements of Horse, 6th. ed. Committee on Nutrient Requirements of Horses: National Academies Press, 2007

Nutritional Requirements of Horses. Merckmanuals.com, reviewer S.L. Ralston Whitehouse Station, NJ: July, 2011

O'Connor, C.I., Lawrence, L.M., Lawrence, A.C., Janicki, K.M., Warren, L.K., and Hayes, S. 2004. The effect of dietary fish oil supplementation on exercising horses. J Anim Sci Oct; 82(10): 2978–84

O'Connor, C.I., Nielsen, B.D., Woodward, A.D., Spooner, H.S., Ventura, B.A., and Turner, K.K. 2008. Mineral balance in horses fed two supplemental silicon sources. J Anim Physio Anim Nutr (Berl) Apr; 92(2): 173–81.

O'Grady, S.E. 2011. How to treat severe laminitis in an ambulatory setting. Proceedings of the 57th Annual Convention of the American Association of Equine Practitioners. Nov: San Antonio.

Oelberg, K. Factors affecting the nutritive value of range forage. Journal of Range Management Archives. Journals.uair.arizona.edu accessed March 17, 2005

Oke, S.L. and McIlwraith, C.W. 2010. Review of the economic impact of osteoarthritis and oral joint-health supplements in horses. Proceedings of the 56th Annual Convention of the American Association of Equine Practitioners. Sep: Baltimore, 12–16.

Pagan, J. D. ed. 2009. Advances in Equine Nutrition IV. Nottingham University Press: UK.

Paradis, M.R. 2012. Feeding the Orphan Foal. Proceedings of the AAEP Annual Convention, Anaheim. Vol. 58. 402–6.

Paradis, M.R. 2012. Normal Foal Nutrition. Proceedings of the AAEP Annual Convention, Anaheim. Vol. 58. 399–401.

Parraga, M.E., Spier, S.J., Thurmond, M., and Hirsh, D. 1997. A clinical trial of probiotic administration for prevention of Salmonella shedding in the postoperative period in horses with colic. J Vet Intern Med Jan-Feb; 11(1): 36–41.

Pfaff, M., Venner, M., and Vervuert, I. 2014. Effects of different forage-based diets on the gastric mucosa in weanlings. Proceeding from the 7th European Workshop on Equine Nutrition, The Impact of Nutrition on Metabolism: 19–20.

Pfister, J.A., Stegelmeyer, B.E., Cheney, C.D., Ralphs, M.H., and Gardner, D.R. 2002 Conditioning Taste Aversions to Locoweed (Oxytropis Sericea) in horses. Journal of Animal Science 80(1): 79–83.

Philippeau, C, Varloud, M., Goachet, A.G., and Julliand, V. 2008. Effect of a moderate dietary fat supplementation on the digestive function in the horse. In Nutrition of the Exercising Horse EAAP Publication No.125, Wageningen Academic Publishers: Netherlands, 97.

Pickard, J.A. and Stevenson Z. 2008, Benefits of yeast culture supplementation in diets for horses. In Nutrition of the Exercising Horse. EAAP Publication No.125, Wageningen Academic Publishers: Netherlands 355

Pierce, K.R., Joyce, J.R., England R.B., and Jones, L.P. 1972. Acute hemolytic anemia caused by wild onion poisoning in horses. JAVMA 160; (3): 323–7.

Popot, M.A., Bonnaire, Y., Guéchot, J., and Youtain, P.L. 2004. Hyaluronan in horses: physiological production rate, plasma and synovial fluid concentrations in control conditions in following sodium hyaluronate administration. Equine Vet J Sp; 36(6): 482–7.

Pratt, S.E., Geor, R.J., and McCutcheon, L.J. 2006. Effects of dietary energy source and physical conditioning on insulin sensitivity and glucose tolerance in horses. Seventh International Conference on Equine Exercise. Aug: Fontainbleu, 192.

Preston, L. Natural Healing for Cats, Dogs, Horses and Other Animals: 150 Alternative Therapies Available to Owners and Caregivers. Skyhorse Publishing: New York, 2011.

Proudman, C.J. 2013. Dietary Management for reducing the risk of gastrointestinal disorders (colic). Feeding for Gastrointestinal Health 6th edition, European Health and Nutrition Congress. Mar: Ghent.

Pugh, D.G. 2007. Feeding the Geriatric Horse. Proceedings of the 53rd Annual Convention of the American Association of Equine Practitioners. Dec: Orlando.

Pugh, D.G. 2008. Feeding the orphaned and hand-raised foal. Proceeding of the AAEP Focus Meeting: First Year of Life. Austin, TX.

Ralston, S. and Harris, P.A. 2013. Chapter 15, Nutritional considerations for aged horses, in Equine Applied and Clinical Nutrition. Saunders Elsevier: NY, Geor, R.J., Harris., P.A., and Coenen, M., eds.

Ramey, D.W. and Duren, S. 2011. Nutritional Content of Five Equine Nutritional Supplements Relative to a 500-kg Working Horse. Proceedings of the Annual Convention of the American Association of Equine Practitioners. Nov: San Antonio. 187–191.

Reinemeyer, C.R. 2008. Parasite control recommendations for horses during the first year of life. Proceeding of the AAEP Focus Meeting: First Year of Life. Austin, TX.

Reisinger, N., Schaumberger, S., and Shatzmayr, G. 2012. Inhibition of lamellar separation caused by endotoxins by Polymixin B in an *ex vivo/in vitro* model of equine laminitis. EEAP Pub. 132: 187–190.

Rezende, A.C.S., Costa, M.L.L., Frraz, V.P., Moreira, G.R., Silva de Moura, R., Silva, V.P., and Lana, A.M.Q. Effects of storage period on the chemical composition and beta-carotene concentration in estilosantes hay varieties for feeding equine (sic). EEAP Pub. 132: 279–88.

Rezende, A.C.S., Freitas, G.P., Costa, M.L.L., Fonseca, M.G., Lage, J., and Leal Jr., H.V. 2012. Nutritional composition of white oat (Avena sativa L.) with different levels of dry matter for use in the diets of horses. EEAP Pu. 132: 274–278.

Rezende, A.C.S., Mauricio, R.M., Carvalho, W.T.V., Moraes, L.F., Santiago, J.M., Ponciano, L.M.A., and Pereira, R.V.G. 2012. Aerobic stability of sugar cane *in natura* hydrolyzed with calcium oxide to be used in equine diets. EEAP Pub 132: 271–274.

Riet-Correa, F., Rivero, R., Odriozola, E., Adrien, M. de L., Medeiros, R.M., and Schild, A.L. November 2013 Mycotoxicois of ruminants and horses. J Vet Diagn Invest 25(6): 692–708.

Robinson, N. E. Robinson's Current Therapy in Equine Medicine, 7th ed. Elsevier Saunders: St. Louis, 2015

Rodiek, A.C. and Stull, C.L. 2005. Glycemic Index of Ten Common Horse Feeds. J Eq Vet Sci 27(5): 205–11.

Roger, C., Harris, P.A., Routledge, N.B.H., Naylor, J.R.J., and Wilson, A.M. 2006. Plasma glutamine concentrations in the horse following feeding with and without oral glutamine supplementation. Seventh International Conference on Equine Exercise. Aug: Fontainbleu, 204

Rohrbach, B.W., Stafford, J.R., Clermont, R.S., Reed, S.M., Schott II, H.C., and Andrews, F.M. 2012. Diagnostic frequency, response to therapy, and long-term prognosis among horses and ponies with pituitary pars intermedia dysfunction, 1993–2004. J Vet Intern Med Jul-Aug; 26(4): 1027–34.

Rubio, M.D. 2012. Assessment of the combined effects of probiotics and training on metabolic response to exercise in andalusian horses. Proceedings of the 18th Annual Meeting of the Italian Association of equine Veterinarians. Feb: Bologna, 246.

Saastamoinen, M., Fradinho, M.J., Santos, A.S., and Miraglia, N. (eds.) 2012. Forages and grazing in horse nutrition. EAAP Publication No. 132: Wageningen Academic Publishers.

Saastamoinen, M.T. and Harris, P.A. 2008. Vitamin requirements and supplementation in athletic horses. In Nutrition of the Exercising Horse EAAP Publication No.125 Wageningen Academic Publishers: Netherlands, 233.

Sadet-Bourgeteau, S., Philippeau, C., Dequiedt S., and Julliand, V. 2014. Comparison of the bacterial community structure within the equine hindgut and faeces using Automated Ribosomal Intergenic Spacer Analysis (ARISA) Dec 8(12): 1928–34.

Sampieri, F., Schott II, H.C., Hinchcliff, K.W., Geor, R.J., and Jose-Cunilleras, E. 2006. Effect of oral electrolyte supplementation on endurance horses competing in 80 km rides. Equine Vet J Suppl Aug; (36): 19–26.

Särkijarvi, S., Kivinen, N., Saastamoinen, M., and Vuorenmaa, J. 2008. Effect of hydrolyzed yeast (Progut™) on the microbial flora of the horse. In Nutrition of the Exercising Horse. EAAP Publication No.125; Wageningen Academic Publishers: Netherlands, 365.

Schott II, H.C. 2013. Chapter 36, Urinary tract disease, in Equine Applied and Clinical Nutrition. Saunders Elsevier: NY, Geor, R.J., Harris, P.A., and Coenen, M., eds.

Schott II, H.C., Axiak, S.M., Woody, K.A., and Eberhart, S.W. 2002. Effect of oral administration of electrolyte pastes on rehydration of horses. Am J Vet Res Jan; 63(1): 19–27.

Schott II, H.C., Düsterdieck, K.F., Eberhart, S.W., Woody, K.A., Refsal, K.R., and Coenen, M. 1999. Effects of electrolyte and glycerol supplementation on recovery from endurance exercise. Equine Vet J Suppl 30: 384–93.

Seidel, S., Kreutzer, R., Smith, D., McNeel, S., and Gillis, D. 2001. Assessment of commercial laboratories performing hair mineral analysis. JAMA 3: 285(1): 67–72.

Sharif, M. T., Tehrani, S.J., Mozaffari, R., Nakhaee, H., Adlparvar, A., and Moosavi, A.A.H. 2012. Evaluation of five point of care glucometers for use in equine practice. Proceedings of the 18th Annual Meeting of the Italian Association of equine Veterinarians. Feb: Bologna, 232.

Silva, S.R., Guedes, C.M., Couto, P., Santos, A.S., and Melo-Pinto, P. 2012. Relationship between body condition and neck crest score systems and subcutaneous fat, tissue and ultrasonic measurements in horses. EEAP Pub. 321: 81–6.

Smith, D.G. and Burden, F. A. 2013. Chapter 16, Practical donkey and mule nutrition, in Equine Applied and Clinical Nutrition. Saunders Elsevier: NY, Geor, R.J., Harris., P.A., and Coenen, M., eds.

Smith, R., Cotten, K., Allman, R., Watson, R., Sena, K., and Keene, T. 2012. Grazing and pasture management considerations from around the world. EEAP Pub. 132: 197–208.

Speirs, V.C. 1997. Clinical Examination of Horses. Saunders: Philadelphia.

Spooner, H.S., Nielsen, B.D., Schott II, H.C., and Harris, P.A. 2010. Sweat composition in Arabian horses performing endurance exercise on forage-based, low Na rations. Equine Vet J Suppl Nov; (38): 382–6.

Spooner, H.S., Nielsen, B.D., Turner, K.K., Ventura, B., Woodward, A.D., and O'Connor, C.I. 2006. Mineral balance in horses fed sodium zeolite. Seventh International Conference on Equine Exercise. Aug: Fontainbleu, 208.

Staniar, W.B. 2013. Chapter 12, Feeding the growing horse, in Equine Applied and Clinical Nutrition. Saunders Elsevier: NY, Geor, R.J., Harris., P.A., and Coenen, M., eds.

Stokes, A.M., Lavie, N.L., Keowen, M.L., Gaschen, L., Gaschen, F.P., Barthel, D. and Andrews, F. 2012. Evaluation of a wireless ambulatory capsule (SmartPill®) to measure gastrointestinal tract pH, luminal pressure and temperature, and transit time in ponies. Equine Vet J Jul; 44(4): 482–6.

Stull, C.L. 2008. The skinny on carbohydrates and body size of horses. Proceedings of the Horse Breeders and Owners Conference. Jan; Alberta.

Swor, T.M., Whittenburg, J.L., and Chaffin, M.K. 2008. Ivermectin Toxicosis in Three Adult Horses. 54th Annual Convention of the American Association of Equine Practitioners. Dec: San Diego.

Swyers, K.L., Burk, A.O., Hartsock, T.G., Ungerfeld, E.M., and Shelton, J.L. 2008. Effects of direct-fed microbial supplementationon digestibility and fermentation end-products in horses fed low- and high-starch concentrates. J Anim Sci Oct; 86(10): 2596–608.

Sykes, B.W., Sykes, K.M., and Hallowell, G.D. 2014. Administration of trimethoprim-sulfadimidine does not improve healing of glandular gastric ulceration in horses receiving omeprazole: a randomized, blinded clinical study. BMC Veterinary Research; 10: 180.

Taintor, J.S., Wright, J., Caldwell, F., Dymond, B., and Schumacher, J. 2014. Efficacy of an extract of blue-green algae in amelioration of Lameness caused by degenerative joint disease in the horse. J Eq Vet Sci. Oct; 34(10): 1197–1200.

Tallon, C. and Andreasen, A. 200. Veterinary Nutraceutical Medicine. Can Vet J Mar; 41(3): 231–4.

Treiber, K., Hess, T., Carter, R., Staniar, W.B., Kronfeld, D., Harris, P., and Geor, R. 2007. Laminitis in ponies is a diabetic-like state. The FASEB Journal 21; 737: 23.

Treiber, K.H., Hess, T.M., Kronfeld, D.S., Boston, R.C., Geor, R.J., Freire, M.S., Silva, A.M.G.B., and Harris, P.A. 2006. Dietary energy sources affect minimal model parameters in trained Arabian gelding during endurance exercise. Seventh International Conference on Equine Exercise. Aug: Fontainbleu, 203.

Trigo, P., Martins, J.A., Almeida, F.A., Silva, V.P., Azevedo, J.F., Oliveira, C.A.A., and Ramos, M.T. 2012. Effects of electrolyte supplementation on colinic contents and faeces in horses. EEAP Pub. 132: 367–70.

Trigo, P., Redondo, A.J., Estévez, I., Muñoz, A., Riber, C., and Castejón, F. 2006. Effects of a high fat diet and aerobic training on carbohydrate and fat utilization during a maximal incremental exercise. Seventh International Conference on Equine Exercise. Aug: Fontainbleu, 202.

Trumble, T.N. 2005. The use of nutraceuticals for osteoarthritis in the horse. Vet Clin N Am Equine Pract (21); 575–597.

Turner, K.K., Nielsen, B.D., O'Connor, C.I., and Rosenstein, D.S. 2006. Silicon and osteochondrotic lesions in two-year-old standardbred. Seventh International Conference on Equine Exercise. Aug: Fontainbleu, 212.

Turner, S.P., Hess, T.M., Treiber, K., Mello, E.B., Souza B.G., and Almeida, F.Q. 2011. Comparison of insulin sensitivity of horses adapted to different exercise intensities. J E Vet Sci Nov; 31(11); 645–9.

United States Equestrian Federation. 2015. General Rulebook.

Uotila, R., Thuneberg, T., and Saastamoinen, M. 2012. The usage of forage analysis in optimizing horse nutrition in Finland. EEAP Pub. 132: 331–34.

Urschel, K. and Lawrence, L.M. 2013. Chapter 6, Amino acids and protein, in Equine Applied and Clinical Nutrition. Saunders Elsevier: NY, Geor, R.J., Harris., P.A., and Coenen, M., eds.

Valle, E. and Bergero, D. 2008. Electrolyte requirements and supplementation in exercising horses. In Nutrition of the Exercising Horse EAAP Publication No.125 Wageningen Academic Publishers: Netherlands, 219.

Vanderweerd, J.M., Coisnon, C., Clegg, P., Cambier, C., Pierson, A., Hontoir, F., Saegerman, C., Gustin, P., and Buczinksi, S. 2012. Systematic Review of Efficacy of Nutraceuticals to Alleviate Clinical Signs of Osteoarthritis. J Vet Intern Med 26: 448–456.

Vega, S. and Domingo, R. 2012. Metaanalysis of the nephrosplenic entrapment in horses. Proceedings of the 18th Annual Meeting of the Italian Association of equine Veterinarians. Feb: Bologna, 230–232.

Venner, M, Lauffs, S., and Deegen, E. 1999. Treatment of gastric lesions in horses with pectin-lecithin complex. Equine Vet J Suppl Apr; (29)91–6.

Vervuert, I. 2008. Major mineral and trace element requirements and functions in exercising horses. In Nutrition of the Exercising Horse EAAP Publication No.125, Wageningen Academic Publishers: Netherlands pp 207.

Vervuert, I, Boethe, C. and Coenen, M. 2004. Effects of corn processing on the glycemic and insulinaemic responses in horses. J Anim Physio Anim Nutr (Berl) Oct; 88(9–10): 348–55.

Vervuert, I., Boethe, C., and Coenen, M. 2007. Glycaemic and insulinaemic responses to mechanical or thermal processed barley in horses. J Anim Physiol Anim Nutr (Berl) Jun; 91(5–6): 263–8.

Vervuert, I. and Ellis, A. 2013. Chapter 32, Developmental orthopedic disease, in Equine Applied and Clinical Nutrition. Saunders Elsevier: NY, Geor, R.J., Harris, P.A., and Coenen, M., eds.

Vervuert, I., Stanik, K., and Coenen, M. 2006. Effects of different levels of calcium and phosphorus intake on calcium homeostasis in exercising horses. Seventh International Conference on Equine Exercise. Aug: Fontainbleu, 213.

Vervuert, I, Voigt, K., Hollands, T., Cudderford, D., and Coenen, M. 2009. Effect of feeding increasing quantities of starch on glycaemic and insulinaemic responses in healthy horses. Vet J Oct; 182(1): 67–72.

Visser, E.K., Ellis, A.D., and Van Reenan, C.G. 2008. The effect of two different housing conditions on the welfare of young horses stables for the first time. App An Behav Sci Dec 1 (114):3-4:521-533

von Samson-Himmelstjerna, G. 2012. Anthelmintic resistance in equine parasites-detection, potential clinical relevance and implications for control. Vet Parasitol Apr 19; 185(1): 2–8.

Warren, H.E. and Codner, L. 2012. Effect of yucca (Yucca schidigera) on ammonia levels from equine excreta in the stable. EEAP Pub. 132: 343–6.

Warren, H.E. and Hale. C. 2012. Effect of inoculation of laminitic-prone equine fecal innocula with varying forage sources with or without live yeast (Sacchaaromyces cerevisiae) on in vitro gas production parameters. EEAP Pub. 132: 323–6.

Warren, L.K., Lawrence, L.M., and Thompson, K.N. 1999. The influence of betaine on untrained and trained horses exercising to fatigue. J Anim Sci Mar; 77(3): 677–84.

Warren, L.K. and Vineyard, K.R. 2013. Chapter 7, Fats and fatty acids, in Equine Applied and Clinical Nutrition. Saunders Elsevier: NY, Geor, R.J., Harris., P.A., and Coenen, M., eds.

Waterfall H.L., Geor, R.J., Larson, L., Stewart-Hunt, L., and McCutcheon, L.J. 2006. Glucose delivery via the gastrointestinal tract limits early post exercise muscle glycogen synthesis. Seventh International Conference on Equine Exercise. Aug: Fontainbleu, 194.

Watts, K. 2010. Pasture management to minimize the risk of equine laminitis. Vet Clin North Am Equine Pract Aug (26)2; 361–9.

Weese, J.S., Anderson, M.E.C., Lowe, A., and Monteith, G.J. 2003. Preliminary investigation of the probiotic potential of *Lactobacillus rhamnosus* strain GG in horses: fecal recovery following oral administration and safety. Can Vet J Apr; 44(4): 299–302.

Weese, J.S. and Martin, H. 2011. Assessment of commercial probiotic bacterial content and label accuracy., Can Vet J 52(1)43–46.

Weese, J.S. and Rousseau, J. 2005. Evaluation of Lactobacillus pentosus WE7 for prevention of diarrhea in neonatal foals. J am Vet Med Assoc Jun 15; 226(12): 2031–4.

Wein, S. and Wolffram, S. 2013. Oral Bioavailability of Quercetin in Horses. J Eq Vet Sci Jun; 33(6): 441–5.

Weiss, B., Eastridge, M., Shoemaker, D., and St. Pierre, N. Distillers Grains. Ohio State University Extension Factsheet. Accessed Oct: 2015.

White, A., Estrada, M., Walker, K., Wisnia, P., Filueira, G., Valdés, F., Araneda, O., Behn, C., and Ramón Martínez. 2001. Role of exercise and ascorbate on plasma antioxidant capacity in thoroughbred race horses. Elsevier Comp Biochem and Phys Part A: 99–104.

Williams, C.A. 2013. Chapter 19, Specialized dietary supplements, in Equine Applied and Clinical Nutrition. Saunders Elsevier: NY, Geor, R.J., Harris, P.A., and Coenen, M., eds.

Williams, C.A. and Carlucci, S. 2006. The effects of oral vitamin E supplementation on vitamin and antioxidant status in intensely exercising horses. Seventh International Conference on Equine Exercise. Aug: Fontainbleu, 198.

Zeyner, A., personal communication.1 Oct 2015.

Zeyner, A. and Harmeyer, J. 1999. Metabolic functions of L-carnitine and its effect as feed additive in horses: a review. Arch Tierernahr 52; (2): 115–138.

Zeyner, A. and Harris, P. 2013. Chapter 9, Vitamins, in Equine Applied and Clinical Nutrition. Saunders Elsevier: NY, Geor, R.J., Harris., P.A., and Coenen, M., eds.

Zeyner, A., Hoffmeister, C. Einspanier, A., Gottschalk, J., Lengwenat, O., and Illies, M. 2006. Glycaemic and insuliaemic response of quarter horses to concentrates high in fat and low in soluble carbohydrates. Equine Vet J Supp Aug; (36): 643–7.

Zeyner, A. and Kienzle, E. 2002. A Method to Estimate Digestible Energy in Horse Feed. J Nutr 132(6): 17715–35.

Zeyner, A., Romanowski, K., Vernuft, A., Harris, P. and Kienzle, E. 2014. Scoring of sweat losses in exercised horses—a pilot study. J Anim Physiol Anim Nutr (Berl) Apr; 98(2): 246–50.

Zeyner, A., Schwartzer, U., and Fuerll, M. 2006. Effects of an oral sodium chloride load at different levels on acid-base balance and renal mineral excretion in horses. Seventh International Conference on Equine Exercise. Aug: Fontainbleu, 205.

Index

Numbers

2, 4-D, 56

2, 4-Dichlorophenooxyacetic acid, 56

2-chloroproprionate, 137

2-CP, 137

3-carbon acid, 52

3-phosphoglyceric acid, 52

4-carbon acid, 51

A

AAEP; *see American Association of Equine Practitioners (AAEP)*

AAFCO; *see American Association of Feed Control Officials (AAFCO)*

abortion, 139-141, 194

acer, 119-120

acetate, 14, 68

acidosis, 15, 32, 62, 72, 78, 147

aconitum columbianum, 119

acrylic, 126

ACTH; *see adrenocorticotropic hormone (ACTH)*

adelfa, 119

adenoma, 194

adipokines, 175

adiposity, 183

adrenocorticotropic hormone (ACTH), 194-196

aerophagia, 16

aflatoxin, 62, 66, 68, 71, 123

agalactia, 123

agropyron cristatum, 55

agrostis hyemalis, 119

Akhal Teke, 130

alanine, 33, 137

alaria, 68

alfalfa, 3, 5-6, 29-30, 32, 37, 44-45, 48, 51, 54, 56, 60, 65, 68, 70-71, 74, 83, 122-123, 129, 131, 138-139, 141-143, 150-152, 154, 159, 161, 163, 166-167, 173, 197, 202, 205

algae, 68, 157

alimentary system, 10

alkali disease, 31

alkaloid, 118, 120, 122

allium, 85

Ally, 56

almond hulls, 67

aloe vera, 80, 83, 86

alpha-linolenic acid, 32, 69, 89-90, 157

alpha-lipoic acid, 89, 135

alsike clover, 51, 121-123

aluminomagnesium silicate, 206

aluminum hydroxide, 206

American Association of Equine Practitioners (AAEP), 19-20, 155-156

American Association of Feed Control Officials (AAFCO), 39

American Quarter Horse, 131, 143, 158, 169, 202

American Yew, 119

amino acid
branched chain, 33, 134, 137
essential , 33, 68, 75, 217
first limiting, 33-34, 68
non-essential, 33, 68

amsinckia menziesii, 118

amylase, 12, 38

amylopectin, 31

amylose, 31

analysis, feed; *see feed testing*

anaplerosis, 134

andropogon gerardii, 54

andropogon hallii, 54

anemia, 85-86, 89, 120, 172

anhydrosis, 194

anionic salts, 198

anterior, 96, 194

anthelmintic, 87, 102, 104-106, 108-114, 141, 145, 159, 167, 196

anti-donkey factor, 169

antioxidant, 27, 64, 86, 88-89, 132, 137, 157

apoptosis, 155

Appaloosa, 130

apple, 25, 66, 82-83, 86, 118, 198

apple cider vinegar, 25, 86

arcade, dental, 93, 99

arginine, 33

argostis gigantean, 54

arsenic, 44, 85

arthritis, 90, 154-155, 158, 182

artificial sweetener, 25

ascarid, 105-106, 150

ascorbate, 85
ascorbic acid, 85
ash, 37-45, 58
ash content, 42
asparagine, 33
aspartic acid, 33
aspirin, 156, 205
astragalus cicer, 54
ASUs; *see avocado-soy unsaponifibles*
avocado-soy unsaponifibles, 157

B
Bach Flower Remedies, 87-88
Bach, Edward, 87
Bacillus
    licheniformis, B., 73
bacteria, beneficial, 15, 61, 72
bahia, 54, 123
BALF; *see bronchoalveolar lavage fluid (BALF)*
Banamine, 156, 205
Banvel, 56
Banvell II, 56
barley, 32, 42, 62-63, 67, 117, 134, 166
barley disease, 166; *see also barley*
BBCH scale, 50
BCAA; *see branched chain amino acids (BCAAs)*
BCS; *see body condition score (BCS)*
beans, 51, 64
bee pollen, 86
beet pulp, 3, 5, 30, 32, 37, 49, 58, 65-66, 70, 76, 79, 82,
    131, 139, 150, 152, 154, 174, 184, 186, 191, 197, 201-202
behavior, 3-4, 6, 10, 20-24, 30, 96-98, 116, 138, 146-147,
    151, 179, 197
belladonna, 85, 119
benzimidazole, 105, 111
Bermuda grass; *see grass*
berteroa incana, 118
beta-carotene, 26-27
beta-phenyl gamma-aminobutyric acid, 85
betaine, 136
bethanechol, 16, 206
bezoar, 83
bicarb, 29
bicarbonate, 11-12, 29, 129, 136-137, 206
Bifidobacterium
    B. animalis, 73
    B. bifidum, 73
    B. coagulans, 73
    B. curtipendula, 54

B. gracilis, 54
B. infantis, 73
B. licheniformis, 73
B. longum, 73
B. subtilis, 73
bin run, 124
bioflavonoids, 157
biotin, 26-27
bird's-foot trefoil, 51, 55
bismuth subsalicylate, 206
bisphenol A (BPA), 125-126
bitter melon, 86
black blotch, 122
black cohosh, 86
black henbane, 118
black oil sunflower seed, 64
black patch, 122
black tea, 86
black walnut, 118, 120
blind staggers, 31
blind wolf teeth, 94, 96
blister beetle, 51, 123-124
blood builder, 86
blood worms, 104
blue block, 75
blue grama, 53-54
blue-green algae, 157
bluegrass, 48, 50, 53-54, 122
Bluestem, 52, 54
body condition score (BCS), 9, 176, 181, 210-212, 219
bolt (food), 15, 97
boot stage, 49
borborygmi, 18
boron, 28
BOSS; *see black oil sunflower seed*
bot fly, 103, 110
bots, 103, 150
botulism, 59, 124-125, 182
boulardii, 73
bouteloua, 54
Bovatec, 71
box elder, 120
BPA; *see bisphenol A (BPA)*
brachygnathism, 96
bracken fern, 115, 118, 121
bran
    rice, 32, 63-65, 67, 70-71, 134, 158, 163
    wheat, 32, 63-65, 71, 83, 139, 155, 163, 187, 197
    bran disease, 166

branched chain amino acids (BCAAs), 33, 134, 137

brassica, 5

brevis, L., 73

brewer's grains, 67, 154

brewer's yeast, 67

broken wind, 199

brome

    common, 54

    meadow, 54

    smooth, 15, 54, 83, 93, 101

bromelain, 157

bromocriptine, 196

bromus biebersteinii, 54

bromus inermis, 54

bromus riparius, 54

bronchii, 199

bronchioles, 199

bronchiolitis, 199

bronchoalveolar lavage fluid (BALF), 200

brown alga, 68

browse, 7, 164-167

Brunner's glands, 12

bruxism, 15, 204

buccal, 94, 96

buffalograss, 54

bulgaricus, L., 73

bull nettle, 120

burning bush, 118

burro, 164

bute; see phenylbutazone

butter-and-eggs, 118

buttercup, 115, 118, 121

butyrate, 14, 68, 134

C

C3, 52

C4, 51

C-phycocyanin, 157

C. difficile, 206

C. perfringens, 206

Ca; see calcium (Ca)

cabbage, 5

caffeine, 83, 86

Cal; see megacalorie (Mcal)

calcitonin, 29

calcium (Ca), 7, 11, 27-30, 35, 43-44, 65, 67, 74, 76, 79-82, 85-86, 91, 131-132, 137, 139, 150, 155, 166, 197-198, 201, 205-206

calcium carbonate, 80, 132, 206

calcium oxalate, 29

calcium:magnesium ratio, 29

calcium:phosphorus ratio, 7, 29, 67, 74

calculi, 197

calculus index (CI), 100

calming aid, 90

calming supplements, 138

calorie, 34-35, 173

camphor, 85

canine teeth, 94

canola, 3, 5, 69-70, 83, 90, 132, 141-142, 154, 205

cantharidin, 123-124

cap, on a tooth, 96

capillary refill, 25

capsaicin, 85, 89

capsicum, 89

carbohydrate (CHO), 7, 31-32, 34, 39-40, 43-52, 57, 65-66, 129, 135, 160-161, 165, 172, 178, 189, 202-203, 216

carbohydrate, storage, 51-52

carbon dioxide, 14, 51, 82

caries, 99

carnitine, 33, 136

carnosine, 136-137

carotenid, 44

carrot, 82-83, 155

cartilage, 29, 31, 151-152, 155, 157, 166

casei, 73

casein, 68

cathartics, 16

cation, 29, 76

cavities, 99

cecum, 10, 12-14, 16, 32, 105

cellulose, 31, 38-39, 43, 49, 178

cellulytic microbes, 14

centaurea, 119

cereal, 45, 61

cerevisiae, 73

cestode, 104, 106

cetyl M, 157

cetyl myristoleate, 157-158

CF; see crude fiber (CF)

CGIT; see combined glucose-insulin test (CGIT)

chaff, 61, 178

chamomile, 85

charlock, 119

chasteberry, 86, 196

cheek teeth, 93-94, 96-97

cherry, 117-118

chewing, 8, 11, 23, 93-94, 97-98, 165, 204

chia, 63-64, 83

chiggers, 102

chloride (Cl), 16, 25, 28-29, 35, 74, 76-77, 79-81, 126, 132, 187-188

chlorine, 28-29

chlorophyll, 122

CHO; see carbohydrate (CHO)

CHO-FR, 45

CHO-FS, 45

CHO-H, 45

chocolate, 83

choke, 10-11, 14-15, 47, 71, 93, 97, 118, 182

chokecherry, 118

cholecalciferol, 27

cholimimetics, 16

choline, 26

chondroitin, 156-158

chondroitin sulfate, 156

chop, 58-60

chromium (Cr), 28, 67, 86, 91, 135, 137, 191

chromosomes, 164, 169

chronic kidney disease (CKD), 197

CI; see calculus index (CI); comfort index (CI)

cicuta maculatum, 118

cicutoxin, 120

cimetidine, 205-206

cinchy, 204

cirrhosis, 186

cirsium arvense, 118

cisapride, 16

citric acid cycle, 136-137

CKD; see chronic kidney disease (CKD)

Cl; see chloride (Cl)

claviceps, 123

clinoptilolite, 74

Clopyralid, 56

clostridium botulinum, 125

Clostridium difficile, 206

Clostridium perfringens, 206

clover, 51, 54, 56, 118, 121-123

clover slobbers, 123

CMPK, 137

Co; see cobalt (Co)

co-enzyme Q10, 136, 157

co-factor, 157

coagulans, 73

coastal hay, 153

COB (corn, oats and barley combination), 62-63

cobalamin, 28

cobalt (Co), 28, 35, 75-76, 91

cock's-foot, 54

cocklebur, 120

coconut, 66

coconut oil, 66, 70, 83

cod liver, 69

colic,
    impaction, 14, 16, 94, 97, 154, 166
    sand, 16-18, 41, 54, 162

colitis, 182, 203-204, 206

collagen, 156

colon, 10, 13-14, 16, 69, 105, 204

colostrum, 135, 142-143, 145-147

combined glucose-insulin test (CGIT), 190

comfort index (CI), 78

comfrey, 85

common cocklebur, 120

compensatory eating, 21

compensatory grazing, 52, 161, 178

conium maculatum, 118

convolvulus, 118

cool season grasses
    bluegrass, 48, 50, 53-54, 122
    brome, 48, 50, 52, 54, 122, 205
    fescue, 50, 52, 54, 56, 122-123, 141
    orchardgrass, 139
    rye, 45, 50, 52, 56, 62-63, 67, 141

copper (Cu), 28-29, 35, 44, 74-76, 91, 150, 187

copper:zinc ratio, 74-75

copra, 66, 70

coprophagia, 8, 149

corn, 3, 6, 32, 62-63, 66-67, 69-71, 83, 134, 139, 143, 147, 165, 173, 190

corn oil, 70, 143, 173

corn syrup, 147, 190

Cornell University, 43

coronilla varia, 51

cortisol, 129, 194, 196

cottonseed meal, 68, 71

COX, 135, 156-157

COX inhibitor, 156

COX-2, 156-157

CP; see crude protein (CP)

Cr; see chromium (Cr)

cranberry, 86, 206

creatine, 134-137

creep feeding, 149, 151-152

crested wheatgrass, 53

cresty neck, 9, 177, 180, 183-184, 194
Cresty Neck Score, 9, 177, 184
crib biting, 23
cribbing, 16, 20, 23-24, 96, 182
crotalaria, 119
crown vetch, 51
crude fiber (CF), 43
crude protein (CP), 42
crypts, 12
Cu; see copper (Cu)
cubes, hay, 201
cuboidal bone malformation, 151
cumarol, 122
curvatis, L., 73
Cushing's Disease, 189, 193
Cushing, Harvey, 193
cutaneous habronemiasis, 107
cutting, hay, 57
CVB, 207
cyanide, 79, 118
cyanocobalamin, 26
cyathostomes, 105, 111
cyathostominosis; see larval cyathostominosis
cyclooxygenase, 135
cynodon dactylon, 54
cypress, 118
cyproheptadine, 196
cysteine, 31, 33, 88
cystine, 31, 33
cytisus scoparius, 119
cytokines, 137
Cytotec, 206

D

dactylis glomerata, 54
Dallisgrass, 123
dandelion, 86
dandelion, false, 193
Dartmoor, 183
datura, 118-119
DCA; see dichloroacetate (DCA)
DCDIC; see disodium cyanodithiomidocarbonate (DCDIC)
DDGS; see distiller's dried grains with solubles (DDGS)
DDM; see digestible dry matter (DDM)
DE; see digestible energy (DE)
deficiency, 24, 26-31, 33, 85, 152, 166, 192
dental arcade, 99
deoxynivalenol (DON), 62
detergent fiber analysis (DFA), 40, 43

devil's claw, 85-86, 89
deworm, 102, 109-110, 173
dexamethasone suppression test, 195-196
dextrose, 79, 137
DFA; see detergent fiber analysis (DFA)
DFM; see direct fed microbials (DFM)
DHA; see docosahexaenoic acid (DHA)
di-tri-octahedral smectite, 206
diaphoresis, 194
diaphragm, 81, 188
diaphragmatic flexure, 13-14
diastema, 93
diatomaceous earth, 87, 113
diatomite, 113
diazepam, 85
dicalcium phosphate, 29
dicamba, 56
dichloroacetate (DCA), 137
Dictocaulus arnfieldi, 200
dicumarol, 122
Dietary Supplement and Health Education Act of 1994 (DSHEA), 85
digestible dry matter (DDM), 38
digestible energy (DE), 38, 44, 49, 165
digestible protein (DP), 42
digitalis purpurea, 118
dimethylglycine, 136-137
dioctyl sodium sulfosuccinate (DSS), 16
diphyodontous, 94
direct fed microbials (DFM), 72
disaccharide, 31
disodium cyanodithiomidocarbonate (DCDIC), 66
distiller's dried grains with solubles (DDGS), 67
dl-a-tocopheryl, 27
DM; see dry matter (DM)
DMD; see dry matter digestibility (DMD)
DMG; see dimethylglycine
DMI; see dry matter intake (DMI)
docosahexaenoic acid (DHA), 69, 135
docosapentaenoic acid (DPA), 69
dolomite, 80
donkey, 7, 107, 164-169
Donkey Sanctuary, The, 165, 168
dorsal colon, 13-14, 204
dorsal curvature, 96
dorsal recumbancy, 106, 150, 204
DP; see digestible protein (DP)
DPA; see docosapentaenoic acid (DPA)
draschia megastoma, 107

dry cob, 63

dry gangrene, 123

dry matter (DM), 40, 42

dry matter digestibility (DMD), 38

dry matter intake (DMI), 45

dry weight (DW), 38

DSHEA; *see Dietary Supplement and Health Education Act of 1994 (DSHEA)*

DSS; *see dioctyl sodium sulfosuccinate (DSS)*

DTO smectite, 206

dulse, 68

DW; *see dry weight (DW)*

dyospirobezoars, 83

dysautonomia, 125

dyschondroplasia, 151

dystocia, 123

E

e. coli, 65, 206

E. faecium, 73

E. thermophilus, 73

eastern black nightshade, 119

easy keeper, 48, 153, 175, 183

Echinacea, 86, 89

echium vulgare, 119

edema, 120, 173

EDM; *see equine degenerative myeloencephalopathy (EDM)*

EE; *see ether extract (EE)*

EFA; *see fatty acid*

EFE; *see epiploic foramen entrapment (EFE)*

egg reappearance period (ERP), 109

eggs per gram (EPG), 107

EGS; *see equine grass sickness (EGS)*

EGUD; *see equine gastroduodenal ulcer disease (EGUD)*

EGUS; *see equine gastric ulcer syndrome (EGUS)*

eicosapentaenoic acid (EPA), 69

elder, box, 120

electrolytes, 1, 25, 28, 33, 51, 65, 70, 76-80, 129, 131-132, 137, 170, 172, 182, 188, 205

elymus lanceolatus, 55

embryo (seed), 61

EMS; *see equine metabolic syndrome (EMS)*

endocrine, 155, 182-183, 193, 196

endophyte, 54, 123, 141

endoscopy, 203-204

endosperm, 61-62

energy, 5, 14, 20, 32, 34-36, 38-42, 44-45, 48-49, 58, 61, 63, 67-70, 76, 111, 129-130, 133-139, 141, 143-144, 146,

150, 152, 159, 161, 164-165, 167, 169, 171-172, 175, 179, 186, 196, 203

enteral fluids, 16

Enterococcus, 72-73

enterolith, 16, 51, 54

enzyme, 12, 32, 64-65, 89, 135-137, 147, 156-157, 205

EPA, 69, 157

EPG; *see eggs per gram (EPG)*

epiphysitis, 151

epiploic foramen entrapment (EFE), 16

EPM; *see equine protozoal myeloencephalitis (EPM)*

EPSM; *see equine polysaccharide storage myopathy (EPSM)*

Epsom salts, 16, 80

equine degenerative myeloencephalopathy (EDM), 27, 140, 192

equine gastric ulcer syndrome (EGUS), 7, 150, 203-204

equine gastroduodenal ulcer disease (EGUD), 203-204

equine grass sickness (EGS), 124-125, 182, 188

equine leukoencephalomalacia, 71

equine metabolic syndrome (EMS), 32, 85, 182, 194

equine motor neuron disease (EMND), 27, 192

equine periodontal disease index, 100

equine polysaccharide storage myopathy (EPSM), 202

equine protozoal myeloencephalitis (EPM), 103

equisetum arvense, 118

Equisyl Advantage, 205

Equus africanus asinus, 164

equus ferus caballus, 164

ER; *see recurrent exertional rhabdomyolysis (RER)*

Eragrostis teff, 55

ergocalciferol, 27

ergogenic, 33, 65, 132-136, 138-139, 157

ergot, 54, 123, 141

ergotism, 123

ERP; *see egg reappearance period (ERP)*

ERS, 201

erythrocytes, 169, 172

ESC; *see ethanol soluble carbohydrate (ESC)*

esomeprazole, 206

esophageal obstruction, 11, 14-15, 65

esophagus, 10-11, 13-14, 110, 201

essential fatty acid; *see fatty acid*

essential oil, 90

ethanol soluble carbohydrate (ESC), 38, 45

ether extract (EE), 42

euthanasia, 17, 113, 116, 187

expectorant, 200

extinction behavior, 24

extruded, 71

extrusion, 64, 71

F

F;*see fluoride (F)*
faecium, E., 73
famotidine, 206
fasciculation, 201, 203
fast twitch, 133
fasting, 21-24, 146, 161, 166, 172, 204
fat, 24, 26, 32, 34, 36, 39-40, 42-44, 48-49, 61, 63,
    65-70, 75, 129, 132, 135, 139, 144, 147-148, 152-154,
    160-161, 165-167, 169, 171-172, 175-177, 179-187, 189,
    194, 196, 203, 210
fat soluble vitamins, 26, 187
fatty acid
    essential, 20, 32-33, 40, 42, 48, 68-69, 75, 90, 114,
        117, 147, 154, 166, 184, 205
    monounsaturated, 69
    non-esterified, 69
    polyunsaturated, 69, 157
    saturated, 69
    volatile, 14, 68, 72
Fe; *see iron (Fe)*
febrile, 88
FEC; *see fecal egg count (FEC)*
fecal egg count (FEC), 102, 107-109, 114, 194, 196
fecal egg count reduction test (FECRT), 109
fecal exam, 17, 107
fecal sand check, 16-17
FECRT; *see fecal egg count reduction test (FECRT)*
feed analysis, 37-40, 43-46, 64, 124
feed testing; *see feed analysis*
Feekes scale, 50
fenbendazole, 105, 111-112
feral horse, 151
ferulic acid, 65, 134
fescue, 50, 52, 54, 56, 122-123, 141
festuca, 54
fiddleneck, 118
field bindweed, 118
field horsetail, 115
field oats, 62
firocoxib, 156, 205
first limiting amino acid, 33-34, 68
fish meal, 68
fish oil, 69
fistulated, 69
flavonoids, 157
flax, 30, 42, 63-64, 68-69, 83, 90, 139, 163, 205

fleas, 102
flies, 24, 102-103, 107, 154
floating, dental, 96, 98-99
flotation tests, 109
flowers-of-sulfur, 31
flunixin meglamine (Banamine), 156, 205
fluoride (F), 28
folic acid, 26
forage, 1, 7-8, 11, 14-16, 18-24, 27, 30-32, 34, 36-37,
    39-40, 43-45, 47-63, 65, 67-69, 71, 73-75, 77, 79, 81,
    83, 89-90, 93-94, 121-123, 125, 129, 131, 135, 138, 141,
    143-144, 147, 149-152, 159-161, 163-167, 178, 184, 188,
    190-191, 196, 199, 201-202, 204-205
forage poisoning, 125
forbs, 48
Forsell's procedure, 23
founder, 18
foxglove, 115, 118
foxtail, 117-119
free radical, 137, 157
fresh weight (FW), 40
fructan, 7, 31, 39, 49-52, 59, 178, 191
fructooligosaccharides, 73-74
fructose, 31, 49
fruit, 25, 66, 82, 118, 191
fumonisin, 62, 71
functional keratin, 156
fungi
    intestinal, 16-17, 104, 110, 194
    nematophagus, 114
fungus, 54, 56, 62, 123
furanocoumarins, 122
fusariotoxin, 123
fusarium, 62
FW; *see fresh weight (FW)*

G

GABA; *see gamma-aminobutyric acid (GABA)*
GAGs, See glycosaminoglycans, 156
galactooligosaccharides, 73
galactose, 31
gallic acid, 118, 120
gamma oryzanol (GO), 65, 134
gamma-aminobutyric acid (GABA), 85, 138
gangrene, 123
garlic, 85-86, 89, 113
gasterophilus, 103
gastric ulcer, 7, 150, 182, 203-204
gastroduodenal ulcer disease (GDUD), 204

gastrointestinal tract (GIT), 10, 13, 16, 18, 25, 51, 64-65,
    72, 74, 87, 102-105, 107, 110, 113, 115, 119, 123, 125, 129,
    131, 135, 141, 146, 149-150, 156, 164, 172-173, 175, 205,
    217
GDUD; see gastroduodenal ulcer disease (GDUD)
GE; see gross energy (GE)
GEH (Gesellschaft fur Ernahrungsphysiologie der
    Haustiere) , 207
gelatin, 134
genetically modified organism (GMO), 66
geophagia, 8, 16
germ, part of a seed, 61-62, 65, 83
ginger, 86
gingivitis index (GI), 100
GIT; see gastrointestinal tract (GIT)
glandular stomach region, 11
glucometer, 191
gluconeogenesis, 186
glucophage, 191
glucosamine, 156-158
glucose, 12, 31, 49, 62, 69, 90, 129, 136, 147, 172, 185-186,
    189, 191, 202
glutamic acid, 33
glutamine, 33
glutathione peroxidase, 132
glycemic index, 31-32, 132, 189, 191
glycemic response, 31-32, 49, 67, 191
glyceride, 69
glycerine, 80
glycerol, 32, 69, 80
glycine, 33, 134
glycogen, 129, 132, 135, 137, 146, 172, 202
glycolytic, 133, 137
glycosaminoglycans (GAGs), 156
glycoside, 118
glyphosate, 5, 66
GMO; see genetically modified organism (GMO)
GO; see gamma oryzanol (GO)
goiter, 30
grain, 6-7, 11, 15, 18-20, 30, 32, 39, 46, 50, 58, 60-64,
    67-68,
70-71, 74, 83, 90, 124, 131, 144, 150, 152, 155, 161, 165-167,
    169, 173, 181, 184, 186, 189, 191, 198, 202-203
grain hay
    oat, 50, 52, 54, 60, 67, 124, 139, 163, 173
    rye, 45, 50, 52, 56, 62-63, 67, 141
grama
    blue, 53-54
    sideoats, 53-54

graminaceous, 62
grass
    bahia, 54, 123
    Bermuda, 45, 48, 52, 54, 122, 153, 205
    Brome, 48, 50, 52, 54, 122, 205
    buffalograss, 54
    coastal, 54, 153
    cock's-foot, 54
    Dallisgrass, 123
    fescue, 50, 52, 54, 56, 122-123, 141
    Indiangrass, 53-54
    Johnson, 53-54, 119, 122, 167
    needlegrass, 54
    oat, 50, 52, 54, 60, 67, 124, 139, 163, 173
    orchardgrass, 52, 54
    red top, 54
    reed canary, 53-54
    rye, 45, 50, 52, 56, 62-63, 67, 141
    Sudan, 52-54, 119, 122, 167
    teff, 53, 55
    timothy, 48, 52-53, 55, 60, 122, 163
    wheatgrass, 53, 55
grass sickness, 124-125, 182, 188
grazing muzzle, 50, 52-53, 161, 178, 190
green chop, 60
green tea, 86
green-lipped mussels, 157
grinders, 93
gross energy (GE), 38
groundsel, 119, 122
growth spurt, 144

H
hair analysis, 90-91
hairy vetch, 51
halitosis, 97
hard keeper, 154
hawthorn, 86
hay
    alfalfa, 3, 5-6, 29-30, 32, 37, 44-45, 48, 51, 54, 56, 60, 65,
        68, 70-71, 74, 83, 122-123, 129, 131, 138-139, 141-143,
        150-152, 154, 159, 161, 163, 166-167, 173, 197, 202, 205
    analysis, 57
    bahia, 54, 123
    Bermuda, 45, 48, 52, 54, 122, 153, 205
    grain, 6-7, 11, 15, 18-20, 30, 32, 39, 46, 50, 58,
        60-64, 67-68, 70-71, 74, 83, 90, 124, 131, 144, 150,
        152, 155, 161, 165-167, 169, 173, 181, 184, 186, 189,
        191, 198, 202-203

grass, 1, 7, 12, 14, 16, 19-20, 31, 41, 45, 47-57, 59-60, 63, 66, 68, 70, 74-75, 83, 93, 96, 104-105, 114, 117-119, 122-125, 138-139, 141, 150-151, 154, 160-161, 165, 167, 178, 180-182, 188, 190, 197, 202, 205

quality, 2-4, 7, 39, 42-44, 46, 53, 57, 59-61, 63, 129, 131, 141-144, 146, 149-152, 154-155, 159-160, 162, 164-165, 171, 178, 185-186, 196

storage, 32, 47, 51-52, 57, 67, 124, 129, 160, 182, 189, 201-202

tifton, 54

timothy, 48, 52-53, 55, 60, 122, 163

hay belly, 45

hay soaking, 188

haylage, 58-60, 125, 201

heart, 8, 18, 81, 99, 104, 118, 129-130, 136, 145, 148, 163, 168, 172, 175-176, 179, 208-209, 211, 214-215, 219

heart girth, 8, 148, 162-163, 168, 175-176, 208-209, 211, 219

heart monitor, 130

heave line, 198

heavy metals, 66

Heinz Body Anemia, 86

Helicobacter, 206

heliotrope, 118, 122

helminth, 102, 111

helveticus, L., 73

hematuria, 124

hemicellulose, 31, 38-39, 43, 49, 178

hemlock, 115, 118, 120

hemoglobin, 136

hemolytic anemia, 120

hemp, 63-64, 69

Henneke body condition score, 9, 152, 167, 176, 210-212

hepatotoxic, 118

herbicide, 56, 66, 124

hermaphrodite worms, 109

heterodontous, 93

high contaminator, 108

high shedder, 108, 114

hindgut acidosis, 15, 32, 62

hinny, 169

hirsutism, 193

histidine, 33, 137

hoary allysum, 118

homeopathic preparation, 87-88

homeopathy, 87

honey, 83, 90

honeybee, 87

hook bone, 172, 210, 212

hooks, on teeth

anterior, 96

caudal, 96

rostral, 96

hops, 85

hordeum jubatum, 117

hordeum vulgare, 62

hormone

adrenocorticotropic, 194-195

insulin, 10, 12, 20-22, 31-32, 39, 43, 47, 50, 52, 62, 82, 90, 121, 129, 140, 160-161, 172-173, 175, 180, 182-185, 188-192, 194-196, 202

leptin, 129, 184

parathyroid, 29

thyrotropin-releasing hormone, 195

troponin, 72

horse nettle, 119-120

horsetail, 115, 118, 121

hound's tongue, 118

hull

almond, 67

peanut, 68, 70, 80, 83

rice, 32, 63, 65, 67, 70-71, 134, 158, 163

soy, 30, 37, 67-69, 76, 90, 154, 157, 163, 166, 191, 202, 205

humeral head, 209-211

husks, 67

hyaluronic acid, 156

hyaluronon, 156-157

hydrated magnesium sulfate, 16

hydrochloric acid, 11-12, 22

hyoscyamus niger, 118

hyper-excitability, 81

hyperalimentation, 88

hypericum perforatum, 119

hyperinsulinemia, 184, 189

hyperkalemic periodic paralysis (HYPP), 30, 47, 83, 187

hyperleptinemia, 184

hyperlipemia, 139, 161, 166, 179, 186

hyperlipidemia, 186

hypernutrition, 88, 173

hypersalivation, 119, 122

hyperthermia, 193

hypertonic, 78, 132, 205

hypertrichosis, 193

hypochaeris radicata, 193

hypokalemic diaphragmatic flutter, 182

hypophosphatemia, 172-173

hypothalamus, 193-194

hypothiaminosis, 173

hypothyroidism, 30, 182
HYPP; *see hyperkalemic periodic paralysis (HYPP)*
hypsodont, 93

I

I;*see iodine (I)*
Icelandic, 163
icterus, 145, 186; *see also jaundice*
IgG; *see immunoglobin G (IgG)*
ileocecal valve, 12, 106
ileum, 12-13, 15
ileus, 15
immunoglobin G (IgG), 143, 146
impaction, 14, 16, 94, 97, 154, 166
in vitro dry matter digestibility (IVDMD), 38
inappetance, 25, 31, 73, 116, 129, 161, 166, 173, 186, 197
incisors, 93-94, 96-97
index,
    calculus, 100
    comfort (CI), 78
    gingivitis (GI), 100
    glycemic, 31-32, 49, 67, 132, 189, 191
    plaque (PI), 100
    sulcular bleeding (SBI), 100
Indiangrass, 53-54
infantis, B., 73
inorganic material, 41-42
INRA (L'Institut National de la Recherche Agronomique), 207
insulin, 10, 12, 20-22, 31-32, 39, 43, 47, 50, 52, 62, 82, 90, 121, 129, 140, 160-161, 172-173, 175, 180, 182-185, 188-192, 194-196, 202
insulin resistant / resistance (IR), 32, 50, 90, 182, 184, 189, 194-195
interdental space, 93
International Units (IU), 26-27
intravenous fluids, 16, 81, 145, 202
intussusception, 16
iodine (I), 28-30, 35, 68, 75-76
ionophore, 71-72, 122, 139
IR; *see insulin resistant / resistance (IR)*
iron (Fe), 28-30, 35, 75-76, 86, 187
ishial tuberosity, 172
isobutyrate, 14
isoleucine, 33, 134
isoquinoline, 111
isotonic, 25, 81
isotonic saline, 25
isovalerate, 14

IU; *see International Units (IU)*
IVDMD; *see in vitro dry matter digestibility (IVDMD)*
ivermectin, 105, 107, 111-113, 122

J

jack sores, 107
jaggery, 82
Japanese Yew, 119
jaundice, 31, 116, 145, 186; *see also icterus*
jejunum, 12-13, 30
jenny, 169
jimson weed, 118-119
jingulan, 86
jockey oats, 32, 63
johimbe, 16
Johnson grass, 53, 119, 122, 167
joint supplements
    avocado-soy unsaponifibles, 157
    cetyl myristoleate, 157-158
    chondroitin, 156-158
    functional keratin, 156
    glucosamine, 156-158
    hyaluronic acid, 156
    keratin, 156
    methylsulfonylmethane (MSM), 157
joule, 34
jugging, 193
juglans nigra, 118

K

K, 26, 28, 137; *see also potassium*
kale, 30
kava kava, 85
Kcal; *see kilocalorie (Kcal)*
KCl, 79, 83, 131; *see also potassium chloride*
kelp, 68
keratin, 156
kidney, 29, 147, 155, 173, 197-198
kilocalorie (Kcal), 34-35
Krebs cycle, 137

L

L-carnitine, 136
L. acidophilus, 73
L. brevis, 73
L. bulgaricus, 73
L. casei, 73
L. curvatis, 73
L. helveticus, 73

L. lactis, 73
L. paracasei, 73
L. plantarum, 73
L. rhamnosus, 73
L. salivarius, 73
L. sporogenes, 73
LAB; *see lactic acid bacteria (LAB)*
lactation, 24, 139-144, 186
lactic acid bacteria (LAB), 15, 59, 61
lactis, L., 73
Lactobacillus, 72-73
lactose, 31, 135
ladino clover, 54
lameness, 9, 19-20, 84, 155-156, 166
lamina, 18
laminitic stance, 19, 165, 167
laminitis, 6, 9-10, 14-15, 18-22, 32, 47, 49-50, 52, 61-62, 87, 116, 118, 121, 160-161, 166-167, 175, 178, 180, 182-184, 189, 193-195
laminitis grading, 9, 19
lansoprazole, 206
large colon, 10, 13-14, 16
large intestine, 6, 10, 12-13, 78
large strongyles, 104-105, 112
larval cyathostominosis, 105
lasalocid, 71, 122
latrine, 55
laurel, 85, 119
lavaging, 15
lavender, 85, 90
lavender oil, 90
lawn clippings, 59
lawns, 55, 59
LDC; *see left dorsal colon*
lecithin, 206
left dorsal colon, 13-14
left ventral colon, 13-14
legume, 31, 51, 55, 64, 68, 165
leopard's bane, 85
leptin, 129, 184
leptospermum scoparium, 90
lespedeza, 51, 54
leucine, 33, 134
levothyroxine sodium, 191
licheniformis, B., 73
licorice root, 86
lidocaine, 16
light salt, 79-80, 83
lignan, 64

lignin, 38, 43, 49-50, 64, 67, 164
ligustrum vulgare, 119
limestone, 80
linaria vulgaris, 118
linoleic acid, 32, 69, 89
linolenic acid, 32, 69, 89-90, 157
lipase, 12, 32, 65
lipid, 42, 157-158
lipidemia; *see hyperlipidemia*
lipoic acid, 88-89, 135
lipomas, 175
lipopolysaccharides (LPS), 19
liver, 13, 15, 27, 51, 104-105, 118-119, 122, 129, 134-135, 137, 145-146, 155, 167, 169, 172-173, 185-187, 214
liver damage, 118-119
lolium perenne, 54
Lontrel 360, 56
lotus corniculatus, 51, 55
low shedder, 108
low starch, 163, 184, 186, 202
low sugar, 163, 186
LPS; *see lipopolysaccharides (LPS)*
lucerne, 51
lumen, 11-12, 17
lung worms, 107
LVC; *see left ventral colon*
lysine, 33-35, 51, 60, 63, 66, 68, 75, 142, 150, 153

M
macrominerals, 27-28, 44, 79, 91, 172, 207
magnesium (Mg), 28, 137
magnesium aspartate, 30
magnesium carbonate, 30, 80
magnesium citrate, 30, 80
magnesium hydroxide, 206
magnesium oxide, 30, 80
magnesium sulfate, 16, 30, 80
maintenance, 24, 34-36, 39, 45, 48, 128-129, 140-143, 155, 178-179, 191, 207-208
maize, 63
mallow, 86
malocclusion, 96
maltase, 147
maltose, 31, 147
mammary glands, 184
Mammoth donkey, 107
mandible, 93, 96
manganese (Mn), 28-29, 35, 76, 157
mange, 102

mannooligosaccharides, 73

manuka honey, 90

maple, 119-120

margo plicatus, 12

marsh mallow, 86

masa harina, 83

maxilla, 93

ME; see metabolizable energy (ME)

meal

    alfalfa, 37, 71, 139, 150, 163, 167

    cottonseed, 68, 71

    flax, 30, 42, 63-64, 68-69, 83, 90, 139, 163, 205

    oilseed, 30

    peanut, 68, 70, 80, 83

    soybean, 32, 37, 68, 71, 129, 139, 141-142, 150-151, 163

meal size, 10, 131, 205

medicago sativa, 54

megacalorie (Mcal), 34-35

megajoule (Mjoule), 34

menadione, 27

menadione sodium bisulfate, 27

menaquinone, 27

metabolizable energy (ME), 44

Metamucil, 205

metformin, 191

methane, 14, 44

methionine, 31, 33

methylsulfonylmethane (MSM), 157

metoclopramide, 16

metronidazole, 206

Mg; see magnesium (Mg)

Mg SO4; see magnesium sulfate

microbes, 7, 13-15, 26-28, 49, 58, 68, 72, 149

microbial population, 7, 14, 18, 26, 74, 149

microbiome, 14

microbiota, 14

microflora, 14, 18, 32, 66, 72-73

microminerals, 27-29, 44, 91, 172

micronizing, 61

middlings, 63, 65, 71, 139, 163

midds, 65

milk teeth, 94

milk thistle, 19

milk vetch, 54

milkshake, 137

millet, 63

milo, 63

mineral oil, 16, 70, 90

minerals, 1, 3, 7-8, 12, 24, 27-30, 34, 41-44, 54, 57-58, 61, 66, 68, 70, 74-76, 79, 88, 91, 137-139, 141, 150, 159, 173, 187-188, 191, 198, 202-203, 207

miniature horse, 161, 163

Missouri Foxtrotter, 180

mite, 106

Mn; see manganese (Mn)

Mo; see molybdenum

Modified Triadan Tooth Numbering System, 99

molars, 93-94, 96-97, 100

molasses, 30, 63, 65, 74

mold, 45, 54, 56, 58-59, 62-63, 115, 122-124, 199, 201

molybdenum, 28-29, 44, 76

Monday morning sickness, 201

monensin, 71, 122, 139

monkey mouth, 96

monkshood, 119

monofloral, 90

monosaccharides, 31

monosodium phosphate, 29

Morgan, 183, 195

mosquitoes, 102

mountain laurel, 119

mouth

    monkey, 96

    parrot, 96

    shear, 96

    sow, 96

    step, 3-4, 6, 58, 66, 93, 96

    wave, 96

moxidectin, 105, 107, 111-112

MSM; see methylsulfonylmethane (MSM)

mucous membranes, 116

muscle, 15, 30-31, 72, 79, 81, 111, 125, 133-134, 136-137, 154-155, 160, 171-172, 186-189, 194, 196, 201-203, 212-214

mussels, 88, 157

Mustang, 139

mustard, 119, 124

muzzle, 23, 50, 52-53, 145, 161, 178, 190

mycotoxicosis, 123-124

mycotoxin, 62

myocarditis, 72

myoglobin, 72, 201-202

myristoleate, 157-158

myristoleic acid, 157

myrtle, 90

N

N, N-dimethylglycine, 136-137

N-propyl disulfide, 89

Na; *see sodium (Na)*

NaCl, 79, 81, 83, 131

NAD; *see neuroaxonal dystrophy (NAD)*

nasogastric, 15-17, 110-111, 137

National Animal Supplement Council, 85

National Research Council (NRC), 35, 75, 130, 150, 164, 207, 213, 216-217

ND; *see not detectable (ND)*

NDF; *see neutral detergent fiber (NDF)*

NDICP; *see neutral detergent insoluble nitrogen (NDIN)*

NE; *see net energy (NE)*

near infrared spectroscopy (NIRS), 40, 43

needlegrass, 54

negative fecal, 107

nematode, 104, 106

nematophagus fungi, 114

neonatal isoerthryolysis (NI), 141, 145-146, 169

neostigmine methylsulfate, 16

nerium oleander, 119

net energy (NE), 44

nettle, 86, 119-120

neuroaxonal dystrophy (NAD), 27, 140, 192

neuromuscular hyper-excitability, 81

neutral detergent fiber (NDF), 9, 38-39, 43-44, 49, 57, 65, 67, 69

neutral detergent insoluble nitrogen (NDIN), 39

New Zealand tea tree, 90

NFC; *see non-fiber carbohydrates*

NFE; *see nitrogen-free extract (NFE)*

NI; *see neonatal isoerthryolysis (NI)*

niacin, 26, 44, 187

nidus, 51

night blindness, 26

nightshade, 83, 85, 119-120, 122

NIRS; *see near infrared spectroscopy (NIRS)*

nitrate, 45

nitrite, 45

nitrogen, 33, 38-39, 42-43, 51, 201

nitrogen-free extract (NFE), 43

nizatidine, 206

no-salt, 79, 83

non-essential amino acid, 33, 68

non-fiber carbohydrates, 39, 45

non-forage, 36, 47-49, 51, 53, 55, 57-59, 61, 63, 65, 67, 69, 71, 73, 75, 77, 79, 81, 83, 144

non-glandular stomach region, 11

non-protein nitrogen (NPN), 39

non-responder, 121

non-squamous, 11

non-starch polysaccharides (NSP), 39

non-steroidal anti-inflammatory drug (NSAID), 156, 205

non-structural carbohydrate (NSC), 15, 39, 47-52, 57, 64-66, 107, 160-161, 167, 178, 183-184, 189-191, 202-203

Norway Maple, 120

not detectable (ND), 38

noxious weeds, 56

NPN; *see non-protein nitrogen (NPN)*

NRC; *see National Research Council (NRC)*

NSAID; *see non-steroidal anti-inflammatory drug (NSAID)*

NSC; *see non-structural carbohydrate (NSC)*

NSH; *see also nutritional secondary hyperparathyroidism (NSH)*

NSP; *see non-starch polysaccharides (NSP)*

nuchal ligament, 183

nucleic acids, 41

nutritional parathyroidism, 65, 166

nutritional secondary hyperparathyroidism (NSH), 29-30, 65, 166

nuts, 70, 121, 191

nylon, 126

O

oak, 117, 119, 121

oat hay, 52, 54, 60, 173

oats

    bin run, 124

    field, 50, 52, 55-56, 62, 101, 118, 124

    high fat, 32, 70, 132, 144

    hull-less, 63, 67

    jockey, 32, 63

    meal, 10, 12, 18, 22-23, 32, 37, 64-65, 68, 71, 83, 129, 131, 139, 141-142, 150-151, 159, 163-167, 181, 184, 188-189, 201, 205

naked, 63, 67

racehorse, 32, 63, 116, 136

Obel laminitis grading scale, 9, 19

Obesity-Associated Laminitis (OAL), 178, 182

OCD; *see osteochondritis dissecans (OCD)*

odonoplasty, 98

ODST; *see overnight dexamethasone suppression test (ODST)*

oenanthe crocata, 119

oil

    canola, 3, 5, 69-70, 83, 90, 132, 141-142, 154, 205

    coconut oil, 66, 70, 83

    corn, 3, 6, 32, 62-63, 66-67, 69-71, 83, 134, 139, 143, 147, 165, 173, 190

    fish, 68-69, 88, 157

flax, 30, 42, 63-64, 68-69, 83, 90, 139, 163, 205
hemp, 63-64, 69
lavender, 90
linseed, 68-69, 141
menhaden, 69
mineral, 16, 70, 90
palm, 69
peanut, 68, 70, 80, 83
rice bran, 32, 65, 70-71, 134, 158, 163
safflower, 69-70, 83, 205
soybean, 32, 37, 68, 71, 129, 139, 141-142, 150-151, 163
sunflower, 30, 64, 69-70
vegetable oil, 65, 83
wheat germ, 65, 83
oilseed meal, 30
Old Dominion endurance riders, 80
oleander, 117, 119, 121, 126
oligosaccharides, 147
OM; see organic matter
omega-3, 64, 69-70, 135, 139, 205; see also alpha-linolenic acid
omega-6, 64, 69-70, 139; see also alpha-linolenic acid
omeprazole, 205-206
onion, 85
onobrychis viciifolia, 54
orange peel, 86
orchardgrass, 139
organic matter, 39, 42
orphan, 145-148
orthopedic disease, 29, 140, 149-151, 182
orthosilic acid (OSA), 74
oryza sativa, 65
osteoarthritis, 154-158
osteochondritis dissecans (OCD), 151, 157
osteochondrosis, 31, 151-152, 182
osteomalacia, 27
ova, 107
overbite, 96
overgrazing, 53, 55, 57
overnight dexamethasone suppression test (ODST), 195-196
overseeding, 126
oxalate, 29
oxaloacetate, 51
oxfendazole, 111
oxibendazole, 111-112
oxidative stress, 27, 88, 133, 135, 137
oxytropis, 118

oxyuris equi, 105

P
P;see phosphorus
pacing, 23
Paint, 121, 187, 202
PAL; see pasture-associated laminitis (PAL)
palm oil, 69
palmaria palmata, 68
pancreas, 10, 12-13, 15, 104
panicum virgatum, 54
pantoprazole, 206
pantothenic acid, 26
paracasei, L., 73
parascaris equorum, 105
parasitic burden, 102, 173
parathyroid, 29
parotid, 11
parrot mouth, 96
pars intermedia, 32, 47, 85-86, 99, 155, 182, 184, 189, 193-195
parts per million (PPM), 28, 44, 75
pascopyrum smithii, 55
Paso Fino, 183
paspalum notatum, 54
passion flower, 85
pastinaca sativa, 120
pasture management, 52-53, 56, 114, 161
pasture-associated laminitis (PAL), 19, 52
pathogenic, 103, 106
pathognomonic sign, 193
pausinystalis johimbe, 16
pawing, 18, 20, 23, 116, 204
PDH; see pyruvate
peanut, 68, 70, 80, 83
peas, 51, 64, 71
pectin, 38-39, 43, 45, 49, 65-66, 73, 147, 178, 206
pellets, 37, 47-48, 58, 60, 65, 70-71, 76, 82-83, 131, 147, 152, 154, 162-163, 191, 200-201, 205, 217
pellets, case-hardened, 71
pelvic flexure, 13-14
pepsin, 12
pergolide mesylate, 196
periodontal disease, 98, 100
Peripheral Cushing's syndrome, 182
peripheral vasodilation, 189
perna canaliculus, 157
persimmon, 83
persin, 83

pH, 10-12, 14-15, 18, 59-61, 69, 74, 81-82, 129, 146, 205

phalaris arundinacea, 54

phenylalanine, 33

phenylbutazone, 156, 205

phleum pratense, 55

phosphate dehydrogenase, 89

phosphate salts, 29

phosphorus, 7, 28-30, 35, 44, 64-65, 67, 74-75, 135, 137, 150, 155, 166, 172, 197

photosensitivity, 51, 85, 116, 118-123

photosynthesize, 48

phrenic nerve, 81

phylate, 30

phylloerythrin, 122

phylloquinone, 27

physiolysis, 151

physitis, 151

phytase, 64

phytate, 29, 64

phytic acid, 29, 64

phytoestrogen, 51

phytolaca americana, 119

phytotoxin, 118

PI; see plaque index (PI)

pica, 8, 16

pickling, 59

pigeon grass, 118

pin bone, 172, 210-212

pinto, 121

pinworms, 105-106, 112

piperazine, 111-112

pituitary adenoma, 194

pituitary gland, 193-195

pituitary pars intermedia dysfunction (PPID), 32, 47, 85-86, 140, 155, 184, 189, 193-196

planatarum, 73

plant protein, 62, 65, 71

plaque index (PI), 106

poa pratensis, 54

points, on teeth, 94, 96, 98

poison hemlock, 120

pollen, 86, 200-201

polydextrose, 73

polydipsia, 194

polyethylene, 126

polymixin B, 19

polysaccharide, 31-32, 39, 189

polysaccharide storage myopathy (PSSM), 32, 47, 160, 201-202

polystyrene, 126

polysulfated glucosaminoglycan (PSGAG), 156

polyunsaturated, 69, 157

polyuria, 194

polyvinyl chloride, 126

POMC; see proopiomelanocortin (POMC)

pony, 3, 7, 138, 161-165, 169, 179-181, 183, 195

potash, 188

potassium, 28-30, 35, 44, 67, 72, 76-77, 79-81, 83, 86, 132, 137, 147, 173, 187-188

potassium chloride, 79, 132

PPID; see pituitary pars intermedia dysfunction (PPID)

praziquantel, 111-112

Pre-Laminitic Metabolic syndrome, 182

prebiotics, 70, 72, 74

precursor, 26, 136

pregnancy, 1, 139-141, 144-145, 186, 194, 209

premolars, 93-94, 96-97, 100

prepuce, 184

Previcox, 156, 205

privet, 119

probiotics, 70, 72-75

processing (grain), 32

prognathism, 96

proline, 33, 134

Pronutrin, 206

proopiomelanocortin (POMC), 194

propionate, 14, 68

propyl disulfide, 89

prostaglandin, 135, 206

protein, 1, 12, 24, 31, 33-35, 37-45, 47-49, 51, 54, 58, 61-68, 71, 81, 107, 129, 131, 134-135, 139, 141-142, 146-147, 150-151, 153-155, 157, 159, 161, 163, 165-167, 172-173, 178, 185, 197, 200-201, 205

proteoglycans, 156

protozoa, 14, 72

proximate analysis, 40, 43

prunus, 118

prussic acid, 118

psathyrostachys juncea, 55

PSGAG; see polysulfated glucosaminoglycan (PSGAG)

PSSM; see polysaccharide storage myopathy (PSSM)

psyllium, 16-17, 73, 205

psyllium hydrophilic mucilloid, 16, 205

psyllium mucilloid, 205

Pteridium aquilinum, 118

ptosis, 125, 188

ptyalism, 14-15, 97, 123, 125, 204

PUFA

pulse, 19, 130, 179-180, 198, 213-216, 219
pyrantel pamoate, 111-112
pyrantel tartrate, 111-112
pyridoxine, 26
pyruvate, 136-137

Q
Quarter Horse, 131, 143, 153, 158, 169, 187, 202
quercetin, 136-138, 157
quercetin dehydrate, 138
quercus, 119

R
rabeprazole, 206
racehorse oats, 32, 63
raffinose, 31
ragwort, 119, 122
ranitidine, 205-206
ranunculus, 118
RAO; see recurrent airway obstruction (RAO)
raowolfia, 85
rape, 5, 124
rat poison, 122
ratio
    calcium:magnesium ratio, 29
    calcium:phosphorus, 7, 29, 67, 74
    copper:zinc, 74-75
ration balancers, 70, 74, 141
rattlebox, 119
rattlepod, 119
rattlesnake, 116
RDC; see right dorsal colon (RDC)
recipe
    baked horse cookies, 83
    creep feed, 71, 150
    electrolyte, 30, 70, 76-81, 129, 131-132, 139, 172, 205
    no-bake horse treats, 82
rectum, 13-14, 105
recurrent airway obstruction (RAO), 198-199
recurrent exertional rhabdomyolysis (RER), 201
red alga, 68
red blood cells, 89, 120, 136, 145-146, 172
red clover, 54
Red Maple, 120
red poppy, 85
red top, 54
red worms, 104
reed canary grass, 53-54
refeeding syndrome, 8, 171, 173

rejected foal, 145-147
relative feed value (RFV), 44
relative forage quality (RFQ), 39, 44-45
relative humidity, 78
RER; see recurrent exertional rhabdomyolysis (RER)
Rescue Remedy, 88
resting pulse, 215, 219
RFQ; see relative forage quality (RFQ)
RFV; see relative feed value (RFV)
rhabdo, 201
rhabdomyolysis, 160, 182, 188, 197, 201-203
rhamnosus, L., 73
rhinitis sicca, 125
rhizoctonia leguminicola, 122
rhodiola rosea, 86
rhododendron, 117
riboflavin, 26, 44
rice bran, 32, 65, 70-71, 134, 158, 163
richweed, 119
rickets, 27
right dorsal colitis, 182, 203-204
right dorsal colon (RDC), 13-14, 204
right ventral colon (RVC), 13
rose laurel, 119
rosehips, 82, 89
rotovirus, 204
roughs, 55
Roundup, 3, 5, 56, 66
roundworms, 105
Rumensin, 71
Russian knapwood, 119
Russian wildrye, 55
RVC; see right ventral colon (RVC)
rye, 45, 50, 52, 56, 62-63, 67, 141
ryegrass, 45, 50, 52, 54, 122-123
ryegrass staggers, 123

S
S; see sulfur (S)
S. boulardii, 73
S. cerevisiae, 73
S. halepense, 54
S. sudanense, 54
S. thermophilus, 73
saccharides, 31
Saccharomyces, 67, 73
Saddlebred, 183
SADMOA; see slow-acting, disease-modifying osteoarthritis
    agent (SADMOA)

sainfoin, 54

Saint John's Wort, 85

saliva, 11, 14, 22, 93, 97, 204-205

salt

    block, 3, 8, 74-76, 139, 143, 174, 187-188, 197

    blue, 53-54, 75-76, 157, 208

    Epsom, 16, 80

    iodized, 79

    kosher, 79, 83

    light, 75, 79-80, 83, 103, 121-122, 128-130, 142, 148, 159, 163, 179, 190-191, 207

    taxidermy, 79

sand colic, 16-17, 162

saponin, 118

saturated fat, 69

SBI; see sulcular bleeding index (SBI)

ScFA; see short chain fatty acid (SCFA)

scFOS; see short chain fructooligosaccharides (scFOS)

sclera, 116, 145, 186

sclerotia, 123

sclerotium, 123

scoring system,

    body condition, 4, 9, 36, 141, 152, 165, 167, 171-172, 174-176, 181, 183, 204, 207-210

    cresty neck, 9, 177, 180, 183-184, 194

    dental, 7, 9, 11, 18, 93-101, 154, 158, 162, 167, 196, 207

    Henneke, 9, 152, 167, 176, 210-212

    sweat, 9, 24-25, 30, 76-79, 148

    ulcer, 7, 22, 146, 150, 182, 203-204, 206

scotchbroom, 119

SDF; see soluble dietary fiber (SDF)

SDG; see seicoisolariciresinol diglucoside (SDG)

Se; see selenium

seabuckthorn berry, 206

seaweed, 68

sedge, 48

seed head, 49-50, 62

seed meal, 68

seicoisolariciresinol diglucoside (SDG), 64

selenium

    and vitamin E, 72

serine, 33

setaria lutescens, 118

shaker foal syndrome, 125

sham eating, 167

shear mouth, 96

Shetland, 183

shivers, 160, 182, 188, 192-193

short chain fatty acid (SCFA), 69

short chain fructooligosaccharides (scFOS), 31, 74

shrill calling, 23

silage, 48, 58-60, 125

silica, 38, 67, 113

silicon, 29, 31, 74, 152

silymarin, 19

skeleton, 29-30, 152, 209

skin tenting, 25

skullcap, 85

slaframine, 122

slobbers, 54, 122-123

slow feeder, 16, 20, 94, 163

slow twitch, 133

slow-acting, disease-modifying osteoarthritis agent (SADMOA), 156

small colon, 10, 13-14

small intestine, 6, 10, 12-16, 29-30, 32, 61, 64, 105

small strongyles, 104-105, 112

SmartPill, 18, 205

snake, 116

snakeroot, 119, 121

soaking

    beet pulp, 65-66, 70, 76, 131-132, 152, 154, 201

    hay, 57-58, 178, 181, 184, 188, 190, 199-201

SOD; see superoxide dismutase (SOD)

sodium (Na), 16, 25, 27-30, 35, 44, 71, 74-77, 79-81, 132, 136-137, 152, 187-188, 191, 206

sodium ferrocyanide, 79

sodium selenite, 132

sodium zeolite, 74, 152

solanum, 119-120, 122

solanum, 119-120, 122

solanum carolinense, 120

solanum elaeagnifllium, 122

soluble dietary fiber (SDF), 39

Somali Wild Ass, 164

sooty blotch, 123

sorghastrum nutans, 54

sorghum, 54, 63, 119, 122

sow mouth, 96

soy, 30, 37, 67-69, 76, 90, 154, 157, 163, 166, 191, 202, 205

soy hulls, 37, 47, 68, 76, 154, 163, 191, 202

soya, 67

soybean, 32, 37, 68, 71, 129, 139, 141-142, 150-151, 163

Spanish Mustang, 183

spider, 116

spindle tree, 118

spinous process, 172

spirulina, 157

spontaneous abortion, 139-141, 194

sprouts, 5, 58, 60

squamous, 11

squirrel grass, 117

stall walking, 23

Standardbred, 136

starch, 1, 6-7, 12, 15, 31-32, 39, 43, 48-53, 59, 61-63, 67, 69, 71-73, 129, 131, 150, 152, 160, 163, 165, 173, 178, 184, 186, 189, 191, 202-205

starch redline, 6-7, 12, 216-217, 219

starvation, 10, 69, 128, 167, 171, 173

step mouth, 96

stereotypic behavior, 10, 20-21, 23-24, 96, 151, 179

sternal flexure, 13-14

sterol, 65, 134

stocking up, 120

stomach worms, 107

stones

    bladder, 12, 29, 185, 198

    enterolith, 16, 51, 54

    urinary, 29, 137

storage carbohydrate, 51-52

stover, 165

straw, 141, 165-166, 200, 205

strawberry bush, 118

Streptococcus, 72-73, 206

stringhalt, 182, 192-193

strongyles, 104-105, 112, 150

strongyloides westeri, 104, 141

strongylosis, 104

Strongylus edentatus (S. edentatus), 104

Strongylus equinus (S. equinus), 104

Strongylus vulgaris (S. vulgaris), 104

subtilis, B., 73

sucralfate, 205-206

sucrose, 31, 49, 147

Sudan grass, 52-53, 122

sugar, 3, 5, 15, 19-20, 31, 40, 45, 49-53, 56-59, 61-62, 65-67, 73, 79-80, 82-83, 87-88, 90, 121, 129, 137-138, 147, 163, 171, 173, 181, 184, 186, 190-191, 194, 196

sugar beet pulp, 3, 5, 58, 65-66

sulcular bleeding index (SBI), 100

sulfadimidine, 206

sulfur (S), 28-29, 31, 33, 35, 74, 76, 89, 157

summer sores, 107

sunburn, 116, 121

sunflower, 30, 64, 69-70

sunflower seeds, 64

supernumerary, 99

superoxide, 29, 89, 137

superoxide dismutase (SOD), 89, 136-137

supplements

    calming, 30, 85, 90, 138

    electrolyte, 30, 70, 76-81, 129, 131-132, 139, 172, 205

    ergogenic, 33, 65, 132-136, 138-139, 157

    joint, 4, 19, 84-85, 88, 90, 154-158

    mineral, 3-4, 7, 16, 25, 27-30, 39-41, 51, 58, 60-61, 65, 70, 72, 74-76, 79, 83, 88, 90-91, 132, 137, 141, 143, 147, 150-152, 154-156, 162-163, 166, 172-173, 187-188, 197-198

    prebiotic, 73-74

    probiotic, 72-73

    vitamin, 3-4, 7, 26-29, 31, 35, 40, 44, 65, 67, 70, 72, 74, 76, 79, 83, 85-86, 88-89, 117, 123, 132, 141, 143, 150-152, 154, 156-157, 160, 162-163, 166, 187-188, 192-194, 198

surrogate mare, 145, 148

sweet feed, 31, 71

switchgrass, 52-54

sympatholytics, 16

synapis, 119

synchronous diaphragmatic flutter, 70, 81, 129, 182

synovial, 155

synthetic vitamin E, 27

T

T. pratense, 54

T. repens, 54

tachycardia, 18, 145

tachypnea, 18, 145

tall butterbups, 121

tannin, 167

tansy ragwort, 122

taxus, 119

TDF; see total dietary fiber (TDF)

tea tree, 90

teeth,

    blind wolf, 94, 96

    canine, 94, 100

    cap, 96

    cheek, 93-94, 96-97

    deciduous, 94, 96

    floating, 96, 98-99

    milk, 19, 54, 68, 94, 104, 119, 123, 135, 139, 141-143, 145-149, 153, 198

    supernumerary, 99

    wolf, 94, 96, 98

teff, 53, 55

temperate grasses, 52

temperature, rectal, 15

Tennessee Walkers, 183

tenting, skin, 25, 214

test,

    ACTH, 194-196

    CGI, 190

    oral sugar, 190

    overnight dexamethasone suppression, 195-196

    TRH Stimulation, 195

tetrahydrocannabinol, 85

tetrahydropyrimidines, 111

Tevis, 25, 170-171

theobromine, 83, 86

thermistors, 130

thermophilus, E., 73

thiamin, 26-27, 44, 117

thiaminase, 26, 117

thiamine, 44, 173

thinopyrum ponticum, 55

Thoroughbred, 131, 158

threadworms, 104, 141, 150

threonine, 33

thumps, 70, 79, 81-82, 129, 139, 182

Thyro-L, 191

thyroid, 30

thyrotropin, 195

thyrotropin-releasing hormone, 195

ticklegrass, 119

ticks, 102

Tifton, 54

timothy, 48, 52-53, 55, 60, 122, 163

TMG, 136

toadflax, 118

tobacco, 113, 167, 199

tocopherol, 132

tomatoes, 83

total dietary fiber (TDF), 39, 69

total digestible nutrients (TDN), 44

toxicity, 26-28, 30-31, 72, 74, 113, 115, 118, 120-121, 123, 187

toxicoinfectious botulism, 125

toxicosis, 113, 122

trace minerals, 27-28, 79, 207

trachea, 14, 88, 199

transverse processes, 172, 210

treats, 60-61, 82-83, 127, 154, 160, 162-163, 179, 181, 187-188, 191-192

trefoil, bird's-foot, 55

tremetol, 121

Triadan system, 99-100

trichloroacetate intermediates, 134

trichothecenes, 62

trickle feeding, 21-22

trifolium, 54, 118, 121

trifolium hybridum, 121

triglyceride, 69

trilostane, 196

trimethoprim, 206

trimethylglycine (TMG), 136

triterpene alcohol, 134

triticale, 50

triticum aestivum, 63

tropical grasses, 51

troponin, 72

trypsin, 64

trypsin inhibitor, 64

tryptophan, 33

tube worming, 110

tuber ischii, 211

tubing, 110

Tum's, 132

turmeric, 89

tush, 94

tusk, 94

tying up, 31

tyrosine, 33

U

ulcer, 7, 22, 146, 150, 182, 203-204, 206

Ultimate Chart, 2, 6, 8-9, 12, 33-36, 61, 68, 70, 110, 131, 154, 161, 163, 176, 179, 190, 207-209

umbilicus, 176-177, 191

unavailable protein (UP), 43

underbite, 96

unsaturated fats, 69

urea, 129

urine, 29, 38, 44, 77, 80, 104, 115-116, 124, 129, 197-198, 201-202

urolithiasis, 198

V

valerate, 14

valerian, 85-86

valine, 33, 134

Valium, 85, 138

Van Soest, Peter J., 43

vanadium, 28

Vanquish, 56

vegetable oil, 65, 83

ventral colon, 13-14

ventral curvature, 96

vertebral malformation, 151

vervain, 85

vetch, 51, 54

VFA; *see volatile fatty acid (VFA)*

vicia villosa, 51

villi, 12

vinegar, 25, 86-87

vipers bugloss, 119

Virginia Tech, 177, 184

vital signs

    pulse, 19, 130, 179-180, 198, 213-216, 219

    temperature, 15

vitamin

    A, 26, 35, 44

    B1 (thiamine), 26, 35, 117

    B12 (cyanocobalamin), 26, 28

    B2 (riboflavin), 26, 35

    B3 (niacin), 26

    B5 (pantothenic acid), 26

    B6 (pyridoxine), 26

    B7 (biotin), 26

    B9 (folic acid), 26

    C (ascorbic acid), 16, 27, 85, 88-89, 125, 157, 187, 194

    D, 15, 25-27, 29, 35, 56, 89, 158, 187

    D2, 27

    D3, 27, 29

    E, 13, 26-27, 31, 35, 57, 65, 72-74, 88-89, 132, 143, 146, 160, 187, 192-193, 206

    K, 26-28, 72, 89, 123, 137, 187

    K1 (phylloquinone), 27

    K2 (menaquinone), 27

    K3 (menadione), 27

vitus agnus castus, 196

VO2, 132

volatile fatty acid (VFA), 14, 68, 72

volvulus, 16

vomitoxin, 62

W

walnut, 69, 118, 120

warm season grasses

    bahia, 54, 123

    Bermuda, 45, 48, 52, 54, 122, 153, 205

    big bluestem, 52

    dallisgrass, 123

    Johnson, 53-54, 119, 122, 167

    sorghum, 54, 63, 119, 122

    Sudan, 52-54, 119, 122, 167

    Warmblood, 48, 183

water dropwort, 119

water soluble carbohydrate (WSC), 39, 58, 178, 199

water soluble vitamins, 26, 187

water,

    salt, 3, 8, 25, 60-61, 64-65, 67, 74-76, 78-81, 83, 131-132, 139, 143, 158, 174, 187-188, 205

watermelon, 82

wave mouth, 96

WBC; *see white blood cell (WBC)*

weaving, 20, 23

Weende analysis, 40

Weende Experimental Station, 40

weight, body, 207-208

Welsh, 183

West Nile Virus, 103, 192

Western Yew, 119

wet matter (WM), 40

wheat

    bran, 3, 7, 32, 61-65, 70-71, 134, 155, 158, 163, 166, 187, 197

    germ, 61-62, 65, 83

    middlings, 63, 65, 71, 139, 163

    midds, 65

wheatgrass

    tall, 48, 50, 54-55, 115, 121

    thickspike, 55

    western, 55, 119, 170

whey protein, 68

white blood cell (WBC), 98

white clover, 51

white muscle disease, 31

white snakeroot, 121

wild barley, 117

wild mustard, 119

wild parsnip, 120-122

wildrye, Russian, 55

willow bark, 86, 89

windsucking, 16, 23

WM; *see wet matter (WM)*

wobbler syndrome, 151, 192

wolf teeth, 94, 96, 98

worming; *see deworm*

worms, 3, 7, 86, 102-113, 173, 196, 204

WSC; *see water soluble carbohydrate (WSC)*

X

xanthium, 120
xanthium stumaritum, 120
xylooligosaccharides, 73

Y

yeast, 67, 73, 137, 163
yellow prussiate, 79
yellow star thistle, 119
yew, 117, 119, 121, 126
yogurt, 73
yohimbe, 16
yohimbine, 16
yucca, 86, 89

Z

Zadoks scale, 50
zea mays, 63
zearalenone, 62
zeolite, 74, 152
zinc (Zn), 28-29, 35, 44, 74-76, 150, 187
Zn; *see zinc (Zn)*
zwitterion, 33
zymogenic cells, 12

About the Author

Lisa Preston is a lifelong equestrienne. Her education includes a Master of Science, Bachelor of Science, and paramedical training. She has also earned certificates in Advanced Equine Nutrition and in Forage Testing. She is a life member of the USDF, USEA, and USEF.

www.lisapreston.com

Acknowledgments

Thank you to Kathryn Mennone, who was so supportive and helped create a shared vision for this project.

I would also like to express my gratitude to the many veterinarians, PhDs, and other scientists who contributed expertise not just via their research, but also through direct communication with me.

Dr. Joe Bertone

Dr. Faith Burden

Dr. Stephanie Caston Auck

Dr. Andrea Ellis

Dr. Greg Fellers

Dr. Patricia Harris

Dr. Tanja Hess

Dr. James (Jamie) Kerr

Dr. Anne Rodiek

Dr. Carolyn Stull

Dr. Ingrid Vervuert

Dr. Annette Zeyner

Finally, a warm thank you to the people who shared stories and photographs:

Stephanie Caston Auck, DVM

Eva Cooley

Lori Crow

Ann Edie

Fred Eiland

Randy Eiland

Valerie Jones-Jackson

Alexandra Kurland

Greg Lange

Evan Leach

Marilyn

Mari Phillips

Katy Preston

Aly Rattazzi

Diane Royall

Dan Taylor

Rosie Taylor

Dr. Lynn Van Wieringen

Alison Sneed

Elisa Wallace

Kathleen Wilson

The author has no conflict of interest to declare. She receives no benefit, gift, or funding from any manufacturer or distributer of any equine feed, supplement, or service, nor does she sell or promote any nutritional product.

Also, she often refers to the horse as "he" in this book. Rest assured, she's not anti-mare; both of her horses are mares.